Financial Economics

Financial Economics

Edited by Edward May

CLANRYE INTERNATIONAL
www.clanryeinternational.com

Clanrye International,
750 Third Avenue, 9th Floor,
New York, NY 10017, USA

ISBN: 978-1-63240-675-0

Cataloging-in-Publication Data

Financial economics / edited by Edward May.
p. cm.
Includes bibliographical references and index.
ISBN 978-1-63240-675-0
1. Finance. 2. Economics. I. May, Edward.
HG173 .F56 2018
332--dc23

For information on all Clanrye International publications
visit our website at www.clanryeinternational.com

Clanrye International

Printed in China.

Contents

Preface

This book aims to highlight the current researches and provides a platform to further the scope of innovations in this area. This book is a product of the combined efforts of many researchers and scientists, after going through thorough studies and analysis from different parts of the world. The objective of this book is to provide the readers with the latest information of the field.

Financial economics is the branch of economics which studies the financial decisions made under uncertain conditions. Decision theory in combination with microeconomics forms the basis of financial economics. The two main areas related to this subject are asset pricing and corporate finance. This book unfolds the innovative aspects of financial economics which will be crucial for the progress of this field in the future. It will serve as a valuable source of reference for graduate and post graduate students.

I would like to express my sincere thanks to the authors for their dedicated efforts in the completion of this book. I acknowledge the efforts of the publisher for providing constant support. Lastly, I would like to thank my family for their support in all academic endeavors.

Editor

1

Survey of Free Market Principles for Encouraging Market: Participation of African American and the Economically Challenged

Amaechi N. Nwaokoro[1]

[1] College of Business, Albany State University, Albany, Georgia, USA

Correspondence: Amaechi N. Nwaokoro, College of Business, Albany State University, 504 College Drive, Albany, Georgia 31705, USA. E-mail: amaechi.nwaokoro@asurams.edu

Abstract

This study targets to challenge African American and other economically challenged to embrace free market principles to enhance their participation in the economy of Albany/Dougherty County, Georgia. With a market-based questionnaire, this study assess the understanding of these principles from among the students of Albany State University, the major educational institution in the county. Among other compelling actions, the responses provided on the survey highlight the need for effective education, increasing interest in taking market risks, elevation of access to capital, and fairer and inclusive society.

Keywords: poverty, inequality, partnership, financial instruments, accessible capital, market principles, free enterprise

1. Introduction

African American, in particular, has a substantially low business ownership in Albany/Dougherty County where African American has a majority status with 60.1%, and the White and Hispanics make up 37.34% and 1.3% respectively of the county's population of 96,065 (Note 1). In this situation, one should expect substantial dimensions of ethnically related poverty and other inequalities where the majority tends to dependent on the white minority to have access to employment, justice and considerations, capital, and to other opportunities. If a representative of African Americans cannot economically stand out in this county, one would wonder how much they fare in other counties. If the low African American business ownership in this county is comparable to those of other counties in the U.S., then a significant discussion must come to bear on ethnic poverty.

Remotely located in Southwest Georgia where southern poverty is prevalent (Note 2), Albany/Dougherty County is income-stratified, non-macro economically harmonized, and is dualistically entrenched by race leading to East and West Albany. Impoverished East Albany is mostly inhabited by African Americans while the White live in the West Albany where African Americans conventionally own faith-based initiatives. The White and recent immigrants have the ownership of most of the small businesses in the East Albany. The county has a substantial economic inequality issues that seem to emanate mostly from an inadequate awareness of the principles of a free market economy. The inequality issues relate to the disparities from the economic and educational achievements, poverty, and unemployment that are prevailing in the county. These adversities tend to disproportionally characterize the ethnic minorities, African American in particular. Inequality issue can arise whereby the would-be-market participants of the African American ethnic group, cannot articulate the exposition of the free market principles and of the activities of the financial market. Income earned from the financial market augments the income from the labor market that most people apply to. Nationally, only 10% of African Americans owns stocks and bonds and only 18% of American Indians receives some kinds of incomes from financial investments, stocks, and property (Lui et al., 2006, pp. 77, 32).

Economic inequality issues could arise due to a limited education most especially from the African American community. Educational achievement is positively related to a non-discriminating wage rate and to other opportunities. As African American's educational achievements lag behind that of the White being minority in the county, the inequality issue will linger. With limited education, labor may not have favorable negotiations on the terms of labor contracts and will most likely be paid a wage rate that is lower than the value of the physical marginal product of labor. Given limited opportunities, a felon with a limited education may have to settle with any wage rate offered. A labor with a limited education or is unskilled is most likely to be a subject to employment shocks most especially where labor and capital are substitutable in the production process. The diverse economic inequalities tend to emanate mostly from a limited understanding of free market principles and from the lagging educational achievements in this remote county that is divided by segregation and discrimination. Due to increasing city vices, there is an exodus of white and middle class African Americans out of the county to the nearest rural counties and this leads to some market failure. All these inequalities lead to a substantial African American and White purchasing power disparity explained by a quotient (Note 3) of (0.545). This estimate shows that the average African American earns roughly fifty-five cents for every one dollar that the average White person earns. Very high unemployment rates characterize the Albany/Dougherty (Georgia Department of Labor, 2010).

The crucial roles of concepts, business partnership, financial institutions, entrepreneurship, and microfinance institutions in a market driven economy seem not to be understood. The ability to understand these market attributes would not only assist in the development of market human capital, they also enable individuals to self-select into the economic activities where they command the greatest comparative advantages. A latent African American market participation is explained by the group's limited understanding of the market specific traits and of entrepreneurship particularly (Lofstron & Bates, 2007; and Ucbasaran et al., 2008). Adams-Cooper (2011) could not highlight African American business partnerships even in the predominantly African American neighborhood. Partnerships are highlighted mostly in non-profit and faith-based initiatives. Business partnership assists in amalgamating funds and other resources that is beyond the resources of an individual to underwrite the initial outlay of business formation. Some small scale partnerships among those with common interests could be the routes to introduce the economically challenged to economic markets. Understanding the roles of the various financial intermediaries in a market economy could assist the economically challenged to locate where there could be a consideration for some small scale capital formation.

It seems most effort is directed toward getting jobs. In the absence of job opportunities, effort seems inhibited and productive people could end up on program incomes. People tend to ignore or have not realize the important role of entrepreneurship in a price-driven economy for increasing their incomes and the incomes and opportunities of others. This market attribute needs to be highlighted for people to realize that there are various dimensions of market risks undertaken by entrepreneurs (risk takers) to effect increase in their incomes and those of others. Even the economically challenged could step out to undertake some calculated risks at some appropriate levels to enhance their expected market rewards. Another market factor that could place and sustain the economically challenged mostly in the market is the microfinance institutions. Besides making concessionary loans and advances, these institutions provide some specialized services that are not handled by the conventional financial intermediaries. These institutions are on record for alleviating poverty in South America, and in Southeast Asia (Khandker & Shahidur, 2005; Morduch, 2002; Ahmed, Chowdhury, & Bhuiya, 2001). These institutions can enhance microenterprise to encourage a shift to economic activities (Servon & Bates, 1998).

Based on the perceived inability of the economically challenged, African Americans in particular, to apply adequately to a market economy, the objective of this study is to use market-based questionnaire to sample the articulation of the exposition of market principles by the would-be-market participants from among the students of Albany State University, the major educational institution in the county and to provide actions for alleviating the market inhibitions. Particularly, the study serves to ignite the latent commercial articulation of the ethnic African American majority, and of other economically challenged in Albany/Dougherty. College students would most likely be educationally-driven entrepreneurs that would have an impact on alleviating the economic and the other inequalities. The questionnaire items focus on the roles of price mechanism, business partnership, entrepreneurship, financial market, and skills acquisition and labor market. Both male and female students applied to the questionnaire.

From the overall responses, there was a failure in recognizing the general activities of a market economy. Cautiously speaking, the survey responses revealed specifically, the students' understandings of the crucial role of entrepreneurship and of profit motive as factors or principles in the economic markets. Compelling actions to address the failure of the performance on the survey items would include but not limited to the need for: effective education, increasing interest in taking market risks, elevating access to capital, and for fairer and inclusive society. The rest of this study is laid out as follows. Section two presents the literature review on the sources of poverty and economic inequalities, on the economic markets, and on the associated crucial factors and institutions. Respectively, sections three and four present the data and methodology, and the research findings and results. Section five handles the conclusion and direction for future study.

2. Literature Review

The literature review will highlight the sources of poverty, the diversity of markets, and the roles of the market supportive institutions.

2.1 Sources of Economic Inequalities in African American Community of Dougherty County, Georgia

Many sources, including the environmental duality caused by segregation and discrimination, the carryovers from slavery, tend to perpetuate poverty and the other inequalities in Albany/Dougherty County. Lack of black entrepreneurship during the slavery tends to hinder the African Americans' contemporary perceptions of free market factors. At the end of slavery, without some capital, African Americans found themselves on marginal lands that lacks macroeconomic framework. Those in impoverished neighborhoods are more restricted from applying to American free enterprise system. It is even rare to have African American entrepreneurs even in the predominantly African American neighborhood where the new immigrants from Asia and white people commercially excel. Instead of having business diversity, African American's effort, when exercised, seems to be directed at creating businesses that are similar to the few petty ones already established. This non-market foresight leads to unhealthy competition. These adversities seem to be the foundation of African American dependency on White's employment and on subsistence activities that perpetuates poverty and the economic inequalities right from the beginning of the African Americans' freedom.

Poverty has been carried over from the colonial America in which only the freed were judged by the incidence of poverty. The poverty of the Blacks then was considered normal since those that were not free did not have the opportunity to use own labor to obtain their economic security. Those that were free and could not acquire economic security by their labor were seem as being morally flawed or morally bankrupt. With much human development in a post-industrial period, poverty is explained by cultural theories. Schiller (2008, p. 156) explains that:

"Most cultural theories of poverty assert that the poor lack sufficient desire and motivation to escape poverty. They allege that the goal of economic security is of lesser importance in the value matrix of the poor. Welfare mothers would rather have kids than jobs. Young men would rather "hustle" on the street corners than accept a regular job. An overriding focus on immediate gratification discourages family planning, the pursuit of education, or the accumulation of savings. Because they are trapped by this culture, the members of the underclass don't behave in ways that would help them escape from poverty."

Some of these characterizations may not be true, but the modern day African American poverty tends to reflect limited understanding of market principles, of the importance of market partnership, and of the crucial role of entrepreneurship in a market economy. In the face of resource scarcity, African American's economic engagements tend to be in a few non-diversified markets. Resource scarcity and limited educational achievements (Note 4) may have compelled some preference to self-select governmental programs and faith-based activities for income securities in a postindustrial era. Also preference tends to be dependence on white establishments for economic security. Perpetuated poverty might have led to some dependency on programs given the non-understanding as to how the market economy works. African American ethnic poverty and the inequalities faced may need to be visited with both striving market principles and substantial level of exogenous capital investment to economically uplift the economies of the restricted neighborhoods.

Poverty tends to perpetuate intergenerational poverty as children of programs dependent families may not be cognizant of how income and wealth can be earned from the economic markets. Though the sources of the African American's economic adversities have been mitigated in both post war eras by legislation, by establishment of HBCU schools, and by encouraging, an increase of African American employment participation, most African Americans may not be aware of the activities in the various markets that make up the market economy. Particularly, they have not fully realized the importance of financial market where incomes can be earned to augment labor market incomes that they are used to. The undiversified nature of the educational institutions in the county tend to limit educational interaction and shared values only within racial groups.

Besides being remotely located, the county is dualistically divided by the Flint River and this situation leads to East and West Albany. These two constraints tend to limit the citizens' market participation and therefore leads to poverty. Most employment, financial, and other opportunities are apparent in the West and North sides of the county. The East is populated mostly by African Americans with 91% of the population and a poverty rate of 45% (Farr & Slade, 2008; Hoynes et al., 2006). An interaction between enlarged poverty and limited education would perpetuate generational poverty and economic inequalities that would grossly affect the benefits of comparative advantage and specialization (Bagi, 2008). The economically disadvantaged in the restricted environments that are being challenged by economic incentives would either drive or are driven to the opportunity areas. Those who do not have the luxury of having work transportation are therefore trapped in the restricted and impoverished areas. Due to the remoteness of the county, it takes approximately three and half, and two and half driving hours respectively to access employment and other opportunities in the nearest industrial cities of Atlanta Georgia and Tallahassee Florida. Georgia's portion of the Interstate 75 constructed in mid 1970s is said to have taken business opportunities from the county's traditional business areas (Farr & Slade, 2008).

White and rich African Americans are leaving the county. Businesses are also relocating out of the county. Firestone, the US. Naval Air Station and Merck Pharmaceuticals have left. These movements that are mostly from the City of Albany tend to be responses to the expected increasing city crimes, to declining educational achievements from the public schools system, and to declining business opportunities. Involuntary unemployment and poverty are the outcomes of these movements (Schmitt, 2004). Discrimination and segregation, and crimes (Note 5) prevent an adequate harmonized economic planning in the county. With the environmental duality, planning does not seem to address the root issue of ethnic related-poverty in the impoverished neighborhoods. Severity of scarcity of resources in this neighborhoods is most likely to attract hedonic consumption and more crimes. The extensiveness and intensiveness of the crimes are likely to depend on the interactions between the substandard education and occupational skills, hedonic consumption, and the extent that racial discrimination and segregation dump citizens in the restricted and impoverished environments. Along with the inadequate applications to economic principles, these adverse and non-market factors tend to perpetuate the economic, educational, wage, and other inequalities, and African American in particular could not adequately apply themselves to the economic markets. Card and Dinardo (2002) present the source of wage inequality as emanating not only from technological competency, but also from non-market factors such as race, gender, and age implications.

2.2 Introducing Economic Markets

A market is a situation where there is an exchange of monetary payment (price) for a receipt of something scarce that has an economic value. American economy is based on market in the system of prices. The prices allocate economic resources among the competing functions. Economic goods and resources are rationed in some specific markets. Minority members, African Americans in particular, tend not to understand the U.S. price-based economy and therefore do not have adequate participation in it. Price is the amount of money that is paid or received in the process of purchasing and selling of economic goods or resources. Price takes different forms in the economic markets for product, labor, bonds, and money. Also known as price mechanism, the price system decides what, how, and when each good is produced. Due to an unawareness of the concept of price mechanism from the general context, some people tend to associate price only to product or service. This is the price that the non-market challenged in particular seem to be very much aware of. They tend not to understand that labor, bonds, and money have their respective prices in terms of wage rate, interest rate, and discount rate. We consume to derive some happiness (utility). The extra happiness that a purchaser of good expects from an extra consumption of the good or service is valued by the price that the purchaser is willing to pay. Also the extra amount that the seller earns by selling one extra good or service is valued by the price received. Understanding the role of the price system, would enable the economically disadvantaged to measure their consumption, the worth of their labor, and the return from financial instruments in the bonds market.

With implied indirect negotiations, both sellers and buyers of economic goods settle prices in the product markets. When both the buyers and the sellers of a particular goods or service agree to a particular price point, the product market will get to its equilibrium situation where the quantity that the buyers purchased is exactly the quantity that the sellers sold. Relating to this simple procedure of the functionality of the product market will guide the economically challenged to becoming market participants.

In the bonds market where borrowers acquire funds from lenders, the price paid for acquiring and for releasing funds takes the form of an interest rate. Non market participants may not understand interest rate as the price that is paid for borrowers to use the savers' funds. This particular price does not seem to be recognized just as the price of a product is recognized. Limited interactive engagements in this elitist market where interest rate is established tends to inhibit the understanding of the interest rate as a price. As in the product market, an agreement of the borrower and lender to a particular interest rate point leads to a market clearing or equilibrium condition where the quantity of funds borrowed is exactly the quantity lent. The understanding of this simple process of the bonds market's interactive adjustments could promote the desire of the economically challenged to engage the activities of this particular market.

In the labor market, price is the wage rate paid to the provider of labor by the receiver of the effort of the labor. As in other economic markets, a common wage point agreed to by both the provider and receiver of the effort of the labor will create the labor market equilibrium where the quantity of labor provided is exactly the same quantity of labor accepted by employers. As applicable to the product market, people tend to be familiar with the labor market that is usually known as the job market. Relating to this particular market will enable the poor to be familiar with the critical issues of wage rate that is expected to be equal to the value of the physical marginal product of labor. Also, increasing participation in this market will lead to increasing awareness of the issue of discrimination, by race and gender, of immigration, of child labor, of employment related benefits, and of fulltime and overtime hours.

Another economic market is the money market. This market involves the Federal Reserve Bank, Fed's ability to control the economy's money supply by changing the discount interest rate and by conducting open market operation. Open market operation involves the policy on the commercial bank's reserve requirements, and buying and selling of the U. S. securities. The discount rate decision which targets the short run control of money supply is also set in the open market operations. If there is a large quantity of money in the economy that will lead to inflation (rise in prices), the Fed will increase the discount rate which is the rate that commercial banks pay to loan money from the Fed. All the interest rates charged by banks, savings and loans, mutual funds, credit cards, retirements funds, and pawnshops are influenced by the discount rate. For example, an increase in the discount rate will lead to an increase in the federal funds rate which is the rate that banks pay to borrow the excesses of other banks. Also, an increase in the discount rate will reduce the ability of the commercial banks to acquire cheap loans from the Fed and the rates that the commercial banks charge their customers will therefore increase. A reduction of a discount rate would increase the money supply to have an expansionary economic effect.

2.3 The Importance of Business Partnerships

Business partnership is a market attribute that brings people with common or in some instances from diverged functional backgrounds to amalgamate the skills and funds required to underwrite the initial outlay of starting a business that seeks to achieve some reasonable level of economies of scale. Specialized talents and enhanced financial resources would lead to operational efficiency for lowering costs to therefore maximize profit. In order words, business partnership enhances the division and specialization of labor to achieve the economies of size that may not be realized where a single partner underwrites the operation. By contributing funds and other resources to have a viable partnership, those who would not have exercised market entrepreneurship would therefore be in the market. More entrepreneurs will therefore be raised. Business partnership is therefore a vital market attribute that is necessary to achieve a reasonable continuity in business (Samuelson & Nordhaus, 2005, p. 119). Business partnerships in existing non-partnered businesses could enable the businesses to strive and to achieve business competitiveness and appreciable longevity. The benefits of comparative advantage could be enhanced where small initial venture capitals are merged to target some specific markets. If understood, business partnership could be the mechanism for alleviating ethnic minority-related poverty.

Businesses and professional partnerships are mostly in law, medicine, and technology, and are not common in petty businesses. Partnerships in small businesses are likely to engage the economic disadvantaged in buying and selling some goods and services. As the poor gathers market experience, their learning curve would most likely be an upward sloping curve. Poverty could diminish as the poor exercise market entrepreneurial activities. Not everyone may be active in some business partnerships. Some partners could be "sleeping partners". These partners, who understand the future value of money invested currently, could contribute funds or some resources or both to establish business or professional partnerships without being active in the day-to-day activities of the businesses. These kinds of partners could be seen as business financiers who expect to share from the profit of the partnered businesses. With limited involvement in the activities of the businesses, the sleeping partners could share from the profit in proportion to their contributions to the businesses. The active partners would expect earnings based on their contributions and for being active in the partnered businesses. The classification of partners as active or sleeping would depend on the charter of the partnerships. Financial institutions could partner with some groups of the economically disadvantaged with some concessionary micro loans to encourage the market participation of this group in the economic market that rewards greater than program incomes. Increased market participation of this group could diminish crimes and incarcerations. The poor, the less educated, and those with less market skills are mostly incarcerated (Georgia Department of Corrections, 2010).

Unfortunately, Dougherty County has not sufficiently realized the benefits of business partnerships as the few businesses that have partners reflect either Caucasian or Asian ethnicities. Even with the majority status of African Americans in the county, African American and White partnered businesses are not common, not even in the faith-based organizations. Even in the restricted economy of East Albany with African American majority, business partnerships are not visible among African Americans (Adams-Cooper, 2011). In this restricted area, black partnerships are visible mostly in nonprofit organizations and faith-based initiatives. In this same restricted economy, various business partnerships are common only among people of other races who understand the values of entrepreneurship and partnership. Generally, lack of partnership seems to emanate from distrust, from perceived disutility from interracial partnering, and from the fear of transferring wealth from one ethnic group to the other groups.

Trust is the denominator for forming enduring business partnerships. In order words, partnership rests on commonly accepted levels of integrity, honesty, and ethical behavior. An absence of a substantial trust from any member has the propensity to adversely affect both the earnings and the business reputation of other members. Unethical issues and violation of the laws can ruin a partnership. Community perceived ethical issues in any business could lead to avoidance of the business. To have a viable business, there must be a sufficient commitment in the different stages of business development. The commitment must be highly pronounced especially in the short run period of a business development when economic losses are possible due to the presence of a fixed cost—cost that must be paid even if production or service has not commenced. A hidden partner's agenda in a partnership is capable of causing some frictions among the members. Operational events reflecting a hidden agenda could drift a partnership from its mission.

The importance of trust in partnership is related to the principle of limited liability. The principle highlights that upon the failure of a partnered business, the partners can lose beyond what they invested in the business to pay creditors. They could lose their investment interest in other endeavors, their homes, and other personal belongings to pay creditors. Legally, upon the failure of the business, the richest partner or partners can assume the responsibility for the obligations of other partners that are financially unable to settle their respective obligations in the partnership. This situation compels the partners to demand the highest-level of trust from each and every partner.

An insinuation of business distrust and disagreement can be minimized with a formal document that provides a detailed expression on all the terms. Some level of self-interest must be compromised for the expected benefits of business partnership. Underwriting the initial capital outlay to have an efficient operation for maximizing profit ought to be important to all the partners. Participating partners need to understand why the current level of consumption is reduced in order to contribute to the optimal outlay to the partnership. Expected higher future levels of consumption relative to the current level must be an incentive to set up partnerships. Generally, partners share the earnings of the partnered business relative to their contributions in the business. Where there are both active and sleeping partners in the partnership, the partnership document must provide how the active members are to be compensated. The economically disadvantaged in Dougherty County could start off with some informal, small-scale partnerships to address some market niches.

2.4 Financial Market

A discussion on the benefits from participating in the financial market can be used to motivate the economically disadvantaged to exit from poverty. Given poverty, some people may not know about the existence of the financial market. Financial market is where the borrowers-spenders borrow money from the lenders-savers with bonds instruments. Issuing bonds instruments enable corporations, municipalities, cities, counties, and schools to raise money for development purposes. It is in the bonds market that the rate of interest (price of borrowing money) is established at the market equilibrium where the quantity demanded is equal to the quantity supplied of the bonds instruments. With reference to the Federal Reserve Bank discount rate, the established rate in the bonds market can decide the rates of interest that are expressed on small market instruments such as certificate of deposit (CD), savings accounts, and mutual funds. Also, bonds rates influence the rates that commercial banks charge their customers to borrow their loans. Banks' interest rate charges on credit cards, and pawn shops, payday and Check cashing rates are also influenced by the bonds rates.

Financial market provides an opportunity where lenders-savers earn extra incomes to augment the incomes from the labor market where the most aggregated income is earned. As the economically disadvantaged acquire market skills and principles, their participation in the financial market could substantially minimize economic inequalities. The economically disadvantaged should be led to realize that the reward from economic markets including the financial market substantially exceed the program incomes that if depended on for a long time, would perpetuate the disparities. Non market rewards may entice the economically disadvantaged since they are used to such rewards. With functional skills and market principles, the economically disadvantaged will understand the incentives for earning rewards from the markets. Expected high future market rewards and consumption must be shown to be positively correlated for the development of the contemporary skills and for engaging the market principles. This market reward challenge will highlight the desire of the economically disadvantaged to want to participate in the economic markets.

2.5 Federal Reserve System and Commercial Banks Activities on the Economy

The various interest rates in the commercial areas are related to the activities of the central bank of America popularly known as The Federal Reserve, Fed. The discount rate from the Fed influences the interest rates in our competitive economy. Just as bank customers pay some kinds of interest rates to borrow from the commercial banks, the commercial banks pay the discount rate to borrow a discount loan from the Fed. The Fed open market operation's policy on buying and selling of U. S. bonds influences the long run control of the money supply that in turn describes economic activities. With inadequate money supply, the Fed will expand the quantity of money in circulation by repurchasing the U. S. securities being held by the customers-purchasers of the bonds. As a result of the payout to the customers, the commercial banks would experience an increase in the amounts held in their vaults. Therefore, at the current or prevailing interest rate, the commercial banks are able to extend more loans to their customers. Entrepreneurs are therefore able to access more capital to expand the capacities of their business activities. Preventing the long term inflation would compel the Fed to encourage a tight monetary policy of selling U. S. bonds or securities. As a result of this policy, the short term discount rate could increase to encourage more investments in the U.S. bonds. An increase in this rate tends to increase the preference for investing in the U.S. secured or guaranteed bonds given that the U.S. government will not default on her instruments. The presentation of the various economic markets will encourage the economically challenged to have participations in them in order to earn the premium market incomes.

2.6 Entrepreneurship

Another market and income enhancement is the multiplier effect of entrepreneurship. Joseph Schumpeter recognized this effect that led him to characterize entrepreneurs as innovative market factor who organize capital and other resources to bring about economic development (Schumpeter, 1989). These creative risk takers are searchers of profit that are able to increase their incomes and those of others. Entrepreneurs are market innovators who take some calculated risks with the objective of maximizing profit. They analyze the possible options for dealing with market issues and then select the options that are deemed sufficient to address the market issues. They are able to engage marginal analysis procedure that weighs the marginal benefits against marginal costs (opportunity costs). Failure is possible in the markets but innovative entrepreneurs tend to persist in their search for profits. To have success, entrepreneurs will retry some other market options that are deemed feasible to engaging some other markets. Entrepreneurs engage market activities that would maximize profit from the appropriate scales of operations. The possible short-run losses due to the presence of the fixed cost may not deter the risk takers from targeting their expected planning horizon being the long run period. In this period, entrepreneurs would acquire more efficiency to diminish the average cost from their optimal plants or from the level of their operational activities.

Entrepreneurship relates to human capital that has both specific and general traits. Ucbasaran et al. (2008) presents that the specific traits characterize business, managerial, technical, and other special qualities. African American entrepreneurship is said to be highly limited due to inhibited specific market traits (Lofstron & Bates, 2007). Limited African American market entrepreneurship tends to lead their preference for values from the political, non-profit, faith-based, and hedonic activities that are non-market activities. Ashenfelter (1978) presents that the acquired general human capital is influenced by factors such as education, job related experience, and trainings. Arrow (1985) presents both quantitative and qualitative education for describing a functional human capital. Limited education and capital are said to hinder African Americans from having ownerships in the hard to enter industries. Even in the easy to enter industries, African Americans are said to have the low entry and high exit rates (Lofstron & Bates, 2007). Bearing on the work of Mr. Schumpeter and from the cited authors, every community needs entrepreneurs that self-select market norms to enhance their economic status and by so doing encourage others to earn market premium incomes. Market premium income is the difference between market income and the average program income from the same period. The difference would become a large positive value as more people self-select market activities instead of depending on income-supportive safeties of a welfare state.

The two kinds of entrepreneurship--specific and general seen not understood and are lacking most especially in African American community of Dougherty County. The specific entrepreneurship is the rare in-born type and could be hereditary. This is the special type of entrepreneurship that could develop early in the gifted people's lives. Parents could be the first to notice this specific type of entrepreneurship. This unique entrepreneurship could have a quick impact on economic development that could enhance the incomes and standard of living across the globe. The other kind of entrepreneurship is the general. This is the entrepreneurship that is acquired from education or from experiences. Generally, education enhances entrepreneurship but individuals' persistent learning and retraining will enhance the different levels of this entrepreneurship.

Schools and parents have the responsibility to reinforce the general entrepreneurship. Schools can encourage this innovation by providing effective, sufficient, and evolving curricula, savvy technology, and relevant internships. Mentoring can also reinforce the general entrepreneurship. Given the market constraints and rigidities, mentoring could focus on encouraging market innovators to create jobs and opportunities that will not only increase the innovators' incomes but the incomes of the others. Generally, African American majority neighborhoods do not have the entrepreneurship that evolved from the neighborhoods. Caucasian and people of Asian ancestry provide the limited entrepreneurship in these neighborhoods. These neighborhoods tend to duplicate faith-based initiative organizations, and businesses such as barbering and hair dressing salon shops whose scopes and scales of production are highly limited. With the limited entrepreneurship in the county, preference seems to be employment acceptances from the government, from faith-based organizations, and from the white minority establishments.

2.7 The Role of Micro-Financing Institutions

The economically challenged mostly could improve their market effectiveness with the presence of institutions such as micro financial institutions that specifically understand the plight of the poor. Relative to production and distribution, these institutions are on record for providing the moral, educational, and financial support to the economically challenged. As discussed in (Lui et al., 2006) communities, most especially the impoverished ones benefit from the presence of micro-financing opportunities. The opportunities could lead to financial shocks especially in the impoverished communities to effect reductions in poverty and in economic inequalities. The economy of Dougherty County has not financially accommodated a large number of the residents with low incomes. Particularly, the members of the African American community do not have an access to investment or production related capital. With the presence of many non-profit and faith-based organizations in the county, it seems they have more access to faith-based initiative loans than they do for commercial loans. Ethnic discrimination and segregation, limited education, and unavailability of collaterals seem to prevent the members of the ethnic African American majority in the county from capital formation.

Also, default from different levels of indebtedness that could arise mostly from consumer loans in a restrictive and impoverished environment such as Dougherty County could prevent a formation of production capital (Lardner & Smith, 2005, p. 74). In this environment the capital formation terms on the contracts of the conventional financial outlets will most likely not be favorable. Bank request from customers of compensating balances can inhibit entrepreneurial goals. Lack of an understanding of the functionality of the financial market most especially by African Americans could lead to their loan denial.

The problem of unavailability of especially small scale loans could be addressed by the introduction of micro financing establishments in the county. These establishment have tractable evidences of emancipating the economically disadvantaged from poverty in South America and in Southeast Asian countries. Micro finance establishments have multiple instruments to address the diverse groups of the economically disadvantaged. These instruments that have diverse attributes can include micro credit, project financing, asset leasing, loans and advances, and deposit and savings. A particular instrument's attributes relate to a specific economically disadvantaged relative to the group's understanding of a particular economic market, ability to bear risks, and willingness to repay concessionary loans. An economically disadvantaged that understand the opportunity cost of the depositors of the loan-able funds and could articulate the functionality of a particular market, could benefit from the higher end of the financial instruments with more attributes than those at the lower end. Some combinations of the instruments could be used to trigger increasing market participation of those that demonstrate some appreciable propensities to succeed in the economic markets. Those that have not participated in the market in the past could be considered for any of the lower end financial instruments. They could be subjects for frequent assessments and monitoring of their credits. A favorable outcome from the assessment could lead to a recommendation for the award of higher end instruments as long as the beneficiaries have market participations and are repaying the respective financial obligations when due.

2.8 Education, Skills, and Employment

Education and market skills as a labor enhancement factors in the labor market are the most commonly accepted for reducing unemployment and economic disparities. These factors add value to human natural endowment and they have significant impact in explaining the average wage rates (equilibrium wage rates) in the labor market. They enhance the average physical product of labor that is the firm's efficiency parameter for determining the wage rates. Also, they can explain employment longevity, upward economic mobility, and the frequency of labor mobility among comparable jobs, among vertical employment levels, and geographically. With the proper education and skills, labor will specialize for diverse functions and the general education acquired enables the training and retraining of labor to enhance their productivity (Theodos & Bednarzik, 2006, p. 43).

On the other hand, an uneducated labor would be expensive to train, to retrain, and also it faces the most employment shocks. Uneducated labor or unskilled labor and capital are substitutes in the production functions. This means that capital could easily replace labor when the price of labor becomes expensive or the price of capital becomes less expensive. Non-specialized labor does not command a reasonable comparative advantage in their respective employment. Hence the opportunity cost that is what is forgone for a particular employment could be comparable to the benefit from the employment. This assertion would imply that a non-specialized labor could be indifferent as to whether to remain in the respective current employment or to go back to the function that was given up. A situation like this does not lead to enhanced wage rates and other employment opportunities. Contrary to this situation, educated and specialized labor stands to enjoy substantial comparative advantages in their respective employment that are associated with the low opportunity costs.

Many studies support substantial returns to education in most circumstances. Generally, educated college graduates earns income that is about twice of the earning of an average high school graduate (Grubb, 1993; Welch, 1973; Hotchkiss, 1993; Theodos & Bednarzik, 2006). High school graduates are most likely to have more difficulties than would the college graduates when searching for jobs and other opportunities. An educated college graduate will most likely invest in the financial market where extra incomes are earned to augment the labor incomes. Given the high school graduation and dropout rates of 57%, 44% (Note 6) respectively, it is apparent that the county has not yet achieved a qualitative education. The limited qualitative education in mostly East Albany that is predominantly African Americans leads to the commercialization of the respective economy by recent Asian immigrants and white people. In this same economy, African Americans tend to focus on achieving the most non-market values from political, social, and faith based activities. Theodos and Bednarzik (2006) and Gardner and Hern (1992) observe that qualitative education correlates with productivity and earnings and with market equity. A low educational endowment is associated with a low level of human capital that could be subjected to a non-market discriminatory low wage rates and upward work advancements. A higher proportion of black women than that of the white women as heads of households with limited education is said to explain the disparity of incomes between the two groups (Browne, 1997). D'Amico and Maxwell (1994) observe that the labor market incomes of both white and black youths are comparable where both have comparable high school educational preparations.

3. Data and Methodology

With a survey instrument on the critical market factors on: partnership, entrepreneurship, financial market, and some other market concepts, data is collected from among the student-body of Albany State University that is predominantly African American. Albany State University is a public institution and part of the Historically Black Colleges and Universities (HBCU). The University is a co-educational institution that is located in Dougherty County of Southwest Georgia where the southern poverty is highly pronounced. The students come from different socio- and economic- backgrounds that need some treatments with the market related principles to ignite their general and any latent specific (in-born) entrepreneurship possessed. College students are most likely to engage in experiential learning that could ignite especially, the educationally driven general entrepreneurship.

It needs to be mentioned again that Dougherty County that houses Albany State University has African America majority that observes very little business ownership. It looks as if the university does not have an appreciable impact on the economy of the county. Therefore, the students in this university would be the adequate testifiers of poverty and economic inequalities. Since poverty and economic inequalities are race-associated, market sampling from this kind of institution will enable the adequate assessment of the extent that economic market principles are understood. Without any concern as to what other students in a diversified student-body think; the sampled audience from this university, would without any inhibition provide the true market data. This data would be the true representative of the respective population for verifying and for elevating the discussion on race related poverty and inequalities.

In Dougherty County that houses the university, preference tends to be expressed for public and private employment, and for activities in faith-based organizations. In this situation, one would expect the sampled data to express a latent entrepreneurship in the county. The students that applied to the survey may have taken or are taking courses in the functional disciplines that are capable of driving up the general entrepreneurship mostly, for the application to the markets. An understanding on how much GPA is related to the market concepts is important to describing market success. Students could be going through college without having pragmatic understanding of the related activities. To cultivate an elevated market disciplines, students need to conceive the market principles and pragmatic activities right from college where knowledge induces the general entrepreneurship.

3.1 Theoretical Models for the Economically Challenged Expected Incentive from the Market

An understanding of the market norms and principles is expected to increase market participation, and earnings from the various economic markets. These market desirables will be necessary to diminish the long run poverty and economic inequalities, and dependence on the income safeties of a welfare state. Therefore, the earning (income) from the market that is above the relative program income will be a function of the extent to which the average would-be- market participant understands the enduring market concepts of: individualized economic markets (mkt), business partnership (buspa), and entrepreneurship (entrep). With formal education, these norms will describe a would-be-market participant. Awareness of the individualized markets would highlight the understanding of the various markets for: products, labor, bonds, and money that characterize the U.S. economy. This general market-income function can be stated as:

$$Market\ income_t = f\ (mkt,\ buspa,\ entrep). \tag{1}$$

Equation one implies that the impact of the exogenous factors will cause the expected improvement of income. Income is positively related to each of these predetermined factors. The idea and activities of partnership would encourage individual's comparative advantage and specialization that will lead to groups' adequate economies of scale and the associated lowest average cost of their operations. Market will reward the knowledgeable participants that understand the functionality of the various markets that make up our competitive market economy. These participants are most likely to understand and to simulate each market to find out what the expected rewards or incentives are.

Market risk premium-income model can also shed light on the income improvement of a market participant. Some market risks included in this model introduce the market participants to some challenges of operating in a competitive economy. With the understanding and willingness to take some basic market risks, the market's individual participant would be expressing more desire to explore market opportunities where the expected income exceeds the program income. The risk premium-income model basically demonstrates the premium income there is from the market activities instead of dependence on a program income. Application to market, not handout or program income would therefore tend toward reducing poverty and inequalities. Relative to the discussion in Mishkin 2001, given the challenges facing market participants, the risk premium income from embracing market factors is the amount by which the expected market income exceeds the program income and is expressed as:

$$Market\ Risk\ premium = RET^e - RET_f = \beta(RET^e_m - RET_f) \tag{2}$$

Where,

RET^e = expected market income from all sources. This income underscores that the poor could attract some additional income on top of the dependent income

RET_f = Risk-free dependent or program income

β = Beta of the market

RET^e_m = Expected income from the market income.

The equation shows that the economically disadvantaged will be motivated to want to learn the market principles for participating in the economic markets where the market return is adjusted by the systematic risk (Note 7) described by beta. This adjusted return is substantially greater than the return from the program income. Where the economically disadvantaged learns and is able to apply to the various economic markets, the following equation shows the associated individual returns and risk parameters as:

$$Risk\ premium = RET^e - RET_f = \beta_1(RET^e_{factor\ 1} - RET_f) + \beta_2(RET^e_{factor\ 2} - RET_f) + \\ +. \ldots\ldots + \beta_K\ (RET_{factor\ K} - RET_f) \tag{3}$$

This equation can be pragmatically explained to financially motive the economically disadvantaged.

4. Research Findings and Results

Six hundred and sixty survey responses on eight market-related questions were drawn from 110 students of the student body at Albany State University irrespective of gender and ethnicity. Questions one to six have the right and wrong answers and the right responses on them are used mostly to describe the students' would-be-market participations. Their understanding of the market requirements and activities could describe the extent that the market could diminish poverty and economic inequalities. Questions seven and eight do not have the right and wrong answers and the responses on them are characterized accordingly. The following Table 1 and Figure 1 highlight the distribution and percentages of the responses on the right options on the survey questions. The number of performance responses from each category is related to the number of the responses on the representative range of the grade point average, GPA (2.9-2.5).

Table 1. Market success performances

Questions and Test	No. of Performances	% of Performances	Ratio of Performances and GPA
QI	64	58	1.2
Q2	72	65	1.4
Q3	57	52	1.06
Q4	89	81	1.68
Q5	98	89	1.85
Q6	30	27	0.57
N=110 responses on each question and 660 responses on all the questions			

Key on the Questions (Qs): Q1=Knowledge of different prices-price of product, wage rate, and interest rate, Q2=Knowledge of business partnership, Q3=Knowledge of financial market, Q4=Knowledge of entrepreneurship, Q5=Knowledge of maximizing business profit relative to cost and output, Q6= Knowledge of competitive product market. Q7 gathers information on Grade Point Average, and Q8 gathers information on African American Market Inhibitors.

The concept of price mechanism as allocator of resources in a competitive economy such as the U.S. has not been understood by a lot of the students. On the question addressing the recognition of competitive pricing in the different economic markets, only 58% of the surveyed students understands the role of the competitive pricing for allocating goods and services, labor services, and bonds in their respective markets. Thirty-eight percent of the responses sees competitive pricing only in the product market. This percentage is not surprising given that everyone goes to the product market to purchase goods and services. Only 0.07% of the responses shows the understanding of a competitive wage rate as a price in the labor market.

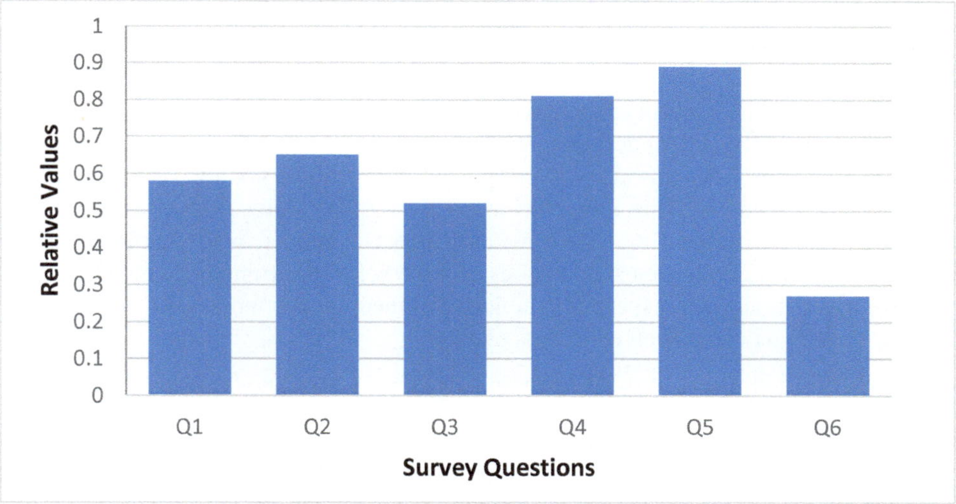

Figure 1. Survey of performance responses

Students need to reinforce their understanding of the importance of business partnerships as a way of amalgamating funds and other resources to underwrite the initial business outlays that are beyond the capability of an individual. Partnership provides a novel avenue to be competitive in small businesses that are expected to survive the short run losses, and for planning for the long run. On the respective question, only 65% of the student responses implies the students' market awareness of the critical role of partnership as a market factor.

This factor could lead to initial entry into the market and if one is struggling in the market, it could lead to diminished average total cost of operation due to the realization of an appropriate economies of scale. Roughly 34% of the responses implies unawareness of the critical role of partnership. Lack of business trust could be inhibiting the knowledge of this factor. By submitting to a legally drafted article on partnership, the members could substantially minimized the mistrust. If applicable, the mistrust could be further reduced by having very few active members to conduct the day to day operations while the silent or "sleeping members" participate only when called. With this arrangement, the active members get compensated for operating the business in addition to their compensation from the profit.

Students could be getting small loans from small financial companies without the basic idea of why individuals participate in the financial market. On the understanding of the basic knowledge for participating in this market, the percentage of the student performance responses is unacceptable. Only 52% of the responses has the common core knowledge that individuals participate in the financial market to lend and to borrow with the applicable instruments. A low percentage such as this could imply that the students are basically acquiring education only for the purpose of getting jobs. They tend not to understand the benefits of being in the financial market. Forty-three percent of the responses implies lack of the knowledgeability of this important market where extra incomes could be earned to augment the popular labor market incomes.

Students may have had entrepreneurship classes to be able to highlight the entrepreneurship factor. Generally, the level of assessment performance responses on the importance of entrepreneurship is acceptable given the associated 81% rate of the responses. Roughly, 19% of the responses would imply lack of understanding of the activities of entrepreneurship. While the rate of the knowledgeability of entrepreneurship portrays a general awareness of the activities of the market entrepreneurs, the specifics on how to observe the entrepreneurship factor need to be explored. Increasing awareness of the specifics on the factor could come from the understanding of the competitiveness of the markets and by engaging the concepts of: marginal analysis, comparative advantage and specialization, and global trade to analyze economic opportunities. Along with the understanding of the importance of market partnership, engaging these concepts and accessing functional capital, would determine whether market risk taking is worthwhile.

Articulation of profit and profit earning procedure is encouraging. On the respective question, roughly 90% of the responses encourages production according to a business' share of the market. The responses suggest that over production and underproduction will lead to producing at a high cost. Cost minimization is necessary to produce the efficiency output that would enable profits to be maximized according to the market competitiveness driven by the market structure. An understanding of the concept of marginal analysis will enable production and price to be pegged at the point where the marginal revenue is equal to marginal cost. Below this production point, increasing production would decrease the cost of production. And beyond this point increasing production would increase the cost of production.

Students have not understood the concept of competitive pricing in a competitive product market. Only 27% of the performance responses implies the understanding of pricing according to the competitiveness of the market. Seventy-two percent of the respondents do not understand competitive pricing. The respondents could be charging wrong prices by not knowing the competitiveness of the market they are in. It is imperative for market participants to realize that in competitive environments that each producer will charge relative to the price charged by the other producers of the comparable goods. A price below the going price could amount to the price going below the average cost and the respective producer will incur an economic loss. Also, an increase of the going price by even a penny will lead to an entire loss of sales.

Most responses on the GPA fall within the GPA range of 2.9-2.5 with a response rate of 48%. The GPA responses within the range of 3.5-3.0 constitute a response rate of 37%. With response rates of 10% and 4.5%, the responses fall within the GPA ranges of 3.6 and up, and 2.4-2.0 respectively. Cautiously speaking, these statistics would support that the students have limited understanding of the market factors. Also, they are highlighting the students' passiveness in college where they are supposed to be drawing meaningful market experiences. There must be leads and encouragements for the students to engage the markets pragmatically to achieve the most expected earnings, given the competitiveness of the markets.

Among other compelling factors, a limited education is mostly blamed for the limitedness of African Americans participation in the economic markets with a response rate of 36%. This is not surprising given a very low student academic achievements from the public school systems. Students may not be well prepared for college success. Students may not be caring enough about the importance of education as an income equalizer. They could be exercising the minimum effort in their pursuit of educational success and would apply to the jobs that do not require education if unsuccessful. To counteract these adversities at the college level, the activities of the institutional factors may need to be enhanced to encourage college related effort (Nwaokoro, 2010).

With a response rate of 30%, a lack of interest in taking risks is the second factor that is blamed for the inactive African American market participation. This is not surprising given that the respondents' cultural, economic, and entrepreneurial backgrounds are yet to reflect strong market requirements. Along with the functional business education, market simulation and workshops, application to pragmatic market activities and to business internships could assist to reducing the market inhibitors. Though discrimination and segregated environments as a factor prevents African Americans' market participation, its impact weighs minimally. Seventeen percent of the responses blames discrimination and segregated environments as being responsible for the inability of the African Americans to participate in the economic market. This low percentage would imply that the society is becoming fairer. The students may not have enough experiences to characterize discrimination and segregated environments.

Sixteen percent of the responses implies that lack of access to capital is the obstacle preventing African Americans' market participation. The responses on the access to capital may reflect the respondents' family experiences since college students are unlikely to ask for access to capital. This factor may not be considered as a strong market inhibitor because the respondents may not know what to do with capital in a market environment, where the White owned businesses have explored most of the benefits of economies of scale. Again this low percentage could be implying that the society is becoming fairer. In a nutshell, among other compelling actions, the responses provided on the survey highlight the need for effective education, increasing interest in taking market risks, elevation of access to capital, and a fairer society.

As expected most responses on the grade point average fall within the range of 2.9-2.5. To have some clue as to how the effect of education could improve market awareness, the number of the responses on this range is related to the number of the responses on each correct option of each question. The respective quotients from this relationship are posted in column four of the Table 1. For example, with a unit point improvement in the GPA, the understanding of the different prices of question 1, will improve by 2.1 points. With this estimate, one could cautiously say that education has impact in the awareness of market factors.

5. Conclusion and Future Study

Dougherty County is characterized by poverty, remoteness, and substantially low academic achievements from the public school system, discrimination and segregation, and the exit of white and rich African Americans from the county. With these adversities, there is a market failure in directing economic outcomes. To measure the awareness of the specific market principles, this study sampled college students' knowledge of the different prices in a competitive economy, of the importance of business partnership, of financial market, of entrepreneurship, of profit motive, and of competitive product market. College students are more likely to exercise the educationally induced market entrepreneurship to alleviate the economic adversities in the county. College education could even lead to a discovery of the latent specific human capital of the naturally gifted individuals that could foster economic development.

The general performance of the students from the survey is mixed and not encouraging. This is to say that most of the market principles are not articulated by the respondents. Specifically, they tend to have a bit of understanding of the principles of entrepreneurship and of the profit motive. More awareness of these fine principles is highly desirable for individuals to tie entrepreneurship with the incentive of profit rewards. Introductory courses in economics and entrepreneurship, if taught on pragmatic basis can highlight these awareness. Students need be asked to recognize the key words, concepts, and issues of significance from these courses and could be asked to apply to assignments that demands constructing market related narratives with the terms.

There is a performance failure in the recognition of the importance of competitive prices (wage, interest rate, and composite price of the goods and services), of business partnership, of the financial market, and of the competitive product market. Improvements on these principles could come from the introductory courses in economics, business, finance, and marketing. Improving GPA is expected to elevate market awareness. Future study on market awareness may have to focus on how quantitative courses could be interestingly taught to students. It is very important for students to enhance their aptitude on ratio and marginal analysis to empirically compare and contrast values—comparing apples to apples, and contrasting apples with oranges.

References

Adams-Cooper, V. (2010). *Addressing the Roots of Black Poverty in the United States: A Proposed Dual*

Macro-Micro, Niche-Market Network Systems Approach [White Paper]. Albany, GA: VAAC Consulting Inc.

Ahmed, S. M., Mushtaque, C., & Abbas, B. (2001). Micro-Credit and Emotional Well-Being: Experience of Poor Rural Women from Matlab, Bangladesh. *World Development, 29*(11), 1957-1966. https://doi.org/10.1016/S0305-750X(01)00069-9

Arrow, K. J. (1985). The theory of discrimination. *Applied Economics, 6*. Belknap Press of Harvard University Press, Cambridge, Massachusetts.

Ashenfelter, O. (1978). Estimating the effect of training program on earnings. *The Review of Economics and Statistics, 60*(1), 47-57. https://doi.org/10.2307/1924332

Bagi, S. (2008). An Analysis of Inequality, Human Development, and Economic Growth. *Southwestern Journal of Economics, x*(2), 69-80.

Browne, I. (1997). Explaining the Black-White Gap in Labor Force Participation Among Women Heading Households. *American Sociological Review*, (62), 236-252. https://doi.org/10.2307/2657302

Card & Dinardo. (2002). Skill-Based Technological Change and Rising Wage Inequality: Some Problem and Puzzles. *Journal of Labor Economics, 20*(4), 733-783. https://doi.org/10.1086/342055

D'Amico, R., & Nan, L. M. (1994). The Impact of Post-School Joblessness on Male Black Wage Differentials. *Industrial Relations*, 184-205. https://doi.org/10.1111/j.1468-232x.1994.tb00335.x

Dougherty County School System. (2002-2009). *DCSS Graduation & Dropout Rates. Dougherty County School System*. Albany, Georgia.

Farr, J. L., & Sibyl, S. S. (2008). *Albany, Georgia: the East Albany Neighborhood*. Federal Reserve Bank Working Paper, Albany Georgia.

Garder, J. M., & Diane, E. H. (1992). Working and Poor in 1990. *Monthly Labor Review*, 20-28.

Georgia Bureau of Corrections. (2010). *Reports: Annual Statistics*. Georgia Department of Corrections, Atlanta, Georgia.

Georgia Department of Labor. (2010). *1990-2009 Unemployment rate: Workforce Professionals: Historical Data*. Georgia Department of Labor, Atlanta, Georgia.

Grubb, N. W. (1993). The varied economic returns to postsecondary education: New evidence from the class of 1972. *Journal Human Resources, XXVIII*(2), 365-381. https://doi.org/10.2307/146208

Hotchkiss, L. (1993). Effects of training, occupation, and training-occupation match on wage. *Journal Human Resources, 28*(3), 482-496. https://doi.org/10.2307/146156

Hoynes, H. W. et al. (2006). Poverty in America: Trends and Explanations. *Journal of Economic Perspectives*, 47-68. https://doi.org/10.1257/089533006776526102

Khandker, S. R. (2005). Microfinance and Poverty: Evidence Using Panel Data from Bangladesh. *The World Bank Economic Review Advance Access, 19*(2), 263-286. https://doi.org/10.1093/wber/lhi008

Lardner, J., & Smith, D. A. (2005). *Inequality matters: The growing economic divide in America and its poisonous consequences*. New York, NY: New Press.

Lofstron, M., & Bates, T. (2007). African Americans' pursuit of self-employment. *Discussion Paper Series* (Discussion Paper No. 3156). Institute for the Study of Labor. Bonn, Germany.

Lui, M., Robles, B., Leondar-Wright, B., Brewer, R., & Adamson, R. (2006). *The color of wealth*. New York, NY: New York Press.

Mishkin, F. (2001). *The Economics of Money, Banking, and Financial Markets* (6th ed.). Addison Wesley, New York, USA.

Morduch, J. (2002). *Analysis of the Effects of Microfinance on Poverty Reduction* (pp. 1-163). NYU Wagner Working Paper. Robert F. Wagner Graduate School of Public Service, New York University.

Nwaokoro, A. N. (2010). An Investigation of Institutional Enhancement Factors on Student College Success. *Contemporary Issues In Education Research, 3,* 1-7. https://doi.org/10.19030/cier.v3i8.221

Riddell et al. (2011). *Economics: A Tool for Critically Understanding Society.* Pearson/Addison Wesley, San Francisco, California.

Samuelson, P. A., & William, D. N. (1998). *Economics 6e*. McGraw-Hill/Irwin, New York.

Schiller, B. (2008). *The Economics of Poverty and Discrimination*. Pearson: Prentice Hall. Upper Saddle River, N.J.

Schmitt, J. (2004). The Rise in Job Displacement, 1991-2004. *Challenge*, 46-68.

Schumpter, J. A. (1989). *Essays: On entrepreneurs, innovations, business cycles, and the evolution of capitalism.* New Brunswick, NJ: Transaction Publishers.

Selig Center for Economic Growth. (2009). The *multicultural economy*. Terry College of Business, University of Georgia. Athens, Georgia.

Servon, L., & Timothy, B. (1998). *Microenterprise As An Exit Route from Poverty: Recommendations for Program and Policy Makers.* Center for Economic Studies, Washington Plaza II, Room 211, Bureau of the Census, Washington, DC. https://doi.org/10.1111/j.1467-9906.1998.tb00430.x

Theodos, B., & Robert, B. (2006). Earnings Mobility and low-wage workers in the United States. *Monthly Labor Review, 34*, 34-47.

Ucbasaran, D., Paul, W., & Mike, W. (2008). Opportunity Identification and Pursuit: Does an Entrepreneur's Human Capital Matter? *Small Business Economics, 30*, 153-173. https://doi.org/10.1007/s11187-006-9020-3

Welch, F. (1973). Black-White Differences in Return to Schooling. *The American Economic Review, 63*(5), 893-907.

Notes

Note 1. The population percentage estimates are retrieved from: http://www.city-data.com/county/DoughertyCounty-GA.html, while the population estimate is retrieved from: http://www.city-data/county/DaughertyCounty-GA.html;http://dougertycounty.georgia.gov/03/home/0,2230,8466851,00.html

Note 2. The south that has one-third of the U.S. population has 40% the U.S. poor (Riddell et al., 2011, p. 269).

Note 3.This estimate is calculated from the purchasing power data of The University of Georgia, Terry college of Business, Selig Center for Economic Growth.

Note 4. High school graduation and dropout rates of 57%, and 44% respectively, and unemployment rate that rose from 7.4% in the early 1990s to 10.2 by 2009 characterize the county.

Note 5. The crimes indexes are accessible at: http://services.georgia.gov/gbi/crimestats/viewCrimeStatReport.do

From 2000 and 2010, the various crimes in the county included vehicle theft, larceny, burglary, assault, robbery, rape, and murder.

Note 6. Dougherty County School System provided these estimates.

Note 7. Systematic risk is measured by beta—measures the behavior (sensitivity) of an instrument's return to the changes in the market portfolio of instrument as

$$\beta = \frac{\%\,\Delta\, in\ instrument's\ value}{\%\,\Delta\, in\ market\ portfolio\ of\ instrument}$$

If the change in asset's value is less than the change in the market portfolio of instruments, the systematic risk is low. Any asset with a high beta is associated with high systematic risk, and is less desirable in the portfolio of assets and therefore should have a high market risk premium.

2

Effect of F Score on Stock Performance: Evidence from Indian Equity Market

Trilochan Tripathy[1] & Bijon Pani[1]

[1] XLRI-Xavier School of Management, Jamshedpur, India

Correspondence: Trilochan Tripathy, XLRI-Xavier School of Management, Jamshedpur, India. E-mail: trilochan@xlri.ac.in

Abstract

This study seeks to examine whether value investing strategy based on F Score when applied to high book to market firms can significantly shift the current and future stock performance in favour of the investor in the Indian market. The study engages the panel data model to analyse the impact of high F Score on contemporaneous and future stock returns (R_t and R_{t+1}), return on equity (ROE_t and ROE_{t+1}) and market to book value ($MTBV_t$ and $MTBV_{t+1}$) as stock performance measures. The study concludes that high book to market firms with high F Score can shift the distribution of contemporaneous and future stock performances in favour of investors in the Indian market. However such observation is most prominent and statistically significant at higher level when applied to future stock valuation measures than the future stock return as measures of stock performance. The outcome of the study would no doubt help the individual value investors, mutual fund managers and value investing strategists who have presence in the Indian market.

Keywords: value investing, F score, firm performance, book to market value, return on equity, high book to price

1. Introduction

Emerging equity markets are increasingly seen as important destination for investment in recent decades. One challenge investors especially those in asset management industry face is that of investing in emerging market deep value stocks. Literature suggests that these stocks are usually categorised as high book to market value and are often illiquid (Fama & French, 1993; Pontiff & Lawrence, 1998). Fishing for investment in distressed area of equity markets is difficult for funds that have to commit to scalability and easy liquid redemption norms along with regulatory rules. Alternative investment and private wealth does better in capturing this value tilt in their portfolios. There is larger upside return surprise in distressed stocks as the market has already discounted all the negative news and overpays for any good news, such as earnings surprise or management strategy. But in high growth stocks, good news is already factored in so more good news has limited upside return potential while negative news has bigger downside price movement risk.

The goal of this study is to examine whether value investing as a strategy based on Piotroski Score (F Score) when applied to a broad portfolio of high book to market firms can significantly shift the current and future stock performance in favour of the investor in the Indian market. Value investing in general and application of F Score as a value investing strategy in particular remain mostly limited to trading in the market space. However empirical evidences of the effect of F Score on stock performance are highly scanty, sporadic and mostly remain limited to the developed markets. This paper seeks to fill the gap in literature in demonstrating the effect of F Score on stock performance in an emerging market context. Firstly, Indian market is an interesting setting to examine the effects of F score on firm performance due to its regulation, risk, liquidity, growth potential compared to mature and frontier markets. Secondly, there is lack of comprehensive study for Indian markets, where investor's base for retail is expanding but limited to only 0.2% of its population, while global institutional investors have active participation after liberalization era (Gondhi & Sarkar, 2011). Further India is a natural choice among the emerging markets due to its strong and consistent growth among its peers.

Engaging panel data model over a period of 6 years on stocks drawn from the third largest stock exchange of the world (National Stock Exchange of India), the study concludes that F Score, when applied to a broad portfolio of high book-to-market firms, can shift the stock performance in favour of investors in the Indian market. F Score can also be used stand alone to measure how strong financially companies are in a stock portfolio or for evaluation of an acquisition target or for effect of management decision on long term financial health of the firm. It is a good measure of the financial soundness of a firm based on its bottom up financial data. The outcome of this study would no doubt influence the individual value investors, mutual fund managers and trading strategists who have presence in the Indian market.

The rest of the paper is organized as follows: Section 1 provides a general overview of the research work and discusses the objectives of the study. Section 2 reviews the major literature on value investing and hypotheses development. Section 3 presents the methodology employed in the study. Section 4 presents results of the study. Robustness examination is carried out in section 5. Section 6 concludes the study.

2. Review of Literature and Hypotheses Development

The book to market effect is probably one of the oldest effects which has been investigated in financial markets. The bigger the book to market ratio is, the more fundamentally cheap is the stock of the firm. Literature suggests that investors overreact to growth aspects for growth stocks, and value stocks remain thus undervalued (Debondt & Thaler, 1985; 1987). It is believed that the stock with high market to book value is often financially distressed and thus the larger returns generated by this stock is simply a compensation for risk (Fama & French, 1993; Pontiff & Lawrence, 1998). Since many decades, investment analysts worldwide have been adopting this value investing strategies to predict the stock and portfolio returns. Debondt and Thaler (1985 and 1987) also conclude that long term past losers outperform the long term past winners. While Jegadeesh and Titman (1993), report that in an intermediate horizon of three to twelve months, past winners continue to outperform past losers. Jegadeesh and Titman's (2001) study affirms that buying winning stocks and selling losing stocks based on their past performance provides abnormal returns and this zero cost momentum strategy provides abnormal returns. Sehgal and Balakrishnan (2002) report continuation of trend in short term and significant high returns of value investing strategy in Indian market from July 1989 to March 1999 for 364 companies. Fama and French (2012) have added momentum as a fourth factor to their three factor model to explain the excess return. Academic literature on value investing has grown leaps and bounds around the momentum strategies. Many of these studies look at company financial statements as a source of prediction of future stock value and price movement. Lev and Thiagarajan (1993) analysed 12 financial ratios and demonstrated their positive effect on future earnings growth. Ou and Penman (1989) similarly showed the predictive power of financial ratios in a firm's future earnings. Mohanram (2005) used financial statement analysis to show that fundamental factors can help pick winning stocks among low Book to Market stocks (Growth stocks) while Piotroski (2000) used it on high Book to Market stocks (Value stocks). The value investing proposition of Joseph D Piotroski (2000) even though aggressively used in the trading practices, has not been given enough scrutiny in the academic literature. Thus this study employs value investing strategies of Piotroski to bridge the gap in the literature in the emerging market context.

Literature amply evidences that portfolio of high book to market (BM) firms out performs the low BM firms in the future (Rosenberg, Reid and Lanstein (1985), Fama and French (1992, 1993, 1995, 1996 & 1998), Lakonishok, Shleifer and Vishny (1994), Kothari, Shanken and Sloan (1995)). Fama and French (1992) affirm that firm's book to market, characterised as a variable, measures the financial distress and in turn future stream of returns of the stock required to be fairly compensated for risk. This high future return attribution to high BM stock emanates from both market efficiency and inefficiency. On one hand literature evidences a strong positive relation between BM, leverage, financial leverage and other risk based measures, which ensure the contribution of market efficiency (Fama & French, 1992; Chen & Zhang, 1998). On the other, the high BM stocks are often mispriced and these stocks surprise with their quarterly earnings and dividends, which remains un-noticed by the market participants (La Porta et al., 1997). Empirical evidence also suggests that market doesn't fully incorporate historical financial information into price formation in future, which shows the inefficiency of the market (Piotroski, 2000). From an investment perspective, financial strategists normally don't choose the poor performing low volume and small capitalised firms (McNichols & O'Brien, 1997; Hayes, 1998). As the high BM firm managers suffers from credibility issue, their forward looking positive information disclosure fails to change the mood of capital market (Koch, 2002; Piotroski, 2000; Miller, 2002). There have been some studies on effectiveness of Piotroski F Score in emerging market which have been country or region specific. Galdi and Broedel Lopes (2009) study the Brazilian (BOVESPA) market where they found a positive relation of F Score to strong value stocks but when adjusted for arbitrage and short selling constraints of Brazilian market, this excess return disappeared; Asian markets has been studied by Kang and Ding (2005) where they found financially strong firms determined by F Score usually outperform weak firms. While Charles Hyde (2013) uses the MSCI Emerging Market Index for his studies which includes a very small portion of Indian listed firms.

Based on the research question of how Piotroski Score influences the stock performances in the Indian market, the following two broad hypotheses and six specific hypotheses are examined in this study:

H1a: There is a positive relationship between F Score and contemporaneous stock performance.

H1.1a: There is a positive relationship between F Score & contemporaneous stock return.

H1.2a: There is a positive relationship between F Score and contemporaneous return on equity.

H1.3a: There is a positive relationship between F Score and contemporaneous market to book value.

H2: Stocks with high BM and high F Score at current period positively influence future stock performance.

H2.1a: Stocks with high BM & high F Score at current period positively influence future stock return.

H2.1a: Stocks with high BM & high F Score at current period positively influence future return on equity.

H3.1a: Stocks with high BM & high F Score at current period positively influence future market to book value.

3. Materials and Methods

This section explains about the nature and sources of data used, variables used in the empirical investigation and their construction methodologies, and models engaged in the study.

3.1 Nature and Sources of Data

This study is based on secondary annual audited end of the year financial statements data obtained from Centre for Monitoring Indian Economy (CMIE) Prowess data base and Bloomberg. It is a challenge to find correct financial data for Indian companies over a long time frame. Databases that do contain financial information have gaps in this record over the study period. To overcome this problem, we used the Bloomberg data source and merged it with the CMIE to build the final dataset. Dataset looks at the NSE Top 500 companies in India across the whole time frame. These are the top 500 companies by market capitalisation listed on the National Stock Exchange, India. Any firm with missing data or erroneous data in the time line that could not be rectified was removed. After doing so, we were left with 266 companies whose data was available for the entire period of our study (2009 till 2015). This spread of companies covers blue-chip as well as medium and small capitalization companies. In 2009, the largest company in the dataset was Reliance Industries Limited with a market capitalization of approximately 2.5 trillion rupees and the smallest company was Geometric Limited with market capitalization of approximately 900 million rupees. The dataset constitutes 266 companies spreading across 9 different sectors such as basic materials, communications, consumer goods, energy, financials, industrial, technology, utilities and diversified. However, the final data set excludes all banking and financial institutions from our study and thus we are left with 215 firms. The financial data set that is used in this study contains the following variables: stock return, price to book value, return on asset, income before extraordinary items, cash flow from operations, total asset, current asset, current liabilities, long term debt, current ratio, gross margin, total sales, total shares outstanding, operating income, cost of goods sold, sector categories, market capitalisation and age of the firm.

3.2 Variables Used

Three stock performance related measures such as stock return, price to book and return on equity are used as dependant variables. The independent variables used in this study are F score, size of the firm, age of the firm and a set of 8 dummy industry variables. The interest variable is F score, which is constructed and used in the model. The stock performance examination is carried out both contemporaneously and with lead indicators of dependant variables. The following subsection presents in detail the F score construction methodology and other variables used in the study.

Following the prescribed scoring methodology of Joseph Piotroski (2000), we have constructed the Piotroski Score (F Score) using the historical financial information from our sample Indian firms. Although Piotroski uses his scoring system on a high book to market portfolio, we have used this on the Top 500 Indian companies listed on the National Stock Exchange of India (NSE) based on the firm's market capitalisation. While constructing the F Score, a scoring system is designed to capture the 9 fundamental signals- 4 profitability signals, 3 leverage and liquidity signals and 2 operating efficiency signals to measure the financial health of the firm. These signals are obtained from the firm's historical information on profitability, financial leverage and operating efficiency measures.

The four profitability signals are obtained from the last reported return on asset (ROA), last reported cash flow from operations (CFO), change in return on asset (ΔROA) and last reported income from extraordinary items

(ACCRUAL). The ROA signal value is 1 if the last reported ROA for the firm is a positive number otherwise 0. If the last reported cash flow from operations for the firm is positive then CFO signal value is 1 else 0. If the change in ROA scaled by total asset of the current year from the previous year is positive, then ΔROA signal value is 1 else 0. The ACCRUAL signal value is 1 if last reported income from extraordinary items for the firm is positive, otherwise 0. Likewise, three leverage and liquidity related signals are change in leverage (ΔLEVERAGE), change in liquidity (ΔLIQUIDITY) and change in equity (ΔEquity). The (ΔLEVERAGE) signal value is 1 if the change in long term borrowing scaled by total assets for the previous year is greater than the current year, otherwise 0. If the difference between current ratio for the current year from the previous year for the firm is positive then, ΔLIQUIDITY signal value is 1, else 0. If the previous year common equity outstanding for a firm is greater than the current year, then ΔEQUITY signal value is 1 else 0. Two operating efficiency signals come from change in margin (ΔMARGIN) and change in turnover (ΔTURNOVER). If the change in total sales scaled by total assets for the current year from the previous year is positive, then (ΔMARGIN) signal value is 1, otherwise 0. The (ΔTURNOVER) signal value is 1 if the change in total sales scaled by total assets for the current year from the previous year is positive, otherwise 0. Each signal output is expressed in terms of a binary response variable 1 as good and 0 as bad for the firm. The conditions used in estimating individual F Score components are given thereof in the Table 1.

Table 1. Conditions used in estimating individual F Score components

ROA>0	IF (ROA>0) then 1 else 0
CFO>0	IF (Cash flow from Operations>0) then 1 else 0
Change in ROA	IF(Current Year ROA/Total Asset - Previous Year ROA/Total Asset) > 0 then 1 else 0
Change in Accruals	IF(CFO- Income before Extraordinary Items)< 0 then 1 else 0
Change in Leverage	IF(Current Year Long Term Debt/Total Asset - Previous Year Long Term Debt/Total Asset) < 0 then 1 else 0
Change in Liquidity	IF(Current Year Current Ratio - Previous Year Current Ratio) > 0 then 1 else 0
Change in Equity	IF(Current Year Shares Outstanding - Previous Year Shares Outstanding) < 0 then 1 else 0
Change in Margin	IF(Current Year Gross Margin/Total Sales - Previous Year Gross Margin/Total Sales) > 0 then 1 else 0
Change in Asset Turnover	IF(Current Year Total Sales/Total Asset - Previous Year Total Sales/Total Asset) > 0 then 1 else 0

All the nine signal outputs are aggregated to arrive at the final F Score for each firm under study. Thus the range of F score obviously lies from a value of 0 to 9. A firm having F Score above 5, up to 4 and at 5 are classified as firms having strong financial health, weak financial health and neutral respectively. F Score may change over the years depending on the changes in the fundamental signal values obtained from 9 aforesaid parameters. F Score can be presented mathematically as follows:

$$F\ Score = ROA + CFO + \Delta ROA + ACCRUAL + \Delta LEVERAGE + \Delta LIQUIDITY + \Delta EQUITY + \Delta MARGIN + \Delta TURNOVER \quad (1)$$

Market to Book Value (MTBV): The MTBV ratio is used as a proxy for firm performance measure. This ratio is also known as Price to Book Ratio, which is normally used as a proxy for measuring firm's market performance. It is calculated as Price/Book Ratio = Stock Price Per Share / Shareholders' Equity Per Share or (Book Value of Equity).

Return on Equity (ROE): ROE is used in this study as a measure of the financial performance of a firm for the shareholders. It is an indicator of how efficiently a firm is managing the funds contributed by the shareholders. It is calculated as ROE = Net Income / Shareholder's Equity

Return (Rt): Return is calculated by taking the difference in start of the year price to end of year price as a percentage. To normalize the return data, we have used lognormal return series in our model.

Size: The variable Size refers to the market capitalisation of the firm. It is calculated using the total number of shares outstanding and the market price per share. Size = Number of Shares Outstanding * Market Price per Share

Age of the firm: It refers to the number of years the firm has been in existence since incorporation till the year under observation in the model.

Industry Dummy Variables: There are 8 industry dummy variables used in this study as per the classification provided by CMIE. These dummy variables refer to the industry sectors that the firms in our study belong to. They are as follows: Basic Materials, Communications, Consumer Goods, Diversified, Energy, Industrials, Technology and Utilities.

3.3 Model Used

In this study we engage two sets of panel model where the first set of model tests the contemporaneous effect of the explanatory variables on the explained variables and the second set of model tests the effect of the explanatory variables on the lead explained variables. To investigate whether F Score including other explanatory variables contemporaneously affect the stock performance indicators measured by stock return (Rt), market to Book Value (MTBV) and return on equity (ROE), we estimated three full panel models. The choice of the panel model whether fixed and random effect is decided based on the result of the Hausman test provided in section IV. The panel model specifications are defined as follows:

$$MTBV_{i,t} = \alpha_i + \beta_1 \text{F Score}_{i,t} + \beta_2 \text{Ln MC}_{i,t} + \beta_3 \text{Ln Age}_{i,t} + \gamma_j \text{D}_{i,j} + \varepsilon_{i,t} \quad (2)$$

$$R_{i,t} = \alpha_i + \beta_1 \text{F Score}_{i,t} + \beta_2 \text{Ln MC}_{i,t} + \beta_3 \text{Ln Age}_{i,t} + \gamma_j \text{D}_{i,j} + \varepsilon_{i,t} \quad (3)$$

$$ROE_{i,t} = \alpha_i + \beta_1 \text{F Score}_{i,t} + \beta_2 \text{Ln MC}_{i,t} + \beta_3 \text{Ln Age}_{i,t} + \gamma_j \text{D}_{i,j} + \varepsilon_{i,t} \quad (4)$$

However, to investigate whether current period F Score including other explanatory variables affect the lead stock performance indicators measured by stock return (Rt), market to Book Value (MTBV) and return on equity (ROE), we estimated three full panel models. The choice of the panel model whether pooled, fixed and random effect is discussed in the section IV. The panel model specifications are defined as follows:

$$MTBV_{i,t+1} = \alpha_i + \beta_1 \text{F Score}_{i,t} + \beta_2 \text{Ln MC}_{i,t} + \beta_3 \text{Ln Age}_{i,t} + \gamma_j \text{D}_{i,j} + \varepsilon_{i,t} \quad (5)$$

$$R_{i,t+1} = \alpha_i + \beta_1 \text{F Score}_{i,t} + \beta_2 \text{Ln MC}_{i,t} + \beta_3 \text{Ln Age}_{i,t} + \gamma_j \text{D}_{i,j} + \varepsilon_{i,t} \quad (6)$$

$$ROE_{i,t+1} = \alpha_i + \beta_1 \text{F Score}_{i,t} + \beta_2 \text{Ln MC}_{i,t} + \beta_3 \text{Ln Age}_{i,t} + \gamma_j \text{D}_{i,j} + \varepsilon_{i,t} \quad (7)$$

Where i stands for the firm, j stands for industry and t stands for time.

4. Results

4.1 Preliminary Findings

This segment analyses the results of descriptive statistics for variables that are used in the empirical examination in the next section. The combined mean ratio of MTBV over the study period is 3.22 which suggest that 72% of Indian firms' market value is not captured in their book value. This finding supports the empirical findings in many countries (Lev & Zarowin, 1999. Khanqah, Khosroshahi, & Ghanavati, 2012, Tripathy, Ranajee, & Mishra, 2015). The descriptive statistics associated with the variables under the study are reported in Table 2. The standard deviation of the MTBV of the sample firms during the study period are observed to be 4.26, which suggests that market to book value of the firms are not stable and varying across the time and firms. The mean and standard deviation of annual return (Rt) and ROEt series are observed to be -0.198 and 0.551 and 14.43 and 23.28 respectively. While the mean age and market capitalisation of the firms under investigation are observed to be 41.4 years and Rs.176905.6 million respectively However, the mean value of the interest variable i.e. F Score is observed to be 5.124 with a minimum of 0 and maximum of 9. The standard deviation, skewness and kurtosis value of F score are observed to be 1.45, -0.41 and 0.04 respectively. Likewise, the skewness and kurtosis statistics associated with all the variables used in this study are not normally distributed. Against this backdrop, to normalize and linearise all the variables we have converted them into natural logarithms.

Table 2. Descriptive statistics for the variables used in the study

2010-2015	F Score	MTBV	Market Capitalization (in Million Rupees)	ROE	Age of Firm (in Years)	Annual Return (in%)
Max	9	80.591	5002493	452.238	115	3.165
Min	0	0.0969	1903.383	-195.691	3	-0.864
Mean	5.124806	3.216	176905.6	14.432	41.416	0.198
Stdev	1.446996	4.264	422595.5	23.289	23.247	0.551
Kurtosis	-0.41476	97.187	35.03284	110.207	0.0287	5.274
Skew	0.04	7.205	5.214629	5.176	0.858	1.731

An attempt is made hereunder to explore a few descriptive statistics for the 1 year ahead lead stock performance indicators which are used as explained variables in the full models (5, 6 and 7). While exploring the mean return difference between the firms having high F Score (6, 7, 8 and 9) and low F Score (0, 1, 2, 3 and 4) for the high book to price firms, it is observed that difference across the years are positive except for the year 2012-13. While estimating the mean difference in MTBVt+1 and ROEt+1 under the said framework, it is observed that the differences are positive for both the stock performance indicators (Table 3). The study here suggests that firms having high book to price with high F Score tend to outperform the firms having high book to price with low F Score. However, this mean difference across the stock performance indicators may be confounding and thus there is a need of formal statistical test to establish the result. This test would be carried out in the result and discussion segment.

Table 3. Differences in lead stock performance measures based on high book to price with F score across time periods

High Book to Price with F Score and Lead MTBV				High Book to Price with F Score Lead Return				High Book to Price with F Score and Lead ROE			
2010-2011	MTBV	σ	CV	Return	σ	CV	N	ROE	σ	CV	N
High (H)	3.39	4.61	135.84	0.27	0.42	158.36	13	16.61	7.27	43.74	7
Neutral	2.13	1.80	84.52	0.20	0.24	122.56	6	23.64	21.05	89.05	3
Low (L)	0.97	1.50	154.09	-0.13	0.47	-356.80	6	13.21	4.53	34.29	5
H-L	2.42	3.11		0.40	-0.04			3.41	2.74		
2011-2012	MTBV	σ	CV	Return	σ	CV	N	ROE	σ	CV	N
High (H)	2.15	2.25	104.67	-0.33	0.35	-106.06	17	12.06	4.60	38.17	5
Neutral	1.50	1.28	85.36	-0.30	0.42	-139.69	8	15.06	3.65	24.22	4
Low (L)	0.79	0.84	106.81	-0.49	0.50	-103.57	12	9.01	5.70	63.23	8
H-L	1.36	1.41		0.15	-0.15			3.05	-1.10		
2012-2013	MTBV	σ	CV	Return	σ	CV	N	ROE	σ	CV	N
High (H)	2.20	3.08	140.15	0.24	0.20	82.94	17	10.86	3.88	35.73	13
Neutral	1.40	1.62	115.78	0.18	0.33	179.37	21	10.40	3.44	33.05	7
Low (L)	1.62	2.97	183.42	0.32	0.26	81.22	22	10.00	4.58	45.76	14
H-L	0.58	0.11		-0.08	-0.06			0.85	-0.70		
2013-2014	MTBV	σ	CV	Return	σ	CV	N	ROE	σ	CV	N
High (H)	2.36	2.96	125.47	0.18	0.37	209.09	17	11.58	4.67	40.36	13
Neutral	1.99	2.88	144.68	0.11	0.31	285.88	20	10.83	4.56	42.10	10
Low (L)	2.15	3.40	157.96	-0.08	0.30	-375.02	29	9.87	5.24	53.11	11
H-L	0.21	-0.43		0.26	0.07			1.71	-0.57		
2014-2015	MTBV	σ	CV	Return	σ	CV	N	ROE	σ	CV	N
High (H)	4.63	4.13	89.38	0.74	0.39	53.04	19	10.54	3.33	31.60	14
Neutral	3.33	5.49	164.70	0.35	0.35	98.36	19	12.50	7.76	62.09	6
Low (L)	6.10	16.27	266.81	0.43	0.51	118.21	27	11.66	3.62	31.03	7
H-L	-1.47	-12.13		0.31	-0.12			-1.13	-0.29		

High denotes F Score value 6,7,8,9 ; Neutral is F Score value 5; and Low is F Score value 0,1,2,3,4.

4.2 Main Findings

The empirical findings are reported under two subsections. The first subsection presents the findings from the contemporaneous model estimation. The second subsection presents, whether firms with higher F Score with high book to market value in ensuing year tend to have better stock performance in the following years. However, before carrying out the empirical examination, there is a need of choosing appropriate panel models and the following section makes such an attempt.

4.2.1 Model Selection Criteria

Table 4 contrasts the output of the pooled Ordinary Least Square (OLS) and four variants of fixed effect estimations such as Least Square Dummy Variable (LSDV), within fixed effect (Within) Models, between fixed effect (between) and fixed effect (FE). All four estimates produce almost different SSE and parameter estimates. However, it reports quite similar standard errors and goodness of fit statistics. While examining the pooled regression data, it is observed that goodness of fit statistic is high and statistically significant but it reports very high standard error and low R square value. Against this backdrop, it points out that the fixed effect model estimations are reasonably better having reasonably high R square value, low standard error and supported by F test at acceptable level of significance. Thus, we may use Fixed effect model for our examination.

Further we conduct Breusch–Pegan Lagrange Multiplier (LM) test to examine whether any random effect exists in our data set under the examination. The null hypothesis associated with the random effect model states that firm specific or time specific error variance components are zero (H0: error variance is zero). If the null hypothesis is not rejected, the Pooled Ordinary Least Square Regression would be preferred over the random effect model. The Breusch–Pegan Lagrange Multiplier (LM) test value turns out to be 1915.38 and significant at 1% level of significance, which suggests that the random effect model is preferred over the Pooled Ordinary Least Square regression model.

Now the challenge at hand is whether to model our data under random effect model or fixed effect model. To resolve this issue, we perform Hausman Test, which examines whether individual effects are uncorrelated with any other regressor in the model. If individual effects are correlated with any other regressor, the random effect model violates a Gauss- Markov assumption and the estimates are no longer best linear unbiased estimators. On the other hand, in the fixed effect model as the individual effects are linked to the intercept and regressor, which doesn't violate the Gauss-Markov assumption and thus estimators are still considered to be best linear unbiased estimator. The null hypothesis associated with the Hausman test is 'Random effect model is preferred over the fixed effect model (H0: differences in coefficient is not systematic. The test statistic associated with Hausman test for random effect turns out to be 7.32 and it is statistically significant at 1% level and thus we reject the null hypothesis. By summarising all the results of pooled regression, fixed effect model and random effect models, we thus conclude to build fixed effect model for the empirical examination.

Table 4. Selecting appropriate base model for empirical examination

Variables	OLS	LSDV	Within	Between	Fixed Effect
Intercept	0.0333 (0.24)	-0.6249*** (-2.78)	0.4453*** (5.88)	-1.056* (-1.86)	1.1771*** (6.00)
Lnfs	0.4260*** (5.01)	0.3679*** (4.49)	0.1672*** (3.56)	1.1103*** (3.13)	0.1672*** (3.56)
Basic Materials		0.4915** (2.51)			
Communications		0.8926*** (4.04)			
Consumer Goods		1.0259*** (5.43)			
Energy		0.3335 (1.48)			
Industrials		0.6799*** (3.59)			
Technology		0.9493*** (4.51)			
Utilities		0.2436 (1.13)			
F Test (Model)	25.29***	17.45***	12.68***	12.98***	
Degrees of Freedom	1288	1281	1074	1074	1074
SSM (Model)	22.20	113.3016	2.482	0.7036	0.1957
SSE (Residual)	1131.01	1039.915	236.02	149.856	210.2
Root MSE (SSE)	0.931	0.901	0.912	0.8388	0.4424
R^2	0.0193	0.0982	0.0117	0.04	0.8279
Adjusted R^2	0.0185	0.0926	0.015		0.8177
F Test (Fixed effect)					21.98***
Number of obs.	1290	1290	1290	1290	1290
LM Test: M value: 1915.38, [p value: <0.0001]			Hausman Test value: 7.32 [p value: <0.0068]		

Note. Figures in the parenthesis are t values.

*, **, *** represent level of significance at 1%, 5% and 10% respectively.

4.2.2 Full Contemporaneous Model

Model (2, 3 and 4) are estimated for the full sample period (2009-2015) with the fixed effect model combining all the firms and across 9 different industry categories. In total, 3 fixed effect models are estimated to examine the effect of F Score of the firms across industries and time on stock performance indicators (MTBV i,t, R i,t and ROE i,t) contemporaneously. In doing so, it is expected that F Score as a composite measure for financial health of the firms would significantly influence financial performances measured across aforesaid stock performance indicators. The estimated results of these models are reported in Table 5.

The observed R square and F values for model 2, 3 and 4 suggest that explanatory variables used in the models are significantly explaining the change in all the stock performance measures engaged under the study. The estimated results under these models also suggest that the coefficient attached to F Score is observed to be statistically significant at accepted levels for all the stock performance regressions. The sign attached to the F score across these models are observed to be positive, which suggests that higher is the F Score better is the firms contemporaneous stock performance and vice versa. These results lend support to our first set of alternative hypotheses under H1 (H1a: H1.1a H1.2a and H1.3a) that there is a positive relationship between F Score & contemporaneous stock performance measures (MTBVt, Rt and ROEt).

Table 5. Contemporaneous effect of F score on stock performance measures

Independent Variables	Dependant Variables		
	Ln (MTBVt)	Ln(ROEt)	Ln (Rt)
Ln (F Score)	0.3548***	.4446***	0.3182***
	(5.06)	(9.80)	(7.23)
Ln (Market Cap)	0.3027***	0.2262***	0.0414***
	(21.45)	(11.59)	(4.67)
Ln(Age)	0.0505	-0.0439	-0.0105
	(1.25)	(0.79)	(-0.41)
Basic Materials	0.2505	-0.0693	-0.0654
	(1.49)	(-0.3)	(-0.62)
Communications	0.5123***	-0.8529***	-0.2147*
	(2.60)	(-3.13)	(-1.74)
Consumer Goods	0.7576***	-0.1802	-0.0069
	(4.64)	(-0.8)	(-0.07)
Energy	-0.2748	-1.6129**	-0.2561**
	(-1.4)	(-2.26)	(-2.08)
Industrials	0.5315***	-0.2037	-0.0332
	(3.27)	(-0.9)	(-0.32)
Technology	0.6968***	0.3122	0.0648
	(3.78)	-1.23	(0.56)
Utilities	-0.1135	-0.4588*	-0.2165*
	(-0.61)	(-1.78)	(-1.85)
Constant	-3.7935***	-1.5805***	-0.6399***
	(-13.52)	(-4.07)	(-3.63)
Adj R-squared	0.3347	0.1933	0.077
F Value	65.85***	31.89***	10.36***

Note. Figures in the parenthesis are t values.

*, **, *** represent level of significance at 1%, 5% and 10% respectively.

4.2.3 Full Lead Model

To test the second objective we have estimated the full model with 1 year ahead lead stock performance indicators as dependent variables and current year F Score and other explanatory variables including industry dummies as independent variables. The model (5, 6 and 7) is estimated for the full sample period (2009-2015) with the pooled regression combining the firms and across 8 different industry categories and the estimated results are captured in Table 6.

Table 6: Effect of F score on future stock performance measures for the high book to price firms

Explanatory Variables	**Explained variables**		
	Ln (Rt+1)	**Ln (MTBVt+1)**	**Ln(ROEt+1)**
Ln (F Score)	0.0954**	0.3006***	0.0743*
	(1.99)	(3.56)	(1.85)
Ln (Market Cap)	-0.0082	0.256***	-0.008
	(-1.13)	(15.04)	(-1.15)
Ln(Age)	-0.0458**	-0.0913*	-0.055**
	(2.22)	(1.94)	(2.043)
Basic Materials	-0.0474	0.3065	0.062*
	(-0.55)	(1.53)	(1.82)
Communications	-0.0403	0.6362***	0.0076
	(-0.4)	(2.71)	(0.72)

Consumer Goods	0.0492 (0.59)	0.8642*** (4.44)	0.01227 (1.22)
Energy	-0.1227 (-1.22)	-0.2116 (-0.191)	-0.0498 (-0.6)
Industrials	-0.0498 (-0.6)	0.5485*** (2.83)	0.177*** (2.57)
Technology	0.1191 (1.26)	0.7817*** (3.57)	0.0314* (1.72)
Utilities	-0.1381 (-1.44)	-0.1314 (-0.59)	-0.216 (-1.5)
Constant	-0.2486 (-1.73)	-3.4403*** (-10.32)	-2.3445*** (-10.45)
Adj R-squared	0.0374	0.259	0.0198
F Value	6.01***	38.57***	3.45**

Note. Figures in the parenthesis are t values.
*, **, *** represent level of significance at 1%, 5% and 10% respectively.

While estimating these models, we intend to examine the effect of high F Score for the firms having high book to price value across the industries and time on one period lead stock performance indicators (MTBV i,t+1, R i,t+1 and ROE i,t+1). The F Score obtained against each firm in each period is categorised into three different categories. The firms having F Score above 5, up to 4 and at 5 are classified as firms with strong financial health, weak financial health and neutral respectively. Further, a firm having book to price ratio above 1 and otherwise are categorised as high book to price firms and low book to price firms. It is expected that firms having better financial health represented by high F Score with high book to market value can significantly shift the future stock performance in favour of the investors. The estimated results of these models are reported in Table 6.

The observed R square and F values for model 5, 6 and 7 suggests that explanatory variables used in the models are significantly explaining the change in all the stock future performance measures engaged under the study. It is also observed that the coefficient attached to F Score is observed to be positive and statistically significant at accepted levels for all the stock performance regressions. However, the F Score coefficient attached to return regression is statistically significant at 10% level of significance which shows that F Score has weak explanatory power to influence the firms' future return compared to two other stock performance indicators. The result here affirms that future stock performance of firms having higher book to market value would be better for the firms having higher F score as against the firms having lower F Score. These results lend support to our first set of alternative hypotheses H2 at least at 10% level of significance (H2a: H2.1a H2.2a and H2.3a). That means there is a positive relationship between current F Score and future stock performance measures (MTBVt+1, Rt+1 and ROEt+1).

5. Robustness Tests

An unobservable correlated with F score and firm performance measures may be present and would make coefficient estimates biased. hence, to justify our results two robustness tests are attempted i.e.one test is calibrated with F Score's concurrent measure and other test calibrated with a year specific cross section regression where a current period (2016) firm performance measure is regressed on the previous period (2015) F score. Further a 'current period enterprise value (EV) as a control variable is also included in the second model. The logic of including EV into the second model emanates from the fact that the EV has a direct linkage with the firm performance. Thus the first model is estimated with concurrent high F score with the contemporaneous firm performance measures. The result suggests that firms with high F score in the current period don't have any statistically significant effect on firm performance measures (Panel A of Table 7). The results here corroborate our findings that a firm high F score in the current period expected to perform better in the future. Second, robustness model is developed where each firm performance measures of the year 2016 are regressed separately on F scores of 2015. It is observed that the firm with high F score in the year 2015 significantly influencing the firm performance in the year 2016 (Panel B of Table 7). Overall analysis suggests that our estimated results are robust and unbiased.

Table 7: Robustness examination results for firm performance measures and F score

Panel A			
Description	MTBV(t)	Return (t)	ROE (t)
Intercept	3.027 (0.383)	-1.221 (-1.259)	-2.446 (-0.038)
LnFS (t)	0.315 (0.079)	0.823 (1.396)	12.582 (0.388)
F value	0.006	2.828*	0.151
R Square	0.000	0.012	0.006
Panel B			
Description	LnMTBV t+1	RETt+1	ROE t+1
Intercept	-12.592*** (-2.577)	-0.045 (-0.183)	-0.530** (-2.014)
LNFS	6.434** (2.013)	0.571*** (3.128)	0.779*** (4.024)
LEV	1.079*** (3.275)	0.037** (2.234)	0.095*** (2.680)
Adjusted R Square	0.046	0.075	0.062
F Statistic	6.214***	8.654***	8.098***

Note. Figures in the parenthesis are t values. *, **, *** represent level of significance at 1%, 5% and 10% respectively.

6. Conclusion

The study has engaged the panel data model to analyse the impact of high Piotroski Score on current and future stock return (R_t and R_{t+1}), return on equity (ROE_t and ROE_{t+1}) and market to book value ($MTBV_t$ and $MTBV_{t+1}$) as stock performance measures. The study concludes that F Score as a simple accounting-based fundamental analysis strategy applied to firms having high book to market value with high F score can shift the distribution of returns earned by an investor in the Indian market. The impact of this single index F Score measure is observed to be statistically significant when applied to future stock valuation rather than on the future stock return at least at 5% level of significance. . The result here affirms that future stock performance of firms having higher book to market value would be better for the firms having higher F score as against the firms having lower F Score. These results lend support to our second set of alternative hypotheses at least at 10% level of significance (H2a: H2.1a H2.2a and H2.3a) that there is a positive relationship between F Score & future stock performance measures (MTBVt+1 Rt+1 and ROEt+1). To the best of our knowledge, until now not much systematic study has empirically investigated the effect of F score on stock performance in the Indian equity market. However this study is not free from limitations. The convergence of data from different sources may have potential problems and our estimated results may be questioned. Thus there is a need for further research to look into this issue more carefully. The results may be further validated with the extended time period and including more firms into the sampling framework. However, the outcome of the study may help the individual value investors, mutual fund managers and value investing strategists who have presence in the Indian market. This paper contributes to the literature by providing evidence and applicability of value investment strategy based on F Score in the emerging market context.

References

Chen, N., & Zhang, F. (1998). Risk and return of value stocks. *The Journal of Business, 71*(4), 501-535. https://doi.org/10.1086/209755

De Bondt, W. F., & Thaler, R. (1985). Does the stock market overreact? *The Journal of Finance, 40*(3), 793-805. https://doi.org/10.1111/j.1540-6261.1985.tb05004.x

De Bondt, W. F., & Thaler, R. (1987). Further evidence on investor overreaction and stock market seasonality. *The Journal of Finance, 42*(3), 557-581. https://doi.org/10.1111/j.1540-6261.1987.tb04569.x

De, S., Gondhi, N. R., & Sarkar, S. (2011). Behavioral biases, investor performance, and wealth transfers between investor groups. *Investor Performance, and Wealth Transfers between Investor Groups* (November 15, 2011). https://doi.org/10.2139/ssrn.2022992

Fama, E. F., & French, K. R. (1992). The cross-section of expected stock returns. *The Journal of Finance, 47*(2), 427-465. https://doi.org/10.1111/j.1540-6261.1992.tb04398.x

Fama, E. F., & French, K. R. (1993). Common risk factors in the returns on stocks and bonds. *Journal of Financial Economics, 33*(1), 3-56. https://doi.org/10.1016/0304-405x(93)90023-5

Fama, E. F., & French, K. R. (1995). Size and book to market factors in earnings and returns. *The Journal of*

Finance, 50(1), 131-155. https://doi.org/10.1111/j.1540-6261.1995.tb05169.x

Fama, E. F., & French, K. R. (1996). Multifactor explanations of asset pricing anomalies. *The Journal of Finance, 51*(1), 55-84. https://doi.org/10.1111/j.1540-6261.1996.tb05202.x

Fama, E. F., & French, K. R. (1998). Value versus growth: The international evidence. *The Journal of Finance, 53*(6), 1975-1999. https://doi.org/10.1111/0022-1082.00080

Fama, E. F., & French, K. R. (2012). Size, value, and momentum in international stock returns. *Journal of Financial Economics, 105*(3), 457-472. https://doi.org/10.1016/j.jfineco.2012.05.011

Hayes, R. (1998). The impact of trading commission incentives on analysts' stock coverage decisions and earnings forecasts. *Journal of Accounting Research, 36*(2), 299-320. https://doi.org/10.2307/2491479

Jaspal, S. K. K. (2015). Adding value to value stocks in Indian stock market: An empirical analysis. *International Journal of Law and Management, 57*(6), 621-636. https://doi.org/10.1108/ijlma-09-2014-0055

Jegadeesh, N., & Titman, S. (1993). Returns to buying winners and selling losers: Implications for stock market efficiency. *The Journal of Finance,* 65-91. https://doi.org/10.1111/j.1540-6261.1993.tb04702.x

Jegadeesh, N., & Titman, S. (2001). Profitability of momentum strategies: An evaluation of alternative explanations. *The Journal of Finance, 56*(2), 699-720. https://doi.org/10.1111/0022-1082.00342

Koch, A. S. (2002). *Financial distress and the credibility of management earnings forecasts.* https://doi.org/10.2139/ssrn.415580.

Kothari, S. P., Shanken, J., & Sloan, R. G. (1995). Another look at the cross-section of expected stock returns. *The Journal of Finance, 50*(1), 185-224. https://doi.org/10.1111/j.1540-6261.1995.tb05171.x

Lakonishok, J., Shleifer, A., & Vishny, R. W. (1994). Contrarian investment, extrapolation, and risk. *The Journal of Finance, 49*(5), 1541-1578. https://doi.org/10.1111/j.1540-6261.1994.tb04772.x

Lev, B., & Zarowin, P. (1999). The boundaries of financial reporting and how to extend them. *Journal of Accounting Research, 37*(2), 353-385. https://doi.org/10.2307/2491413

McNichols, M., & O'Brien, P. C. (1997). Self-selection and analyst coverage. *Journal of Accounting Research, 35*, 167-199. https://doi.org/10.2307/2491460

Miller, G. S. (2002). Earnings performance and discretionary disclosure. *Journal of Accounting Research, 40*(1), 173-204. https://doi.org/10.1111/1475-679x.00043

Piotroski, J. (2000). Value investing: The use of historical financial statement information to separate winners from losers. *Journal of Accounting Research, 38*, 1-41. https://doi.org/10.2307/2672906

Pontiff, J., & Lawrence, D. S. (1998). Book-to-market ratios as predictors of market returns. *Journal of Financial Economics, 49*(2), 141-160. https://doi.org/10.1016/s0304-405x(98)00020-8

Porta, R. L., Lakonishok, J., Shleifer, A., & Vishny, R. (1997). Good news for value stocks: Further evidence on market efficiency. *The Journal of Finance, 52*(2), 859-874. https://doi.org/10.1111/j.1540-6261.1997.tb04825.x

Rosenberg, B., Reid, K., & Lanstein, R. (1985). Persuasive evidence of market inefficiency. *The Journal of Portfolio Management, 11*(3), 9-16. https://doi.org/10.3905/jpm.1985.409007

Salteh, H. M., Ghanavati, E., Khanqah, V. T., & Khosroshahi, M. A. (2012). Capital structure and firm performance; Evidence from Tehran Stock Exchange. *International Proceedings of Economics Development & Research, 43*, 225-230.

Sehgal, S., & Balakrishnan, I. (2002). Contrarian and momentum strategies in the Indian capital market. *Vikalpa, 27*(1), 13-20. https://doi.org/10.1177/0256090920020103

Tripathy, T., Ranajee, & Mishra, A. K. (2015). Time-varying momentum return in Indian stock market. *International Journal of Behavioural Accounting and Finance, 5*(3-4), 203-241. https://doi.org/10.1504/ijbaf.2015.075330

Seasoned Equity Offerings as Technical Market Anomalies: Long-Term Temporal Trading Functionalities

Vasiliki A. Basdekidou[1]

[1] SRFA Aristotle University of Thessaloniki, Greece

Correspondence: Vasiliki A. Basdekidou, Special Research Fund Account (ELKE), Aristotle University of Thessaloniki, Greece. E-mail: Vasiliki.Basdekidou@gmail.com

Abstract

The main goal of this paper is to approach the Seasoned Equity Offerings (SEO) trading opportunities as technical market anomalies and under the prism of a number of temporal (time-based) long-term trading functionalities (long-term TTF) introduced for the first time in corporate finance literature. The long-term is defined, for the purposes of this paper, as the 3-year time period, traded usually with daily, weekly and monthly time-frames. Trading is a temporal (i.e. time-based) historical living system with a number of functions, like: SEO, IPO, stock (instrument) price action Gaps, Breakouts, etc. In this domain, a number of warning long-term and short-term dynamics timing functionalities is available, like: candlestick patterns breaks, price action patterns pivotal-lines breaks, on open gup-ups (ooGUp), on open gup-downs (ooGDn), morning breakouts (mB), etc. All these time-based functionalities are regarded as 2nd level functions (i.e. functions of functions; because of the timing involved) with great trading opportunities, and they are defined –for the first time in the corporate finance literature- by this paper as temporal (timing) trading functionalities. In particular, the SEOs with the embedded long-term TTF functionalities are great trading opportunities for the institutions, the individual (non-commercial) market investors, the swing traders, and the speculators. Data analysis shows that during the seasoned equity offerings time, shareowners significantly increase their share-holding, including offerings that would be classified as overpriced at that time; hence, the involved trading volatility is increased resulting in great trading and profit opportunities. This paper contributes to corporate finance literature by examining the SEOs functions and define and document their inherit TTF functionalities. For this purpose, four categories of share-holders are regarded: The long-term institution & non-commercial traders (investors), the swing momentary institution traders (institutions), the short-term non-commercial traders (speculators) and the intraday non-commercial traders (speculators). Paper concludes that, in SEO/long-term TTF trading, apart from the insiders, the swing traders (usually the smart-money and the institutions) are more benefited, at the expense of momentary short-term and intraday speculators, while the long-term investors are not affected by the SEO offerings.

Keywords: equity issue timing, corporate ownership, liquidity, market timing, seasoned equity offerings (SEO), temporal (timing) trading functionalities (TTF), technical market anomalies

1. Introduction

The main goal of this paper is to approach the Seasoned Equity Offerings (SEO), as technical market anomalies and trading opportunities, under the prism of a number of temporal (time-based) long-term trading functionalities (long-term TTF) introduced for the first time in corporate finance literature. The long-term is defined, for the purposes of this paper, as the 3-year time period, traded usually with daily, weekly and monthly time-frames.

1.1 Problem Introduction

Trading is regarded as a temporal historical living system (Styliadis, 2007; Styliadis & Vassilakopoulos, 2005) with a number of time-based company initiatives operating as trading functions. Historically, trading company initiatives is undertaken by insiders and technical analysis speculators without semantic temporal influence in their plans and strategies. In these initiatives, the issuing company allocates securities (and particularly "shares" and not other securities like bonds, warrants, etc.) to new owners resulting in company's outstanding capital growing. One of these company initiatives is the SEO which, like the IPO initiative (Choie, 2016), has a great temporal (timing) trading functionality (Hovakimian & Hu, 2016; Demiralp et al., 2011), resulting in excellent profit & wealth growth opportunities (Ogden & Wu, 2013; Basdekidou, 2015). In this domain, economics and finance literature reasoning that the companies "time" their SEOs and IPOs to months of relatively high stock prices, mainly because the CEOs and officers think that the prices of the shares (company stocks) will probably be overbought at such "times" (an encapsulated TTF functionality).

The observed mispricing, as a typical technical market anomaly, concealed such as trading timing and could be regarded as the result of the lack of any available TTF information (for the investors, traders, institutions and speculators) for the embedded time-based behavioral biases dominant in securities (equities), Forex and option markets (Basdekidou, 2016a; Basdekidou, 2016b; Basdekidou & Styliadou, 2017). The reason that long-term investors (institutions) could buy overbought shares in SEOs/TTF is the same, in regard also with Edelen, Ince, and Kadlec (2015), who provide evidence that long-term investors, traders and speculators prefer to purchase shares classified as overbought (momentum trading psychology) based on a number of classical equities-trading strategies ("trend-follow" trading, but without any TTF functionality in this case).

Corporate financing approach emphasizes that disengagement of holding and domination has as a result the clash of interest between outside shareowners, CEOs, and governors (Jensen, 1986). In this domain, the literature reasoning is that big corporate shareowners (not interested in short-term trading; not using TTF functionalities in their trading plans) can alleviate such things as clashes by positioning, observing and controlling CEOs and governors through the SEC reports (Hartzell & Starks, 2003; Myers & Majluf, 1984).

Trading (Myers & Majluf, 1984) and trading timing (Baker & Wurgler, 2002) approaches of economics and finance try to clarify such attitude, assuming that the shares trading decisions (i.e. open/close positions; lot trade size, etc.) are formed for the regard of old non-speculative shareowners (investors), who adequately take profit from SEO shares just as a consequence of right-timing SEO initiatives/issues based on long-term (year) time trading functionalities (SEO/long-term TTF) and not as a result of a well-designed, based on long-term TTF, trading strategy. The current paper agrees that the data are consistent and produce profit with such expectations, as far as the timing of the company's SEO initiatives is regarded as a long-term TTF functionality.

1.2 Problem Importance Exploration

In the situation of equities and non-equities SEO "timing" (stocks, options, Forex, etc.), Cesari, Espenlaub, Khurshed, and Simkovic (2012) argues on the effects of share-holding and stock liquidation on the SEO/TTF timing transactions of open and close position (i.e. "*buy*" in case of a short position; and "*sell*" in case of a long position), but no more details for long-term TTF functionalities were given; and Demiralp, D'Mello, Schlingemann, and Subramaniam (2011) state that old-issue share returns and passive trading, are both strongly connected with the coexisting old-issue changes in corporate holding for a time period up to 3 years after the SEO/TTF time. This 3-year period is regarded as too big, even for the "*buy-and-hold*" investors, for nowadays swing and volatile securities markets (leveraged 3x ETFs; Gold, Silver, WTI Oil, and Natural Gas ETNs; etc.).

In this article, the author concludes that her results are persistent with the control acting of long-term passive-trading investors. Also, in this case the TTF functionalities were not discussed. Furthermore, Hao (2014) states that companies with higher short-term non-commercial shareowners (speculators) enjoy more negative atypical results at the report release (TTF timing) of SEOs and concludes that momentary corporate shareowners and speculators are not prompted to control the usage of the lifted trading capital and profit (Choie, 2016; Hovakimian & Hu , 2016).

1.3 Relevant Scholarship Description

The current article is relevant to some other articles that investigate corporate share-holding under the prism of the SEO/TTF timing. In this frame, some articles (Choie, 2016; Markoulis & Neofytou, 2016) targeted on the information asset and stock-taking intelligence of corporate investors, while others (Hao, 2014; Baker, Stein, & Wurgler, 2003) targeted the trading strategies and plans, but in both cases no TTF information was given. Gibson, Safieddine, and Sonti (2004) report that seasoned equity and option SEO initiatives, with the bigger boost in corporate share-holding, are detected between the (relative to SEO/TTF, SEO timing) quarters −1 and +1; these long-term investors reported that their positions outperform in the subsequent the SEO issue year and qualify this outperform to their competitive convenience asset position. Chemmanur, He, and Hu (2009) find that long-term passive-trading investors (as opposed to non-commercial short-term investors and traders) are likely to experience bigger share positions in SEOs hoping on better results (profit) and their transactions somewhat greatly exceed a (even a well designed) passive "*buy-and-hold*" trading plan by the share-holding investors (Nguyen & Tran, 2016; Basdekidou, 2016a; Basdekidou & Styliadou, 2017).

In accordance to the above situation, Edelen, Ince, and Kadlec (2015), examined corporate trading and securities return divergences, and discovered that corporate firms prefer to purchase shares categorized as overbought and this is regarded as a non-positive association (i.e. relationship functionality) between corporate open-position and future trading (close-position) result. In opposition to these articles that spotlight on whether long-term investors and old-shareowners are better-informed (i.e. insiders functionality), the current research article targets on the dominant relationship and the underlined trading functionalities between the corporate shareowners and the CEO/managers (Basdekidou, 2016b).

Alti and Sulaeman (2012) also expressed a disaggrement to these articles, by pointing out how company SEO issuing initiative is influenced by corporate and non-commercial trading. In their paper, they support the position that strong securities trading results and profit trading trigger equity derivation only if the later is connected with a great pre-issue corporate investor demand, as it is regarded to be consistent with the new corporate holdings (swing momentary traders). Alti and Sulaeman also clarify their results as logical and dependable with SEO initiatives using the corporate investor demand as a gauge of the market's interest in the company's equity SEO initiative.

In this domain, the main target of the current article is disparate. Actually, I investigate whether old shareowners (as long-term investors), gain profit from the SEO/TTF timing. It is notable that, the results obtained do not depend on the supposition and conclusion that SEOs/governors are gauged to sell overbought shares for the interest and profit of such kind of shareowners (corporate investors as opposed to non-commercial momentary speculators).

1.4 Paper's Structure

The rest of the article is organized as follows: Section 2 ("*Share-holding & Trading Data*") describes the share-holding data as the corporate share-holding variables; Section 3 ("*Temporal (timing) Trading Functionality*") documents the introduced TTF term by examining the relation between SEO timing and institutional & non-commercial share purchases, as well as the impact of corporate & non-commercial holdings on SEO timing; Finally, Section 4 ("*Conclusions & Discussion*") summarizes the conclusions and discusses paper's innovations and contributions.

2. Share-holding & Trading Data (Institutions and Non-Commercial Traders)

For the current paper, the share-holding information, the changes in insider holdings & some sample profit/losses trading data (1990-2016) –used in this paper as the share-holding & profit variables- came from many resources. The Barron's information databases and sources, a Wall Street Journal affiliate (Barron's, 2016); the StockCharts.com initiative; the Securities & Exchange Commission/SEC notices, releases & announcements; the Commitments of Traders (CoT) / CFTC speculative net positions reports; the Yahoo! Finance insiders data feed; the SEC EDGAR database; individual filings at: http://www.sec.gov/cgi-bin/srch-edgar; SEC's Forms 4 (CEO) & 14a (Directors & Officers); and the Thomson Financial corporate holdings SEC's Form 13f database, which reports corporate share-holdings and profit/losses on a calendar-quarter base ending in the last day of March, June, September, and December. The United States SEC requires that all commercial investors and traders with a total position more than $100 million of securities or equities positions greater than 10,000 shares or positions in individual shares greater than $200,000, must report their holdings, using the SEC's Form 13f, quarterly.

In this paper, the above numbers were used to estimate, with an acceptable standard deviation (st. dev.), total corporate securities holdings and position changes (if applicable). Also, the current paper identifies long- and short-term corporate investors, traders and speculators based on their average portfolio "*security turnover*" (defined as a measure of security liquidity; calculated by dividing the total number of securities traded over a period by the average number of securities outstanding for the same period. Obviously, the higher the "*security turnover*" number, the more volatile the trading and more opportunities for profit after applying a trading strategy based on long-term TTFs) in the last four quarters (Yan & Zhang, 2009).

Additionally, for each of the above four (4) quarters, the traders involved in SEO were sorted into four categories ("quadrants") according to their temporal (time-based) corporate holdings as the percentage of total shares outstanding at the end of each of these quarters. In the first category, I placed the institutions ranked in the bottom "quadrant" after having the lowest "*security turnover*"; they are classified as Long-term corporate passive investors (LT share-holding Investors) (Table 1). In the second category, I placed the institutions ranked in the top "quadrant" after having the highest "*security turnover*"; they are classified as Momentary corporate swing-trading investors (swing ST institution share-holding Traders) (Table 1). Then, the rest group is divided into two equal categories (third & fourth "quadrant"). In the third category, I placed the individual traders involved in swing SEO trading (ST non-commercial share-holding Speculators) (Table 1). Finally, in the forth category the detected intraday individual traders were placed (Intraday non-commercial share-holding Speculators) (Table 1).

The result is an unbalanced panel, covering the sample time period from January 1st 2000 to June 30th 2016, with more than 100,000 Non-SEO and more than 3,100 SEO observations. The sample period starts from 2000 because from this year the data (share-holding, transaction, etc.) are available in a digital format with a relatively low cost.

While quarterly data allow me better and more accurately to associate share-holding changes with SEO/TTF, time longer (annual) results are presented for two reasons. First, because they help me to understand how unusual the changes in ownership at the time of SEO are; and second, the annual (fiscal year) long-term data provide firmness as well as flexibility with any following throwbacks, which are estimated using (fiscal year) long-term annual data. The statistics for the sample time period are presented in the following Table 1, which displays the summary numbers of SEO initiatives and Non-SEO initiatives from 1st January 2000 to 30th June 2016 (Seasoned equity offerings are obtained from SEC/SDC).

Table 1. Sample share-holding statistics

	Equity SEO initiatives				Non-SEO initiatives				
	Obs.	Mean	Median	St.dev.	Obs.	Mean	Median	St.dev.	Differences*
A. Firm characteristics									
Size	3105	4.54	4.54	1.92	100,005	4.70	4.87	2.05	−0.16
Return	3105	0.50	0.25	1.25	100,005	0.15	0.04	0.87	0.35
Market-to-book	3105	2.31	1.82	1.59	100,005	1.69	1.25	1.22	0.62
Total share-holding	3105	51.62	49.88	26.50	100,005	35.04	29.59	26.92	16.58
LT share-holding Investors	3105	8.68	6.92	7.26	100,005	9.55	7.47	9.72	−0.87
Swing ST Traders	3105	12.27	10.46	10.48	100,005	10.10	7.00	11.58	2.17
ST Speculators	3105	14.70	11.41	12.54	100,005	11.35	7.57	12.30	3.35
Intraday Speculators	3105	16.67	15.49	17.40	100,005	12.88	8.02	13.66	3.79
B. Changes in share-holding									
Continuing share-holding	3984	5.42	3.07	8.30	100,740	0.98	0.32	5.44	4.44
LT Continuing share-holding	3504	1.54	0.95	2.77	100,200	0.61	0.22	2.48	0.93
ST Continuing share-holding (Traders & Speculators)	3504	1.09	1.03	5.39	80,900	0.12	0.02	4.44	0.97
Liquidations									
LT liquidations	2552	−1.19	−0.51	1.42	62,802	−1.26	−0.22	2.05	-0.07
ST liquidations (Traders & Speculators)	3884	−4.25	−3.92	4.71	77,300	−4.90	−2.03	6.23	0.65
Initiations									
LT initiations (new Investors)	4223	2.31	2.57	3.03	90,009	2.04	1.35	3.69	0.27
ST initiations (Traders)	4196	12.42	10.83	10.02	81,770	4.77	2.33	6.06	7.65

*Changes significantly different from zero at 5% level.

Note. Size: The natural Logarithm of Sales;

Return: The Stock return measured over the fiscal year;

Market-to-book: The (total assets − book equity + market equity) / total assets;

LT: The Long-term corporate share-holding (Corporate investors' ownership-period is identified from their portfolio "*security turnover*" over the last four quarters);

ST: The Momentary corporate share-holding (Corporate investors' ownership-period is identified from their portfolio "*security turnover*" over the last four quarters);

Continuing share-holding: This term is referred to corporate investors, as shareowners, both at the beginning and at the end of the fiscal year (annual data);

Liquidations: This term is referred to cases where institutions own shares at the beginning of the fiscal year but liquidate their holdings by the end of the fiscal year (annual data);

Initiations: This term is referred to cases where institutions own no shares at the beginning of the fiscal year but establish new positions by the end of the fiscal year (annual data);

Difference: The difference in Means between SEO initiatives and Non-SEO initiatives. Another version of Table 1 sample statistics would support quality interpretations based on the "Medians" (usually used in corporate finance and securities trading literature) rather than the "Means".

3. Temporal (timing) Trading Functionalities (TTFs)

In this section, the innovative term *Temporal (timing) Trading Functionality* (TTF) is introduced, analyzed and documented.

3.1 Equity SEO Initiative Timing & Corporate Share-Holding around Equity SEO Initiatives

Hovakimian and Hu (2016) first well examine the arrangement of changes in corporate share-holding around equity SEO initiatives and then (just) present the time-series functionalities of mean Market-to-Book ratios and stock returns for 3 years before and 3 years after the year of equity issue (SEO) without a temporal TTF functionality. Their findings rise for future researchers some questions about the interpretation of SEO timing (i.e. TTF functionalities) reflected in candlestick and price action patterns as attempt and strain to buy oversold and to sell overvalued securities (Choie, 2016; Nguyen & Tran, 2016; Nickerson, 2016).

3.2 Corporate Share-Holding around the Equity SEO Initiatives

Chen, Harford, and Li (2007) and Hao (2014) argue that long-term institutions tend to be passive traders and, therefore, are not interested in the SEO/TTF functionalities. On the other hand, momentary, swing, and intraday trading institutions (and speculators as well) usually have better quality data and therefore tend to trade actively the SEO initiatives to benefit from their own informational convenience asset position. The significant information, gained by Figure 1, is the comparison tests between the share-holdings changes during the indicated period to share-holdings changes in period 0 (i.e. SEO timing).

The results in Figure 1 show that momentary swing trading corporate shareowners, clearly and strongly increment (boost positions) their security position during the year of the SEO; and mainly in the current quarter of the SEO initiative. Actually, these share-holding changes are significantly different from zero. On the other hand, the level of share acquisitions by the long-term passive-trading institution shareowners remains inflated for at least three (3) years after the SEO initiative; whereas the level of withdrawals (liquidations) for the short-term speculators and the swing traders constantly and continuously increases just after the SEO initiative. The results also show that the level of new share-holding position initiations rises in the year and particularly at the current quarter of the SEO initiative (insiders). Figure 1 presents stock's price action chart (rich in candlestick and price action patterns, as long-term TTF warning dynamics trading signals), in a Year time-frame format, from Year -3 to Year +3 relative to the SEO issue year.

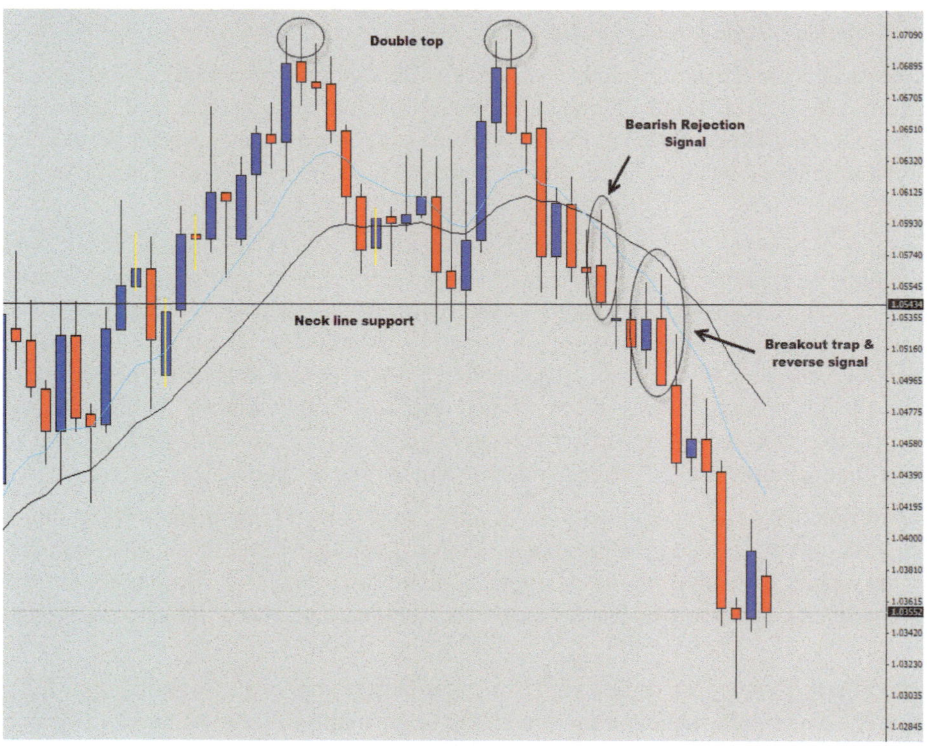

Figure 1. Market timing of equity SEO initiatives (Year time-frame)

Note. Market-to-Book: The price defined as: (total assets – book equity + market equity) / total assets.

Return: The security return measured over the fiscal year. Year (timing) 0: The SEO issuing year (current quarter).

Following, Table 2 presents the time-series profiles of mean Market-to-Book ratios and Returns of equity SEO initiatives from year −3 to +3 relative to the SEO issue years (Year time-frame: long-term TTF functionality). The changes are statistically significant at 1% level.

Table 2. The (Year time-frame) time-series profiles of mean market-to-book ratios & returns

	Levels							Changes*		
Year	−3	−2	−1	0	1	2	3	−3 to −1	−1 to 0	−1 to 3
Market-to-Book	1.72	2.01	2.78	2.30	2.09	1.58	1.77	0.22	−0.21	−0.71
Return	0.36	0.32	0.22	0.55	0.32	0.09	0.15	0.42	−0.11	−0.52

Note. *Changes significantly different from zero at 1% level.

Market-to-Book: The price is defined as: (total assets – book equity + market equity) / total assets.

Return: The stock return measured over the fiscal year.

Year (timing) 0: The SEO issuing year (current quarter).

The results in Table 2 show that, similarly to insiders and unlike the long-term corporate shareowners, existing momentary swing trading corporate shareowners sharply increase their share purchases in the year and especially in the current quarter of the SEO initiative (TTF functionality). Then, in the period following the SEO initiative, the level of share purchases by continuing short-term swing trading shareowners drops below the pre-SEO initiative level.

The level of liquidations increases somewhat during the year and the current quarter of the SEO initiative and shows further increase after the SEO initiative, substantially exceeding the pre-SEO initiative level. The results also show that the level of new share-holding position initiations rises in the year and the quarter of the SEO issue and then drops back to the pre-SEO initiative levels.

Overall, these results suggest that the existing long-term institution shareowners act as if they are not concerned about SEO/TTF timing. Furthermore, the fractional share-holding level of existing momentary corporate investors and speculators increases in the SEO quarter, which implies that SEO's fractional allocation to these shareowners exceeds their fractional pre-existing stakes in the firm. This means that existing long-term corporate shareowners do not benefit from SEO timing.

3.3 The Temporal (Timing) Trading Functionality

Company initiatives and particular the SEO ones, offer great trading opportunities (leverage, options, CfDs, long/short positions, etc.) for all kind of traders (investors, institutions, insiders, individual non-commercial market investors, and speculators). Trading these initiatives is a time sensitive procedure that requires to have and to obey a strict time-based strategy. So, in trading, the need for a 2nd level timing function of the SEO trading opportunities is obvious.

The innovative term "*Temporal (Timing) Trading Functionalities*" (TTFs) is defined as an array of temporal functionalities applied to traditional company initiatives like SEO & IPO, and stock price action patterns like *Gaps* ("*Windows*" in technical analysis terminology) and *Breakouts*. These TTF temporal functionalities are both short-term (popular price action time-frames: [5-minute], [30-minute], [1-hour], [2-hour]) and long-term (popular price action time-frames: [day], [week], [month]); and they could be documented by time-targets in trading securities (stocks, options, futures, Forex, bonds, warrants, etc.) as follows: define swing, momentary & intraday trading strategies based on specific time-targets; and open/close long/short positions at a specific time-target. These time-targets could be the SEO announcement time and the SEO actual time.

The TTF temporal functionalities operate as great warning dynamics trading signals when they are related to particular candlestick and price action pattern-targets. Following, Table 3 presents a small number of initiatives (functions) and the related warning dynamics temporal (timing) long-term TTF functionalities acting actually as time-based pattern-targets in securities (shares), options, futures, and Forex short-term, swing and intraday trading.

For the TTF-based trading strategies, these long-term pattern-targets operate as warning dynamics signals (w!D signals), awaiting the final confirmation/triggering signal (e.g. candlestick *Break*; Jesse Livermore's resistance pivotal-line *Breakout*; Jesse Livermore's support pivotal-line *Breakdown*) just before the executive order (i.e. Open / Close position).

Table 3. Company initiatives, fed meetings, reports & long-term TTF (pattern-targets)

Company Initiatives, Fed Meetings, Report	Time-based Pattern-Targets (long-term TTF trading)
SEO company initiative	SEO announcement time & SEO actual time
Day Trading	1-candle Hammer & inverted Hammer Candlestick Patterns (Hammer; Shooting Stars)
Fed/FOMC monetary policy meetings	Price Action Patterns (Head & Shoulders / Neckline)
Fed/FOMC monetary policy meetings	2-candle Engulfing Candlestick Patterns (Bullish Engulfing; Bearish Engulfing)
Fed Members Speeches	Three White Soldiers (after down-trend: Bullish Pattern); Three Black Crows (after up-trend: Bearish Pattern)
Non-Farm Payrolls reports	3-candle Stars Candlestick Patterns (after down-trend: Morning Star; after up-trend: Evening Star)
API reports for WTI (USO) inventories	1-cabdle Dojis Candlestick Patterns
EIA reports for WTI (USO) inventories	Price Action Patterns (Cups; Uprising Triangles; Head & Shoulders / Neckline; etc.)

Comparative analysis shows that the TTF temporal (year) functionalities better apply to the following four categories of traders:

(1) Long-term Institution Investors ("*LT Investors*")

(2) Short-term Swing Traders ("*ST_1 Traders*")

(3) Momentary Short-term Traders ("*ST_2 Speculators*")

(4) Intraday Traders ("*ST_3 Speculators*")

Following, Table 4 presents, in summary, the ownership % (share-holding position) & the trading results (profit %) for these four categories of traders. The data used were those presented in Section 2 "*Share-holding & Trading Data*" (1st January 2000 – 30th June 2016).

Table 4. Ownership (%) & trading results (%)

Ownership & (Share-holding Position %)	Trading Results (%)			
	Before SEO date	@SEO date (time)	After SEO date	Profit
Long-term Investors (LT Investors)	100%	81.90%)	100%	0%
Short-term Swing Traders (ST_1 Traders)	0%	5.10%	0%	9%
Momentary Short-term Traders (ST_2 Speculators)	0%	8.40%	0%	-2.5%
Intraday Traders (ST_3 Speculators)	0%	4.60%	0%	-6.5%

4. Conclusions & Discussion

The main goal of this paper is to approach the seasoned equity offerings (SEO) trading opportunities under the prism of a number of temporal (time-based) long-term trading functionalities (long-term TTF) introduced for the first time in corporate finance literature. The long-term is defined, for the purposes of this paper, as the 3-year time period, traded usually with daily, weekly and monthly time-frames.

The seasoned equity offerings trading functions offer great temporal (i.e. time-based) trading opportunities (i.e. Temporal Trading Functionalities, SEO/TTF: time-based leverage, options, CfDs, Long/Short positions, etc.) for the institutions, the insiders, the individual non-commercial market investors, and the speculators. Data analysis shows that during the SEO time, shareowners significantly increased their share ownership -including offerings that would have been categorized as overpriced during that SEO period- resulting in increasing volatility and trading profit opportunities (Nickerson, 2016).

Due to the fact and in the sense that corporate shareowners can control and restraint CEOs, governors and managers, the SEO/long-term TTF initiatives are expected to be in the interest of such shareowners. According to the corporate finance literature, these sort of shareowners are expected to be disappointed with companies' CEOs, governors and managers. Obviously, not all corporate shareholders benefit from these SEO/long-term TTF initiatives. Actually, the swing traders profit at the expense of the short-term speculators.

One could argue that any kind of management should be expected to act especially in the interest of existing corporate shareholders with continued share-holding interest, since shareowners who liquidate their share-positions, actually abandon and drop-out their claims, benefits and power to control the CEOs, the governors and the managers.

In this paper, I assume that the managers' motivation is to sell overbought equities and options in SEO/long-term TTF initiatives, to boost the pre-existing old corporate shareholder holding and to drop-out of the corporate shareowner presence in the SEO initiatives. Hence, my proposed trading plan is to investigate, control and document how SEO/long-term TTF timing is functioning within shareowners (i.e. institutions vs. non-commercial individual traders vs. speculators) and if the prepared SEO and the corporate shareholder trades are logical, steady and dependable with the assumption that SEO/long-term TTF timing profits the issuing company's old corporate shareowners.

In the process to examine the functionalities of corporate share-holding at SEO, the paper categorizes corporate share-holders along with two compatible and consistent functions. First, I isolate the trading -as a long-term TTF functionality- of the old corporate shareowners (old Investors) from those investors that open positions just on the announcement of the SEO initiative (new Investors). Then, I further isolate old shareowners that continue to hold their securities and after the SEO announcement & the SEO actual timing from those shareowners that liquidate their positions around or about the time of the SEO itself (short-term TTF functionality). In this paper, I follow Gaspar et al. (2005), as well as Yan and Zhang (2009) in order to categorize corporate investors according to their short or long position, investment and trading attitude.

With respect to the fact that the corporate shareowners seem to be found in the basis of both the pragmatic and speculative options, in the current paper I also separate corporate investors that are more possible to control and discipline from those investors (traders, speculators) that are not. Economics and finance literature proposes that some corporate investors control, plan and invest for the long run; whereas others (traders and speculators) focuses their skills on spotting on undervalues and then trade heavily to profit from their informational convenience asset positions.

It is also found that trading behavior of corporate investors at SEO/long-term & short-term TTF suggests and denotes that such ~~as~~ traders, in a large scale, boost their share-holdings just before or at the time of the SEO. ~~I~~ Furthermore, I discover no evidence that these increases take into consideration the Table 3's SEO pattern-targets (i.e. no TTF functionality is detected). These SEO pattern-targets are valid for both groups of corporate shareowners (i.e. for both: institutions with long and institutions with short investment horizons). Finally, the results show that firms with higher corporate share-holdings are in favor to employ less time from their SEOs.

The above conclusion is further supported by my findings that SEO/long-term TTF timing does not transfer wealth (profit) from the SEO swing-trading temporal investors and speculators to the old shareowners (passive-trading institutions). Explicitly, I also find (from the 2000-2016 Barron's data sources analyzed) that the companies decide the SEO initiative when the share prices are relatively high. These results signify and suggest that SEO/TTF timing does not, normally, offer benefit to long-term corporate and short-term non-commercial shareowners.

As long as the corporate swing-trading shareholders purchase shares in SEO and hence, they cannot discipline the CEO & the managers, the results further imply that the timing of SEOs is unlikely to be impulsive (catalyst functionality) by the intention of trading overbought equities, options, futures and Forex pairs.

Paper contributes to corporate finance literature by: (a) the introduction and documentation of the innovative term "*temporal (timing) trading functionality*" (TTF) as a 2nd level timing function of the casing SEO function; and (b) the executive application in SEO initiatives as technical market anomalies: (i) the long-term TTF functionalities (design a trading strategy for long/short positions at a particular period, according to candlestick patterns, like "*bullish engulfing*", "*hammer:morning star*", and "*inverted hammer: evening star*", as well as to price action patterns, like "*cups*", "*uprising triangles*", and "*head & shoulders / neckline*"); and (ii) the short-term TTF functionalities (apply swing & intraday time-based trading strategies for open/close positions at a particular time during the daily trading session: 09:30 am – 04:00 pm EST, according to the "*price action Jesse Livermore's resistance/support pivotal-lines breakout/breakdown*" confirmation/triggering signal).

The SEOs were discussed under the TTF prism for four categories of shareowners: The long-term institution & non-commercial traders (investors), the swing momentary institution traders (institutions), the short-term non-commercial traders (speculators) and the intraday non-commercial traders (speculators).

The data analysis applied in this paper, demonstrated that swing momentary institution traders (institutions) and insiders (CEO, Governors, Officers, etc.) increase their share share-holding just before or at the announcement of the Seasoned Equity Offerings and they gain benefit at the expense of short-term and intraday non-commercial speculators, while the long-term institution and non-commercial investors' wealth position is not affected significantly by these SEO offerings (accepted standard deviation prices).

Acknowledgments

The financial support (covering the CoT/CFTC and the Barron's & WSJ.com market data expenses) from the EU/LLP Programme "EPOCHE 2013" (with Project No. 2012-1-GR-ERA10-10609) is gratefully acknowledged.

Conflict of Interests

The author has not declared any conflict of interests.

References

Alti, A., & Sulaeman, J. (2012). When do high stock returns Trigger Equity Issues? *Journal of Financial Economics, 103*, 61-87. http://dx.doi.org/10.1016/j.jfineco.2011.08.007

Baker, M., & Wurgler, J. (2002). Market Timing and Capital Structure. *The Journal of Finance, 57*, 1-32. http://dx.doi.org/10.1111/1540-6261.00414

Baker, M., Stein, J. C., & Wurgler, J. (2003). When does the Market Matter? Stock Prices and the Investment of Equity-dependent Firms. *The Quarterly Journal of Economics, 118*, 969-1005. http://dx.doi.org/10.1162/00335530360698478

Barron's Financial Investment News and Market Data. (2016). Retrieved from http://www.barrons.com/data; and http://www.wsj.com; and http://www.wsj.com/europe

Basdekidou, V. A. (2015). *Functionality, Returns and Efficiency before and after the Debt Crisis: An Empirical Analysis of the Greek Stock Market* (Unpublished doctoral dissertation). Bulgarian Academy of Sciences – Economic Research Institute, Bulgaria.

Basdekidou, V. A. (2016a). IPO Trading with Short-term and Intraday Temporal Functionalities. *Business and Economics Journal, 7*(4). http://dx.doi.org/10.4172/2151-6219.1000257

Basdekidou, V. A. (2016b). Personalized Temporal Trading Functionalities Engaged in Calendar Market Anomalies: Empirical Evidences from the 2007 and 2009 Financial Crises. *Journal of Business & Financial Affairs, 5*(4). http://dx.doi.org/10.4172/2167-0234.1000225

Basdekidou, V. A., & Styliadou, A. A. (2017). Technical Market Anomalies: Leveraged ETF Trading with Daily and Intraday Temporal Functionalities. *Business and Economics Journal, 8*(1). http://dx.doi.org/10.4172/2151-6219.1000275

Cesari, A. D., Espenlaub, S., Khurshed, A., & Simkovic, M. (2012). The Effects of Ownership and Stock Liquidity on the Timing of Repurchase Transactions. *Journal of Corporate Finance, 18*, 1023-1050. http://dx.doi.org/10.1016/j.jcorpfin.2012.06.004

Chemmanur, T. J., He, S., & Hu, G. (2009). The role of Iinstitutional Investors in Seasoned Equity Offerings. *Journal of Financial Economics, 94*, 384-411. http://dx.doi.org/10.1016/j.jfineco.2008.12.011

Chen, X., Harford, J., & Li, K. (2007). Monitoring: Which institutions matter? *Journal of Financial Economics, 86*, 279-305. http://dx.doi.org/10.1016/j.jfineco.2006.09.005

Choie, K. S. (2016). Factors of IPO Underpricing. *International Journal of Economics and Finance, 8*(2), 107-114. http://dx.doi.org/10.5539/ijef.v8n2p107

Demiralp, I., D'Mello, R., Schlingemann, F. P., & Subramaniam, V. (2011). Are there Monitoring Benefits to Institutional Ownership? Evidence from Seasoned Equity Offerings. *Journal of Corporate Finance, 17*, 1340-1359. http://dx.doi.org/10.1016/j.jcorpfin.2011.07.002

Edelen, R. M., Ince, O., & Kadlec, G. B. (2015). Institutional Investors and Stock Return Anomalies. *E- Journal SSRN*. http://dx.doi.org/10.2139/ssrn.2359744

Gaspar, J. M., Massa, M., & Matos, P. (2005). Shareholder Investment Horizons and the Market for Corporate Control. *Journal of Financial Economics, 76*, 135-165. http://dx.doi.org/10.1016/j.jfineco.2004.10.002

Gibson, S., Safieddine, A., & Sonti, R. (2004). Smart investments by smart money: Evidence from seasoned equity offerings. *Journal of Financial Economics, 72*, 581-604. http://dx.doi.org/10.1016/j.jfineco.2003.05.001

Hao, G. Q. (2014). Institutional shareholder investment horizons and seasoned equity offerings. *Financial Management, 43*, 87-111. http://dx.doi.org/10.1111/fima.12038

Hartzell, J. C., & Starks, L. T. (2003). Institutional Investors and Executive Compensation. *Journal of Finance, 58*, 2351-2374. http://dx.doi.org/10.1046/j.1540-6261.2003.00608.x

Hovakimian, A., & Hu, H. (2016). Institutional Shareholders and SEO Market Timing. *Journal of Corporate Finance*, *36*, 1-14. http://dx.doi.org/10.1016/j.jcorpfin.2015.09.009

Jensen, M. C. (1986). Agency Cost of free cash flow, Corporate Finance, and Takeovers. *The American Economic Review*, *76*, 323-329. http://www.jstor.org/stable/1818789

Markoulis, S. N., & Neofytou, N. (2016). An Empirical Analysis of the Relationship between Oil Prices and Stock Markets. *International Journal of Economics and Finance,* *8*(12), 120-131. http://dx.doi.org/10.5539/ijef.v8n12p120

Myers, S. C., & Majluf, N. S. (1984). Corporate Financing and Investment Decisions when Firms have information that Investors do not have. *Journal of Financial Economics*, *13*, 187-221. http://dx.doi.org/10.1016/0304-405X(84)90023-0

Nguyen, X. M., & Tran, Q. T. (2016). Dividend Smoothing and Signaling Under the Impact of the Global Financial Crisis: A Comparison of US and Southeast Asian Markets. *International Journal of Economics and Finance,* *8*(11), 118-123. http://dx.doi.org/10.5539/ijef.v8n11p118

Nickerson, D. (2016). Asset Price Volatility, Credit Rationing and Rational Lending Discimination. *International Journal of Economics and Finance,* *8*(10), 140-158. http://dx.doi.org/10.5539/ijef.v8n10p140

Ogden, J. P., & Wu, S. (2013). Reassessing the Effect of Growth Options on Leverage. *Journal of Corporate Finance*, *23*, 182-195. http://dx.doi.org/10.1016/j.jcorpfin.2013.08.008

Styliadis, A. D. (2007). E-learning Documentation of Historical Living Systems with 3-d Modeling Functionality. *Informatica*, *18*(3), 419-446. Retrieved from http://www.mii.vu.lt/informatica/pdf/INFO686.pdf

Styliadis, A. D., & Vassilakopoulos, M. G. (2005). A Spatio-Temporal Geometry-based Model for Digital Documentation of Historical Living Systems. *Information & Management*, *42*(2), 349-359. http://dx.doi.org/10.1016/j.im.2004.01.006

Yan, X., & Zhang, Z. (2009). Institutional Investors and Equity Returns: Are Short-term Institutions Better Informed? *The Review of Financial Studies*, *22*, 893-924. http://dx.doi.org/10.1093/revfin/hhl046

4

Antecedents of E-Banking Services by Customers for the Selected Commercial Banks in Sylhet, Bangladesh

Mohammad Zahed Hossain[1]

[1] Senior Lecturer, Department of Business Administration, Leading University, Sylhet

Correspondence: Mohammad Zahed Hossain, Senior Lecturer, Department of Business Administration, Leading University, Sylhet. E-mail: zahedbtc@gmail.com

Abstract

This study is conducted to identify customers view regarding cost effectiveness, time savings and security of different types of e-banking products like online banking, ATM banking, internet banking, mobile banking and telephone banking. E-banking is the alternative delivery channels that banks adopted for providing efficient banking services through the help of internet, computers, mobile phone etc. Banks' customers were considered as population and primary data were collected through questionnaire. Descriptive statistics and Chi-square test were used for analyzing the data. The results indicated that customers prefer ATM banking services most, next to follow mobile banking and online banking. The customers believed that all types of e-banking products save time and except telephone banking others types of e-banking products were secured. Online banking and ATM banking services were not considered as cost effective. Analysis indicated no relationship between online banking and different demographic variables. ATM banking services was highly influenced by most of the demographic variables whereas internet banking, mobile banking and telephone banking influenced by few demographic variables i.e. age groups, education level, and monthly income. The results help banks to develop varieties of e-banking products and formulate strategies by considering the demographic characteristics of the customers. Customers expect more users friendly e-banking products along with diversify features and suggested to develop latest e-banking products like mobile apps based banking for ensuring long term customers relationship, attracting potential customers and keeping existing customers that may ensure consistent growth and profit as well.

Keywords: E-banking, cost effective, alternative delivery channels, commercial banks

1. Introduction

E-banking or electronic banking is the alternative way of providing banking services through electronic means i.e. pc, tab, telephone etc. with the help of internet. E-banking service offered as online banking, internet banking, telephone banking, sms banking, Automated Teller Machine (ATM) service etc. Customers can withdraw and deposit money at any branches of the respective bank where they maintain their account and they also can be informed about current status of their account through online banking services. Internet banking empowering customers to do transaction like fund transfer; utilities bill payments, mobile recharge, online purchase payments etc by themselves. ATM card enable customers withdraw money anytime from ATM booth as well as make payments for purchase. Through Mobile banking customers are able to do transactions their own. Transactions can be done by instructing bankers through telephone by the customers. Today customers chose bank (s) base on different types of e-banking services offered by banks for making their financial transactions. Through e-banking products banks able to provide customize services that create long term customer relationship. Electronic banking has become important weapon for competing with rivalries that ensure sustainable growth and profitability.

Previous studies have identified that despite the attractiveness of electronic commerce for corporation, customers might be reluctant to utilize it (Riasi & Pourmiri, 2015). Peoples react differently to adoption of technology some think that it may save time by making task easier while others concern about its perspective risk (Dillon & Morris, 1996). Some developed countries introduced electronic banking through Automated Teller Machine (ATM) since 1980 then telephone banking was introduced in 1990. USA launched internet banking in 1995 (Sohail & Shanmugham, 2003). Technology adoption helps organizations to reach their customers more easily

(Lu et al., 2005; Winch & Joyce, 2006). Through electronic banking services banks are able to provide quality services and gain competitive advantage (Jayawardhena & Foley, 2000). E-Banking save customers' time and they can access more services any time that are not available in the bank branches (Baraghani, 2007). Sankari et al. (2015) proved that trust and perceived ease of use has positive and significant impact on adoption of internet banking. Devi and Malarvizhi (2010) concluded that ATM is more popular which is most cost effective. Spaho and Ramaj (2014) found that education and income level were significantly related to the use of electronic banking services. Rotchanakitumnual and Mark (2003) indicated that security of the internet is a major factor inhibiting wider adoption. Hanafizadeh et al. (2014) after analyzing 165 articles suggested some research opportunities like in Asia internet banking adoption is affected by some specific regional factors along with that they also encouraged for studying the comparative effects of a broader set of descriptive variables as they impact internet banking adoption.

Since electronic banking has different types of products like ATM banking, online banking, internet banking telephone banking and mobile banking but most of the previous works were conducted by considering only anyone of e-banking products. Very few comparative studies have been done to show association among demographic variables and different types of e-banking. Such types of work are not conducted in our country.

This study emphasized to derive relationship for each types of electronic banking with different demographic variables. This study focused on the relationship among different demographic variables i.e. gender, age groups, education levels, income levels & occupations and various features of different types electronic banking products like online banking, ATM banking, internet banking, mobile banking and telephone banking.

The objectives of this paper are to identify customers view regarding cost effectiveness, time savings and security of different types of e-banking products; to find association with clients' demographic variables and cost effectiveness, time savings and security of different types of e-banking products like online banking, ATM banking, internet banking, mobile banking and telephone banking; to understand the views of customers to electronic banking compare to traditional banking and to understand customers responses to electronic banking based on awareness program.

2. Literature Review

E-commerce literature has studied the phenomenon of e-banking from different perspectives. Some researcher analyzed the adoption and growth of e-banking, whilst others describe the challenges and benefits to be gained from e-banking services as far as the organization is concerned.

Karimzadeh (2012) found that increased competition, changing business environments, globalization and the advancement of Information and Communications Technology are the important factors along with that have forced Banking and Financial services to change. Ridzwanl et al. (2012) noticed that Innovativeness and Familiarity significantly influence users acceptance of e-Banking in this urban district in Malaysia. Vishnoi et al. (2014) observed that people are aware of e-banking as they feel it has advantages like convenience and saves time but they also feel that factors like security and privacy, trust, familiarity and speed seems hurdle in the acceptance of e-banking. Singh (2014) said that customer can do multiple things from the comforts of home or office with e-Banking - a one stop solution for all banking needs. They proposed top three critical success factors of e-banking, cost and promotion; security and privacy; ease of use. Dixit and Datta (2010) investigates many factors like security & privacy, trust, innovativeness, familiarity, awareness level increase the acceptance of e-banking services among Indian customers. Their finding shows that in spite of users' security and privacy concern, adult customers are willing to adopt online banking if banks provide users necessary guidance. Khurshid (2014) showed that risk involved in e-banking is insignificant compared to its usefulness. Devi and Malarvizhi (2010) understand that the customers are satisfied with the quality of e-banking services. But they face technical as well as administrative and procedural problems. Karjaluoto et al. (2002) their finding depicts that bank managers can, by knowing the basic beliefs consumers hold about internet banking, create more effective customer communication, improve software and target prospects better concerning internet banking. There is wide agreement that internet banking will on the one hand have a great impact on the whole bank market, and on the other hand will be considered the most important retail banking delivery channel in the near future. Ismail and Osman (2012) identified eleven factors that affect the adoption of e-banking in Sudan. These factors include frequent breakdown of ATMs, inconvenient locations of ATMs and Electronic Points of Sale (EPOS), inaccessible internet, lack of means reporting technical problems, unclear legislations protecting e-transactions, slow banks response for correcting erroneous transactions, weak banks' role in raising clients awareness, unclear e-banking guidelines and instructions, frequent power cut offs, and high e-banking services' fees. Alam et al. (2010) present that banks perceive online banking as a powerful 'value-added' tool to attract and retain new customers while helping to eliminate costly paper handling and teller interactions. Online banking has managed to provide customers the convenience, efficiency, effectiveness, and most importantly, the speed needed in today's dynamic world.

3. Research Methodology

The study was mainly based on primary data. A questionnaire including both open-ended and close-ended questions was used for collecting raw data. Population of this study was the existing clients of the different commercial banks in Sylhet, Bangladesh. 200 useful samples were collected from existing customers of different commercial banks out of 300, representing 66.67% response rate. Data were collected in Sylhet, and conveniences sampling technique was used.

Factors included in this study were adopted from different published articles and determined by interview with bank executives. Data were analyzed through descriptive statistical tools and chi-square test. To measure the data five point Likert Scaling technique was used within the range of "strongly disagree" to "strongly agree". Higher mean value indicates positive consent of the respondents on respective issues. The p-value less or equal to 0.05 indicates the association between demographic variables and features of different types of e-banking products. SPSS was used for conducting the analysis.

4. Results and Discussion

The data analysis has been found out by the opinion of the respondents. While presenting, data charts and tables are used at relevant places. The demographic profile of the respondent is one of the factors that influence the adoption/non- adoption of technology based products and services. The demographic characteristics of the E-Banking users of the sample respondents are given below:

Table 1. Profile of the respondents

Gender	Male			Female	
Number	**146**			**54**	
Percentage of respondents	**73**			**27**	
Age(Years)	20 and less	21-30	31-40	41-50	50 and above
Number	**5**	**84**	**64**	**34**	**13**
Percentage of respondents	**2.50**	**42.00**	**32.00**	**17.00**	**6.50**
Education	SSC/HHC and below	Undergraduate	Post Graduate	M.phil And/or Ph.D.	Others
Number	**26**	**47**	**114**	**4**	**9**
Percentage of respondents	**13**	**23.50**	**57.00**	**2.00**	**4.50**
Occupation	Businessman	Professionals	Self employed	Service holder	Students
Number	**45**	**11**	**13**	**121**	**10**
Percentage of respondents	**22.50**	**5.50**	**6.50**	**60.50**	**5.00**
Monthly Income (TK.)	10,000 and less	10,001-20,000	20,001-50,000	50,001-1,00,000	100000 and above
Number	**7**	**44**	**97**	**47**	**5**
Percentage of respondents	**3.50**	**22.00**	**48.50**	**23.50**	**2.50**

* Self employed= dairy, poultry, building workers, mechanics.

From Table 1, it was observed that among the respondents, 73% are males and the rest 27% are females. About 45% of the respondents were below 30 years of age and 32% were between 31 to 40 years of age. Majority 57% of the respondents have completed post graduates and 23% have completed graduate degree. Almost 60% respondents were service holders, 22.50% were businessmen. Around 50% of the respondents had monthly income between tk.20,000 - tk.50,000 and near about 25% had monthly income below tk.20,000.

Table 2. Preferences for E-banking services

E-Banking Services	**R-1**	**R-2**	**R-3**	**R-4**	**R-5**	**R-6**	**R-7**	**Total Scores**
ATM	70	60	40	30	0	0	0	1170
Mobile Banking	40	30	30	50	30	20	0	940
Online Banking	27	29	38	20	36	49	1	840
Internet Banking	18	23	34	20	41	42	22	743
Tele Banking	0	21	12	22	43	55	47	560

From Table 2, it was observed that respondents were requested to give their preferences among E-banking services between rank 1 to rank 7 and scoring in opposite direction like rank 1 equal to score 7, rank 2 equal to score 6 and so on. Based on the score given by the respondents it was revealed that highest preferences given to ATM services score 1170, next preference was given to mobile banking with score 940 after that online banking is in third position with score 840. Respondents were reluctant to telephone phone banking having minimum score 560. These findings are same as the findings of Devi and Malarvizhi (2010). The most frequent usage of ATM compared with others types of e-banking services is supported by (Spaho & Ramaj, 2014; Mohamed & Mohammed, 2012; Izogo et al., 2012; Wan et al., 2005).

Table 3. Cost effectiveness of different E-banking products

	Cost effectiveness of Online banking	Cost effectiveness of ATM banking	Cost effectiveness of Internet banking	Cost effectiveness of Mobile banking	Cost effectiveness of Tele banking
Mean	3.0800	2.6150	3.8200	3.8350	3.5850
Std. Deviation	1.26555	1.35126	0.93915	0.90658	1.10402

From Table 3, it was observed that in respond to the cost effectiveness of different e-banking products respondents believed that they were paying more for ATM services compare to Online banking, Internet banking, Mobile banking, and Tele banking services. Among the different e-banking products respondents believed Mobile banking most cost effective, next to follow Internet banking, Tele banking, and Online bank. Findings differ from Devi and Malarvizhi (2010).

Table 4. Customers' response to the statement- "E-banking products save times"

	Online banking save time	ATM banking save time	Internet banking save time	Mobile banking save time	Tele banking save time
Mean	4.2700	4.5650	4.1500	4.1950	3.6600
Std. Deviation	0.92812	0.76728	0.87827	0.69959	1.06775

From Table 4, it was observed that all most every respondent believed that all e-banking products save time. Among the various types of e-banking products respondents highly believed that ATM services enabled to save their times next online banking, mobile banking, internet banking and telephone banking. Since through all the e-banking products customers are able to do banking without physically visit to bank premises, waiting in line and paper work etc. so that e banking products are competent enough to save times.

Table 5. Customer response regarding security and privacy issues of E-banking products

	Online banking is secure	ATM banking is secure	Internet banking is secure	Mobile banking is secure	Tele banking is secure
Mean	3.9750	4.1500	3.4650	3.1250	2.3600
Std. Deviation	1.20066	.86093	1.22322	1.39251	1.05640

From the Table 5, it was noticed that except telephone banking others e-banking products online, ATM, internet and mobile banking services were secured. Respondents opined ATM services more secured next to follow online banking, internet banking and mobile banking.

Table 6. Chi Square results p-value for cost effectiveness of different types of e-banking services

	Age	Gender	Education	Occupation	Monthly Income
Online Banking					
Chi-square value *(df)*	11.821 (16)	2.356 (4)	10.594 (16)	12.765 (16)	19.152 (16)
p-value	0.756	0.671	0.834	0.690	0.261
ATM Banking					
Chi-square value *(df)*	28.011 (16)	12.606 (4)	29.003 (16)	19.054 (16)	29.093 (16)
p-value	**0.032**	**0.013**	**0.024**	0.266	**0.023**

Internet Banking					
Chi-square value *(df)*	35.051 (16)	5.074 (4)	10.594 (16)	8.775 (16)	12.281 (16)
p-value	**0.004**	0.280	0.834	0.922	0.724
Mobile Banking					
Chi-square value *(df)*	25.064 (16)	4.795 (4)	36.773 (16)	20.281 (16)	21.172 (16)
p-value	0.069	0.309	**0.002**	0.208	0.172
Telephone Banking					
Chi-square value *(df)*	32.393 (16)	1.115 (4)	25.327 (16)	20.025 (16)	30.904 (16)
p-value	**0.009**	0.892	0.064	0.219	**0.014**

From Table 6, it was observed that the results of chi square test indicated significant association between the demographic variables and cost effectiveness of different e-banking products. From the analysis it is found that ATM banking has association with all democratic variables except occupation, internet banking showed association with different age groups, mobile banking has an strong association with education level and telephone banking indicated relation with age groups and relation with income level.

Table 7. Chi Square results p-value for time savings of different types of e-banking services

	Age	Gender	Education	Occupation	Monthly Income
Online Banking					
Chi-square value *(df)*	10.735 (16)	8.433 (4)	24.516 (16)	17.090 (16)	22.844 (16)
p-value	0.826	0.077	0.079	0.380	0.118
ATM Banking					
Chi-square value *(df)*	19.844 (12)	0.706 (3)	14.427 (12)	21.439 (12)	16.921 (12)
p-value	0.070	0.872	0.274	**0.044**	0.153
Internet Banking					
Chi-square value *(df)*	26.283 (16)	4.042 (4)	33.532 (16)	12.407 (16)	23.676 (16)
p-value	**0.050**	0.400	**0.006**	0.716	0.097
Mobile Banking					
Chi-square value *(df)*	32.382 (12)	4.465 (3)	23.996 (12)	9.931 (12)	16.518 (12)
p-value	**0.001**	0.215	**0.020**	0.622	0.169
Telephone Banking					
Chi-square value *(df)*	19.112 (16)	13.905 (4)	22.378 (16)	11.646 (16)	39.775 (16)
p-value	0.263	**0.008**	0.131	0.768	**0.001**

From Table 7, it was observed that the results of chi square test indicated significant relation between the demographic variables and time savings benefit of different e-banking products. The result indicated relation between ATM banking and age, internet banking has association with age and education, mobile banking also showed relation with age and education, telephone banking has association with gender and income level.

Table 8. Chi Square results p-value for security of different types of e-banking services

	Age	Gender	Education	Occupation	Monthly Income
Online Banking					
Chi-square value *(df)*	14.430 (16)	4.909 (4)	18.062 (16)	20.836 (16)	20.939 (16)
p-value	0.567	0.297	0.320	0.185	0.181
ATM Banking					
Chi-square value *(df)*	32.817 (16)	4.541 (4)	36.144 (16)	21.847 (16)	36.568 (16)
p-value	**0.008**	0.338	**0.003**	0.148	**0.002**
Internet Banking					
Chi-square value *(df)*	40.447 (16)	2.034 (4)	48.271 (16)	22.316 (16)	23.970 (16)
p-value	**0.001**	0.730	**0.000**	0.133	0.090
Mobile Banking					
Chi-square value *(df)*	29.961 (16)	6.659 (4)	15.530 (16)	17.436 (16)	21.234 (16)
p-value	**0.018**	0.155	0.486	0.358	0.170
Telephone Banking					
Chi-square value *(df)*	15.666 (16)	10.078 (4)	14,551 (16)	19.048 (16)	34.842 (16)
p-value	0.477	**0.039**	0.558	0.266	**0.004**

From the analysis of the Table 8, it was notice that security issue of ATM banking services has association with different age groups, education level and income level. Internet banking security issue showed strong relation with age groups and education level. Mobile banking security has relation with age groups. Telephone banking security indicated association with gender and income level.

There were no association between demographic variables and online banking's cost effectiveness, time savings and security aspect. In Bangladesh all banks are providing online banking services because it is now become basic banking services along with that without online banking services bank can't provide others type of e-banking services.

4.1 Customers' Response to the Statement- "E-Banking Services Are Relatively Better than Traditional Manual Banking"

Table 9. Percentage of the respondents' opinion

	Yes	No
Number of respondents	144	56
Percentage of respondents	**72**	**28**

From Table 9, it was observed that through e-banking customers are empowered to do some transactions like fund transfer, installment payments of loan/deposit, utilities bills payment etc. and they also can make request for check book and stop check payments etc. without visiting bank premises physically. Since e-banking services are prompt, less burdensome and offer different types of benefits about 72% respondents believe that e-banking services are better than traditional banking services.

4.2 Customers' Response to the Question: Do You Think Banks Need to Take Various Types of Awareness Programs to Inform Customers about the Benefits of E-Banking Products?

Table 10. Respondents' opinions regarding awareness programs

	Yes	No
Number of respondents	173	27
Percentage of respondents	**86.50**	**13.5**

From Table 10, it was observed that maximum respondents, 86.50%, opined that banks need to adopt promotional activities for disseminating information regarding the benefits of different types of e-banking products since they were not informed about the benefits.

5. Conclusion

E-Banking is the latest inclusion in banking transactions has opened up new window of opportunity to the banks and financial institutions. Data were analyzed through descriptive statistical analysis and chi-square test. All most every bank maintaining their own websites but all of them are not offering full fledges e-banking facilities in Bangladesh. Most of the e-banking users are young which indicates the bright prospects of e-banking services. Customers prefer ATM service most although they perceived that ATM service is not cost effective. All the respondents unanimously believe that e-banking products save time. Respondents also have positive views regarding security of e-banking products except telephone banking. About all customers opined that e-banking services are better than traditional banking services.

Analysis indicated no relation between online banking and different demographic variables. Cost effectiveness of different types of e-banking products have shown the following association; ATM banking with most of the demographic variables, internet banking and mobile banking has strong association with different age groups and education levels respectively; telephone banking has association with age groups and income level. In case of time savings of different e-banking products following relations have found ATM banking with occupation, both internet banking and mobile banking with age groups and education level and mobile banking with gender & income level. Security of internet banking has strong association with age groups and education level; ATM banking has association with age, education & income. Awareness program may increase e-banking users as they believe e-banking is better than traditional banking. Customers expect more users friendly e-banking products along with diversify features and they also suggested to develop latest e-banking products like mobile apps based banking for ensuring long term customers relationship, attracting potential customers and keeping existing customers that may ensure consistent growth and profit as well. The findings of this study help banks to develop different types of e-banking products that can be able to meet the needs of the customers.

The study findings are only suggestive since those findings rely solely on the use of questionnaires that might not capture the full nature and all the factors. Moreover, it might be difficult to generalize the findings of the present study given the shortness of the sample which was restricted to a very small number out of the total customers of different banks. Furthermore, there might be biased responses, and, therefore, might influence the findings and conclusions of the study.

Limitations all the demographic factors that influence e banking may not cover. Data were collected from concentrated area rather entire country. In some cases Respondents were given their opinions without enjoying the services.

Further research can be conducted to identify the factors that tempted potential users to adopt e-banking services such as: development of technology, changing lifestyle, essay access to internet, online payment facilities, social status, hazardous paper tasks in bank premises, queue in branches, risk of carrying cash, banks' promotional activities.

References

Alam, N., Magboul, I. H. M., & Raman, M. (2010). Challenges Faced by Sudanese Banks in Implementing Online Banking: Bankers' Perception. *Journal of Internet Banking and Commerce, 15*(2), 1-9.

Baraghani, S. N. (2007). *Factors Influencing the Adoption of Internet Banking* (Unpublished Master's Thesis). Lulea university of Technology. Sweden. Retrieved from http://www.diva-portal.org/smash/get/diva2:1017415/FULLTEXT01.pdf

Devi, P. A., & Malarvizhi, V. (2010). Customers' Perception of E-banking: Factor Analysis. *IUP Journal of Management Research, 10*(6), 7-19.

Dillon, A., & Morris, M. (1996). User acceptance of new information technology: theories and models. In M. Williams (Ed.), *Annual Review of Information Science and Technology* (Vol. 31, pp. 3-32). Medford NJ: Information Today. Retrieved from http://www.ischool.utexas.edu/~adillon/BookChapters/User%20acceptance.htm

Dixit, N., & Datta, S. K. (2010). Acceptance of E-banking among Adult Customers: An Empirical Investigation in India. *Journal of Internet Banking and Commerce, 15*(2), 1-17.

Hanafizadeh, P., Keating, W. B., & Khedmatgozar, R. H. (2013). A systematic review of Internet banking adoption. *Telematics and Informatics, 31*(3), 492-510. http://dx.doi.org/10.1016/j.tele.2013.04.003

Ismail, M. A., & Osman, M. A. Y. (2012). Factors Influencing the Adoption of E-banking in Sudan: Perceptions of Retail Banking Clients. *Journal of Internet Banking and Commerce, 17*(3), 1-16.

Izogo, E. E., Nnaemeka, O. C., Onuoha, O. A., & Ezema, K. S. (2012). Impact of Demographic Variables on Consumers' Adoption of E banking in Nigeria: An Empirical Investigation. *European Journal of Business and Management, 4*(17), 27-39.

Jayawardhena, C., & Foley, P. (2000). Changes in the banking sector – The case of Internet banking in the UK. *Journal of Internet research:Electronic Networking Application and Policy, 10*(1), 19-30. https://doi.org/10.1108/10662240010312048

Karimzadeh, M. (2012). Electronic Banking Challenges in India: An Empirical Investigation. *Interdisciplinary Journal of Contemporary Research in Business, 4*(2), 31-45.

Karjaluoto, H., Mattila, M., & Pento, T. (2002). Electronic banking in Finland: Consumer beliefs and reactions to a new delivery channel. *Journal of Financial Services Marketing, 6*(4), 346-361. https://doi.org/10.1057/palgrave.fsm.4770064

Khurshid, A., Rizwan, M., & Tasneem, E. (2014). Factors contributing towards adoption of E-banking in Pakistan. *International Journal of Accounting and Financial Reporting, 4*(02), 437-455. http://dx.doi.org/10.5296/ ijafr.v4i2.6584

Lu, H., Hsu, C., & Hsu, H. (2005). An empirical study of the effects of perceived risk upon intention to use online applications. *Information Management & Computer Security, 13*(2), 106-120. http://dx.doi.org/10.1108/09685220510589299

Riasi, A., & Pourmiri, S. (2015). Effects of online marketing on Iranian ecotourism industry: Economic, sociological, and cultural aspects. *Management Science Letters, 5*(10), 915-926.

Ridzwan1, I. U., Zain, N. A. M., Raizal, N. F., & Khamsan, N. S. (2012). Factors Affecting Users'Acceptance of E-Banking in Damansara, Malaysia. *International Proceedings of Economics Development and Research, 55*(33), 163-166.

Rotchanakitumnual, S., & Mark, S. (2003). Barriers to Internet banking adoption: A qualitative study among corporate customers in Thailand. *The International Journal of Bank Marketing, 21*(6/7), 312-323. http://dx.doi.org/10.1108/02652320310498465

Sankari, A., Ghazzawi, K., Danawi, S.,E., Nemar, S., E., & Arnaout, B. (2015). Factors affecting the adoption of internet Banking in lebanon. *International Journal of Management (ijm), 6*(3), 75-86. Retrieved from http://citeseerx.ist.psu.edu/viewdoc/download?doi=10.1.1.695.3682&rep=rep1&type=pdf

Singh, M. (2014). Critical Success Factors in E-Banking: An Indian Perspective. *International Research Journal of Management Science & Technology, 5*(9), 38-52.

Sohail, M. S., & Shanmugham, B. (2003). E-banking and customer preferences in Malaysia: An empirical investigation. *Information Sciences-Informatics and Computer Science. An international Journal, 150*(3-4), 207-217. http://dx.doi.org/10.1016/S0020-0255(02)00378-X

Spaho, A., & Tedis, R. (2014). Electronic Banking in Albania: A Statistical Analysis. *International Journal of Research in Business Management, 2*(12), 1-10.

Vishnoi, S., Varma, S., & Thomas, G. (2014). A study of customers perception towards services of e banking (with special reference to gwalior city). *Global Journal of Multidisciplinary Studies, 4*(01), 95-101.

Wan, W. W. N., Luk, C. L., & Chow, C. W. C. (2005). Customers' adoption of banking channels in Hong Kong. *International Journal of Bank Marketing, 23*(3), 255-272. http://dx.doi.org/10.1108/02652320510591711

Winch, G., & Joyce, P. (2006). Exploring the dynamics of building, and losing, consumer trust in B2C eBusiness. *International Journal of Retails and Distribution Management, 34*(7), 541-555. http://dx.doi.org/10.1108/09590550610673617

5

Bilateral Trades between Egypt and Malaysia: Issues and Opportunities for Further Development

Muhamad Muda[1], Siti Nurazira Daud[1] & Ibrahim Mohamed Ibrahim Eldeeb[2]

[1] Faculty of Economic and Muamalat, Universiti Sains Islam Malaysia, Nilai, Malaysia

[2] Master candidate in Faculty of Economic and Muamalat, Universiti sains Islam Malaysia, Nilai, Malaysia

Correspondence: Ibrahim Mohamed Ibrahim Eldeeb, Batu Laban 8, Gombak, Malaysia.
E-mail: ibrahimeldeeb1980@gmail.com

Abstract

Egypt and Malaysia are both belong to the Organization of Islamic Conference (OIC), have a similar historical background that both have been under the British colony and have enjoyed independence at almost within the same period. However, trades between the two countries are relatively small, and if based on the socio-economic background the magnitude of trades between the two countries can be further improved. This paper traces the historical development of bilateral trade relationship between Egypt and Malaysia to understand the strength and weaknesses. The aim is to develop possible proposals for further enhancement of the relationship. The main objective of this paper is to investigate factors that may enhance integration and cooperation between Egypt and Malaysia. The research used qualitative analysis approach by looking at the trade sectors and volumes over the period of 2000-2012, based on the phenomenological case study method. It is found that Egypt and Malaysia enjoyed significant bilateral trade relations since the independence of Malaysia in 1957, especially in the fields of culture and education. Because of the appreciation of the Malaysian citizens to the Islamic-based education such as Islamic studies, medicine, and pharmacy particularly the world-renowned institution of Al-Azhar University, thousands of Malaysians have enrolled and graduated from this university and other related institutions. On the other hand, Malaysia is falling behind Argentina, Brazil and India regarding export to Egypt. However recently, Malaysia has been becoming popular for the Egyptian tourists. The paper explores a proposal for further improvement regarding bilateral trades based on Islamic approach.

Keywords: bilateral trade, Egypt, Malaysia, international trade, development economics

1. Introduction

The main purpose of pursuing the current study on trade relations between Malaysia and Egypt is to enhance the inter-trade between them to find a suitable way to the economic cooperation. This study is embarked and driven by some factors. First, there seems to be a desire to promote the economic relations between the two countries which are constantly developing. It is worth mentioning that the exports and imports between Malaysia and Egypt are very weak since 1960 through to 1979. However, in the early 80s, there appears a new era in Malaysia towards the implementation of economic reform policies to improve the level of per capita income, which greatly forge the rise in its exports and imports. The results of this economic reform can be seen whereby the exports rise to its highest level in 2012. This perhaps also explains the commitment of the Malaysian government towards the implementation of the socio-economic plan in Vision 2020, which will move Malaysia to be among the developed countries. This plan has been drawn to the economic strategies policies to develop simple and medium projects toward achieving some important objectives such as enhancement of the ability competitiveness of Malaysian industries, improvement of industrial infrastructure. This plan also helps Malaysia in the Malaysian transformation industries and production of intermediate goods to the final products (Gomez, 1999).

1.1 Background on Egypt and Malaysia

Both countries starting from a similar point, both under British colonial and after independence they began the way of development. Furthermore, Egypt after obtaining independence on 23 June 1952, attempts to implement the socialist economic system by focusing on developing public sectors. The main characteristics of this era are furnished on knowledge in public universities although there is a lack of political freedom. Consequently, the Egyptian economic system is more centralized. In addition, Egypt was also constantly engaged in wars that might have disrupted its economic development. In 1978, Egyptian authorities signed a peace convention with Israel after the war that could pave the way for peace and improve concentration on economic development. Moreover, the slowdown in economic growth as a result of the wrong economic policy that led to corruption in each sector and increased the rate of unemployment (Hassan, 2001). The gross domestic product also (GDP) is equal to the total expenditures for all final goods and services produced within the country in a stipulated period. Egyptian GDP reflects big problems faced Egyptian economy. Egyptian GDP increased slowly until 2002. After that GDP increased dramatically from 2002 to 2012. Egyptian GDP reflects big problems faced Egyptian economy. It worth mention that a big gap in the Egyptian economic policies. In spite of the current situation of deficit trade balance and increased the unemployment problems and raised the rate of inflation and also deflation. And also the lack of political stability leads to economic instability in light of the lack of security. Furthermore, Policy of rising support for goods and services to fill the budget deficit and the instability of the market exchange rate.

Figure 1 explains the GDP since 1960 to 1979; it may seem the enhancement in the Egyptian domestic gross product since 1970 until 1979 because the GDP rapidly increased because focusing on other development aspects of the community. It worth to note that it may interpret developed all outputs of Egyptian economic sectors. Additionally, Egypt in this period has been promoted in several economic aspects. Unfortunately, Egypt lost their some its economic power because of preoccupation with some political issues such as the war with Israel since 1960 until 1973. However, the most important effects of revolution are the escape of foreign investments. It should be noted that the instability of the political situation leads to a more economic crisis in Egypt. Some of the employees lost their jobs in the last decade, and some factories have been closed, and more social factors have been raised. Egypt in this period has been promoted in several economic aspects. Unfortunately, Egypt lost they're some its economic power because of preoccupation with some political issues such as the war with Israel since 1960 until 1973. However, the most important effects of revolution are the escape of foreign investments. It should be noted that the instability of the political situation leads to a more economic crisis in Egypt. Some of the employees lost their jobs in the last decade, and some factories have been closed, and more social factors have been raised. It has been seen obvious that all of exports and imports do not reach to the situation that reduced the deficit trade balance. Moreover, Egyptian import volumes reached US $43.98 billion in 2009, a 24 percent rise from the previous year's level. It has been clear that a surplus import. Egypt has had a negative balance of trade (trade deficit) since the 1980s. Also, the indicator of import and export has been increased after the financial crisis since 2008 to 2010. During this time Malaysia starts the way of development since independence in 1957. At this time since 30 years, Prime Minister Mahathir Mohamed begins to improve industry sector.

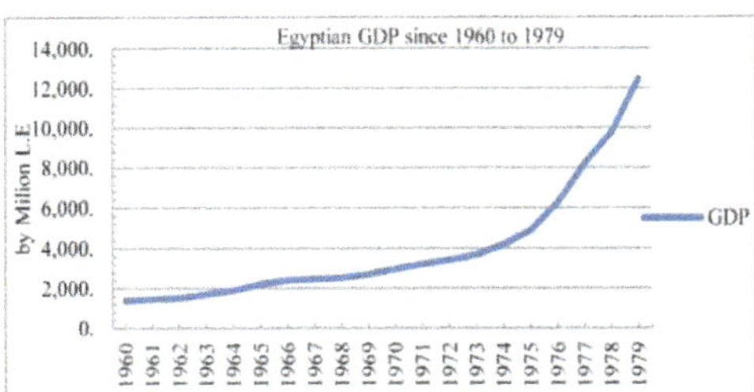

Figure 1. Egyptian gross domestic products since 1960 to 1979

Source: CAPMAS (2014).

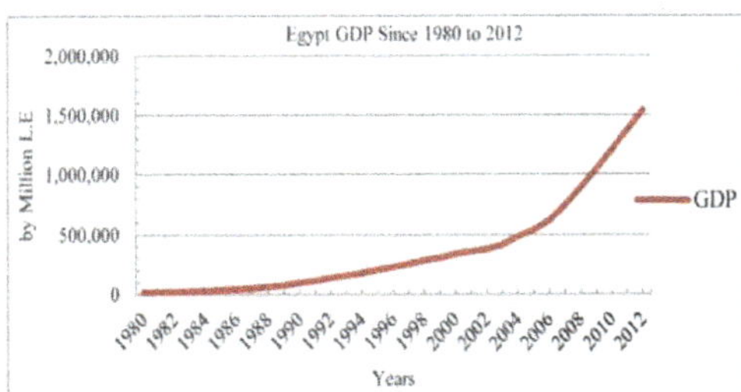

Figure 2. Egyptian gross domestic products since 1980 to 2012

Source: CAPMAS (2014).

Figure 2 reveals the gross domestic products since 1960 to 2012. It should be pointed out that the stability of gross domestic product since 1960 to 2012. It should be noted that during this time in Malaysia struggle to improve the industrial sector. In addition, Figure 2 interprets the transformation from agriculture community to the industrial community by the successful economic policy (Porter, 2000). This figure also reveals the way that Malaysia enhanced the manufacturing development. It may promote the cluster-based concept by improving some relations that can organize production process and between some other activities (Ketels, 2003). Figure 2 also reveals the GDP in Malaysia recorded the highest point in 1997. It should be noted that the GDP increased dramatically. It also refers to economic improvement. The diagram also emphasizes that the Malaysian economy struggles to achieve the target vision 2020.The diagram also reflects the successful economic approach as discovering the basis of the pursuit of successful economic policies toward the target 2020. However, the big significant challenge facing the country is raising gap between the actual growth rate and the projected growth rate required to reach the targets to shift the country from a middle-income economy to a high-income economy by 2020. Moreover, Malaysia going very fast to another development stage by improving the heavy industrial sector. Also, Malaysia also developed the education system and open the way for utilities from exchange expertise. Nevertheless, both countries have similar Islamic vision about integration under the unity of Muslims (Daugbjerg, 2015). Also, the historical relations between both countries encourage to strength this relation by implement more agreements especially after signed and ratified a full agreement in 2013. Both Egypt and Malaysia have embraced economic policies that are different from each country, and some of its objectives follow the economic system whereby others have embraced a market economy and others a mixture of both. Both countries followed different versions of economic policies, whether for industrial goods, agricultural or services. Moreover, these countries have not benefited regarding industrial raw materials or competitiveness in the different industries or agricultural commodities; it is a result of these policies' deepening dependency to the outside market.

1.2 Bilateral Trade between Egypt and Malaysia

In fact, the simplest form of economic integration which provides the free trade between two or more countries (Guan, 2005). According to the simplest principle of economic integration theory among two countries, the relation between Malaysia and Egypt is one of the most important bilateral relationships in Southeast Asia and North Africa. It is one of the best examples to enhance bilateral trade between two countries. Harun (2009) reveals that the balance of trade is inclined towards Malaysia due to the remarkable activity of Malaysian businessmen to explore the Egyptian markets and the opportunities of exporting to Egypt, in addition to the existence of a "Malaysian National Trade Promotion Agency" office in Cairo to support Malaysian businessmen. Both Malaysia and Egypt have many common characteristic and traits; these include common frames of reference in vision, culture, and religion. Malaysia is one of the most important Islamic countries that were able to go beyond the defaults and proceed to development in various fields of life and living conditions ranging from the economy through education, technology and the end of the health and culture. In addition, Egypt also is the largest Muslim country in the Middle East and it's achieved a good position because of high levels of trade with Islamic countries, which leads to enhancing and promote trade volume for a move towards economic integration between two countries. Currently, Egypt has a lot of educational relation with Malaysia more clearly than ever before. Egypt and Malaysia share a lot of views and at the multilateral level, as they continue to be active in the OIC, NAM, and the UN which is useful in promoting co-operation between both countries, as well as the other member states. This strong cooperation contributes to finding solutions to global problems and in establishing common ground rules that will guide the best conduct of international relations. Originally, the balance of trade is inclined towards Malaysia due to the remarkable activity of Malaysian businessmen to explore the Egyptian markets and the opportunities of exporting to Egypt, in addition to the existence of a "Malaysian National Trade Promotion Agency" office in Cairo to support Malaysian businessmen. In fact, both Malaysia and Egypt need to devote efforts to start a free movement of goods, services, and labor to achieve the cooperation and integration markets between them. It also provides free movement of production factors allows optimum allocation of labor and capital. Moreover, cooperation and integration between Egypt and Malaysia led to overcome the problem of entrepreneurs to shift their capital from places of low return to other high return places. However, capital movements the willingness to integrate is less obvious because cooperation and integration may lessen the effectiveness of critical macroeconomic instruments. Confirming the importance of policy cooperation and integration and taking into account the role of the state in enhancing economic welfare by correcting imperfection of markets and in realizing some political objectives such as an equitable income distribution. Furthermore, if objectives of two governments are inconsistent, the policy of one country will frustrate that of the other. Consequently, policy cooperation and integration may bring the economic benefit that leads to recovery of effectiveness in policy making. In addition, the transaction cost between governments increases with the increase in the numbers of negotiators and the diversity of paradigms in which they work.

There seem to be a need for joint investments and to promote the economic relations between the two countries which are constantly developing. It is worth mentioning that the exports and imports between Malaysia and Egypt are modest and very simple since 1960 and until 1979.However, in the early80s there a new era in Malaysia towards the implementation of economic reform policies and improve the level of per capita income, which greatly affected the rise in exports and imports from Malaysia. This can be seen up to its highest level in 2012. It also explains the commitment of the Malaysian government towards the implementation of the plan in 2020, which will move Malaysia to be among the developed countries.

2. Literature Review

The mechanism and process of economic integration have been the focus of many scholars in this area of which we will look at in this section. However, for a startup in the economic integration effort as this study is investigating, we will also look at the definition of what integration means. In addition, what is equally important is to understand why countries would want to integrate, what benefits they will reap as the result of the outcome. In lights of the recent "Brexit" incident which could be seen as reverse integration, this has raised some lights into whether the benefits expected from integration could be realistic. However, in our view, that will be a major issue to consider and is outside the scope of this study. At this moment we will focus on the conventional factors that motivate countries, particularly the developing ones like Malaysia and Egypt, to economically integrate. According to Machlup (1977), integration is the process of combining separate economies into one larger economic region. Machlup and Staley (1977) indicates that integration is concerned with the utilization of all potential opportunities and efficient division of labor. Umo (2002) on the other hand, refers to integration as the unification of neighboring countries working within a framework to promote free movement of goods, services, and factors of production to coordinate and harmonize their policies. Two factors have been identified that facilitate the regional economic integration, firstly, the neighboring countries have common history and interests and may be more willing to coordinate. Secondly, countries who are not neighbors (integration agreements) but if their ideologies are similar. According to Madyo (2009), economic integration is a process that includes procedures led to removing discrimination among different countries. One of the most notable trends in the global economy in recent years has been an accelerated movement toward regional economic integration such as ASEAN, AFTA, NAFTA, APEC, and EU. Linking countries together making them more dependent on each other by entering into regional agreements, group countries aim to reduce trade barriers more rapidly than can be achieved. All countries can benefit if each country specializes in the production of those goods it can produce best and satisfy their other wants and needs by trading for them. Balassa (1961) emphasized that there are a wide range and various reasons why countries accepted the agreement of economic integration. The economic cooperation and integration between Egypt and Malaysia would lead to solving the economic problems in both countries by using Islamic concepts to enhance and improve the bilateral trade movements. Furthermore, improve economic cooperation and integration between Egypt and Malaysia by using Islamic concepts taking into account the global economic condition, diversify and create new opportunities in trade relations, enhance participation in decision-making at international level, and improve standards of living. In the last few years, Malaysia and Egypt have adopted many common views on the international level and in the multilateral forums, which they are members of the OIC organization and the non-aligned movement organization and the UN, which support cooperation between two countries. Moreover, contributing to finding solutions to global problems and to establish common rules to support economic relationship, Egypt, and Malaysia shares the views on global issues such as human rights and environmental issues, and refugee issues. The desire to strengthen cooperation led both countries to try to use new economic policies through signing and ratifying bilateral trade agreements since 2013 (Egypt Embassy, 2014).

Considering the importance of promoting the relationship between Malaysia and Egypt and putting in mind the unity of Muslim countries, there are two valuable concepts; Firstly, to encourage the free movement of goods, services, and factors of production between the member's state. Secondly, to increase cooperation in the field of fiscal and monetary policy that also follows the liberalization of trade between the members' states to activate preferential trade agreements, which will lead to the reduction of trade barriers between each. Egypt and Malaysia desire to improve the bilateral trade since Egyptian revolution in 25th January 2011 to alleviate the effects of negative political that happened in Egypt other (El-Said, 2014). However, economic integration offers additional opportunities to share risks and have smooth consumption temporally (Kalemli Ozcan, 2001). Another aspect that has been the focus of integration literature is on its mechanism. In this paper, we will also explore how Egypt and Malaysia should place their attention in the process of integration. Hitiris (1991) mentions that economic integration among developed countries concentrate on the changing of trade pattern as undeveloped countries seek economic agglomeration to enhance development in making essential structural production to be able to generate a sizeable trade. Consequently, Regional Trade Agreements form a key part of the institutional structure of the world economy. For this kind of agreement, there is no general reduction on internal tariffs without a common external tariff. Tariffs between the members of the agreement are reduced (or eliminated) only for some goods or services, sometimes unilaterally (Ahmed, 1970). Viner (1950) focused on the impact of the formation of the Customs Union on the production. This theory has been developed by Lipsey (1960) and Meade (1953). The Customs Union in literature occurs when two or more countries agree to eliminate tariffs between themselves and set a common external tariff on imports from the rest of the world. Viner (1950) also used this analysis of neoclassical theory in foreign trade and uses religious duties such as full competition, the stability of production costs and lack of transportation costs. However, there is another approach in customs union theory which does not lay emphasis on welfare improving effects of liberalization, but views economic integration as a means for a continuation of national import of substitutions policies on a wider regional level (Corden, 1972). The Customs Union avoids the problem of developing complicated rules of origin but introduces the problem of policy coordination. With a customs union, two countries or more must be able to agree on tariff percentages across many different import industries. Lipsey (1960) emphasizes in terms of trade of the member states. Viner focused on short-term effects. Viner (1950) also used this analysis of neoclassical theory in foreign trade and uses religious duties such as full competition, the stability of production costs and lack of transportation costs. Viner (1950) referred on the improvement of transportation costs, and he also assumes that the importance of proximity as a factor in granting preferential tariff. Balassa (1960) referred to the proximity between the member states of the Customs Union has raised the positive economic integration. Egypt and Malaysia share a common objective to improve multilateral trade level as they continue to be active in the OIC, NAM, and the UN. This is useful in promoting co-operation between both countries. This strong desire to cooperate contributes to finding solutions to trade problem and in establishing common ground rules that will guide the best conduct of international relations. Initially, the balance of trade is inclined towards Malaysia due to the remarkable activity of Malaysian businessmen to explore the Egyptian markets and the opportunities of exporting to Egypt. In addition, this success is also assisted by the existence of Malaysian National Trade Promotion Agency office in Cairo to support the Malaysian businessmen (Harun, 2009). Maximum integration is permitted between the economies of the member states. Full economic integration is through the emergence of an immediate nature organizations or supranational. It had the authority to put monetary and fiscal policies, trade and implemented without reference to the member states, and this is what distinguishes this power under full economic integration (Twana, 2010).

3. Methodology

The qualitative research allows to deeply understanding the phenomenon of weakness of bilateral trade between Egypt and Malaysia. It has been clearly obvious that using qualitative research definitely provide a full discussion of this type of case study between both countries. The main task of using qualitative approach is to deeply understand; in this case, the Islamic view that existed in pre and post-Islam integration. In fact, by using a qualitative approach, the reader can take the economic practices from both conventional and Islamic eras to provide the best solution to the phenomenon of weakness of bilateral trade between both countries. In turn, a process can be determined for both countries in bilateral relations to undergo to achieve a successful economic relationship. Phenomenology theory enables researchers to generate theories that offer an explanation of behavior, creation of a new theory, application in worldly practices, and providing a general perspective. Regarding behaviourism, it provides clear hypotheses that are ideal for further research (Denzin, 2009). Freebody (2004) lists the criteria of a case study which is the framework for this study. Therefore, it allows the exploration of different perspectives to achieve their goals (Lindgren & Kehoe, 1981 cited in Vaughn et al., 1986; Henry, 2008). It should be noted that the phenomenological case study approach is a qualitative research to explain more details about the phenomenology of the weakness of bilateral trade between both countries (Henry, 2008).

4. Discussion

Figure 1 illustrates the movement of goods and services in Malaysia from 1980 to 2012. It should be noted that the movement of exports and imports slightly increased in 1983 and sharply increased from 1986. The Malaysian export consists mainly of agriculture, manufacturing and mining goods. The economic indicator shows that the most exported good is Palm oil (45 percent), optical & scientific equipment (17 percent) and non-Metallic Mineral products (11 percent). Furthermore, the Malaysian import indicators show that textiles, clothing & footwear is 3% of the total Malaysian imports. Moreover, this may explain the implementation of the strategic development plan since 1980 to 2012. Although there is fluctuation in the trend of Malaysian import and export, however, the movement of import and export has improved since 2000 because of the implementation of some economic recovery policies.

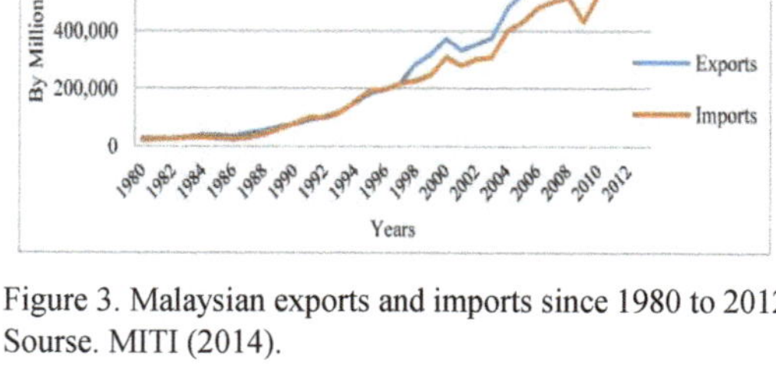

Figure 3. Malaysian exports and imports since 1980 to 2012
Sourse. MITI (2014).

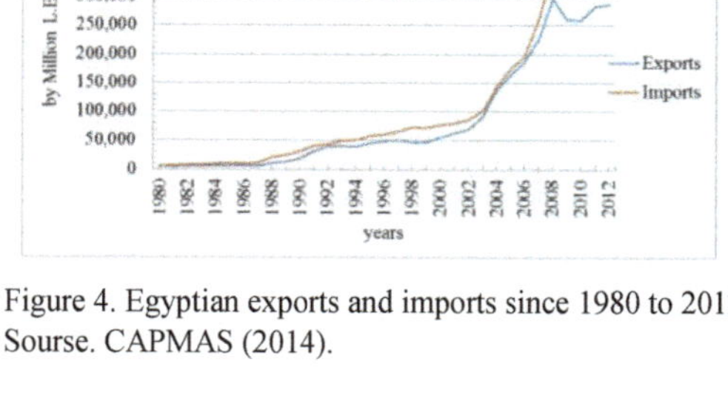

Figure 4. Egyptian exports and imports since 1980 to 2012
Sourse. CAPMAS (2014).

Figure 3 shows a rapid increase in exports and imports and successful policies up till 1999. It also reflects the trade movements in goods and services. The figure also reveals the significant performance of goods and services in the last decade. In addition, exports and imports have been promoted since last ten years. Moreover, assessment of the movement of exports and imports in last ten years led to putting economic policies as a model for other Muslim countries particularly Egypt. The fluctuation of imports and exports since 2008 to 2010 illustrated the reasons for the decline of both. However, the economic reforms by Malaysian government lead to rapid growth and refer to the structural change in equality. In addition, the government has sought through an economic model of 2010 to put the economy back on the growth for Malaysia to be in a high degree income country by 2020. Furthermore, it shows the trade policy and commitment of consequences of liberalized trade.

Figure 4 reveals the movements of exports and imports of goods and services since 1980 to 2012. It has been seen obvious that all of exports and imports do not reach to the situation that reduced the deficit trade balance. Moreover, Egyptian import volumes reached US $43.98 billion in 2009, a 24 percent rise from the previous year's level. It has been clear that a surplus import. Egypt has had a negative balance of trade (trade deficit) since the 1980s. In addition, the indicator of import and export has been increased after the financial crisis since 2008 to 2010. Since the 1980s, the government has pioneered several economic reforms through foreign donor aid. However, it has measurable benefits of these economic reforms. The economy is highly dependent on oil exports, which are its major source of foreign income together with tourism receipts and US financial and military aid. It has to import most of its food, other commodities, and equipment since both its agricultural and industrial sectors are not well-developed. Additionally, the problem in Export and import since 1980 to 2002 is not achieving the suitable level and not achieve the required level of international trade. Since the 1980s, the government has pioneered several economic reforms through foreign donor aid. However, it has measurable benefits of these economic reforms. The economy is highly dependent on oil exports, which are its major source of foreign income together with tourism receipts and US financial and military aid. It has to import most of its food, other commodities, and equipment since both its agricultural and industrial sectors are not well-developed. Additionally, the problem in Export and import since 1980 to 2002 is not achieving the suitable level and not achieve the required level of international trade.

Table 1. Egyptian Trade Exchanges with some of the non-OIC member under trade partner countries group (2008-2011) by million L.E

	2008				2009				2010				2011			
Countries	Exports	Imports	Trade balance	Trade Volume	Exports	Imports	Trade balance	Trade Volume	Exports	Imports	Trade balance	Trade Volume	Exports	Imports	Trade balance	Trade Volume
Argentina	595.6	5532.8	-4937.3	6128.4	124.8	2556	-2431.2	2680.8	45	10845.9	-10800.9	10890.9	141.3	5031.8	-4890.5	5173.1
Brazil	681.3	7873.2	-7191.9	8554.5	250	6870	-6620	7120	1615.1	14335.6	-12720.5	15950.7	1194.1	9835.2	-8641.1	11029.3
Chile	29.7	361.7	-332	391.4	1.3	122	-120.7	123.3	236.8	184.3	52.5	421.1	405	78	327	483
Colombia	33.8	32.2	1.6	66	27.5	12	15.5	39.5	83.5	91.9	-8.4	175.4	35.5	97.7	-62.2	133.2
India	9045.6	9586.6	-541	18632.2	8095	6998	1097	15093	13414	9738.9	3675.1	23152.9	7188.4	8830.1	-1641.7	16018.5
Jamaica	2	------	2	2.0	1.1	-------	1.1	1.1	1.3	--------	1.3	1.3	1.1	-------	1.1	1.1
Kenya	625.8	1097.7	-471.9	1723.5	646.6	1155	-508.4	1801.6	1348	2008.4	-660.4	3356.4	1418.1	1168.6	249.5	2586.7
Mexico	1519.3	593.3	926.1	2112.6	362.2	401	-38.8	763.2	149.6	407.8	-258.2	557.4	204.6	473	-268.4	677.6
Peru	14.2	34.8	-20.5	49	10.2	17	-6.8	27.2	14.5	58.2	-43.7	72.7	19	20.4	-1.4	39.4
Srilanka	178	73.7	104.2	251.7	87.6	82	5.6	169.6	77.6	128.9	-51.3	206.5	89.1	85	4.1	174.1
Venezuela	22.7	456.5	-433.8	479.2	14.7	300	-285.3	314.7	35.3	20.7	14.6	56	15.1	272.5	-257.4	287.6
Zimbabwe	6.6	2.7	4	9.3	17.2	2	15.2	19.2	67.2	5.7	61.5	72.9	76.9	95.5	-18.6	172.4

Source: CAPMAS (2014).

Table 1 shows the trade volume and trade balance between Egypt and some non-OIC countries under fifteen group from 2008 until 2011. It should be mentioned that all these countries are under fifteenth countries group. It has been obvious that the trade volume between some of these countries is much higher than the trade volume between Egypt and Malaysia such as India, Mexico, Brazil, and Argentina. Consequently, the Islamic perspective could be a good motive to enhance and promote the bilateral trade between Egypt and Malaysia (CAPMAS, 2014).

Table 2. Egyptian trade exchange with some of OIC member trade partner countries group (2008-2011) by million L.E

Countries	2008			2009			2010			2011		
	Exports	Imports	Trade balance	Exports	Imports	Trade balance	Exports	Imports	Trade balance	Exports	Imports	Trade balance
Algeria	1031.70	2697.40	-1665.70	2119.4	2101	18.40	2306.7	4079	-1772.30	1510.9	2338.2	-827.30
Iran	332.60	185.10	147.50	486.70	187	299.70	556	207.10	348.90	790.30	246.70	543.60
Indonesia	400.20	4142.60	-3742.30	532.10	2965	-2432.9	549.30	5356.4	-4807.10	606.80	3017.1	-2410.30
Malaysia	199.50	3052.40	-2852.80	147	2882	-2735	738.40	4572.5	-3834.10	1177	4444.8	-3267.80
Nigeria	2551.10	0.8	2550.30	505.40	4	501.40	671.30	9.30	662	832.30	6.80	825.50
Senegal	132.40	8.20	124.30	125	5	120	139.60	5.60	134	178	7	171

Source: CAPMAS (2014).

Table 2 illustrates the bilateral trade between Egypt and some of the OIC countries under trade partners group from 2008 until 2011. It should be mentioned that the trade volume and trade balance between Egypt and other countries is much higher than the trade volume between Egypt and Malaysia such as Indonesia. It can be clearly seen that OIC play an important role to collect between these countries to enhance trade together to alleviate poverty. It worth mentioning that the fluctuation of trade volume shows the weakness of movement in goods, services, and labors, it may reflect the deep gap problem in cooperation and integration policy among these countries (CAPMAS, 2014).

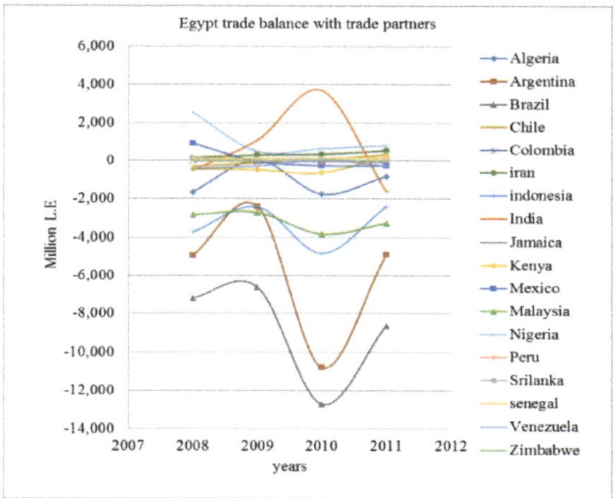

Figure 5. Egypt trade balance with trade partners since 2008 to 2011
Source: CAPMAS (2014).

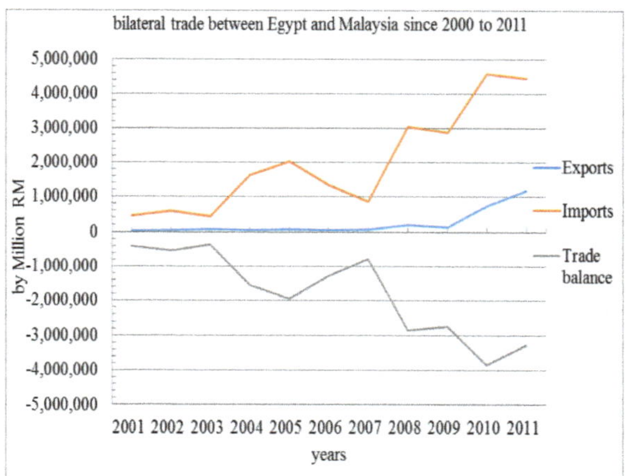

Figure 6. Bilateral trade between Egypt and Malaysia since (2001-2011)
Source: CAPMAS (2014).

Figure 5 reveals that Egypt has a deep problem in bilateral trade with fifteenth countries. It has been obvious that the bilateral trade increased only in natural resources. It also shows the deficit of trade volume in bilateral trade between Egypt and most of the fifteenth countries group. The best example here is the bilateral trade with India. Only if we promote the bilateral trade between Egypt and Malaysia such as India, we will undoubtedly be gain the ultimate benefits of what provides us toward enhancing bilateral trade-economic.

Line chart 6 reveals the bilateral trade between Egypt and Malaysia since 2001 until 2011. It worth be noted that the trade balance was slumped to increasing the gap of deficit among export and import. Consequently, the chart illustrates unbalanced movements between imports and exports especially from 2005 to 2011. It can be clearly seen that imports remained stable from 2001 to 2007. In contrast, it should be mentioned that imports line dramatic rise since 2007 to 2011.

Table 3. The trade volume between Egypt and Malaysia since 2001 to 2011 million L.E

Years	Exports	Imports	Trade balance
2001	38727	445212	-406485
2002	50883	589021	-538138
2003	81086	434983	-353897
2004	65210	1623795	-1558585
2005	78882	2020274	-1941392
2006	52352	1339656	855041

2007	77073	855041	-777968
2008	199500	3052400	-2852900
2009	147000	2882000	-2735000
2010	738400	4572500	-3834100
2011	1177000	4444800	-3267800

Source: CAPMAS (2014).

It can be clearly seen that the volume of Trade between the two countries does not rise to the level of distinguished relations that combine between Egypt and Malaysia. The clear deficit has been shown in the movement of exports and imports between these countries. The previous table also reveals the fluctuation of trade volume between Egypt and Malaysia and the lowest level of cooperation between two countries. In fact, they cooperate in a few products such as liquefied natural gas projects, palm oil, wood, electrical appliances, computers, cocoa, wheel tires, detergents, and copper. Without forgetting the main concept of Islamic unity that tends to enhance and promote the cooperation and integration between Muslim countries in general, especially countries under OIC organization such as Egypt and Malaysia and without forgetting the importance of these two countries in Asia and Africa as well. This research focuses on the current scenario of bilateral trade between Egypt and Malaysia. It should be noted that both countries have significant criteria and they struggle to achieve their goals by increase economic activity. Additionally, both countries also have a good geographical position in the southeast of Asia and the north of Africa, especially in Arab countries. Cooperation and economic integration between Egypt and Malaysia have its advantages, as it prepares for the two countries expanded market, but since the existence of a common market between Egypt and Malaysia, it is understood that the industry needs to have a wide market to be economically produced.The cooperation and economic integration between Egypt and Malaysia derive its legitimacy from the call of Islam to the Muslims of cooperation and brotherhood and unity even in the areas of economic activity, and economic aspects of life. It is agreed among scholars, is free trade between Islamic regions, which means prevent the imposition of customs duties on Muslims trade where there is justification for that, as a Muslim capital will be subject to the commitment of essential financial, zakat and the imposition of the toll or tariff means repetition of the financial obligation for a Muslim capital.

References

Balassa, B. (1961). *The theory of economic integration: Limits and Prospects* (p. 36). Allen and Unwin, London.

Convery, I., Soane, I., Dutson, T., & Shaw, H. (2010). Mainstreaming LEADER Delivery of the RDR in Cumbria: An Interpretative Phenomenological Analysis. *Sociologia Ruralis, 50*(4), 370-391. https://doi.org/10.1111/j.1467-9523.2010.00519.x

Cooper, C. A., & Massell, B. F. (1965). A New Look At Customs Union Theory. *The Economic Journal, 75*(300). https://doi.org/10.2307/2229672

Corden, W. M. (1972). Economies of Scale and Customs Union Theory. *The Journal of Political Economy, 80*(3). https://doi.org/10.1086/259899

Daugbjerg, C., & Swinbank, A. (2015). Globalization and new policy concerns: The WTO and the EU's sustainability criteria for biofuels. *Journal of European public policy, 22*(3), 429-446. https://doi.org/10.1080/13501763.2014.927520

Denzin, N. K., & Lincoln, Y. S. (2009). *Qualitative research.* Yogyakarta: PustakaPelajar.

El-Said, H., & Harrigan, J. (2014). Economic reform, social welfare, and instability: Jordan, Egypt, Morocco, and Tunisia, 1983-2004. *The Middle East Journal, 68*(1), 99-121. https://doi.org/10.3751/68.1.15

Freebody, P. (2004). *Qualitative Research in Education-Interaction and Practice*. London: Sage Publishers.

Gomez, E. T., & Jomo, K. S. (1999). *Malaysia's Political Economy, Politics, Patronage and Profits* (pp. 173-174). Cambridge University Press.

Guan, B. T. C. (2005). ASEAN's Regional Integration Challenge: The ASEAN Process. *The Copenhagen Journal of Asian Studies, 20*, 70-94.

Harun, R. (2009). In Pursuit Of National Interest: Change And Continuity In Malaysia's Foreign Policy Towards The Middle East. *Jurnal Antarabangsa Kajian Asia Barat, 1*, 23

Hasaan, K. M. (2001). An Empirical Investigation of Economic Cooperation Among OIC Member Countries. Working Paper 0212, ERF Working Paper Series, Egypt.

Henry, A., Casserly, A., Coady, M. & Marshall, H. (2008). *A Phenomenological Case Study Exploring Different*

Perspectives on Inclusion within One Post-Primary School.in the North West of Ireland. Sligo, Ireland: St. Angela's College and NUI Galway.

Husin, T. S. (2002). Forging An Economic Integration: The Case Of ASEAN (Order No. 3052488, Argosy University/Sarasota). Proquest Dissertations and Theses (pp. 155-155).

Ketels, C. (2003). The Development of the cluster concept–present experiences and further developments. In *NRW conference on clusters, Duisburg, Germany* (Vol. 5).

Machlup, F. (1977). *A History of Thought on Economic Integration* (p. 50). New York: Columbia University Press. https://doi.org/10.1007/978-1-349-03171-9

Madyo, M. R. (2009). *The importance of regional economic integration in Africa* (p. 125). University of South Africa.

Molle, W. (2001). *The Economics of European Integration Theory* (4th ed., p. 32).

Molle, W. (2006). *The economics of European integration: Theory, practice, policy* (p. 45). Ashgate Publishing, Ltd.

Pardo, S. (2004). Europe of Many Circles: European Neighbourhood Policy. *Geopolitics, 9*(3), 731-737. https://doi.org/10.1080/14650040490478756

Porter, M. E., Takeuchi, H., & Sakakibara, M. (2000). *Can Japan Compete?* Basic Books.

Salvatore, D. (1995). *International Economics* (5th ed., p. 300). Prentice Hall International, Inc., Englewood Cliffs, New Jersey, U.S.A.

Todaro, M. P. (2000). *Economic Development* (7th ed., p. 130). Pearson Education Limited, English.

Twana, S. (2010). *Topical Problems of European Integration Process* (Dissertation Thesis, p. 9). University Of Pardubice.

Vaitsos, C. V. (1978). Crisis in Regional Economic Cooperation (Integration) Among Developing Countries: A Survey. *World Development, 6*(6), 719-769. https://doi.org/10.1016/0305-750X(78)90041-4

Van Bavel, B., Campopiano, M., & Dijkman, J. (2014). Factor markets in early Islamic Iraq, c. 600-1100 AD. *Journal of the Economic and Social History of the Orient, 57*(2), 262-289. https://doi.org/10.1163/15685209-12341349

Viner, J. (1950). *The Customs Union Issue*. New York: Carnegie Endowment for International Peace.

Williams, T. N. (2002). EU– NATO Cooperation in the Fight against Islamic Fundamentalist Terrorism. In J. Krause, A. Wenger, & L. Watanabe (Eds.), *Unravelling the European Security And Defence Policy Conundrum* (pp. 189-204). Zurich: Peter Lang Publishers.

Website:

http://studies.alarabiya.net/hot-issues/2014

http://www.Capmas. gov.eg/2014

http://www.Icci-Oic.org/2014

http://www.Icdt.org. 2014

http://www.mfa.gov.eg/english/Pages/default.aspx/2014

http://www.miti.gov.My/2014

http://www.Oic-Oic.Org/2014

http://www.Worldbank.Org/2014

6

Financial Development and Poverty in Developing Countries: Evidence from Sub-Saharan Africa

Pam Zahonogo[1]

[1] Université Ouaga II, Burkina Faso

Correspondence: Pam Zahonogo, Université Ouaga II, 03 BP 7164, Ouagadougou 03, Burkina Faso. E-mail: pzahonogo@gmail.com

Abstract

The paper investigates how financial development affects poverty indicators in developing countries. We implement this analysis with a poverty model using data from 42 Sub-Saharan African countries and covering the period 1980-2012. We employ the System Generalized Method-of-Moment (GMM) that is appropriate to control country specific effects and the possible endogeneity. The empirical evidence shows that there indeed exists a financial development threshold below which financial development has detrimental effects on poor and above which financial development could be associated with less poverty. The evidence then points an inverted U curve type response and the findings are robust to changes in poverty measures and to alternative model specifications, suggesting thus the non-fragility of the linkage between financial development and poverty for sub-Saharan African countries. Our findings are then promising and support the view that the relation between financial development and poverty reduction is not linear for sub-Saharan African countries.

Keywords: financial development, poverty, Sub-Saharan Africa

1. Introduction

Poverty reduction represents a major challenge for all countries and specifically for developing ones. The international organizations such as World Bank and the International Monetary Fund have incorporated the objective of poverty reduction in most of their development programs. Therefore, and to fight against this scourge, priority was given to pro-growth policies because it has been shown that countries whose experienced high rates of economic growth are those that are managed to reduce their poverty rates. Since the seminal work of McKinnon (1973) and Shaw (1973), economists generally consent that financial development enhances economic growth. Africa remains the poorest continent of the world. Yet, at the same time, Sub-Saharan Africa countries have experienced improvements in financial development. It seems that the large gains expected from developed financial sector have, to date, been limited in Africa, especially for poor people.

The relationship between financial development and poverty reduction has generated a substantial and inconclusive literature both theoretical and empirical fronts in recent years. Theory provides conflicting predictions while empirical results have been equally mixed. Some claim that, by allowing more entrepreneurs to obtain financing, financial development improves the allocation of capital, which has a particular large impact on the poor while others argue that it is primarily the rich and the politically connected who benefit from improvements in the financial system (Singh & Huang, 2015).

Theoretically, financial development may affects poverty through two channels. The first channel shows that financial development affects poverty directly by improving the access of the poor to financial services (Odhiambo, 2009; Pradhan, 2010; and Akhter et al., 2010). The second channel indicates that financial development affects poverty indirectly by stimulating economic growth through increased investment rates (King & Levine, 1993; Levine, 2005). There seems to be an implicit assumption in existing research that if financial development improves growth, then this automatically translates into reduction in poverty. But some argue that financial development has been identified as cause of financial crisis and an unstable macroeconomic environment (Kaminsky & Reinhart, 1999) and these have been identified as detrimental to the poor (Easterly & Fischer, 2001). Theoretical poverty studies suggest at best a very complex relationship between financial development and poverty reduction.

Like theoretical analyses, the empirical literature on the interaction between financial development and poverty provides mostly inconclusive findings. Some studies argue that financial development has a strong positive impact on the income of the poor and contribute to poverty reduction (Jallian & Kirkpatrick, 2002; Honohan, 2004; Beck et al., 2007; Odhiambo, 2009; Boukhaten & Bochra, 2012) while others find that financial development does not affect the poor (Dollar & Kraay, 2002; Fowowe & Abidoye, 2012). Clarke et al. (2003) opined that there is a negative relationship between financial development and income inequality rather than an inverted-U shaped relationship suggested by Greenwood and Jovanovick (1990).

The lack of clear correlation between financial development and poverty could be because financial development almost certainly requires combination with other appropriate policies that encourage access to financial services and investment for poor, allow effective conflict resolution and promote human-capital accumulation. So, institutions can help explain the heterogeneity in financial development-poverty relationship. On policy perspective, since financial sector reform is frequently addressed in policy prescription packages by World Bank and International Monetary Fund to enable poor accessing financial services, it is important to know how and through which mechanisms financial development affects poverty alleviation. The main policy conclusion is that a poverty reduction strategy should not be based solely on financial development, but also on good macroeconomic policies and efficient institutions, which seem to be more robust in poverty regression.

The contribution of this paper is to assess if the relation between financial development and poverty differs between more developed and less developed financial sector. Such distinction is important as there are theoretical models and empirical results suggesting that there was a certain threshold level of financial development that an economy need to attain before it can get the full indirect benefit to reduce poverty. Particularly for developing countries, the lack of investment in human capital and good institutions may hamper expected poverty reduction from developed financial sector through access to financial services. This paper re-examine the role of financial sector on poverty and make contribution to the literature by empirically analyzing the threshold effects and testing for non-linearities in the financial development-poverty relationship based on panels data for sub-Saharan Africa countries. The empirical experience is based on poverty model using data from 42 sub-Saharan Africa countries and covering the period 1980-2012.We employ the System Generalized Method of Moment (GMM) estimator that is appropriate to control country-specific effects and the possible endogeneity of control variables with poverty. Our findings support the view that the relation between financial development and poverty is not linear for Sub-Saharan Africa and points to an inverted U curve type response.

The remainder of the paper is organized as follows. Section 2 reviews the theoretical and empirical literature linking financial development and poverty reduction. Section 3 presents the model and discusses the econometric issues. Section 4 presents data used to implement the model. Section 5 summaries and analyses the empirical results. Section 6 concludes the paper and draws the main economic policy implications.

2. The Link between Financial Development and Poverty Reduction

The lack of access to financial services is one of the main factors explaining persistent poverty (Levine, 2008). The role of financial development has been a key debate in poverty reduction strategy. Theory suggests that access to finance allows poor to better investment and education (Jacoby & Skousfias, 1997; Beegle et al., 2003). Financial development is recognized as a mean that can lead to the reduction of poverty by helping poor to diversify their sources of income through self-employment. The development of financial sector can ease the credit constraint hitherto faced by poor households and which limited their abilities to undertake productive investment. The question of the existence and nature of the link between financial development and poverty has been the subject of considerable interest and debate. However, neither the existing theoretical models nor empirical findings have produced definite conclusion.

Theoretically, financial development can directly contribute to poverty reduction by improving the opportunities for the poor to access formal finance and enables them to achieve a sustainable livelihood (Stiglitz, 1998; Jalilian & Kirkpatrick, 2002). Financial development can also indirectly reduce poverty and income inequality through enhancing economic growth and the gains from growth are channeled to the poor. One of the way in which financial development enhances economic growth is through the mobilization of funds from inefficient to efficient use. Theory provides, however, conflicting predictions about the impact of financial development on the income of the poor. Singh and Huang (2015) argue that if financial markets were perfect, the availability of finance would allow individuals to fund education, training or business opportunities. In this framework, financial development would contribute to equalize opportunities by reducing the importance of initial wealth and then would favor the poor. But others theories suggest that financial deepening would favor the rich because financial institutions operate in settings where complete information is often unavailable. In this context, projects from entrepreneurs that have different probabilities of success are indistinguishable and the information asymmetry requires banks to screen application so as to grant loans only to the most promising projects (Singh, 1992). Finally, the relation between financial development and poverty may be nonlinear. Greenwood and Jovanovic (1990) present a model where income inequality first rises as the financial sector develops but then declines as more people gain access to the system. The financial sector acquires greater capacity and interest to bear the high costs of small credits as it becomes stronger and more competitive (Rajan & Zingales, 2003).

Like theoretical analyses, empirical investigations are controversial. The evidence pointed that the degree of financial intermediation has a strong and positive impact on the income of the poor (Jalilian & Kirkpatrick, 2002; Beck et al., 2007; Boukhatem & Bochra, 2012). Financial development can improve the opportunities for the poor to access formal finance by addressing the causes of financial market failures such as information asymmetry (Stiglitz, 1998). Also, financial development can enable the poor to start microenterprises, which generates more employment and higher income and thereby reduces poverty. Some others findings suggested that financial development may trickle down to the poor trough its positive effect on economic growth because of the positive effect of economic growth on poverty reduction (Ravallion & Datt, 2002; Fan et al., 2000). Uddin et al. (2014) found that a long-run relationship between financial development, economic growth and poverty reduction exists in Bangladesh and financial development helps to reduce poverty but its effect is not linear. Shabhaz and Rehman (2013) find that financial development causes poverty reduction in Pakistan. For African countries, Quartey (2005), and Odhiambo (2009) reach the same result for Ghana, Zambia and South Africa, respectively.

In contrast, some studies find that financial development does not affect the poor (Dollar & Kraay, 2002; Fowowe & Abidoye, 2012). Guillaumont-Jeanneney and Kpodar (2011) find that the contribution of finance in alleviating poverty depends on the transmission channel. For example, their findings suggest that if financial development is measured by the ratio of M3 to GDP, there is a positive relationship between financial development and poverty. But if private credit is used as financial development proxy, the association turns out to be statistically insignificant. They conclude that the poor benefit primarily from the ability of the banking system to facilitate transactions and provide savings opportunities rather than reaping the benefit of greater access to credit.

The benefits of financial development are not automatic and policies aimed at macroeconomic stability and institutional reforms needed to accompany financial development (Singh & Huang, 2015). Jalilian and Kirkpatrick (2005) and Uddin et al. (2014) found that financial development contributes to poverty reduction and the effect varies with the level of economic development. It seems that there was a certain threshold level of financial development that an economy need to attain before it can get the full indirect benefits and reduce the risks of capital account liberalization.

Some reasons why the literature on financial development-poverty link is inconclusive relate to the fact that different studies use different proxies for financial development and rely on different methodologies. Most empirical studies based on cross-country regressions suggest a significant poverty-reduction effect of financial development, although these have been criticized for poor data quality and inadequate control for the endogeneity (Singh & Huang, 2015; Uddin et al., 2014; Dhrifi & Maktouf, 2013; Ho & Odhiambo, 2011). The inconclusive results can be explained by the fact that financial development almost certainly requires combination with other appropriate policies and linear regression models would not be able to capture such complementary dynamics (Beck et al., 2007).

This paper complements the previous literature on financial development and poverty link by providing new cross-country empirical evidence, taking into account the threshold effects of financial development across Sub-Saharan Africa countries. Moreover, other than just focusing on the direct and indirect effects of financial development shown in the previous literature, the paper also goes further to explore other channels through which financial development can affects poverty reduction, for example governance, trade openness and education.

3. Model and Econometric Issues

In the lines of Dollar and Kraay (2002) and Clarke et al. (2006), we estimate a standard poverty model, where poverty depends on financial development, and a set of control variables. The model specification is as follows:

$$Poverty_{i,t} = \delta_1 FD_{i,t} + \delta_2 X_{i,t} + \vartheta_t + \mu_i + \varepsilon_{i,t} \quad (1)$$

where the subscripts i and t represent country and time period, respectively, Poverty is the log of poverty indicator, X is the matrix of control variables, FD is a measure of financial development, ϑ_t corresponds to time effects, μ_i denotes unobserved country-specific effects, and $\varepsilon_{i,t}$ the error term.

Following Chang et al. (2009), we then introduce interacting terms to allow the poverty-financial development relationship to vary with some country characteristics (education, governance, trade openness). Now, the regression equation is the following:

$$Poverty_{i,t} = \delta_1 FD_{i,t} + \delta_2 X_{i,t} + \delta_3 FD_{i,t} \times x_{i,t} + \vartheta_t + \mu_i + \varepsilon_{i,t} \quad (2)$$

where $x_{i,t}$ corresponds alternatively to education, governance and trade openness in the country i at time t.

To control for country-specific effects and the possible endogeneity of control variables with poverty, we estimate the coefficients of our model by using the System Generalized Method-of-Moment (GMM) estimator developed by Blundell and Bond (1998). To verify the consistency of the GMM estimator, we have to make sure that lagged values of the explanatory variables are valid instruments in the poverty equation. This issue is examined by considering the Hansen test of over-identifying restrictions. The no rejection of the null hypothesis implies that instrumental variables are not correlated with the residual and are satisfying the orthogonality conditions required.

4. Data and Variables Definitions

The study works with pooled cross-country and time-series data for forty-two Sub-Saharan Africa countries averaged over five-year period from 1980 to 2012. The choice of the period of study is related to the availability of data on interest variables such as financial development and poverty. The data come from the databases of the World Bank and International Monetary Fund. The dependent variable is poverty indicator, measured by poverty headcount index and poverty gap. We also include a set of control variables that are commonly used in poverty equations.

Poverty. There are many definitions and measures of poverty but the most popular indicator is the poverty headcount index which measures the percentage of population living with per capita consumption or income below the poverty line. It is a measure of absolute poverty. Another popular measure is the poverty gap which takes into account the distance of the poor from the poverty line. This measure characterizes how far below the poverty line lies the average income of the poor and provides some sense of distribution. Unlike the headcount index, this indicator captures a decrease or increase in the income of the poor even when it does not cross the poverty line. As dependent variable, we use the poverty headcount index and the poverty gap considering the $1.25 poverty line.

Financial development. Financial development can improve the opportunities for the poor to access formal finance by reducing the cost of lending to small borrowers that may reduce poverty. The well-functioning financial system may enable the poor to access financial services, thereby enabling the poor to achieve a sustainable livelihood. We use the ratio of private credit to GDP (PC/GDP) to measure financial development. This measure of financial development is frequently used in the literature (Ho & Odhiambo, 2011; Uddin et al., 2014; Le Goff & Singh, 2014).

Control variables. We also include a set of control variables commonly used in poverty equations overall income per capita (GDP per capita) to capture the contribution of economic development. We expect a negative effect of this variable. We add growth of the consumer price index (Inflation) to control for the macroeconomic instability. We also introduce an indicator of institutional quality. Institutional quality impacts positively economic growth (Asiedu, 2003; Acemoglu et al., 2012) and may reduce poverty (Singh & Huang, 2015). Institutional quality is captured by a governance index (IGOV) through the average of the six measures of institutions presented by Kaufmann et al. (1999), namely: voice and accountability, political stability and absence of terrorist violence, government effectiveness, regulatory quality, rule of law and control of corruption. We add the trade openness (sum of exports and imports as a share of GDP) to capture the degree of international openness. Finally we add a measure of human capital proxied by the logarithm of gross secondary enrollment rate (WDI, 2014). Education is a key determinant of poverty reduction and we expect a negative effect of this variable.

5. Empirical Results

5.1 Unit Root Tests

The existence of unit root is tested using tests of Levin et al. (2002), Im et al. (2003) and Maddala and Wu (1999). These tests are performed on the variables of the model in level. The null hypothesis of the presence of a unit root is rejected, if at least two of the three tests simultaneously confirmed that hypothesis. According to the statistics of the three types of unit root tests, all the variables of the model are stationary in level (Table A1 of Appendix 1).

5.2 GMM Estimates

The GMM estimation results are summarized in Tables 1-2.

The estimate results point out a nonlinear relationship between financial development and poverty and the evidence is robust to alternative poverty measures: headcount index and poverty gap. The results shown the presence of inverted U curve (Laffer Curve of financial development). As the financial sector develops, however, this positive association tends to fade away, the coefficient of the square term being significant and of the opposite sign. These results are consistent with Clarke et al. (2006) and Sing and Huang (2015) and confirm that financial development is significantly associated with higher level of poverty to a threshold and above this threshold, the effect becomes negative. For the headcount index, the threshold is estimated to 10.64%. In other words, financial sector is associated with higher level of poverty up to private credit account for 10.69% of GPD. According to poverty gap, the findings point out a threshold of 1.19%, suggesting that financial sector increases poverty gap until private credit account for 1.19% of GDP (Table 2 of Appendix 1). These results indicate that financial sector can be a relevant driver of poverty reduction for Sub-Saharan Africa countries but needed certain level of its development before it can get the full benefit to reduce poverty.

The results related to the control variables are mostly in line with expectations. The results demonstrate that per capita income has a significant poverty-reduction effect. The negative and significant coefficient of income per capita for headcount index reveals that other things being equal, more developed countries then have lower levels of poverty. Interestingly, the results also show a significant positive effect between income per capita and poverty gap, which could indicate that income inequality is higher in the richer Sub-Saharan Africa countries. The results also indicate that education is negatively correlated with poverty, whether measured by headcount index or the poverty gap, but the effect is not significant for poverty gap. We find a significant negative association between governance and poverty gap. The same effect is found for trade openness. Inflation has no significant effect on poverty. This result is consistent with the study of Le Goff and Sing (2014).

While the first regression only considers financial development effects, we examine next the influence of some structural country characteristics in the financial sector-poverty relationship. The results with the interaction terms are presented in models 2, 3 and 4 of Tables 1-2.

We first test the role of human capital in the financial development-poverty relationship (Model 2). The coefficient of the interaction is negative and significant for the headcount index and the poverty gap equation. The beneficial impact of an increase in financial development is larger when the investment on human capital is stronger. We find that an increase in gross secondary enrollment rate is associated with lower poverty rate. This result is consistent with theoretical models suggesting that the effect of financial development on poverty may depend on the human capital stock.

Model 3 examines whether the relationship between the financial development and the poverty rate may hinge on a country's institutional environment. The results suggest governance significantly enhance the association between financial development and poverty reduction. As we expected, the poor benefit more from financial development in countries with high quality of governance, which allows the emergence of new enterprises, improving the poor income.

Finally, we test whether financial development-poverty relationship would change with the trade openness (Model 4). The coefficient of the interaction term with the trade openness measure is negative and significant for the headcount index and the poverty gap equation. These results suggest that a more developed financial sector is associated with lower levels of poverty when trade is more developed. In other words, more trade openness may allow the poor to benefit more from access to cheaper credit.

Table 1. Financial development (Private Credit PC) and poverty headcount index in Sub-Saharan Africa-GMM system

	Poverty headcount (log)			
	(1)	(2)	(3)	(4)
Inflation (log)	0.0045	0.0044	0.0067*	0.0056
	(0.0035)	(0.0036)	(0.0039)	(0.0037)
Trade openness (log)	0.0172	0.0179	0.0135	-0.1500*
	(0.0155)	(0.0160)	(0.0169)	(0.0803)
Igov	-0.0104	-0.0108	0.1202***	-0.0079
	(0.0105)	(0.0106)	(0.0368)	(0.0109)
Private credit (PC) (log)	0.1405***	0.1362**	0.1362***	-0.4512
	(0.0445)	(0.0542)	(0.0478)	(0.2837)
PC^2	-0.0297***	-0.0296***	-0.0300***	0.0295
	(0.0085)	(0.0085)	(0.0091)	(0.0293)
LEdu (log)	-0.0292***	-0.0324	-0.0334***	-0.0313***
	(0.0066)	(0.0241)	(0.0068)	(0.0069)
LGdpc (log)	-0.0323***	-0.0321***	-0.0307***	-0.0328***
	(0.0052)	(0.0052)	(0.0056)	(0.0054)
PC*Ledu		-0.0272***		
		(0.0062)		
PC*Igov			-0.0335**	
			(0.0134)	
PC*Openess				-0.6999**
				(0.3313)
Constant	-0.2658***	-0.2598*	-0.2296*	-0.1083
	(0.1281)	(0.1372)	(0.1380)	(0.1505)
Observations	164	164	164	164
Number of countries	42	42	42	42
Sargan test	0.102	0.566	0.114	0.1131

Note. data are averaged over five years. ***Significant at 1%. ** Significant at 5%. * Significant at 10%. Standard errors in parentheses.

Table 2. Financial development (Private Credit PC) and poverty gap in Sub-Saharan Africa-GMM-sytem

	Poverty gap (log)			
	(1)	(2)	(3)	(4)
Inflation (log)	0.0313	0.0321	0.0341	0.0452**
	(0.0215)	(0.0219)	(0.0216)	(0.0212)
Trade openness (log)	-0.1975**	-0.2000**	-0.199**5	-0.5369***
	(0.0888)	(0.0978)	(0.0926)	(0.1756)
Igov	-0.1641**	-0.1655**	0.0975	-0.1380*
	(0.0756)	(0.0769)	(0.1970)	(0.0753)
Private credit (PC) (log)	0.0205**	0.0212**	0.0212**	0.0098
	(0.0085)	(0.0104)	(0.0088)	(0.0099)
PC^2	-0.0580*	-0.0549	-0.0632**	-0.0490
	(0.0300)	(0.0380)	(0.0305)	(0.0315)
LEdu (log)	0.00001	-0.0364	-0.0606	-0.0742*
	(0.00001)	(0.2137)	(0.0442)	(0.0423)
LGdpc (log)	1.2086***	0.00001	0.1131*	0.1224*
	(0.3519)	(0.00001)	(0.0644)	(0.0678)
PC*Ledu		-2.0273**		
		(0.8647)		
PC*Igov			-0.1776**	
			(0.0705)	
PC*Openess				-0.0018*
				(0.0009)
Constant	-0.0591	1.1877***	0.3542	1.4236**
	(0.0424)	(0.4007)	(0.5252)	(0.6894)
Observations	164	164	164	164
Number of countries	42	42	42	42
Sargan test	0.102	0.566	0.114	0.1131

Note. data are averaged over five years. *** Significant at 1%. ** Significant at 5%. * Significant at 10%. Standard errors in parentheses.

6. Conclusions

In this paper, we have tested a poverty model in the context of Sub-Saharan African countries and two measures of poverty: headcount index and poverty gap. Our results suggest that financial development may impact favorably the poverty indicators. However, the effect is not linear and our results show the presence of inverted U curve and confirm that financial development has a detrimental effect on poverty to a threshold and above this threshold, financial development is associated with less poverty. The no linear relationship between financial development and poverty suggests that the benefits of financial development are not automatic. Then, the poverty effects of financial development may differ according to the development of financial sector. The results then suggest that policies to accompany financial development are needed. These policies would aim at encouraging the quality of institutions, the ability to adjust and learn new skills and the openness of the economy. These policies would then allow resources to be allocated away from less productive activities to more promising ones. Financial development should therefore not be seen in isolation and additional policies will be needed to enhance its impact on poverty reduction strategy. Sub-Saharan African countries should carry on relevant policies such as those that encourage trade openness, allow effective governance and promote human capital accumulation.

This paper provides some interesting findings at the study of financial development and poverty whose can be improved upon. Since informal financial sector is important in Sub-Saharan African countries, future research should work to develop financial development index that will capture the development of both informal and formal financial sector. Being the fact that poverty is multi-dimensional, further empirical studies using multi-dimensional poverty indicators could be carried out to produce more relevant findings.

References

Acemoglu, D., & Robinson, J. A. (2012). *Why Nations Fail: The Origins of Power, Prosperity, and Poverty* (pp. 1-571). Crown Publisers, Crown Publishing Group, a Division of Random House. https://doi.org/10.1355/ae29-2j

Akhter, S., Liu, Y., & Daly, K. (2010). Cross country evidence on the linkages between financial development and poverty. *International Journal of Business and Management, 5*.

Asiedu, E. (2003). Debt Relief and Institutional Reform: A Focus on Heavily Indebted Poor Countries. *The Quarterly Review of Economics and Finance, 43*(3), 614-26. https://doi.org/10.1016/S1062-9769(03)00038-3

Beck, T., Demirguc-Kunt, A., & Levine, R. (2007). Finance, Inequality and the Poor. *Journal of Economic Growth, 12*, 27-49. http://dx.doi.org/10.1007/s10887-007-9010-6

Beegle, K., Dehejia, R., & GAtti, R. (2003). *Child labor, crop shocks, and crediditi constraints.* NBER Working Paper 10088. Cambridge, MA: National Bureau of Economic Research. https://doi.org/10.3386/w10088

Blundell, R., & Bond, S. (1998). Initial conditions and moment restrictions in dynamic panel data models. *Journal of Economics, 87*(1), 115-143. https://doi.org/10.1016/S0304-4076(98)00009-8

Boukhatem, J., & Bochra, M. (2012). Effects directs du développement financier sur la pauvreté: Validation empirique sur un panel de pays à bas et moyen revenu. *Mondes en Développement, 160*, 133-148. http://dx.doi.org/10.3917/med.160.0133

Chang, R., Kaltani, L., & Loayza, N. V. (2009). Openness can be good for growth: The role of policy complementarities. *Journal of Development Economics, 90*(1), 33-49. https://doi.org/10.1016/j.jdeveco.2008.06.011

Clarke, G., Xu, L. C., & Zou, H. (2003). Financial and income inequality: Test of alternatives theories. *World Bank Policy Research Paper,* WPS 2984. The World Bank, Washington DC.

Clarke, G., Xu, L. C., & Zou, H. (2006). Financial and income inequality: What do the data tell us? *Southern Economic Journal, 72*, 578-596. http://dx.doi.org/10.2307/20111834

Dhrifi, A., & Maktouf, S. (2013). Financial liberalization and poverty: The Threshold Effect of Financial Development. *International Journal of Business and Management Invention, 2*(1), 1-10.

Dollar, D., & Kraay, A. (2002). Growth is good for the poor. *Journal of Economic Growth, 7*, 195-225. https://doi.org/10.1023/A:1020139631000

Easterly, W., & Fischer, S. (2001). Inflation and the poor. *Journal of Money, Credit and banking, 33*(2), 160-178. https://doi.org/10.2307/2673879

Fan, S., Hazell, P., & Thorat, S. (2000). Government spending, growth and poverty in rural India. *American Journal of Agricultural Economics, 82*, 1038-1051. https://doi.org/10.1111/0002-9092.00101

Fowowe, B., & Abidoye, B. (2012). *A quantitative assessment of the effect of financial development on poverty in African countries*. Department of Economics, University of Ibadan, Nigeria. http://dx.doi.org/10.1111/j.1467-9957.2012.02302.x

Greenwood, J., & Jovanovic, B. (1990). Financial Development, Growth, and the Distribution of Income. *Journal of Political Economy, 98*(5), 1076-1107. http://dx.doi.org/10.1086/261720

Guillaumont-Jeanneney, S., & Kpodar, K. (2011). Financial development and poverty reduction: Can there be a benefit without cost? *Journal of Development Studies, 47*(1), 143-163. https://doi.org/10.1080/00220388.2010.506918

Ho, S. Y., & Odhiambo, M. N. (2011). Finance and poverty reduction in China: An empirical investigation. *International Business & Economic Research Journal, 10*, 103-114. https://doi.org/10.19030/iber.v10i8.5382

Honohan, P. (2004). *Financial Development, Growth and Poverty: How Close are the link?* World Bank Policy Research Working Paper 3203, Washington D.C: World Bank. http://dx.doi.org/10.1596/1813-9450-3203

Im, K. S., Pesaran, M. H., & Shin, Y. (2003). Testing for Unit Roots in Heterogeneous Panels. *Journal of Econometrics, 115*(1), 53-74. https://doi.org/10.1016/S0304-4076(03)00092-7

Jacoby, H., & Skoufias, E. (1997). Risk, financial markets, and human capital. *Review of Economic Studies, 64*, 311-335. http://dx.doi.org/10.2307/2971716

Jalilian, H., & Kirkpatrick, C. (2002). Financial development and poverty reduction in developing countries. *International Journal of Finance and Economics, 7*, 97-108. http://dx.doi.org/10.1002/ijfe.179

Jalilian, H., & Kirkpatrick, C. (2005). Does financial development contribute to poverty reduction? *Journal of Development Studies, 41*(4), 636-656. https://doi.org/10.1080/00220380500092754

Kaminsky, G. L., & Reinhart, C. M. (1999). The Twin Crises: The Causes of Banking and balance-Of-Payments Problems. *American Economic Review, 89*(3), 473-500. https://doi.org/10.1257/aer.89.3.473

Kaufmann, D., Kraay, A., & Zoido-Lobaton, P. (1999). *Aggregating Governance Indicators*. Policy Research Paper 2195, The World Bank. https://doi.org/10.2139/ssrn.188548

King, R. G., & Levine, R. (1993). Finance and Growth: Schumpeter Might be Right. *Quarterly Journal of Economics, 108*(3), 717-737. https://doi.org/10.2307/2118406

Le Goff, M., & Singh, R. J. (2014). Does trade reduce poverty? A view of Africa. *Journal of African Trade, 1*(2014), 5-14. https://doi.org/10.1016/j.joat.2014.06.001

Levine, A., Lin, C. F., & Chu, C. (2002). Unit Root Test in Panel: Asymptotic and Finite Sample Properties. *Journal of Econometrics, 108*(1), 1-24. https://doi.org/10.1016/S0304-4076(01)00098-7

Levine, R. (2005). Finance and Growth: Theory and Evidence. In P. Aghion, & S. Durlauf (Eds.), *Handbook of Economic Growth* (Vol. 1, Part A, pp. 865-934).

Levine, R. (2008). Finance and the poor. *The Manchester School, 76*, 1-13. http://dx.doi.org/10.1111/j.1467-9957.2008.01078.x

Maddala, G. S., & Wu, S. (1999). A Comparative Study of Unit Root Tests with Panel Data and a New Simple Test. *Oxford Bulletin of Economics and Statistics, 61*, 631-652. https://doi.org/10.1111/1468-0084.61.s1.13

McKinnon, R. I. (1973). *Money and Capital in Economic Development.* Washington D.C: Brookings Institution.

Odhiambo, N. M. (2009). Finance-growth-poverty nexus in South Africa: A dynamic causality linkage. *Journal of Socio-Economics, 38*, 320-325. http://dx.doi.org/10.1016/j.socec.2008.12.006

Pradhan, R. P. (2010). The nexus between finance, growth and poverty in India: The cointegration and causality approach. *Asian Social Science, 6*, 114-122. https://doi.org/10.5539/ass.v6n9p114

Quartey, P. (2005). *Financial sector development, savings mobilization and poverty reduction in Ghana*. UNU-WIDER Research Paper No. 2005/71, Helsinki: UNU World Institute for Development Economics Research. http://dx.doi.org/10.4337/9781845424602.00008

Rajan, R. G., & Zingales, L. (2003). *Banks and markets: The changing character of European finance*. CEPR Discussion Paper No. 3865, London: Centre for Economic Policy Research.

http://dx.doi.org/10.3386/w9595

Ravallion, M., & Datt, G. (2002). Why has economic growth been more pro-poor in some states of India than others? *Journal of Development Economics, 68*, 381-400. https://doi.org/10.1016/S0304-3878(02)00018-4

Shahbaz, M., & Rehman, I. U. (2013). *Multivariate-based Granger causality between financial development and poverty: The case of Pakistan.* MPRA paper No. 50834, Munich. http://dx.doi.org/10.1007/s11135-013-9952-z

Shaw, E. S. (1973). *Financial Deepening in Economic Development*. New York: Oxford University Press.

Singh, R. (1992). *An imperfect information approach to the structure of the financial system.* UNCTAD Discussion Paper No. 86, Geneva, UNCTAD.

Singh, R. J., & Huang, Y. (2015). Financial Deepening, Property Rights, and Poverty: Evidence from Sub-Saharan Africa. *Journal of Banking and Financial Economics, 1*(3), 130-151. https://doi.org/10.7172/2353-6845.jbfe.2015.1.6

Stiglitz, J. (1998). The role of the state in financial markets. In M. Bruno, & B. Pleskovic (Eds.), *Proceedings of the World Bank Annual Conference on Development Economic* (pp. 19-52). World Bank, Washington DC.

Uddin, G. S., Shahbaz, M., Arouri, M., & Teulon, F. (2014). Financial development and poverty reduction nexus: A cointegration and causality analysis in Bangladesh. *Economic Modelling, 36*, 405-412. https://doi.org/10.1016/j.econmod.2013.09.049

Appendix 1

Panel Unit root test and threshold effects

Table A1. Panel unit root test

	Niveau		
Variables	**LLC**	**IPS**	**MW**
lpovhead	-0,004***	-0.8743	709.39***
	(0.000)	(0.1910)	(0.000)
lpovgap	3.3706	-2.760***	667.23***
	(0.9996)	(0.0029)	(0.0000)
linf	-0,01***	-11.235***	235.122***
	(0.000)	(0.000)	(0.000)
lopeness	-8.9230***	1.5357	10.746***
	(0.000)	(0.9377)	(0.000)
igov	-37.0912***	-0.7361	226.75***
	(0.000)	(0.2308)	(0.000)
lpc	-81.0326***	-20.925***	378.03***
	(0.0000)	(0.0000)	(0.0000)
ledu	-12.3771***	0.2986	199.61***
	(0.0000)	(0.6174)	(0.0000)
lgdpc	-0.016***	-0.013***	1153.8***
	(0.0000)	(0.0000)	(0.0000)

Note. Standard errors in parentheses; ***, **, * specify that coefficients are statistically significant at the 1%, 5% and 10% levels.
Source : Author calculations with data provided.

Table A2. Testing threshold effects

	Private Credit (PC)
poverty incidence	10,64
poverty gap	1,193

Note. the thresholds values are in percentage of GDP.

Appendix 2.

List of countries in the sample

Country	Country	Country
Angola	Gabon	Niger
Benin	Gambia, The	Nigeria
Botswana	Ghana	Rwanda
Burkina Faso	Guinea	Senegal
Burundi	Guinea-Bissau	Seychelles
Cameroon	Kenya	Sierra Leone
Cape Verde	Lesotho	South Africa
Central African Republic	Liberia	Sudan
Chad	Madagascar	Swaziland
Comoros	Malawi	Tanzania
Congo, Dem. Rep.	Mali	Togo
Congo Rep.	Mauritania	Uganda
Cote d'Ivoire	Mauritius	Zambia
Ethiopia	Mozambique	Zimbabwe

Source: Author.

7

Forecasting Volatility Stock Return: Evidence from the Nordic Stock Exchanges

Nikolaos Dritsakis[1] & Georgios Savvas[2]

[1] Professor, Department of Applied Informatics, School of Information Sciences, University of Macedonia, Thessaloniki, Greece

[2] Post-Graduate Student, Master of Science in Applied Informatics, Department of Applied Informatics, School of Information Sciences, University of Macedonia, Greece

Correspondence: Georgios Savvas, Department of Applied Informatics, School of Information Sciences, University of Macedonia, Thessaloniki, Greece. E-mail: mai16058@uom.edu.gr

Abstract

The purpose of this study is to explore the volatility and secondary effects in the four Nordic stock exchanges of Norway: Oslo Børs Linked all-share index AXLT Denmark: OMX Copenhagen 20, Sweden: OMX Stockholm 30 and Finland: OMX Helsinki 25. Keeping in mind that there is an ARCH effect in the returns of the four stock exchanges, we move on to the evaluation to the evaluation of models ARCH (q), GARCH (p, q) και GARCH-M (p, q). Evaluating the parameters became possible through the use of the maximum likelihood method using the BHHH algorithm of (Berndt et al., 1974) and the three distributions (normal, t-Student, and the Generalized normal distribution GED). The results of this study indicate model ARMA(0,1)-GARCH-M(1,1) with t-student distribution as the appropriate one to describe the returns of the all Nordic stock exchanges except that of Sweden, where model ARMA(0,3)-GARCH-M(1,1) describes it best. Lastly, for forecasting the models ARMA(0,1)-GARCH-M(1,1) and ARMA(0,3)-GARCH-M(1,1) of the current stock exchanges we use both the dynamic and static process. The results of this study indicate that the static process forecasts better than the corresponding dynamic.

Keywords: stock returns, GARCH models, forecasting volatility, Nordic stock exchanges, BHHH algorithm

1. Introduction

In recent years the financial world is in a serious instability. Modeling financial series is a complex matter for most economists. This complexity derives not only from the various financial market products (interest rate, exchange rates, reserves etc.) but also from the effect of political incidents. These incidents create volatility in time-series, resulting to the difficulty of creating various stochastic models. Assets evaluation becomes possible using their return, which is conventionally defined as the logarithmic price changes, which is close to the relative price change. This return is depicted as follows:

$$R_t = ln(X_t / X_{t-1}) \tag{1}$$

where R_t is a financial asset with value X_t at time t and X_{t-1} at time t-1. The return is scale-free, which facilitates comparisons between assets.

The theory of option pricing is an important topic in the financial literature. The Black, and Scholes (1973) study was the beginning of the European-style purchase options. Consequently it was discovered that the prices of Black and Scholes models differ from the market prices, therefore the literature for evaluating the purchase options formulated a series of theoretical models designed to capture these empirical biases. Various empirical studies related to the price dynamics of current assets, indicated that the assets features in time is the volatility, the non-normality and leverage effect, thus, they should be taken into consideration in financial data. Therefore the various models and developed techniques should incorporate some or all of the above properties.

As previously stated volatility clustering has been used instead of a constant variable in volatility functions depended on the asset value and time. Furthermore time-series are regarded as a stochastic process which can be analysed in two elements:

$$R_t = m_t + u_t \tag{2}$$

$$u_t = \sigma\varepsilon_t \quad (3)$$

Where m_t is a predictable process, and u_t is a nondeterministic process driven by a random noise ε_t is iid with zero mean value and variance one.

GARCH symmetrical models cannot define asymmetry and leptokurtosis in financial data. For this particular reason the GARCH-in-mean model is used in this study, which adds a heteroscedastic term in the equation mean which is determined as a risk premium and incorporates a type of assymetry.

The research on the return and volatility of the Nordic stock markets was carried out for the following reasons:

- There is a strong financial cooperation between those countries.
- The monetary and tax systems of the researched markets are similar and a close association exists between these countries.
- These four Nordic countries have similar industries, therefore their stock markets display a strong correlation.
- They have common trade partners.
- Their stock markets opening and working times coincide.

This research differs from past ones which researched the Nordic market for the following reasons:

1) The past studies of researching volatility and the relationship between the Nordic markets used data from 1988 to 1994 Booth et al. (1997), while Hyytinen (1999) used weekly data and only for three markets (Finnish, Norwegian and Swedish market) from 1983 to 1997. The expansion of data in this study and the conclusions analysis are important for investors who want to diversify their portfolios.
2) The results of this study indicate that every one of these markets are described better from model ARMA(0,1)-GARCH-M(1,1) with t-Student distribution, unlike Booth's et al. (1997) study which uses the EGARCH asymmetric model, and Hyytinen's (1999) which uses the TGARCH asymmetric model for Sweden and GARCH symmetric models for Finland and Norway.
3) Furthermore, the results of this study agree with those of Booth's et al. (1997) that the volatility in the four markets indicate that ill news are stronger than good news. The research on the returns and the volatility of secondary effects in the Nordic markets dictate the enactment of a common Nordic stock market, to create the fourth bigger stock market in Europe after the ones of London, Paris and Frankfurt.

In this paper a short introduction of financial return is presented in section 1. The rest of this paper is as follows: section 2 contains the literature review, section 3 presents the methodological analysis, section 4 describes the data and the descriptive statistics, in section 5 the empirical results of this study are given, while in section 6 the forecasting results are presented. Last but not least, in section 7 the conclusions of this study are given.

2. Literature Review

Time-series performance analysis has troubled financial researchers in recent years. One of the first evaluation tries was conducted from Eun and Shim (1989) when they researched the daily returns of the Australia, Hong Kong, Japan, France, Canada, Switzerland, Germany, the United States and Britain stock exchanges. The results of their study indicated that there are substantial interdependencies among these markets, most of which are with the U.S. stock market. European and Asian stock exchange dependencies are strong but with one day delay.

Hamao, et al. (1990) used daily data from April 1985 to March 1988 from three stock indexes, Nikkei 225 of the Japan stock exchange, FTSE of the Great Britain stock exchange and S & P 500 of the U.S.A. stock exchange. Using model GARCH-M(1,1) they resulted that Nikkei 225 is influenced both from S & P 500 and FTSE, while FTSE is influenced only from S & P 500.

Booth et al. (1997) in their study used a multivariate exponential generalized autoregressive conditionally heteroscedastic (EGARCH) model to research the interaction of the four Scandinavic stock markets in period May 2nd 1988 to June 30th 1994. The results of their study indicate that volatility in the asymmetric model used is being more pronounced for bad than good news.

Hyytinen (1999) studies the development of conditional volatility of returns in three Scandinavian countries (Finland, Norway and Sweden) using weekly data from 1983-1997. The results of the paper shown that the asymmetric EGARCH model is most suitable for Sweden's data whereas the symmetric model GARCH (1,1) is more preferable for the other two countries.

Ng (2000) examined the magnitude and changing nature of volatility spillovers from Japan and the US to six

Pacific–Basin equity. He used indexes Hang Seng of Hong Kong, the Korean Composite Stock Price Index, the Kuala Lumpur Stock Exchange Composite Index (Malaysia), the Stock Exchange of Singapore All Share Index, the Taiwan Stock Exchange Weighted Price Index, the Stock Exchange of Thailand Index, the Tokyo Stock Price Index, and the Standard and Poor's 500 Index. The results of his study indicated that four of six Pacific Basin Region stock exchanges are influenced less than 10% weekly from a change in the returns of Japan and USA stock markets.

Lee (2004) in his study researches the transition mechanism of the stock market return via wavelet analysis. He used the wavelet analysis instead of CARCH models, claiming that his analysis researches the potential and possible interactions of international stock markets. Using daily data from the USA and Korean stock exchange he resulted that developed markets volatility one-way influence the developing ones.

Trang Nha Le and Makoto Kakinaka (2010) researched volatility and secondary effects in three major stock markets, such as these of Japan, USA and China, as well as two emerging ones of Indonesia and Malaysia from the years 2005 to 2007. Using CARCH models they found that there are significant mean spillover effects from the three major markets to the two emerging markets. Furthermore they found that the size of the USA stock market influence upon the emerging ones is greater than those of Japan and China. Lastly, the results of their study indicated that the USA stock market influence upon the Indonesian market is greater than in the Malaysian.

Prashant (2014) researched the return and volatility among the indexes BSE and DJIA of India and US Stock Markets respectively. To do this he used model GARCH-BEKK from January 2, 2012 to April 4, 2014. His study results indicated that DJIA index exercises more influence on BSE in terms of shocks and volatility transmission . Furthermore, he proved that total volatility is greater in the USA stock exchange.

Thenmozh and Chand (2016) in their study showed that forecasting returns based on global reserves attributed better in day trading both in emerging and major markets. Forecasting the returns, the researchers used vector regression for six stock markets, namely those of USA (Dow Jones, S&P500), UK (FTSE-100), India (NSE), Singapore (SGX), Hong Kong (Hang Seng) and China (Shanghai stock exchange) for the period 1999-2011. The empirical analysis shows that models with other global market price information outperform forecast models based merely on auto-regressive past lags and technical indicators.

3. Methodology

Uncertainty plays an essential role in economic analysis and is usually measured with volatility. There are time-series, mainly financial, who display periods of mass volatility. These time-series experience periods with dramatic increases and decreases, during which their variance is varying over time. Therefore, researchers can test the variance of this particular time-series in the varying period, namely the conditional variance. Hence, we can describe the time-series models with conditional variance as conditional heteroscedastic models. Engle (1982) suggested that the varying variance can be described through an autoregressive model depending on its former values. Specifically this model is described as Autoregressive Conditional Heteroscedastic Model, known as ARCH model.

Therefore, based on a structured model, variance can be measured and forecasted. Variance forecasting is crucial to pricing and risk management. In various studies, several variance models have been suggested to be able to include the features of financial time-series efficiency or an asset. The features of an asset's efficiency that researchers acknowledge are as follows:

- The variance of an asset develops with time, in a constant way.
- Periods of great movement in prices, alternate with periods where prices don't move. This feature is known as volatility clustering.
- The variance of an asset does not tend to infinity.
- There is an asymmetric movement in variance.
- Usually, extreme kurtosis or fat-tailedness is observed in variance.

3.1 ARCH-GARCH Varying Models

ARCH-GARCH varying models are consisted of two equations. The first one (mean equation) describes the data over another variable (if present) adding the standard error. The second one (covariance equation) define the evolution of conditional covariance of the error, from the mean equation as a variance of the past conditional covariance of the lagged error.

The mean equation in ARCH – GARCH models is depicted as:

$$R_t = \mu + \varepsilon_t \text{ (ARCH model)} \quad (4)$$

The error term εt in a simple mean equation is linear unrelated, but not time-independent.

$$R_t = \mu + \beta\sigma_t^2 + \varepsilon_t \text{ (GARCH model)} \quad (5)$$

Covariance equation in ARCH – GARCH models is depicted as:

$$\sigma_t^2 = \omega + \sum_{i=1}^{q} a_i \varepsilon_{t-i}^2 \text{ (ARCH model)} \quad (6)$$

The non-linear dependency that the error term εt depicts can be described through the use of squared lagged errors Parameters ω, α_1, α_2,...,α_q are unknown and because covariance is a positive number, meaning that the positive terms are in place, where $\omega>0$ and $\alpha_1,\alpha_2,\ldots,\alpha_q \geq 0$.

$$\sigma_t^2 = \omega + \sum_{i=1}^{q} \alpha_i \varepsilon_{t-i}^2 + \sum_{j=1}^{p} \beta_j \sigma_{t-j}^2 \text{ (GARCH model)} \quad (7)$$

We hypothesize that, for $p\geq 0$ and $q>0$, the parameters are unknown and because of covariance being a positive number the following conditions are in place $\omega\geq 0$ and $\alpha_i\geq 0$ for $i=1,\ldots,q$ and $\beta_i\geq 0$ for $j=1,\ldots,p$

ARCH(1,1) model is depicted as:

$$\sigma_t^2 = \omega + \alpha_1\varepsilon_{t-1}^2 \quad (8)$$

where $\omega\geq 0$ and $\alpha_i\geq 0$ for the positive number of σ_t^2

GARCH(1,1) model is depicted as:

$$\sigma_t^2 = \omega + \alpha_1\varepsilon_{t-1}^2 + \beta_1\sigma_{t-1}^2 \quad (9)$$

where $\omega\geq 0$, $\alpha_i\geq 0$ and $\beta_i\geq 0$ for the positive number of σ_t^2

3.3 ARCH- GARCH Models Features

ARCH – CARCH model according to Engle(1982) is based on the two following hypothesis:

- The error term ε_t in a simple mean equation ($y_t = \mu_t + \varepsilon_t$) is linear unrelated, but not time-independent.
- The non-linear dependency that the error term ε_t depicts can be described through the use of squared lagged errors

3.4 ARCH-GARCH Models Test and Evaluation

Evaluation of ARCH-GARCH models is possible through the use of maximum likelihood method. The logged equation of maximum likelihood is depicted as:

$$lnL(\theta) = -(1/2)\sum_{t=1}^{n}\left[ln(2\pi) + ln\left(\sigma_t^2(\theta)\right) + z_t^2(\theta)\right] \quad (10)$$

where

θ is the vector of parameters (μ, ω, α, β) estimated that maximize the objective function $\ln L(\theta)$,

z_t represents the standardized residual calculated as $(\Delta y_t - \mu)/\sqrt{\sigma_t^2}$.

3.5 Diagnostic Checking of the Model ARCH-GARCH

There are plenty diagnostic tests for the analysis of ARCH- GARCH modeling. The residual correlogram is used to test the residual autocorrelation, while the squared residual correlogram is used to test the autocorrelation of the conditional heteroscedasticity of residuals. To define if the time-series presents autocorrelation or heteroscedasticity we use the Ljung and Box (Q-statistics) (1978). This statistics are depicted as:

$$Q_m = n(n+2)\sum_{k=1}^{m} e_k^2/(n-2) \quad (11)$$

where:

e_k is the residual autocorrelation in lag k.

n is the residual number.

m is the time-lags number tested.

The model is appropriate when the probability of Ljung and Box Q-statistics is higher than 5%.

3.6 The GARCH-M Model

Engle, Lilien, and Robins (1987), build on the ARCH(q) methodology for the purpose of conditional covariance influencing the mean order. In other words we could say that Engle, Lilien, and Robins (1987) restructured the conditional variance model in order that the mean of a sequence to be depended on the conditional covariance. These models are named ARCH-M and are adequately adjusted to the study of the return of financial products. The model that Engle, Lilien and Robins built is the following:

$$R_t = \mu + other\ terms + \delta\sigma^2_{t-1} + \varepsilon_t \text{ (mean equation)} \quad (12)$$

$$\sigma^2_t = \omega + \sum_{i=1}^{q} \alpha_i \varepsilon^2_{t-i} + \sum_{j=1}^{p} \beta_j \sigma^2_{t-j} \text{ (covariance equation)} \quad (13)$$

where:

μ is the conditional mean of the stock market return in time t.

σ^2_t is the conditional covariance that reflects the risk premium.

ω is a constant term.

ε_t is the error term in time t.

μ, δ, ω, α_i and β_j are parameters for evaluation.

In this study the model GARCH-M (1,1) is used, considering the study of Bollerslev (1986), where he claims that the length of the time lag of the squared error and the conditional variance is enough for the stock market return model.

GARCH-M (1,1) model equation can be depicted as:

$$R_t = \mu + other\ terms + \delta\sigma^2_{t-1} + \varepsilon_t \text{ (mean equation)} \quad (14)$$

$$\sigma^2_t = \omega + \alpha_1\varepsilon^2_{t-1} + \beta_1\sigma^2_{t-1} \text{ (covariance equation)} \quad (15)$$

3.7 Forecasting Performance

ARCH-GARCH models are used for forecasting the variance return. Forecasting in ARCH-GARCH models is estimated both in-sample, and out-of-sample. The best forecasting price is given from the mean squared error. Furthermore, other indexes that are usually used for forecast return are the Mean Absolute Error (MAE), Root Mean Square Error (RMSE), Mean Absolute Percentage Error (MAPE) and the inequality index of Theil (U-Theil) (1967).

These indexes are depicted as follows:

$$MSE = (1/T)\sum_{t=1}^{T}(\hat{Y}_t - Y_t)^2 \quad (16)$$

$$MAE = (1/T)\sum_{t=1}^{T}|\hat{Y}_t - Y_t|^2 \quad (17)$$

$$RMSE = \sqrt{(1/T)\sum_{t=1}^{T}(\hat{Y}_t - Y_t)^2} \quad (18)$$

$$MAPE = (1/T)\sum_{t=1}^{T}|(\hat{Y}_t - Y_t)/Y_t|^2 \quad (19)$$

the inequality index of Theil is given as:

$$U = \left(\sqrt{(1/T)\sum_{t=1}^{T}(\hat{Y}_t - Y_t)^2}\right) / \left(\sqrt{(1/T)\sum_{t=1}^{T}(\hat{Y}_t)^2} + \sqrt{(1/T)\sum_{t=1}^{T}(Y_t)^2}\right) \quad 0 \leq U \leq 1 \quad (20)$$

where:

Y_t: Actual value of endogenous variable Y at time t.

$\hat{Y}_t$: Redacted value of endogenous variable Y at time t.

T: Number of observations in the simulations (of the sample).

If the inequality index of Theil U=0, then the actual prices of the time-series, would equal the predicted ones $Y_t = \hat{Y}_t$ for all t, therefore in this case we can say that there is a "perfect fit" between actual and predicted data. Otherwise if variable U=1, there is no right forecast for the studied model. Consequently the individual indexes of Theil are presented, known as inequality proportions, and are depicted as:

- Bias proportion: indicates the systematic differences in actual and forecasted values.

$$UM = ((\bar{\hat{Y}} - \bar{Y})^2)/((1/T)\sum_{t=1}^{T}(\hat{Y}_t - Y_t)^2) \quad (21)$$

where:

$\bar{\hat{Y}}$ and $\bar{Y}$ are the time-series mean of $\hat{Y}_t$ and Y_t correspondingly. Bias proportion counts the distance between the mean of the simulated series and the mean of the actual one.

- Variance proportion: indicates unequal variances of actual and forecasted values.

$$US = ((\hat{S}_{\hat{Y}} - S_Y)^2)/\ ((1/T)\sum_{t=1}^{T}(\hat{Y}_t - Y_t)^2) \quad (22)$$

where:

$\hat{S}_{\hat{Y}}$ and S_Y are the standard deviations of series $\hat{Y}_t$ and Y_t correspondingly. Variance proportion counts the distance between the variance of the simulated series and the variance of the real one.

- Covariance proportion: indicates the correlation between the actual and forecasted values (zero=perfect correlation between actual and forecasted values).

$$UC = (2(1-\rho)\, \hat{S}_{\hat{Y}} S_Y) / \left((1/T)\textstyle\sum_{t=1}^{T}(\hat{Y}_t - Y_t)^2\right) \quad (23)$$

where:

ρ is the correlation variable between $\hat{Y}_t$ and Y_t. Covariance proportion counts the balance of the non-systematic error of simulation.

The forecasting ability of a model is sufficient, when the bias and covariance proportions are low.

The relationship between the above proportions is:

$$UM+US+UC=1 \quad (24)$$

4. Data and Descriptive Statistics

The data for this study was collected from the websites www.nasdaqomxnordic.com for the OMX Copenhagen 20, OMX Stockholm 30 and OMX Helsinki 25 indexes and from the website www.oslobors.no for the AXLT index of Oslo Børs. The data covers the period from January 3rd 1983 to April 7th 2016 for the Norwegian Index and contains 8347 observations, the period from October 10th 1996 to May 11th 2016 for the Danish Index and contains 4893 observations, the period from September 30th 1986 to May 11th 2016 for the Swedish Index and contains 7434 observations and lastly the period from September 3rd 2001 to May 11th 2016 for the Finnish Index and contains 3687 observations.

The daily return of stock markets is calculated as:

$$R_t = \ln(X_t/X_{t-1}) * 100 = (\ln X_t - \ln X_{t-1})*100 \quad (25)$$

where,

X_t is the daily closing price of stock market at time t,

R_t is the daily return of stock market.

The daily closing prices of the AXLT, OMX Copenhagen 20, OMX Stockholm 30 and OMX Helsinki 25 Indexes and their returns are presented at Figures 1 and 2, correspondingly.

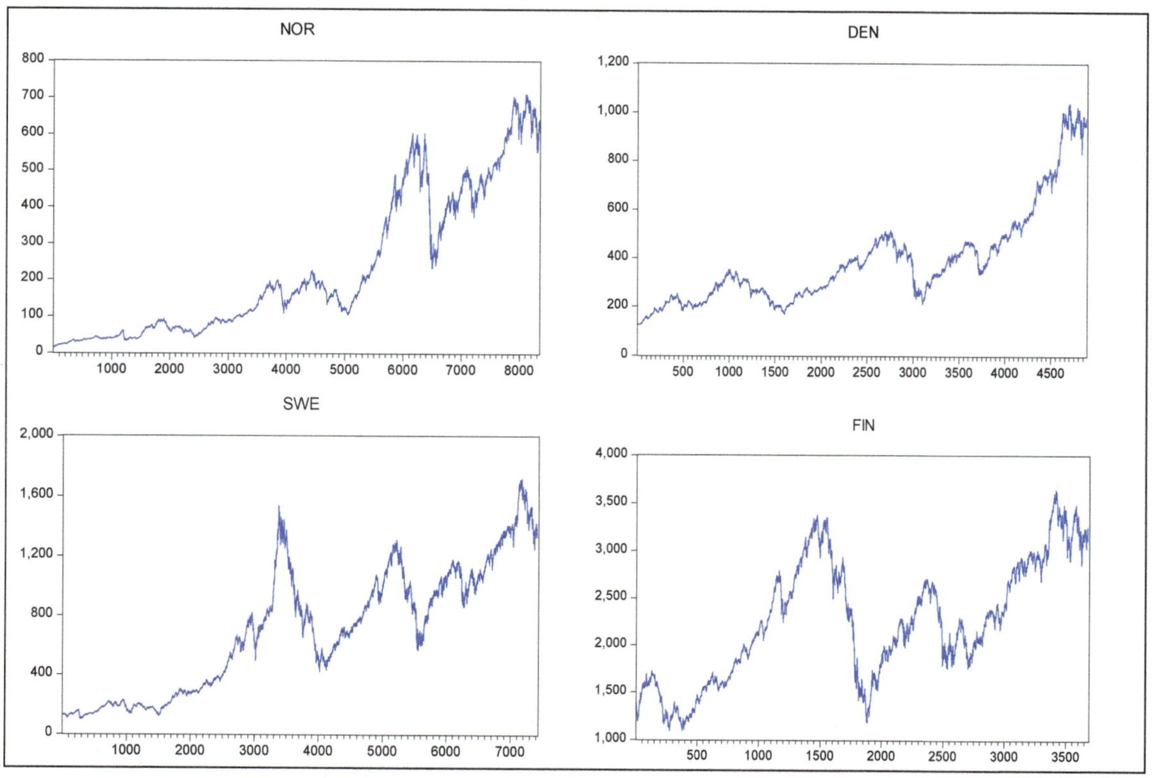

Figure 1. Daily closing prices of the Norwegian, Danish, Swedish and Finnish stock markets

From Figure 1 we can assume that the daily closing prices of all stock markets display a random walk.

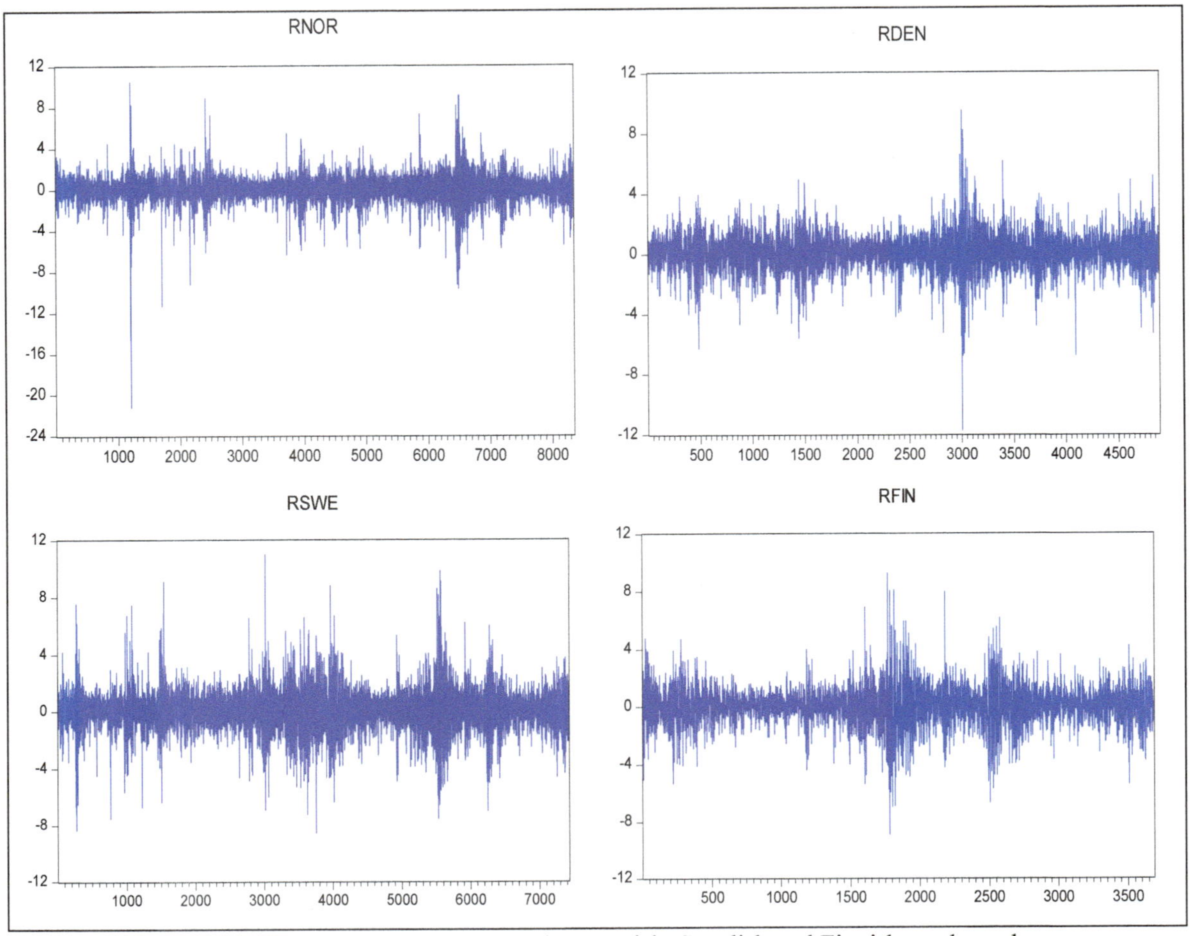

Figure 2. Daily returns of the Norwegian, Danish, Swedish and Finnish stock markets

From Figure 2 we can assume that the daily returns of all the stock markets are stationary. Consequently we can move on to Tables 1 and 2 of correlograms and check if autocorrelation exists in the daily returns of stock markets, as well as the form of autocorrelation in the correlograms of the daily squared returns.

Table 1. Correlogram of the daily return of the Norwegian, Danish, Swedish and Finnish stock markets

Sample: 1 8347
Included observations: 8346

Autocorrelation	Partial Correlation		AC	PAC	Q-Stat	Prob
		1	0.061	0.061	30.978	0.000
		2	-0.012	-0.016	32.165	0.000
		3	-0.024	-0.023	37.144	0.000
		4	0.009	0.012	37.886	0.000
		5	-0.022	-0.024	41.951	0.000
		6	-0.005	-0.002	42.121	0.000
		7	0.051	0.051	63.734	0.000
		8	0.019	0.011	66.617	0.000
		9	0.028	0.029	73.401	0.000
		10	0.015	0.014	75.356	0.000
		11	0.011	0.009	76.281	0.000
		12	0.005	0.008	76.519	0.000
		13	0.024	0.025	81.423	0.000
		14	0.027	0.023	87.594	0.000
		15	0.037	0.035	99.291	0.000
		16	0.020	0.016	102.76	0.000
		17	-0.003	-0.005	102.82	0.000
		18	-0.017	-0.016	105.27	0.000
		19	-0.004	-0.003	105.44	0.000
		20	0.001	-0.001	105.44	0.000
		21	0.010	0.007	106.30	0.000
		22	0.000	-0.007	106.30	0.000
		23	0.014	0.009	107.88	0.000
		24	0.001	-0.004	107.89	0.000
		25	0.036	0.035	118.59	0.000
		26	0.014	0.010	120.23	0.000
		27	-0.009	-0.010	120.85	0.000
		28	-0.009	-0.008	121.51	0.000
		29	0.007	0.005	121.87	0.000
		30	0.002	-0.001	121.90	0.000
		31	-0.022	-0.022	125.96	0.000
		32	0.014	0.014	127.58	0.000
		33	-0.013	-0.017	128.98	0.000
		34	0.002	0.002	129.00	0.000
		35	-0.019	-0.020	132.09	0.000
		36	0.017	0.016	134.64	0.000

Sample: 1 4893
Included observations: 4892

Autocorrelation	Partial Correlation		AC	PAC	Q-Stat	Prob
		1	0.041	0.041	8.3529	0.004
		2	-0.030	-0.032	12.689	0.002
		3	-0.024	-0.021	15.428	0.001
		4	0.022	0.024	17.906	0.001
		5	-0.033	-0.036	23.150	0.000
		6	-0.021	-0.017	25.245	0.000
		7	-0.009	-0.008	25.606	0.001
		8	-0.004	-0.006	25.667	0.001
		9	0.014	0.015	26.671	0.002
		10	0.011	0.009	27.256	0.002
		11	0.034	0.033	32.798	0.001
		12	0.000	-0.002	32.798	0.001
		13	-0.001	0.001	32.800	0.002
		14	0.026	0.028	36.192	0.001
		15	0.001	-0.002	36.194	0.002
		16	0.014	0.018	37.121	0.002
		17	0.001	0.003	37.127	0.003
		18	-0.012	-0.012	37.830	0.004
		19	0.005	0.009	37.956	0.006
		20	0.007	0.005	38.178	0.008
		21	-0.014	-0.013	39.077	0.010
		22	0.009	0.011	39.465	0.012
		23	0.000	-0.003	39.465	0.018
		24	-0.013	-0.014	40.315	0.020
		25	0.034	0.034	45.909	0.007
		26	-0.021	-0.027	48.128	0.005
		27	-0.015	-0.012	49.193	0.006
		28	-0.001	0.001	49.195	0.008
		29	0.038	0.034	56.186	0.002
		30	0.005	0.004	56.319	0.003
		31	-0.019	-0.018	58.176	0.002
		32	-0.004	-0.000	58.256	0.003
		33	-0.004	-0.007	58.319	0.004
		34	-0.003	-0.003	58.373	0.006
		35	-0.011	-0.007	58.931	0.007
		36	0.001	-0.002	58.936	0.009

Sample: 1 7432
Included observations: 7431

Lag	AC	PAC	Q-Stat	Prob
1	0.022	0.022	3.6006	0.058
2	-0.028	-0.028	9.2403	0.010
3	-0.034	-0.033	17.700	0.001
4	0.001	0.001	17.702	0.001
5	-0.008	-0.010	18.156	0.003
6	-0.035	-0.036	27.373	0.000
7	0.008	0.009	27.826	0.000
8	0.015	0.012	29.462	0.000
9	0.019	0.017	32.156	0.000
10	-0.019	-0.019	34.838	0.000
11	0.015	0.017	36.479	0.000
12	0.022	0.021	40.223	0.000
13	0.014	0.013	41.606	0.000
14	0.011	0.014	42.582	0.000
15	0.023	0.026	46.588	0.000
16	0.022	0.022	50.319	0.000
17	0.013	0.015	51.497	0.000
18	-0.026	-0.022	56.644	0.000
19	-0.037	-0.033	66.698	0.000
20	-0.001	0.000	66.700	0.000
21	-0.003	-0.005	66.764	0.000
22	-0.001	-0.002	66.768	0.000
23	0.032	0.031	74.418	0.000
24	0.021	0.015	77.665	0.000
25	0.059	0.057	103.30	0.000
26	0.011	0.012	104.20	0.000
27	-0.005	-0.001	104.42	0.000
28	0.001	0.004	104.42	0.000
29	0.024	0.025	108.81	0.000
30	0.007	0.008	109.17	0.000
31	-0.022	-0.018	112.93	0.000
32	-0.016	-0.015	114.82	0.000
33	-0.001	-0.001	114.83	0.000
34	-0.011	-0.014	115.80	0.000
35	-0.023	-0.020	119.78	0.000
36	0.028	0.025	125.43	0.000

Sample: 1 3687
Included observations: 3686

Lag	AC	PAC	Q-Stat	Prob
1	0.031	0.031	3.4375	0.064
2	-0.012	-0.013	3.9425	0.139
3	-0.025	-0.024	6.2420	0.100
4	0.000	0.002	6.2422	0.182
5	-0.062	-0.062	20.220	0.001
6	-0.021	-0.017	21.785	0.001
7	0.013	0.013	22.414	0.002
8	0.025	0.021	24.684	0.002
9	-0.020	-0.022	26.122	0.002
10	-0.021	-0.023	27.823	0.002
11	0.017	0.016	28.847	0.002
12	-0.009	-0.010	29.122	0.004
13	-0.012	-0.009	29.698	0.005
14	0.015	0.014	30.495	0.007
15	0.007	0.001	30.668	0.010
16	0.038	0.039	35.947	0.003
17	0.033	0.033	39.957	0.001
18	-0.043	-0.046	46.777	0.000
19	-0.011	-0.005	47.188	0.000
20	0.003	0.006	47.220	0.001
21	0.008	0.011	47.454	0.001
22	0.018	0.021	48.646	0.001
23	0.001	-0.005	48.651	0.001
24	-0.030	-0.033	51.947	0.001
25	0.053	0.057	62.244	0.000
26	0.019	0.022	63.629	0.000
27	-0.004	-0.005	63.701	0.000
28	-0.011	-0.010	64.136	0.000
29	0.049	0.049	72.905	0.000
30	0.018	0.019	74.093	0.000
31	-0.039	-0.036	79.654	0.000
32	-0.015	-0.010	80.459	0.000
33	0.023	0.016	82.432	0.000
34	-0.043	-0.038	89.171	0.000
35	-0.020	-0.005	90.611	0.000
36	0.038	0.031	96.008	0.000

Ljung and Box (Q-statistics) indicate that a serial correlation exists for all time lags of the autocorrelation function.

Table 2. Correlogram of the squared daily return of the Norwegian, Danish, Swedish and Finnish stock markets.

Sample: 1 8347
Included observations: 8346

Lag	AC	PAC	Q-Stat	Prob
1	0.307	0.307	787.39	0.000
2	0.148	0.059	969.55	0.000
3	0.143	0.091	1139.3	0.000
4	0.162	0.099	1357.8	0.000
5	0.153	0.073	1553.3	0.000
6	0.137	0.056	1710.2	0.000
7	0.157	0.082	1916.5	0.000
8	0.150	0.057	2104.5	0.000
9	0.143	0.051	2275.1	0.000
10	0.120	0.025	2394.8	0.000
11	0.133	0.049	2542.8	0.000
12	0.154	0.063	2741.8	0.000
13	0.137	0.033	2899.7	0.000
14	0.167	0.077	3132.7	0.000
15	0.147	0.033	3314.0	0.000
16	0.168	0.068	3551.0	0.000
17	0.127	0.006	3686.2	0.000
18	0.112	0.010	3791.2	0.000
19	0.111	0.010	3894.2	0.000
20	0.073	-0.035	3938.4	0.000
21	0.104	0.024	4029.2	0.000
22	0.100	0.003	4112.7	0.000
23	0.109	0.019	4213.1	0.000
24	0.069	-0.029	4252.5	0.000
25	0.096	0.025	4329.6	0.000
26	0.079	-0.014	4382.2	0.000
27	0.082	0.007	4438.8	0.000
28	0.088	0.006	4503.2	0.000
29	0.078	-0.001	4554.7	0.000
30	0.072	-0.010	4598.0	0.000
31	0.065	-0.004	4633.6	0.000
32	0.069	0.003	4673.6	0.000
33	0.068	0.003	4712.8	0.000
34	0.057	-0.005	4740.0	0.000
35	0.074	0.019	4786.0	0.000
36	0.055	-0.007	4811.0	0.000

Sample: 1 4893
Included observations: 4892

Lag	AC	PAC	Q-Stat	Prob
1	0.216	0.216	228.55	0.000
2	0.291	0.257	644.53	0.000
3	0.224	0.137	890.82	0.000
4	0.237	0.127	1166.0	0.000
5	0.375	0.280	1856.3	0.000
6	0.181	0.013	2016.2	0.000
7	0.252	0.071	2328.5	0.000
8	0.187	0.029	2500.4	0.000
9	0.248	0.083	2800.9	0.000
10	0.214	0.016	3025.4	0.000
11	0.184	0.024	3190.7	0.000
12	0.262	0.105	3527.5	0.000
13	0.161	-0.005	3654.7	0.000
14	0.197	-0.001	3845.7	0.000
15	0.170	0.018	3987.5	0.000
16	0.193	0.038	4171.1	0.000
17	0.222	0.048	4413.9	0.000
18	0.155	0.004	4532.7	0.000
19	0.159	-0.014	4656.3	0.000
20	0.100	-0.059	4705.8	0.000
21	0.217	0.076	4937.2	0.000
22	0.169	0.026	5078.2	0.000
23	0.168	0.025	5217.2	0.000
24	0.096	-0.065	5263.0	0.000
25	0.099	-0.022	5310.8	0.000
26	0.128	-0.031	5391.0	0.000
27	0.113	-0.006	5453.5	0.000
28	0.157	0.043	5575.2	0.000
29	0.068	-0.033	5597.8	0.000
30	0.085	-0.033	5633.6	0.000
31	0.077	-0.018	5662.5	0.000
32	0.110	0.036	5722.4	0.000
33	0.122	0.014	5796.2	0.000
34	0.076	-0.001	5824.9	0.000
35	0.075	-0.014	5852.7	0.000
36	0.075	0.016	5880.4	0.000

Sample: 1 7432
Included observations: 7431

Lag	AC	PAC	Q-Stat	Prob
1	0.218	0.218	351.74	0.000
2	0.217	0.178	701.84	0.000
3	0.234	0.170	1108.9	0.000
4	0.185	0.091	1364.7	0.000
5	0.210	0.112	1691.1	0.000
6	0.174	0.060	1915.9	0.000
7	0.192	0.083	2191.5	0.000
8	0.159	0.035	2378.9	0.000
9	0.175	0.060	2605.6	0.000
10	0.184	0.064	2856.3	0.000
11	0.179	0.059	3094.1	0.000
12	0.158	0.027	3279.3	0.000
13	0.161	0.035	3471.4	0.000
14	0.143	0.013	3624.7	0.000
15	0.145	0.022	3781.6	0.000
16	0.152	0.031	3954.5	0.000
17	0.135	0.013	4089.9	0.000
18	0.152	0.035	4263.2	0.000
19	0.126	0.005	4382.3	0.000
20	0.105	-0.017	4465.1	0.000
21	0.147	0.038	4626.0	0.000
22	0.132	0.022	4756.4	0.000
23	0.106	-0.009	4840.7	0.000
24	0.114	0.005	4938.2	0.000
25	0.144	0.045	5092.5	0.000
26	0.096	-0.016	5161.3	0.000
27	0.114	0.012	5259.0	0.000
28	0.123	0.020	5372.3	0.000
29	0.082	-0.023	5422.0	0.000
30	0.114	0.020	5519.2	0.000
31	0.116	0.023	5619.8	0.000
32	0.098	-0.001	5690.9	0.000
33	0.100	0.006	5764.9	0.000
34	0.103	0.010	5843.8	0.000
35	0.112	0.021	5936.8	0.000
36	0.094	0.002	6003.3	0.000

Sample: 1 3687
Included observations: 3686

Lag	AC	PAC	Q-Stat	Prob
1	0.139	0.139	71.500	0.000
2	0.227	0.212	262.16	0.000
3	0.212	0.168	427.55	0.000
4	0.156	0.080	517.32	0.000
5	0.303	0.229	855.51	0.000
6	0.190	0.097	989.57	0.000
7	0.179	0.049	1108.3	0.000
8	0.145	0.005	1186.5	0.000
9	0.198	0.087	1331.3	0.000
10	0.178	0.042	1448.0	0.000
11	0.228	0.106	1639.6	0.000
12	0.188	0.061	1771.1	0.000
13	0.173	0.047	1881.8	0.000
14	0.174	0.023	1993.3	0.000
15	0.130	-0.017	2055.6	0.000
16	0.209	0.059	2217.2	0.000
17	0.196	0.068	2359.2	0.000
18	0.175	0.037	2473.2	0.000
19	0.168	0.025	2578.0	0.000
20	0.123	-0.018	2633.9	0.000
21	0.199	0.054	2781.2	0.000
22	0.175	0.027	2894.7	0.000
23	0.184	0.038	3021.0	0.000
24	0.118	-0.035	3072.4	0.000
25	0.165	0.036	3173.8	0.000
26	0.143	-0.000	3249.5	0.000
27	0.133	-0.017	3315.7	0.000
28	0.184	0.033	3441.2	0.000
29	0.096	-0.030	3475.1	0.000
30	0.147	0.000	3555.2	0.000
31	0.113	-0.012	3602.6	0.000
32	0.144	0.021	3679.7	0.000
33	0.147	0.014	3760.7	0.000
34	0.140	0.020	3834.0	0.000
35	0.182	0.066	3957.9	0.000
36	0.119	0.007	4011.1	0.000

Results of Table 2 indicate that Ljung and Box (Q-statistics) for all time lags is statistical significant, therefore an ARCH effect exists.

Table 3. Descriptive statistics of the daily return of the Norwegian, Danish, Swedish and Finnish stock markets

	NOR	DEN	SWE	FIN
Mean	0.045110	0.041417	0.031782	0.021683
Median	0.092587	0.085747	0.069711	0.063065
Maximum	10.48099	9.496355	11.02284	9.285563
Minimum	-21.21879	-11.72319	-8.526937	-8.905445
Std. Dev.	*1.320211*	1.289933	1.462234	1.444397
Skewness	-1.012962	-0.268218	0.025068	-0.036580
Kurtosis	17.89832	7.847888	7.250442	6.317618
Jarque-Bera	78613.88	4849.151	5594.544	1691.251
Probability	0.000000	0.000000	0.000000	0.000000
Sum	376.4856	202.6100	236.1706	79.92401
Sum Sq.Dev.	14544.98	8138.264	15886.28	7687.956
Observations	8346	4892	7431	3686

Table 4. Stationarity test of the daily return of the Norwegian, Danish, Swedish and Finnish stock markets

Variable	ADF		P-P	
	C	C,T	C	C,T
RNOR	-85.93(0)*	-85.95(0)*	-86.51[25]*	-86.50[25]*
R SWE	-84.31(0)*	-84.31(0)*	-84.32[15]*	-84.32[15]*
RFIN	-58.86(0)*	-58.85(0)*	-58.87[11]*	-58.86[11]*
RDEN	-67.09(0)*	-67.08(0)*	-67.03[14]*	-67.02[14]*

Note. 1. *, ** and *** show significant at 1%, 5% and 10% levels respectively.

2. The numbers within parentheses followed by ADF statistics represent the lag length of the dependent variable used to obtain white noise residuals.

3. The lag lengths for ADF equation were selected using Schwarz Information Criterion (SIC).

4. Mackinnon (1996) critical value for rejection of hypothesis of unit root applied.

5. The numbers within brackets followed by PP statistics represent the bandwidth selected based on Newey West (1994) method using Bartlett Kernel.

6. C=Constant, T=Trend..

After the stationarity detection with tests Dickey-Fuller (1979, 1981) and Phillips-Perron (1988) of all time-series we can define the form of model ARMA (p, q) from the correlogram of Table 1. Parameters p and q can be defined from the partial autocorrelation and correlation variable, correspondingly, comparing them with the critical value $\pm 2 / \sqrt{n} = \pm 2 / \sqrt{8347} = \pm 0.022$ for the Norwegian stock exchange, ± 0.028 for the Danish stock exchange, ± 0.023 for the Swedish stock exchange and ± 0.032 for the Finnish stock exchange.

Therefore for Norway and Finland p value will be $0<p<1$ and q value will be $0<q<1$, for Denmark p value will be $0<p<2$ and q value will be $0<q<2$ and lastly for Sweden p value will be $0<p<3$ and q value will be $0<q<3$. Consequently we can create Table 5 as such:

Table 5. Comparison of models within the range of exploration using AIC, SIC and HQ

ARIMA model	AIC	SC	HQ
RNOR			
(1,0,0)	3.3903	3.3928	3.3912
(0,0,1)	**3.3902**	**3.3927**	**3.3911**
(1,0,1)	3.3904	3.3938	3.3915
R DEN			
(0,0,1)	**3.3462**	**3.3502**	**3.3476**
(0,0,2)	3.3469	3.3512	3.3478
(1,0,0)	3.3463	3.3503	3.3477
(1,0,1)	3.3463	3.3516	3.3482
(1,0,2)	3.3468	3.3524	3.3481
(2,0,0)	3.3462	3.3510	3.3476
(2,0,1)	3.3463	3.3524	3.3481
(2,0,2)	3.3462	3.3532	3.3480

R SWE				
	(0,0,1)	3.5979	3.6017	3.5989
	(0,0,2)	3.5975	3.6012	3.5988
	(0,0,3)	**3.5965**	**3.6012**	**3.5981**
	(1,0,0)	3.5979	3.6017	3.5989
	(1,0,1)	3.5980	3.6017	3.5993
	(1,0,2)	3.5968	3.6015	3.5984
	(1,0,3)	3.5968	3.6024	3.5987
	(2,0,0)	3.5974	3.6012	3.5987
	(2,0,1)	3.5968	3.6014	3.5983
	(2,0,2)	3.5969	3.6025	3.5989
	(2,0,3)	3.5970	3.6035	3.5993
	(3,0,0)	3.5966	3.6013	3.5982
	(3,0,1)	3.5969	3.6025	3.5988
	(3,0,2)	3.5971	3.6036	3.5993
	(3,0,3)	3.5965	3.6039	3.5990
R FIN				
	(1,0,0)	3.57368	3.57874	3.57548
	(0,0,1)	**3.57366**	**3.57872**	**3.57546**
	(1,0,1)	3.5741	3.5809	3.5765

The results from Table 5 indicate that according to the criteria of Akaike (AIC), Schwartz (SIC) and Hannan-Quinn (HQ) model ARIMA (0,0,1) is the fittest for the Norwegian, Finnish and Danish stock while model ARIMA (0,0,3) for the Swedish one.

Table 6. ARMA models estimation

Dependent Variable: RNOR
Method: ARMA Maximum Likelihood (OPG - BHHH)
Date: 09/08/16 Time: 10:04
Sample: 2 8347
Included observations: 8346
Convergence achieved after 65 iterations
Coefficient covariance computed using outer product of gradients

Variable	Coefficient	Std. Error	t-Statistic	Prob.
C	0.045099	0.016066	2.807182	0.0050
MA(1)	0.062339	0.004407	14.14640	0.0000
SIGMASQ	1.736120	0.009588	181.0735	0.0000

R-squared	0.003804	Mean dependent var	0.045110
Adjusted R-squared	0.003565	S.D. dependent var	1.320211
S.E. of regression	1.317856	Akaike info criterion	3.390249
Sum squared resid	14489.65	Schwarz criterion	3.392776
Log likelihood	-14144.51	Hannan-Quinn criter.	3.391112
F-statistic	15.92906	Durbin-Watson stat	2.001003
Prob(F-statistic)	0.000000		

Inverted MA Roots	-.06

Dependent Variable: RDEN
Method: ARMA Maximum Likelihood (OPG - BHHH)
Date: 09/20/16 Time: 13:27
Sample: 2 4893
Included observations: 4892
Convergence achieved after 19 iterations
Coefficient covariance computed using outer product of gradients

Variable	Coefficient	Std. Error	t-Statistic	Prob.
C	0.041419	0.019522	2.121716	0.0339
MA(1)	0.043848	0.009314	4.707982	0.0000
SIGMASQ	1.660569	0.018323	90.62963	0.0000

R-squared	0.001814	Mean dependent var	0.041417
Adjusted R-squared	0.001406	S.D. dependent var	1.289933
S.E. of regression	1.289026	Akaike info criterion	3.346264
Sum squared resid	8123.502	Schwarz criterion	3.350247
Log likelihood	-8181.962	Hannan-Quinn criter.	3.347662
F-statistic	4.442121	Durbin-Watson stat	2.002324
Prob(F-statistic)	0.011818		

Inverted MA Roots	-.04

Dependent Variable: RSWE
Method: ARMA Maximum Likelihood (OPG - BHHH)
Date: 09/28/16 Time: 13:31
Sample: 2 7432
Included observations: 7431
Convergence achieved after 23 iterations
Coefficient covariance computed using outer product of gradients

Variable	Coefficient	Std. Error	t-Statistic	Prob.
C	0.031768	0.016839	1.886558	0.0593
MA(1)	0.021677	0.007570	2.863561	0.0042
MA(2)	-0.027264	0.007630	-3.573291	0.0004
MA(3)	-0.036572	0.007491	-4.882066	0.0000
SIGMASQ	2.132627	0.020084	106.1845	0.0000

R-squared	0.002438	Mean dependent var	0.031782
Adjusted R-squared	0.001901	S.D. dependent var	1.462234
S.E. of regression	1.460843	Akaike info criterion	3.596578
Sum squared resid	15847.55	Schwarz criterion	3.601230
Log likelihood	-13358.09	Hannan-Quinn criter.	3.598176
F-statistic	4.537761	Durbin-Watson stat	1.999909
Prob(F-statistic)	0.001163		

Inverted MA Roots	.35	-.19+.26i	-.19-.26i

Dependent Variable: RFIN
Method: ARMA Maximum Likelihood (OPG - BHHH)
Date: 09/20/16 Time: 13:29
Sample: 2 3687
Included observations: 3686
Convergence achieved after 15 iterations
Coefficient covariance computed using outer product of gradients

Variable	Coefficient	Std. Error	t-Statistic	Prob.
C	0.021689	0.024894	0.871258	0.3837
MA(1)	0.031205	0.012778	2.442078	0.0146
SIGMASQ	2.083729	0.029878	69.74029	0.0000

R-squared	0.000954	Mean dependent var	0.021683
Adjusted R-squared	0.000411	S.D. dependent var	1.444397
S.E. of regression	1.444100	Akaike info criterion	3.573664
Sum squared resid	7680.624	Schwarz criterion	3.578720
Log likelihood	-6583.263	Hannan-Quinn criter.	3.575464
F-statistic	1.757709	Durbin-Watson stat	2.000585
Prob(F-statistic)	0.172584		

Inverted MA Roots	-.03

After the model estimation we test the existence of conditional heteroscedasticity (ARCH(q) test), from the squared residuals of the last model. Table 7 presents us with the results.

Table 7. ARCH(q) effect test

Sample: 1 8347
Included observations: 8346

Autocorrelation	Partial Correlation		AC	PAC	Q-Stat	Prob
		1	0.340	0.340	963.11	0.000
		2	0.156	0.046	1165.9	0.000
		3	0.147	0.091	1345.8	0.000
		4	0.164	0.095	1569.3	0.000
		5	0.160	0.075	1783.0	0.000
		6	0.135	0.046	1936.1	0.000
		7	0.159	0.084	2148.1	0.000
		8	0.152	0.052	2341.2	0.000
		9	0.145	0.051	2517.6	0.000
		10	0.127	0.029	2652.1	0.000
		11	0.133	0.045	2799.9	0.000
		12	0.149	0.055	2985.3	0.000
		13	0.139	0.034	3146.2	0.000
		14	0.172	0.080	3392.5	0.000
		15	0.148	0.027	3575.6	0.000
		16	0.172	0.073	3823.3	0.000
		17	0.121	-0.009	3946.3	0.000
		18	0.116	0.020	4059.0	0.000
		19	0.111	0.006	4162.5	0.000
		20	0.074	-0.033	4207.9	0.000
		21	0.104	0.026	4298.0	0.000
		22	0.102	0.005	4385.4	0.000
		23	0.111	0.019	4487.7	0.000
		24	0.071	-0.028	4530.2	0.000
		25	0.094	0.025	4603.5	0.000
		26	0.080	-0.014	4657.3	0.000
		27	0.085	0.011	4717.3	0.000
		28	0.091	0.008	4786.2	0.000
		29	0.078	-0.003	4836.8	0.000
		30	0.073	-0.009	4881.5	0.000
		31	0.067	-0.000	4919.7	0.000
		32	0.068	-0.001	4958.6	0.000
		33	0.070	0.007	5000.0	0.000
		34	0.053	-0.012	5023.6	0.000
		35	0.079	0.027	5075.7	0.000
		36	0.055	-0.011	5101.4	0.000

Sample: 1 4893
Included observations: 4892

Autocorrelation	Partial Correlation		AC	PAC	Q-Stat	Prob
		1	0.210	0.210	215.02	0.000
		2	0.286	0.254	616.67	0.000
		3	0.219	0.135	851.11	0.000
		4	0.232	0.125	1114.2	0.000
		5	0.382	0.292	1828.1	0.000
		6	0.169	0.003	1968.0	0.000
		7	0.252	0.072	2278.2	0.000
		8	0.178	0.024	2432.8	0.000
		9	0.243	0.082	2722.2	0.000
		10	0.210	0.013	2938.2	0.000
		11	0.174	0.023	3087.3	0.000
		12	0.260	0.106	3420.2	0.000
		13	0.150	-0.009	3530.4	0.000
		14	0.194	-0.000	3716.0	0.000
		15	0.163	0.018	3846.1	0.000
		16	0.189	0.039	4021.1	0.000
		17	0.220	0.048	4258.1	0.000
		18	0.152	0.010	4371.4	0.000
		19	0.154	-0.017	4487.2	0.000
		20	0.098	-0.054	4534.3	0.000
		21	0.212	0.073	4754.4	0.000
		22	0.169	0.029	4895.2	0.000
		23	0.166	0.028	5031.2	0.000
		24	0.094	-0.064	5074.7	0.000
		25	0.094	-0.023	5118.1	0.000
		26	0.126	-0.031	5196.6	0.000
		27	0.108	-0.010	5253.6	0.000
		28	0.154	0.041	5369.7	0.000
		29	0.065	-0.031	5390.2	0.000
		30	0.084	-0.030	5424.8	0.000
		31	0.074	-0.017	5452.2	0.000
		32	0.105	0.033	5506.8	0.000
		33	0.124	0.018	5581.9	0.000
		34	0.072	-0.002	5607.3	0.000
		35	0.076	-0.013	5635.7	0.000
		36	0.072	0.018	5661.4	0.000

Sample: 1 7432
Included observations: 7431

Autocorrelation	Partial Correlation		AC	PAC	Q-Stat	Prob
		1	0.225	0.225	376.24	0.000
		2	0.224	0.183	749.71	0.000
		3	0.240	0.172	1178.3	0.000
		4	0.189	0.089	1443.1	0.000
		5	0.213	0.111	1779.9	0.000
		6	0.177	0.058	2012.1	0.000
		7	0.194	0.081	2293.0	0.000
		8	0.160	0.033	2483.4	0.000
		9	0.173	0.055	2705.7	0.000
		10	0.184	0.063	2956.8	0.000
		11	0.174	0.053	3182.7	0.000
		12	0.155	0.023	3360.9	0.000
		13	0.157	0.030	3543.4	0.000
		14	0.143	0.015	3695.4	0.000
		15	0.147	0.026	3856.4	0.000
		16	0.149	0.028	4021.6	0.000
		17	0.133	0.013	4154.1	0.000
		18	0.148	0.032	4317.4	0.000
		19	0.127	0.007	4436.7	0.000
		20	0.109	-0.011	4524.8	0.000
		21	0.146	0.039	4683.1	0.000
		22	0.129	0.019	4806.6	0.000
		23	0.105	-0.009	4888.1	0.000
		24	0.115	0.008	4986.7	0.000
		25	0.144	0.046	5140.8	0.000
		26	0.096	-0.015	5209.7	0.000
		27	0.113	0.012	5305.5	0.000
		28	0.118	0.015	5408.8	0.000
		29	0.082	-0.020	5459.0	0.000
		30	0.114	0.021	5555.3	0.000
		31	0.121	0.030	5664.1	0.000
		32	0.096	-0.003	5733.0	0.000
		33	0.101	0.008	5809.1	0.000
		34	0.100	0.006	5883.1	0.000
		35	0.112	0.022	5976.0	0.000
		36	0.094	0.001	6042.3	0.000

Sample: 1 3687
Included observations: 3686

Autocorrelation	Partial Correlation		AC	PAC	Q-Stat	Prob
		1	0.138	0.138	70.711	0.000
		2	0.225	0.210	257.54	0.000
		3	0.211	0.167	421.10	0.000
		4	0.154	0.079	508.55	0.000
		5	0.304	0.232	850.28	0.000
		6	0.186	0.092	977.46	0.000
		7	0.179	0.050	1095.3	0.000
		8	0.143	0.004	1170.5	0.000
		9	0.198	0.089	1315.5	0.000
		10	0.179	0.044	1433.8	0.000
		11	0.226	0.106	1622.4	0.000
		12	0.186	0.059	1750.6	0.000
		13	0.166	0.041	1852.8	0.000
		14	0.172	0.022	1962.7	0.000
		15	0.127	-0.018	2022.1	0.000
		16	0.208	0.059	2181.9	0.000
		17	0.191	0.065	2316.7	0.000
		18	0.176	0.042	2431.8	0.000
		19	0.163	0.022	2530.2	0.000
		20	0.123	-0.016	2586.1	0.000
		21	0.196	0.051	2728.7	0.000
		22	0.171	0.026	2836.9	0.000
		23	0.183	0.037	2960.6	0.000
		24	0.117	-0.031	3011.2	0.000
		25	0.162	0.034	3108.1	0.000
		26	0.138	-0.003	3179.3	0.000
		27	0.132	-0.016	3243.9	0.000
		28	0.182	0.034	3366.6	0.000
		29	0.092	-0.031	3398.2	0.000
		30	0.146	0.002	3477.1	0.000
		31	0.112	-0.009	3523.8	0.000
		32	0.139	0.018	3596.1	0.000
		33	0.149	0.017	3678.7	0.000
		34	0.139	0.023	3750.6	0.000
		35	0.183	0.069	3875.3	0.000
		36	0.119	0.009	3928.3	0.000

Table 7 results indicate that the autocorrelation and partial autocorrelation variables are statistically significant. Therefore the null hypothesis for the absence of ARCH or GARCH effect is rejected.

5. Empirical Results

Keeping in mind that the ARCH effect exists in the returns of the stock markets of Norway, Denmark, Sweden and Finland we can move on to the evaluation of the models ARCH(q), GARCH(p, q) and GARCH-M(p, q). The parameters are evaluated with the BHHH algorithm (Berndt et al., 1974). The evaluation of models ARCH-GARCH-GARCH-M is presented in Tables 8a, 8b, 8c and 8d using three distributions for every country.

Table 8a. Estimated ARCH-GARCH-GARCH-M models for the daily returns of Norway

Parameter	Normal	t-Student	GED
ARMA(0,1)-ARCH (1,0)			
Parameter	Normal	t-Student	GED
ω	1.049(0.000)	1.058(0.000)	1.018(0.000)
α_1	0.401(0.000)	0.408(0.000)	0.387(0.000)
		D.O.F=4.226(0.000)	PAR=1.142(0.000)
LL	-13400.04	**-12834.64**	-12896.37
Jarque-Bera	11940.87(0.000)	13041.28(0.000)	13068.85(0.000)
ARCH(1)	1.364(0.242)	1.753(0.1855)	1.616(0.204)
$Q^2(1)$	1.365(0.243)	1.754(0.185)	1.615(0.2037)
ARMA(0,1)-GARCH(1,1)			
Parameter	Normal	t-Student	GED
ω	0.056(0.000)	0.036(0.000)	0.043(0.000)
α_1	0.162(0.000)	0.126(0.000)	0.138(0.000)
β_1	0.808(0.000)	0.852(0.000)	0.837(0.000)
		D.O.F=7.686(0.000)	PAR=1.405(0.000)
LL	-12591.19	**-12360.71**	-12410.64
Jarque-Bera	10895.61(0.000)	1428.65(0.000)	12761.06(0.000)
ARCH(30)	23.758(0.783)	30.736(0.428)	27.712(0.586)
$Q^2(30)$	23.390(0.799)	30.490(0.441)	28.059(0.567)
ARMA(0,1)-GARCH-M (1,1)			
Parameter	Normal	t-Student	GED
ω	0.056(0.000)	0.036(0.000)	0.043(0.000)
α_1	0.162(0.000)	0.126(0.000)	0.138(0.000)
β_1	0.809(0.000)	0.852(0.000)	0.837(0.000)
		D.O.F=7.686(0.000)	PAR=1.405(0.000)
LL	-12591.18	**-12360.70**	-12410.60
Jarque-Bera	10899.43	14212.21(0.000)	12742.25(0.000)
ARCH(30)	23.821(0.780)	30.697(0.430)	27.914(0.575)
$Q^2(30)$	23.453(0.796)	30.449(0.0443)	27.564(0.594)

Note. 1.Values in parentheses denote the *p*-values. 2. LL is the value of the log-likelihood.

Table 8b. Estimated ARCH-GARCH-GARCH-M models for the daily returns of Denmark

Parameter	Normal	t-Student	GED
ARMA(0,1)-ARCH (1,0)			
Parameter	Normal	t-Student	GED
ω	1.154(0.000)	1.179(0.000)	1.138(0.000)
α_1	0.315(0.000)	0.319(0.000)	0.311(0.000)
		D.O.F=4.888(0.000)	PAR=1.243(0.000)
LL	-7952.25	-7757.382	-7771.147
Jarque-Bera	1703.559(0.000)	1723.106(0.000)	1719.885(0.000)
ARCH(1)	5.540(0.018)	5.242(0.022)	5.437(0.019)
$Q^2(1)$	5.544(0.019)	5.246(0.022)	5.441(0.020)
ARMA(0,1)-GARCH(1,1)			
Parameter	Normal	t-Student	GED
ω	0.050(0.000)	0.044(0.000)	0.047(0.000)
α_1	0.111(0.000)	0.117(0.000)	0.115(0.000)
β_1	0.856(0.000)	0.856(0.000)	0.855(0.000)
		D.O.F=9.752(0.000)	PAR=1.523(0.000)
LL	-7557.238	-7499.126	-7507.439
Jarque-Bera	556.6304(0.000)	611.3892(0.000)	584.5145(0.000)
ARCH(30)	24.802(0.734)	26.952(0.625)	25704(0.690)
$Q^2(30)$	24.540(0.747)	26.284(0.661)	25274(0.712)
ARMA(0,1)-GARCH-M (1,1)			
Parameter	Normal	t-Student	GED
ω	0.050(0.000)	0.044(0.000)	0.047(0.000)
α_1	0.111(0.000)	0.117(0.000)	0.115(0.000)
β_1	0.856(0.000)	0.856(0.000)	0.855(0.000)
		D.O.F=9.745(0.000)	PAR=1.523(0.000)
LL	-7557.204	**-7499.085**	-7507.436
Jarque-Bera	553.5764(0.000)	615.2196(0.000)	585.4903(0.000)
ARCH(30)	24883(.0.730)	26.859(0.630)	25.678(0.691)
$Q^2(30)$	24.623(0.743)	26.190(0.665)	25.249(0.713)

Note. 1.Values in parentheses denote the *p*-values. 2. LL is the value of the log-likelihood.

Table 8c. Estimated ARCH-GARCH-GARCH-M models for the daily returns of Sweden

ARMA(0,3)-ARCH (1,0)			
Parameter	Normal	t-Student	GED
ω	1.4888(0.000)	1.515(0.000)	1.452(0.000)
α_1	0.317(0.000)	0.349(0.000)	0.323(0.000)
		D.O.F=4.377(0.000)	PAR=1.186(0.000)
LL	-13013.86	-12645.75	-12674.25
Jarque-Bera	2991.354(0.000)	3154.959(0.000)	3118.569(0.000)
ARCH(1)	3.749(0.052)	5.957(0.014)	5.037(0.024)
Q^2(1)	3.751(0.053)	5.960(0.015)	5.040(0.025)
ARMA(0,3)-GARCH(1,1)			
Parameter	Normal	t-Student	GED
ω	0.038(0.000)	0.025(0.000)	0.030(0.000)
α_1	0.097(0.000)	0.095(0.000)	0.096(0.000)
β_1	0.884(0.000)	0.894(0.000)	0.890(0.000)
		D.O.F=9.038(0.000)	PAR=1.499(0.000)
LL	-12242.42	-12109.21	-12145.77
Jarque-Bera	2594.030(0.000)	3443.449(0.000)	3004.152(0.000)
ARCH(30)	11.953(0.998)	16.746(0.975)	14.541(0.992)
Q^2(30)	11.986(0.999)	16.301(0.980)	14.378(0.993)
ARMA(0,3)-GARCH-M (1,1)			
Parameter	Normal	t-Student	GED
ω	0.038(0.000)	0.025(0.000)	0.030(0.000)
α_1	0.097(0.000)	0.095(0.000)	0.096(0.000)
β_1	0.883(0.000)	0.894(0.000)	0.890(0.000)
		D.O.F=9.016(0.000)	PAR=1.498(0.000)
LL	-12242.21	**-12109.09**	-12145.69
Jarque-Bera	2567.730(0.000)	3465.321(0.000)	3020.694(0.000)
ARCH(30)	11.895(0.998)	16.785(0.975)	14.581(0.991)
Q^2(30)	11.929(0.999)	16.345(0.980)	14.420(0.993)

Note. 1.Values in parentheses denote the *p*-values. 2. LL is the value of the log-likelihood.

Table 8d. Estimated ARCH-GARCH-GARCH-M models for the daily returns of Finland

ARMA(0,1)-ARCH (1,0)			
Parameter	Normal	t-Student	GED
ω	1.586(0.000)	1.673(0.000)	1.565(0.000)
α_1	0.262(0.000)	0.275(0.000)	0.261(0.000)
		D.O.F=4.206(0.000)	PAR=1.161(0.000)
LL	-6490.810	-6317.607	-6318.631
Jarque-Bera	1053.977(0.000)	1051.303(0.000)	1050.031(0.000)
ARCH(1)	4.779(0.028)	4.711(0.030)	4.949(0.026)
Q^2(1)	4.784(0.029)	4.716(0.030)	4.954(0.026)
ARMA(0,1)-GARCH(1,1)			
Parameter	Normal	t-Student	GED
ω	0.019(0.000)	0.016(0.000)	0.018(0.000)
α_1	0.078(0.000)	0.078(0.000)	0.078(0.000)
β_1	0.911(0.000)	0.913(0.000)	0.912(0.000)
		D.O.F=11.939(0.000)	PAR=1.598(0.000)
LL	-6043.635	-6023.131	-6021.973
Jarque-Bera	80.132(0.000)	83.137(0.000)	81.579(0.000)
ARCH(1)	1.387(0.238)	1.228(0.267)	1.303(0.253)
Q^2(1)	1.389(0.239)	1.230(0.267)	1.304(0.253)
ARMA(0,1)-GARCH-M (1,1)			
Parameter	Normal	t-Student	GED
ω	0.019(0.000)	0.016(0.000)	0.018(0.000)
α_1	0.079(0.000)	0.078(0.000)	0.078(0.000)
β_1	0.911(0.000)	0.913(0.000)	0.912(0.000)
		D.O.F=11.966(0.000)	PAR=1.599(0.000)
LL	-6043.226	**-6023.118**	-6023.968
Jarque-Bera	76.780(0.000)	82.487(0.000)	81.195(0.000)
ARCH(1)	1.452(0.228)	1.240(0.265)	1.311(0.252)
Q^2(1)	1.453(0.228)	1.242(0.265)	1.312(0.252)

Note. 1.Values in parentheses denote the *p*-values. 2. LL is the value of the log-likelihood.

The last tables presented us the evaluations and the standard errors for the parameters with the value of log-likelihood function, as well as the tests of normality, autocorrelation and conditional heteroscedasticity. The result of each table revealed the statistical significance of coefficients, in every country, model and distribution. Also, no autocorrelation or conditional heteroscedasticity issue is found. Furthermore, models ARMA(0,1)-GARCH-M(1,1) models, and model ARMA(0,3)-GARCH-M(1,1) in case of Sweden, are the ones with the max Log Likelihood value using the t-Student distribution. Therefore, these models can be used for forecasting.

6. Forecasting

In forecasting the Nordic stock markets using the models ARMA(0,1)-GARCH-M(1,1) and ARMA(0,3)-GARCH-M(1,1) we applied both the dynamic and static process. The dynamic process forecasts the time periods after the first time period of the sample, using the last forecast values from the lags of the dependent variable and the ARMA terms. This process is known as n-step ahead forecasts. The static process uses real, and not forecasted values, of the dependent variable. This process is known as one step- ahead forecast.

In Figures 3, 4, 5 and 5 we present the criterions of the evaluation of stock markets forecasting using the dynamic and static process, respectively.

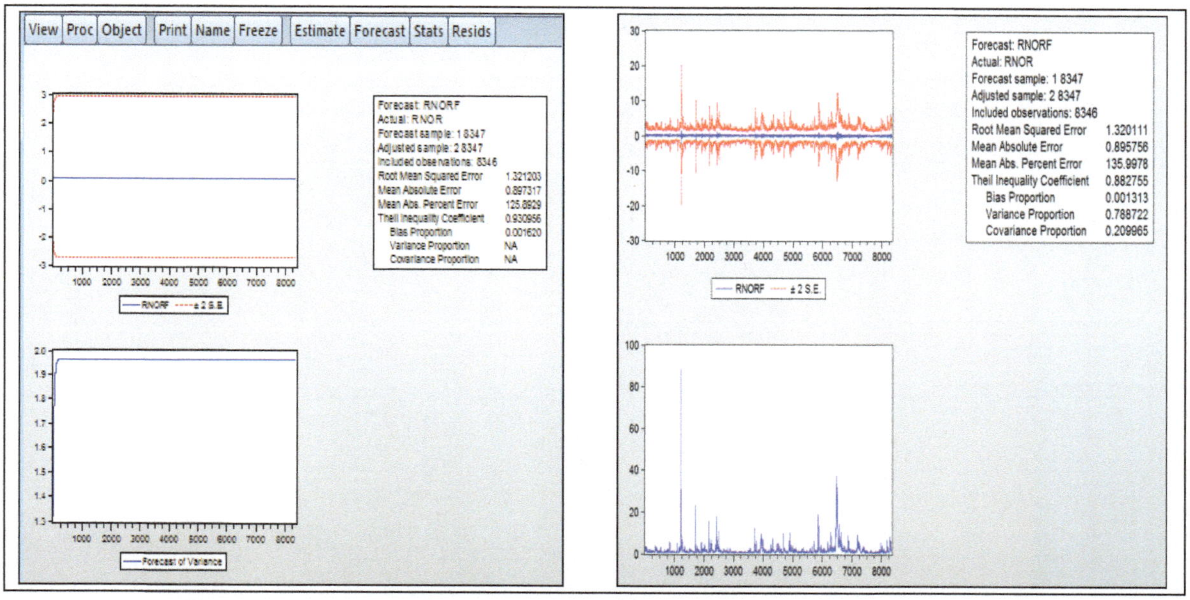

Figure 3. Dynamic and static forecast of the daily returns of Norwegian stock

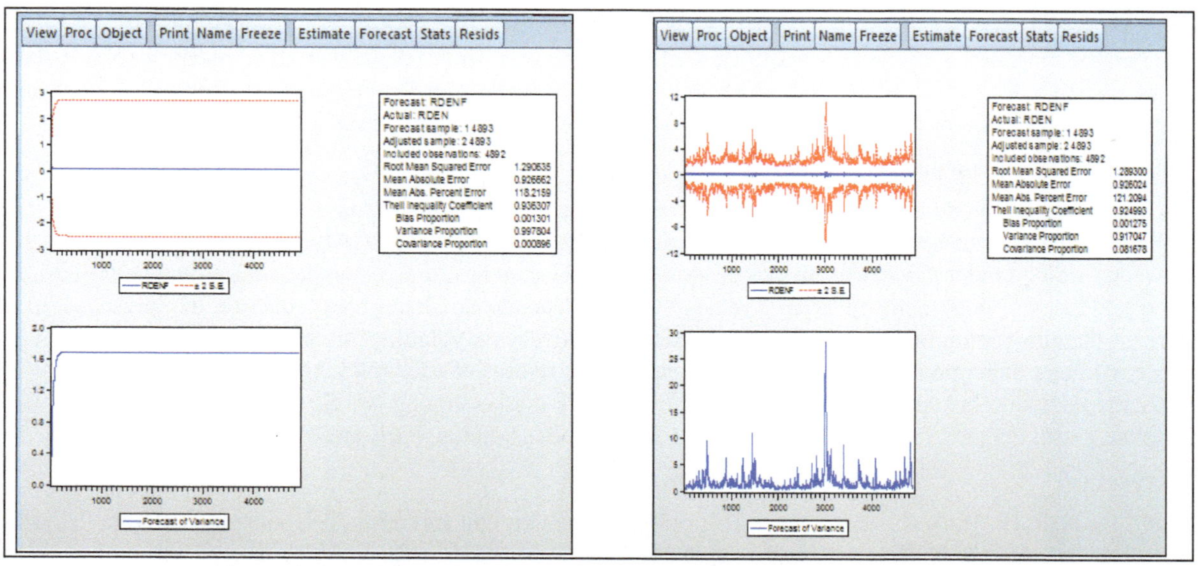

Figure 4. Dynamic and static forecast of the daily returns of Danish stock

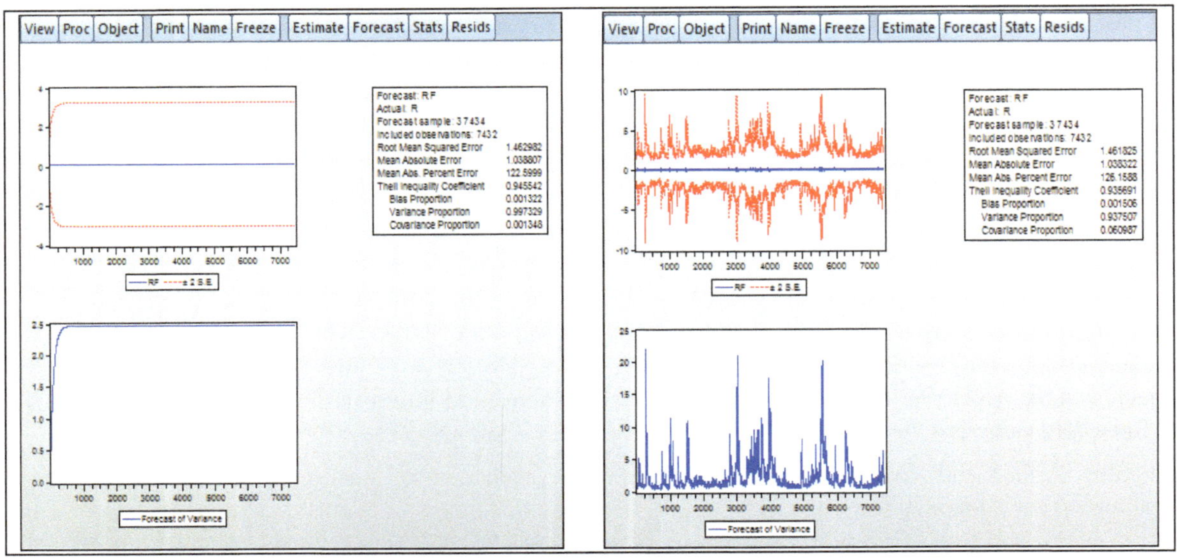

Figure 5. Dynamic and static forecast of the daily returns of Swedish stock

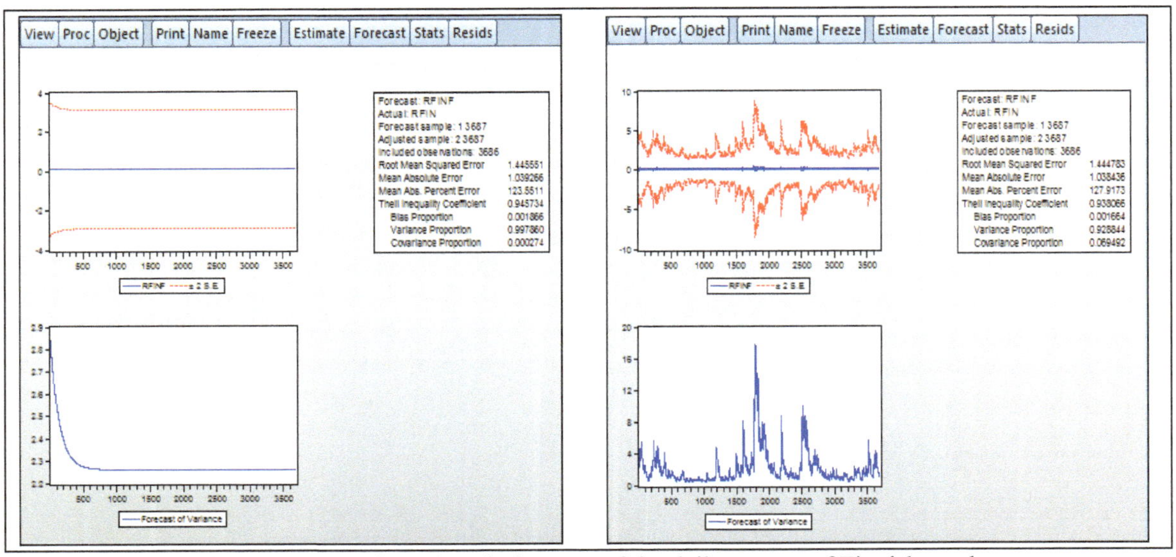

Figure 6. Dynamic and static forecast of the daily returns of Finnish stock

Based on the diagrams above we observe that static process gives better results than the dynamic one in each of the researched stock market (Theil index is lower in static process). But the fact that the Theil index is close to number one indicates that there is no appropriate forecast for the researched model.

7. Discussion and Conclusion

This study aims at modeling the volatility and the secondary effects at the four Nordic stock exchanges. The results indicated that each of the markets is well described by an ARMA(0,1)-GARCH-M(1,1) model except that of Sweden which model ARMA(0,3)-GARCH-M(1,1) describes it best. Each market's returns and volatilities are strongly dependent on their own past values. Linear dependence is probably due to the presence of a time-varying risk premium or in a form of market ineffectiveness. Volatility in each one indicated that the ill news is stronger than good news. Research of volatility and returns of each market, is motivated by the ongoing discussion related to the enactment of common Nordic stock market among Nordic countries. This merging will create the fourth biggest stock exchange market in Europe, after London, Paris and Frankfurt.

References

Berndt, E., Hall, B., Hall, R., & Hausman, J. (1974). Estimation and Inference in Nonlinear Structural Models. *Annals of Economic and Social Measurement, 3*, 653-665. Retrieved from http://EconPapers.repec.org/RePEc:nbr:nberch:10206

Black, F., & Scholes, M. (1973). The Pricing of Options and Corporate Liabilities. *Journal of Political Economy, 81*(3), 637-654. https://doi.org/10.1086/260062

Bollerslev, T. (1986). Generalized Autoregressive Conditional Heteroscedasticity. *Journal of Econometrics, 31*, 307-327. https://doi.org/10.1016/0304-4076(86)90063-1

Booth, G. G., Martikainen, T., & Tse, Y. (1997). Price and Volatility Spillovers in Scandinavian Stock Markets. *Journal of Banking & Finance, 21*(6), 811-823. https://doi.org/10.1016/S0378-4266(97)00006-X

Børs, O. (2016). *Equity indices / Market data / Products and services / Oslo Børs / Home - Oslo Børs*. Retrieved from https://www.oslobors.no/ob_eng/Oslo-Boers/Products-and-services/Market-data/Equity-indices

Dickey, D. A., & Fuller, W. A. (1979). Distributions of the Estimators for Autoregressive Time Series with a Unit Root. *Journal of American Statistical Association, 74*(366), 427-431. https://doi.org/10.2307/2286348

Dickey, D. A., & Fuller, W. A. (1981). Likelihood Ratio Statistics for Autoregressive Time Series with a Unit Root. *Econometrica, 49*(4), 1057-1072. https://doi.org/10.2307/1912517

Engle, R. F. (1982). Autoregressive Conditional Heteroscedasticity with Estimates of the Variance of United Kingdom Inflation. *Econometrica, 50*(4), 987-1007. https://doi.org/10.2307/1912773

Engle, R. F., Lilien, D. M., & Robins, R. P. (1987). Estimating Time Varying Risk Premium in the Term Structure: The Arch-M Model. *Econometrica, 55*(2), 391-407. https://doi.org/10.2307/1913242

Eun, C., & Shim, S. (1989). International Transmission of Stock Market Movement. *The Journal of Financial Quantitative Analysis, 24*(2), 241-255. https://doi.org/10.2307/2330774

Hamao, Y. R., Masulis, R. W., & Ng, V. K. (1990). Correlations in Price Changes and Volatility Across International Stock Markets. *Review of Financial Studies, 3*, 281-307. https://doi.org/10.1093/rfs/3.2.281

Hyytinen, A. (1999). *Stock Return Volatility on Scandinavian Stock Markets and the Banking Industry: Evidence from the Years of Financial Liberalisation and Banking Crisis*. Bank of Finland Research Discussion Paper 19 (1999). Retrieved from https://helda.helsinki.fi/bof/bitstream/handle/123456789/7861/91744.pdf?sequence

Lee, H. S. (2004). International transmission of stock market movements: A wavelet analysis. *Applied Economics Letters, 11*, 197-201. https://doi.org/10.1080/1350485042000203850

Ljung, G. M., & Box, G. E. P. (1978). On a Measure of a Lack of Fit in Time Series Models. *Biometrika, 65*(2), 297-303. https://doi.org/10.1093/biomet/65.2.297

MacKinnon, J. G. (1996). Numerical Distribution Functions for Unit Root and Cointegration Tests. *Journal of Applied Econometrics, 11*(6), 601-618. https://doi.org/10.1002/(SICI)1099-1255(199611)11:6<601::AID-JAE417>3.0.CO;2-T

Nasdaqomxnordic.com. (2016a). *Historical prices OMXC20, OMX Copenhagen 20, (DK0016268840) - NASDAQ OMX NORDIC*. Retrieved from http://www.nasdaqomxnordic.com/indexes/historical_prices?Instrument=DK0016268840

Nasdaqomxnordic.com. (2016b). *Historical prices OMXH25, OMX Helsinki 25, (FI0008900212) - NASDAQ OMX NORDIC*. Retrieved from http://www.nasdaqomxnordic.com/indexes/historical_prices?Instrument=FI0008900212

Nasdaqomxnordic.com. (2016c). *Historical prices OMXS30, OMX Stockholm 30 Index, (SE0000337842) - NASDAQ OMX NORDIC*. Retrieved from http://www.nasdaqomxnordic.com/indexes/historical_prices?Instrument=SE0000337842

Newey, W. K., & West, K. D. (1994). Automatic lag selection in covariance matrix estimation. *Review of Economic Studies, 61*(4), 631-654. https://doi.org/10.2307/2297912

Ng, A. (2000). Volatility Spillover Effects from Japan and the U.S. to the Pacific Basin. *Journal of International Money and Finance, 19*, 207-233. https://doi.org/10.1016/S0261-5606(00)00006-1

Phillips, P. C. B., & Perron, P. (1998). Testing for a Unit Root in Time Series Regression. *Biometrika, 75*, 335-346. https://doi.org/10.1093/biomet/75.2.335

Prashant, J. (2014). Volatility Interactions among India and US Stock Markets. *Case Studies in Business and Management, 1*(1), 107-117. https://doi.org/10.5296/csbm.v1i1.5830

Theil, H. (1967). *Economics and Information Theory*. Chicago: Rand McNally and Company.

Thenmozh, M., & G. Sarath, C. (2016). Forecasting stock returns based on information transmission across global markets using support vector machines. *Neural Computing and Applications, 27*(4), 805-824. https://doi.org/10.1007/s00521-015-1897-9

Trang, N. L., & Makoto, K. (2010). International transmission of stock returns: Mean and volatility spillover effects in Indonesia and Malaysia. *The International Journal of Business and Finance Research, 4*(1), 115-131. International Transmission of Stock Returns Mean and Volatility Spillover Effects in Indonesia and Malaysia. Retrieved from https://www.researchgate.net/publication/228241200

8

Domestic Policies as Strategic Measures in Multinational Markets

Ali Dadpay[1]

[1] Professor of Economics, The Bill Munday School of Business, St. Edward's University, United States

Correspondence: Ali Dadpay, Professor of Economics, The Bill Munday School of Business, St. Edward's University, 3001 South Congress Avenue, Austin, TX 78704-6489, United States. E-mail: adadpay@stedwards.edu

Abstract

This paper studies the role of privatization and subsidization policies as trade strategies in a single multinational market where private and public firms of different nationalities interact. The paper finds that when a country subsidizes its industry the rival country would have the incentive to retaliate by adopting a subsidization regime to prevent a free riders' situation from happening when said country moves to liberalize the market. However, this step does not eliminate the free rider problem governmentsare face in a market when they privatize their public firms unilaterally.

Keywords: Oligopoly, Cournot model, quantity competition, public enterprises and market performance

1. Introduction

The defining characteristic of mixed oligopoly markets has been the presence of a welfare-maximizing public firm competing with private profit-maximizing firms. Governments regulate their domestic markets, or respond to the actions of rival governments, by choosing the production levels of their respective public firm. This choice has allowed authors to explore the strategic interactions between governments and private sectors both in the domestic and multinational markets. Recently, several authors have studied the government's role when they can maximize their individual social welfare through a public firm and subsidization. While some authors have studied multinational mixed oligopoly markets and some have studied subsidization in mixed oligopoly markets, few have studied subsidization and its consequences in multinational markets. This paper is the first, to the best of the author's knowledge, to investigate a multinational mixed oligopoly market.

Initially introducedoriginally by Merrill and Schneider (1966), mixed oligopoly analysis was used to study the interactions between the public sector and private firms in domestic markets. Since then, its applications have been growing steadily from the study of domestic mixed oligopoly markets (Harris & Wiens, 1980; Sertel, 1988; Cremer, Marchand, & Thisse, 1989, 1991; DeFraja & Delbono, 1989, 1990; Fershtman, 1990; Nilssen & Sorgard, 2002; Matsumura & Kanada, 2005), to analysing the role of foreign competition in such markets (Fjell & Pal, 1996; Pal & White, 1998; Fjell & Heywood, 2002; Heywood & Ye, 2010). Recently, a growing number of authors have used a mixed oligopoly structure to study multinational markets (Pal & White, 2003; Dadpay & Heywood, 2006; Heywood & Ye, 2009; Dadpay, 2010). It is well established that in a multinational mixed oligopoly, governments utilize their public firms to react strategically to their rivals' actions and policies.

The policy implications remain at best ambiguous. Dadpay and Heywood (2006) demonstrate how in a single multinational mixed oligopoly market, governments face a prisoner's dilemma. Any unilateral attempt to liberalize markets would improve the rival country's social welfare while advancing the global welfare. Heywood and Ye (2009), who study the role of timing, discover that for all endogenousthatly emerged timings, privatization will always lower domestic welfare, but its influence on global welfare is ambiguous. Dadpay (2010) demonstrates that the government's emphasis on producer surplus might discourage them from joining a coordinated privatization process with other governments. Thus, governments do not always face a prisoners dilemma in privatizing their national firms as previously suggested. The same can be said when a government has already subsidized its industry (Dadpay, 2007).

Several authors have studied the consequences of subsidization in a mixed oligopoly market. Pal and White (1998), Poyago-Theotoky (2001), Fjell and Heywood (2002), Myles (2002) show that in domestic mixed oligopoly markets, subsidization would achieve the first-best pricing. However, in a multinational mixed oligopoly market, when a government implements subsidization, to evade the prisoner's dilemma in privatization (Dadpay & Heywood, 2006), subsidization does not achieve first-best pricing (Dadpay, 2008).

These findings inspire this question: "Facing rivals who have implemented subsidization, would a country have the incentive to retaliate by subsidizing its industry?" This question becomes more significant during the process of globalization. Globalization has brought into close contact, governments with different approaches to industry and production. Would free market-oriented governments adopt subsidization or similar policies interacting with the governments that traditionally support the local industries through subsidization?

The present article studies a single multinational mixed oligopoly market where consumers of different nationalities share the consumers' surplus, and private firms of different nationalities maximize their profits. It assumes the market shares to be exogenous because the size of the consumers' populations varies across the various countries. In the first stage, governments choose a subsidy rate to maximize their social welfares. Then, private and public firms move simultaneously to maximize their objective functions. The paper finds that the governments could improve their social welfare by privatizing their national firms unilaterally by adjusting the optimal subsidy rate to prevent welfare loss. Privatization does not eliminate the prisoners' dilemma, which was originally suggested by Dadpay and Heywood (2006). A government does not have any incentive to privatize its national firms following a unilateral privatization by its rival government. Subsidization prevents a welfare loss, but it does not eliminate the free rider situation.

This article is organized into five sections. After the Introduction, the model, and the equilibrium is presented in Section 2. Section 3 analyses the equilibrium results. Section 4 examines privatization effects in this model, and Section 5 offers our conclusion.

2. Model

Assume that a multinational market is shared by two countries, domestic and foreign; in this market are one domestic public firm, one foreign public firm, *m* domestic private firms and *n* foreign private firm. It is assumed that all firms produce a homogenous commodity and there is a universal demand for this commodity. All firms use the same technology in producing this commodity, so the cost structure is the same for all of the firms. Several authors (Pal & White, 1998; Fjell & Heywood, 2002; Dadpay & Heywood, 2006) have used quadratic cost functions to study mixed oligopoly markets:

$$C(q) = .5kq^2 + f \rightarrow MC = kq, \frac{\partial^2 C}{\partial q^2} \tag{1}$$

The quadratic cost function allows a linear marginal cost with slope $k > 0$.

Private firms maximize profits, and public firms maximize the social welfare functions of their respective societies. The government pays subsidies to both private and public firms. These subsidies are proportional to the firm's outputs. In the existing mixed oligopoly literature, authors usually assume subsidies are proportional to the firm's outputs (White, 1996; Poyago-Theotoky, 2001; Myles, 2002; Fjell & Heywood, 2002). Thus, the total subsidy that a firm receives are a linear function of its output:

$$S_d = s_d * q_i^d \tag{2}$$

$$S_f = s_f * q_j^f$$

Where s_d is the domestic subsidy rate and s_f is the domestic subsidy rate. Demand in the market is linear and can be written as:

$$P = a - (q_o^d + q_o^f + \textstyle\sum_{i=1}^m q_i^d + + \sum_{j=1}^n q_j^f) \tag{3}$$

In (3), P is price, q^d_o is the domestic public firm's output, q^f_o is the foreign public firm's output, q^d_i is the domestic private firm *i's* output ($i = 1,...,m$) and q^f_j is the foreign private firm *j*'s output ($j = 1,..,n$). Based on the demand function, consumer surplus in this multinational market can be written as:

$$CS = .5(q_o^d + q_o^f + \textstyle\sum_{i=1}^m q_i^d + + \sum_{j=1}^n q_j^f)^2 \tag{4}$$

Using equation (4), domestic consumers' surplus and foreign consumer surplus are defined as:

$$CS_d = .5\theta(q_o^d + q_o^f + \textstyle\sum_{i=1}^m q_i^d + + \sum_{j=1}^n q_j^f)^2 \tag{5}$$

$$CS_f = .5(1-\theta)(q_o^d + q_o^f + \textstyle\sum_{i=1}^m q_i^d + + \sum_{j=1}^n q_j^f)^2 \tag{6}$$

where θ is the domestic customers' share of consumer surplus, to which this article also refers to market share.

Since the domestic and the foreign governments subsidize their industries, firm's profit functions include subsidy rate as an exogenous parameter.

Public domestic firm profit is as follows:

$$\pi_o^d = Pq_o^d - f - .5kq_o^{d^2} + s_d q_o^d \tag{7}$$

Private domestic firm profit function is as follows:

$$\pi_i^d = Pq_i^d - f - .5kq_i^{d^2} + s_d q_i^d \qquad (i=1,\ldots,m) \tag{8}$$

Foreign public firm profit function is as follows:

$$\pi_o^f = Pq_o^f - f - .5kq_o^{f^2} + s_f q_o^f \tag{9}$$

Foreign private firm profit function is as follows:

$$\pi_j^f = Pq_j^f - f - .5kq_j^{f^2} + s_f q_j^f \qquad (j=1,\ldots,n) \tag{10}$$

The introduction of subsidy also changes the social welfare function in the domestic country. Its social welfare function is written as the sum of consumer surplus and total profits and because a subsidy is paid, it must be deducted from the total. The domestic social welfare function and the foreign social welfare are written as follows:

$$W_d = .5\theta\left(q_o^d + q_o^f + \textstyle\sum_{i=1}^m q_i^d + + \sum_{j=1}^n q_j^f\right)^2 + \pi_o^d + \sum_{i=1}^m \pi_i^d - s_d\left(q_o^d + \sum_{i=1}^m q_i^d\right) \tag{11}$$

$$W_f = .5(1-\theta)\left(q_o^d + q_o^f + \textstyle\sum_{i=1}^m q_i^d + + \sum_{j=1}^n q_j^f\right)^2 + \pi_o^f + \sum_{j=1}^n \pi_j^f - s_f\left(q_o^f + \sum_{j=1}^n q_j^f\right) \tag{12}$$

Assuming those governments have set the subsidy rate in the first stage, private and public firms move simultaneously to choose their outputs. Private firms maximize their profits, and public firms maximize the social welfare in a Cournot game. Solving the ensuing first order condition's equations yields the following results.

Domestic private firm's equilibrium:

$$q_i^{d^*} = \frac{ak(k+1)+s_d(k+1)(k+2)+nk(s_d-s_f)}{(k+1)(k^2+mk+nk+3k+2)} \tag{13}$$

Foreign private firm's equilibrium:

$$q_j^{f^*} = \frac{ak(k+1)+s_f(k+1)(k+2)+mk(s_f-s_d)}{(k+1)(k^2+mk+nk+3k+2)} \tag{14}$$

Domestic public firm's equilibrium output:

$$q_o^{d^*} = \frac{(k+1)\{a\theta[k(m+n+2)+2] + ak(k+1-m) - s_d m(k+2) - k(1-\theta)(ms_d+ns_f)\} - mnk(s_d-s_f)}{(k+1)[k^2(k-1)+k(k+1)(m+n+5)+2]} \tag{15}$$

Foreign public firm's equilibrium output:

$$q_o^{f^*} = \frac{(k+1)\{amk(1-\theta) - s_f n(k+2) - k\theta(ms_d+ns_f)\} + a[2(1-\theta)(1-2k) - \theta nk] + mnk(s_d-s_f)}{(k+1)[k^2(k-1)+k(k+1)(m+n+5)+2]} \tag{16}$$

Equilibrium total output:

$$Q^* = \frac{2a+k(ms_d+ns_f)+ak(m+n+2)}{(k^2+mk+nk+3k+2)} \tag{17}$$

Equilibrium price:

$$P^* = \frac{k[a(k+1)-(ms_d+ns_f)]}{(k^2+mk+nk+3k+2)} \tag{18}$$

Firms' outputs in social welfare functions are substituted with their equilibrium values. Governments maximize the new presentations of social welfare functions on subsidy rates. Solving first order conditions, one can derive governments' subsidization best response functions. The optimal domestic and foreign subsidy rates are derived by substituting best response functions. The optimal subsidy rates are illustrated as follows:

$$s_d^* = h(a,k,m,n,\theta) = a\frac{A_6'k^6 + A_5'k^5 + A_4'k^4 + A_3'k^3 + A_2'k^2 + A_1'k + A_0'}{B_6'k^6 + B_5'k^5 + B_4'k^4 + B_3'k^3 + B_2'k^2 + B_1'k + B_0'} \tag{19}$$

$$s_f^* = g(a,k,m,n,\theta) = a\frac{A_6''k^6 + A_5''k^5 + A_4''k^4 + A_3''k^3 + A_2''k^2 + A_1''k + A_0''}{B_6''k^6 + B_5''k^5 + B_4''k^4 + B_3''k^3 + B_2''k^2 + B_1''k + B_0''} \tag{20}$$

where A_0' through B_6'' are complicated functions of the number of firms, market share, the slope of marginal cost and demand; *m, n, θ, k & a*. Assuming that there are one domestic private firm and one foreign private firm in the market, $m = 1$ and $n = 1$, and these expressions can be rewritten as follows:

$$s_d^* = a\frac{(4\theta-1)k^4-(4\theta^2-22\theta+3)k^3-(6\theta^2-42\theta+5)k^2-(2\theta^2-32\theta+2)k+8\theta}{k^5+11k^4+43k^3+2k^2(k+1)\theta(\theta-1)+72k^2+58k+16} \quad (21)$$

$$s_f^* = a\frac{(3-4\theta)k^4-(4\theta^2+14\theta-15)k^3-(6\theta^2+30\theta-31)k^2-(2\theta^2+28\theta-28)k+8(1-\theta)}{k^5+11k^4+43k^3+2k^2(k+1)\theta(\theta-1)+72k^2+58k+16} \quad (22)$$

Plugging in the optimal subsidy rates in the equilibrium, as described by equations 13 to 18 yields the equilibrium values. This new presentation of the equilibrium in a multinational mixed oligopoly market provides new insights into government incentives and private firm's profit-maximizing behavior. The next section analyses this new equilibrium in which countries use their public firms as well as subsidization to engage each other strategically.

3. Equilibrium Analysis

The present study departs from the existing literature by assuming a more complex model, in which industries are subsidized, and governments set both subsidy rates and public firm's outputs to maximize social welfare. While the model captures the reality of markets more thoroughly than previously studied models, it is har der to interpret. However, such complexity is not rare in the mixed oligopoly literature. Facing challenging situations, different authors have adopted different approaches. Pal and White (2003) base their conclusions on assuming one private and one public firm in the market while Dadpay and Heywood (2006) and Dadpay (2010) use numerical simulations to analyze market dynamics with different numbers of foreign and domestic private firms. In analyzing the equilibrium results, this paper adopts the approach of Pal and White (2003) to develop some insights into market dynamics. Studying privatization effects in the next section, it adopts Dadpay and Heywood's (2006) numerical simulation approachorder to identify the effects of privatization in different market structures.

Proposition 3.1. The difference between domestic and foreign firms' outputs, both public and private, is proportional to the difference of subsidy rates they receive.

Proof. Substituting s_d and s_f by their optimal values from equations (21) and (22) yields the following for $m = 1$ and $n = 1$:

$$s_d^* - s_f^* = \frac{(2\theta-1)(k+1)(2k+1)(k^2+3k+4)}{k^5+11k^4+43k^3+72k^2+58k+16-2\theta(1-\theta)k^2(k+1)} \quad (23)$$

$$q_o^{d^*} - q_o^{f^*} = \frac{(2\theta-1)(k+1)(k^2+4k+2)}{k^5+11k^4+43k^3+72k^2+58k+16-2\theta(1-\theta)k^2(k+1)} \quad (24)$$

$$q_i^{d^*} - q_j^{f^*} = \frac{(2\theta-1)(2k+1)(k^2+3k+4)}{k^5+11k^4+43k^3+72k^2+58k+16-2\theta(1-\theta)k^2(k+1)} \quad (25)$$

It must be noted that similar formulas can be derived for other combinations of m and n. It can be shown that the difference between private firms and the difference between public firms both are linear functions of the difference of optimal subsidy rates:

$$q_o^{d^*} - q_o^{f^*} = \frac{(s_d^*-s_f^*)}{(2k+1)} \quad (26)$$

$$q_i^{d^*} - q_j^{f^*} = \frac{(s_d^*-s_f^*)}{(k+1)} \quad (27)$$

Proposition 3.1 shows that the general asymmetry in the market, as suggested by Dadpay and Heywood (2006), does not hold in this market structure. However, that symmetry exists under one specific condition, as described by Proposition 3.2.

Proposition 3.2. If the ratio of countries' shares of consumers' surplus is equal to the ratio of the number of their firms, then the optimal subsidy rate does not change from one country to the other.

Proof. In equation (23), if $\theta = 0.5$, the domestic optimal subsidy rate equals the foreign optimal subsidy rate. This can be extended to the following condition:

$$\frac{1-\theta}{\theta} = \frac{n+1}{m+1} \rightarrow s_d^* = s_f^*$$

Should this ratio hold in any market structure, the optimal domestic subsidy will equal to the foreign one. This result is confirmed for any combination *m* and *n* as well as solving for the model when $\theta = (m+1)/(m+n+2)$.

This finding is most intuitive since it shows that the symmetry suggested by the previous authors could exist despite subsidization. Thus, the private firms would produce the same output independent of their nationality as suggested by Dadpay and Heywood (2006). However, this goes further in the case of this study because public firms also produce the same output independent of their nationality. This finding departs from Dadpay and Heywood (2006) and indicates that symmetry in subsidized multinational markets is not the outcome of competition but the result of market structure. The governments' decision to subsidize their industries makes the profit-maximizing private firm conscious of its country's market share. This decision explains the similarities between governments' subsidization policies when their population's share of consumer surplus is equal to their industry's share of production in regional markets. A good example is a similarity between fuel pricing policies in Persian Gulf countries with similar population size and oil production capacity.

Proposition 3.3. When both governments use subsidization as a strategic trade instrument, the domestic public firm always decreases its output in response to a domestic private firm's entry while it increases its output in response to a foreign private firm's entry if θ is above a critical level.

Proof. Solving the model, the equilibrium values are derived for $m = 1$ and $n = 1$ to provide the benchmark. Then, the equilibrium is estimated for $m = 1$ and $n = 2$ for a foreign private firm's entry and for $m = 2$ and $n = 1$ for a domestic private firm's entry. Estimating the size of the change in the domestic public firm's output for each case, a set of polynomials are derived, in which coefficients are functions of θ for the case of $k = 1$; these changes can be written as the following:

$$\Delta q_o^{d^*} = q_o^{d^*}{}_{m=1,n=2} - q_o^{d^*}{}_{m=1,n=1} = -\frac{a(3723-7669\theta+31400\theta^2+2120\theta^3)}{(23\theta^2+43\theta+1044)(4\theta^2-4\theta+201)} \tag{28}$$

$$\Delta q_o^{d^*} = q_o^{d^*}{}_{m=2,n=1} - q_o^{d^*}{}_{m=1,n=1} = -\frac{a(4782+16153\theta-38960\theta^2+1240\theta^3)}{(23\theta^2+43\theta+1044)(4\theta^2-4\theta+201)} \tag{29}$$

Solving equations (28) and (29) for θ, it is shown that equation (29) is always negative for the range of values θ, and the domestic market share can have from 0 to 1. Equation (28) is positive if θ is above a certain value. As the slope of marginal cost changes, this critical level changes, however, there is always a market share above which the domestic public firm increases its output when a foreign private firm enters the market.

Proposition 3.4. The domestic optimal subsidy rate decreases if a domestic private firm enters the market, and increases if a foreign private firm enters the market if θ is below a critical level.

Proof. Solving the model, the equilibrium values for the domestic subsidy rates are derived for $m = 1$ and $n = 1$ to provide the benchmark. Then, the equilibrium is estimated for $m = 1$ and $n = 2$ for a foreign private firm's entry and for $m = 2$ and $n = 1$ for a domestic private firm's entry. Estimating the size of the change in the domestic optimal subsidy rate, a set of polynomials are derived, in which coefficients are functions of θ for the case of $k = 1$ these changes can be written as the following:

$$s_{d\,m=1,n=2}^* - s_{d\,m=1,n=1}^* = \frac{a(4449-1589\theta-36500\theta^2+4200\theta^3+88\theta^4)}{(23\theta^2+43\theta+1044)(4\theta^2-4\theta+201)} \tag{30}$$

$$s_{d\,m=2,n=1}^* - s_{d\,m=1,n=1}^* = -\frac{a(7086+21985\theta-93840\theta^2+13640\theta^3-48\theta^4)}{(23\theta^2-89\theta+1110)(4\theta^2-4\theta+201)} \tag{31}$$

Solving equations (30) and (31) for θ, it is shown that equation (30) is always positive for the range of values θ, and domestic market share can have from 0 to 1. However, equation (31) is always negative for all values of θ. For all other values of *k*, the slope of marginal cost holds for this argument, since those values are positive and the sign of expressions depends on the values of θ.

Propositions 3.3 and 3.4 summarize the effects of entry into the market; they demonstrate that governments respond strategically to new entries using subsidization and their public firm's output. When a domestic private firm enters the market, its entry increases total output and thus improves consumers' surplus. Since the new entrant improves consumers' surplus, the government lowers the subsidy rate it pays the industry, and the domestic public firm reduces its output. This causes the equilibrium price to increase and the producers' surplus in the domestic market to improve. When a foreign private firm enters the market, the foreign producer's surplus increases and thus the domestic government increases the subsidy rate to improve the domestic social welfare through consumers' surplus. Surprisingly, the optimal subsidy rate reacts to the new entry in the same way that the public firms respond to the new entry. Dadpay and Heywood (2006) demonstrate that the entry of a domestic private firm causes the output of the domestic public firm to decrease and entry of a foreign private firm causes the output of the domestic public firm to decrease. The present study confirms that in a mixed oligopoly market, governments use the means at their disposal to maximize their social welfare either through producers' surplus or consumers' surplus or both. It also shows that despite subsidization, the government still benefits from having a public firmorder to guarantee a high level of social welfare in its respective society. The question is if both countries benefit from a simultaneous liberalization of the market, as suggested by Dadpay and Heywood (2006). The next section summarizes the effects of privatization in this market.

4. Privatization

This section reviews the consequences of unilateral and simultaneous privatization in a single market of multinational mixed oligopolies where both governments are subsidizing their respective industries. It analyses the changes in optimal subsidy rates and social welfare levels as governments liberalize their industries, either unilaterally or simultaneously. There is symmetry in the market, in that both governments use subsidization and both countries have public firms. We already know that both governments utilize subsidization as a strategic trade instrument. This paper determines the directions of change for different combinations of numbers of private domestic and foreign firms, *m & n,* at different values of market share ($\theta = 0, .25, .5, .75, 1$), to study the effects of privatization in this market structure. The effects of privatization process are captured through estimating the difference of equilibrium values, as follows:

In the case of domestic unilateral privatization:

$$\Delta s_i^* = s_{i_{dpriv}}^* - s_i^*,\ \ i = f\ or\ d \qquad (32)$$

$$\Delta W_i^* = W_{i_{dpriv}}^* - W_i^*,\ \ i = f\ or\ d \qquad (33)$$

And in the case of simultaneous privatization:

$$\Delta s_i^* = s_{i_{sim}}^* - s_i^*,\ \ i = f\ or\ d \qquad (34)$$

$$\Delta W_i^* = W_{i_{si,}}^* - W_i^*,\ \ i = f\ or\ d \qquad (35)$$

Since the equilibrium values for optimal subsidy rates and social welfares are complicated mathematical models, I utilize numerical simulations to study these changes. In these simulations, $a=1$ & $k=1$ with different combinations of *m & n* from 1 to 5 and different values of θ=0, .25, .5, .75 and 1 are used to calculate the size of changes and to determine their signs. The results are presented in Tables 1 to 6 and propositions 4.1 through 4.3 offer conclusions based on these results.

The results in Table 1 show that any government that carries on unilateral privatization pays an increased subsidy rate and its individual welfare improves as well asof its rival country, where the optimal subsidy rate declines. As one may observe for any given number of domestic private firms and foreign ones, the domestic government increases the optimal subsidy rate it pays the domestic firms. Although, when the number of foreign private firms in the market is large, the size of the increase in the optimal subsidy rate is smaller, nonetheless for the domestic social welfare to improve, the optimal subsidy rate must increase. It must be pointed out that the increase in the optimal subsidy rate is increasing iton the domestic share of consumers' surplus. The larger the domestic customer's share of the market is, the larger the increase in the optimal subsidy rate must be.

When a government privatizes its public firms, total output in the market declines and thus the equilibrium price increases. The domestic government pays a higher subsidy rate to lower prices and to maximize social welfare through consumer surplus as well. A significant share of market amplifies the significance of consumers' surplus in the domestic social welfare. This share results in an even larger increase in the optimal subsidy rate.

Proposition 4.1. When both governments use subsidization as a strategic trade instrument, and one privatizes unilaterally, the other has no incentive to follow its example.

Proof. The results of simulations for equations (33) and (35) are reported in Tables 2 and 3, while Tables 5 and 6 report the consequences of simultaneous privatization on domestic and foreign social welfare levels. The social welfare increases in both countries in both unilateral and simultaneous privatization. However, in most cases, when the domestic government privatizes unilaterally, foreign social welfare improves more than domestic social welfare.

The social welfare improves in both countries as a result of simultaneous privatization, as demonstrated in Tables 5 and 6. However, the foreign social welfare increases less than the case where the domestic government liberalizes its public firm unilaterally. Thus, it is less likely that the foreign government will follow the domestic country in privatizing its public firm. Such a step causes foreign social welfare to decline from its newly achieved level.

Proposition 4.2. When governments decide to privatize simultaneously, the government whose own population share of the market is smaller than its rival increases the optimal subsidy rate while its rival decreases the optimal subsidy rate.

Proof. Table 4 presents the results of numerical simulations of the effects of simultaneous privatization. The domestic government increases the optimal subsidy rate when $\theta < 0.5$ and reduces it when $\theta > 0.5$. The foreign government follows the same path when $1\text{-}\theta < 0.5$ and $1\text{-}\theta > 0.5$. Thus, when the domestic government reduces the optimal subsidy rate, the foreign government increases the optimal subsidy rate.

When the domestic country share of the market is small, the domestic government seeks to increase social welfare by increasing its respective producers' surplus. Increases in the optimal subsidy rate give domestic private firms a comparative advantage over their foreign rivals so they can produce more. At the same time, the foreign government reduces the optimal subsidy rate. The foreign country's citizens are benefiting from the increase in subsidies paid by the domestic government, so the foreign consumers' surplus is already improved.

Proposition 4.3. If countries' share of consumer surplus equals their share of production, then either unilateral or simultaneous privatization does not alter either their welfare or optimal subsidy rate.

Proof. When countries' share of consumers' surplus equals their share of production, the loss in consumers' surplus is compensated by their gain in producers' surplus and vice versa. Thus, the privatization process, which usually results in reduced consumers' surplus and increased producers' surplus, does not increase the producers' surplus more than the fall in the consumers' surplus. This can be shown by solving the model with:

$$\frac{1-\theta}{\theta} = \frac{n+1}{m+1}$$

The consequences of privatization change when both governments exercise subsidization. First, both countries can gain from their rival's unilateral privatization, but the country that carries it on has no choice but to pay an increased optimal subsidy rate to improve its welfare, while its rival can pay a reduced optimal subsidy rate. Neither country has any incentive to privatize when its rival privatizes unilaterally. Thisactually causes its welfare to decline and for its gains to be lost. Thus, the free rider problem continues to exist even when both governments are paying subsidies to their respective industries.

5. Conclusion

This study answers the question asked in the beginning, "Would a government adopt subsidization when it engages a rival government that has already adopted this policy?" The answer is yes. By subsidizing foreign firms, the foreign government prevents the loss of welfare to the domestic country when it liberalizes its industry unilaterally. However, the government, which carries on a unilateral privatization, has to increase the subsidy rate its pays its respective industry. The free rider issue continues to exist in multinational mixed oligopoly markets, although not in the form of welfare loss. Both countries benefit most when the other carries on a unilateral privatization. The symmetry in the market is created structurally and not by competing for private firms seeking to maximize their profits as suggested by previous studies. The perfect symmetry exists where a country's share of consumers' surplus equals its share of production. In this market, neither government has any incentive to liberalize its markets.

Further studies should investigate if governments adopt other forms of policies already adopted by their rivals in a single multinational market. Mixed oligopoly analysis offers an intuitive way to study and to understand the market dynamics between competing governments interacting with their private firms.

Table 1. Domestic privatization effects on the domestic & foreign optimal subsidy rates (s_d^* & s_f^*) for (*a=1, k=1*, θ=0, .25, .5, .75,1) (Case retaliation)

M \ N		1	2	3	4	5
	Δsd*	.07,.12,.2,.36,.57	.08,.12,.2,.28,.42	.08,.11,.16,.23,.33	.08,.1,.14,.19,.26	.08,.09,.12,.15,.2
1	Δsf*	-.02,-.03,-.03,-.02 ,.004	-.02,-.04,-.04,-.04,-.03	-.01,-.04,-.05,-.05, -.04	-.001.-.04,-.05,-.06,-.06	-.01,-.04,-.06,-.07,-.07
	Δsd*	.05,.1,.2,.35,.57	.06,.1,.18,.28,.42	.07,.1,.16,.23,.33	.07,.1,.14,.19,.26	.07,.09,.12,.16,.22
2	Δsf*	-.02,-.02,-.02,-.01,-.01	-.01,-.02,-.03,-.02,-.01	-.01,-.02,-.03,-.03,-.03	-.003,-.02,-.03,-.04,-.04	-.002,-.02,-.04,-.04,-.05
	Δsd*	.03,.1,.2,.33,.56	.05,.1,.17,.27,.41	.06,.1,.15,.22,.32	.06,.1,.13,.19,.26	.07,.09,.12,.16,.22
3	Δsf*	-.01.-.02,-.01,-.01,-.01	-.01,-.01,-.02,-.01,-.005	-.003,-.01,-.02,-.02,-.02	-.001,-.01,-.02,-.03,-.03	.001,-.01,-.02,-.03,-.03
	Δsd*	.02,.1,.18, 33,.56	.04,.09,.16,.26,.41	.05,.09,.14,.22,.32	.06,.09,.13,.19,.26	.06,.09,.12,.16,.22
4	Δsf*	-.01,-.01,-.01,-.004,-.01	-.01,-.01,-.01,-.01,-.02	-.002,-.01,-.01,-.01,-.01	.001,-.01,-.02,-.02,-.02	.002,-.01,-.02,-.02,-.02
	Δsd*	.01,.1,.17,.32,.56	.04,.08,.15,.26,.4	.05,.09,.14,.21,.31	.05,.08,.13,.18,.26	.06,.08,.12,.16,.22
5	Δsf*	-.01,-.01,-.01,-.003,.01	-.005,-.008,-.009,-.007,0	-(.001,.006,.01,.01,.007)	.002,-.005,-.01,-.01,-.01	.004,-.005,-.01,-.02,-.02

Table 2. Domestic privatization effects on domestic welfare ($a = 1$, $k = 1$, $\theta = 0$, .25, .5,.75, 1)

M \ N	1	2	3	4	5
1	+,+,**0**,+,+	+,+,+,+,.002	+,+,+,+,.002	+,+,+,.001,.003	+,**0**,+,.001,.003
2	+,+,+,+,+	+,+,**0**,+,.001	+,+,+,+,.001	+,+,+,+,.002	+,+,+,.+,.002
3	+,+,+,+,+	+,+,+,+,+	+,+,**0**,+,+	+,+,+,+,+	+,+,+,+,.001
4	+,+,+,+,+	+,+,+,+,.002	+,+,+,+,.002	+,+,**0**,+,+	+,+,+,+,.001
5	+,+,+,**0**,+	+,+,+,+,+	+,+,+,+,+	+,+,+,+,+	+,+,**0**,+,+

Note. + stands for a very small but positive number, numbers larger than .001 are reported.

Table 3. Domestic privatization effects on the foreign welfare ($a=1$, $k=1$, θ=0, .25, .5, .75,1)

M \ N	1	2	3	4	5
1	+,+,**0**,.001,.005	+,+,+,.002,.007	.001,+,+,.003,.01	.001,+,+,.004,.01	.001,**0**,+,.005,.01
2	.001,+,+,+,.002	.001,+,**0**,+,.004	.001,+,+,.001,.005	.001,+,+,.006,.002	.001,+,+,.003,.007
3	.001,+,+,+,.001	.002,+,+,+,.003	.001,+,**0**,+,.002	.002,+,+,+,.004	.001,+,+,.002,.005
4	.001,+,+,+,.001	.001,+,+,+,.002	.002,+,+,+,.002	+,+,**0**,+,+	.001,+,+,+,.004
5	.002,+,+,**0**,+	.002,+,+,+,.001	.002,+,+,+,.002	.002,+,+,+,+	.002,+,**0**,+,.003

Table 4. Simultaneous privatization effects on the domestic & foreign optimal subsidy rates (s_d^* & s_f^*) for ($a = 1$, $k = 1$, $\theta = 0$, .25, .5, .75, 1) (Case Retaliation)

M \ N		1	2	3	4	5
	Δs_d^*	.05,.02,**0**, -.01,-.02	.05,.02,-.01,-.03,-05	.04,.01,-,-.04,-.06	.04,+, -.02,-.05,-.07	. 04, **0**, -, -, -.08
1	Δs_f^*	-.02,-.01,**0**, .02,.05	-.01, -, +, .02, .05	-, - , +, .02, .04	- , - ,+ , .02, .03	- , **0**, + , .02, .03
	Δs_d^*	.05, .02, +, - , -	.04, .02, **0**, -.02,-.02	.04,.02, - , -.02,-.03	.04,.01,-.01,-.03,-.04	.04, +,-.02,-.04,-.05
2	Δs_f^*	-.04,-.03, -,+, .05	-.02,-.01, **0**,.02,.04	-.01, - , +,.02,.04	- , -, +, .02,.04	- , -, +, .02,.03
	Δs_d^*	.04, .02, +, - , -	.04, .02, +, - , -.01	.04,.02, **0**,-.01,-.02	.04, .02, - ,-.02, -.03	.03, .01, -, -.02, -.04
3	Δs_f^*	-.05,-.04,-.01,.01,.04	-.04,-.02, - ,+ ,.04	-.02,-.01, **0**, .02, .04	-.02, -, +, .02, .03	-.01, -, +, .02, .03
	Δs_d^*	.03, .02, +, -, -	.04, .02, +, - , -	.04, .02, +, - , -.02	.04,.02, **0**, -.01 , -.02	.03,.01, -,-.02,-.03
4	Δs_f^*	-.07,-.05,-.02, +, .04	-.04,-.03,-.01,.01,.04	-.03,-.02, -,.02,.04	-.02,-.01, **0**,.02,.03	-.02, -, +, .02, .03
	Δs_d^*	.03, .02, +, **0**, -	.03, .02, +, - , -	.03, .02, +, - , -.01	.03, .02, +, - , -.02	.03,.01, **0**, -.01, -.02
5	Δs_f^*	-.08,-.06,-.03, **0**, .04	-.05,-.04,-.02,+,.04	-.04,-.02, -, +,.03	-.03,-.02, -, .01,.03	-.02,-.01, **0**, .01,.03

Table 5. Simultaneous privatization effects on domestic welfare ($a = 1$, $k = 1$, $\theta = 0$, .25, .5, .75, 1) (Case retaliation)

M \ N	1	2	3	4	5
1	+, +, **0**, +, +	+, +, +, +, +	+, +, +, +, .01	+, +, +, +, .01	+, **0**, +, +, .01
2	.01, +, +, +, +	+, +, **0**, +, +	+, +, +, +, +	+, +, +, +, +	+, +, +, +, .01
3	.01, +, +, +, +	+, +, +, +, +	+, +, **0**, +, +	+, +, +, +, +	+, +, +, +, +
4	.02, +, +, +, +	.01, +, +, +, +	+, +, +, +, +	+, +, **0**, +, +	+, +, +, +, +
5	.02, +, +, **0**, +	.01, +,+, +, +	+, +, +, +, +	+, +, +, +, +	+, +, **0**, +, +

Table 6. Simultaneous privatization effects on the foreign welfare ($a = 1$, $k = 1$, $\theta = 0$, .25, .5, .75, 1) (Case retaliation)

M \ N	1	2	3	4	5
1	+, +, **0**, +, +	+, +, +, +, .01	+, +, +, +, .01	+, +, +, +, .02	+, **0**, +, +, .02
2	+, +, +, +, +	+, +, **0**, +, +	+, +, +, +, +	+, +, +, +, .01	+, +, +, +, .01
3	.01, +, +, +, +	+, +, +, +, +	+, +, **0**, +, +	+, +, +, +, +	+, +, +, +, +
4	.01, +, +, +, +	.01, +, +, +, +	+, +, +, +, +	+, +, **0**, +, +	+, +, +, +, +
5	.01, +, +, **0**, +	.01, +,+, +, +	+, +, +, +, +	+, +, +, +, +	+, +, **0**, +, +

References

Ali, D. (2007). *Three essays on applied mixed oligopoly theory and policy implications*. Doctoral Dissertation, the University of Wisconsin–Milwaukee.

Cremer, H., Marchand, M., & Thisse, J. F. (1989). The Public Firm as an Instrument for Regulating an Oligopolistic Market†. *Oxford Economic Papers*, *41*(2), 283-301.

Dadpay, A. (2010). Governments and Producers in Multinational Markets: A Mixed Oligopoly. *Applied Economics Quarterly*, *56*(3), 211-229. https://doi.org/10.3790/aeq.56.3.211

Dadpay, A., & Heywood, J. S. (2006). Mixed oligopoly in a single international market. *Australian Economic Papers*, *45*(4), 269-280. https://doi.org/10.1111/j.1467-8454.2006.00292.x

De Fraja, G., & Delbono, F. (1989). Alternative strategies of a public enterprise in oligopoly. *Oxford Economic Papers*, *41*(2), 302-311.

Debashis, P., & Mark D. W. (1998). Mixed oligopoly, privatization, and strategic trade policy. *Southern Economic Journal,* 264-281.

Fershtman, C. (1990). The interdependence between ownership status and market structure: The case of privatization. *Economica*, 319-328. https://doi.org/10.2307/2554937

Fjell, K., & Heywood, J. S. (2002). Public Stackelberg leadership in a mixed oligopoly with foreign firms. *Australian Economic Papers*, *41*(3), 267-281. https://doi.org/10.1111/1467-8454.00164

Fjell, K., & Pal, D. (1996). A mixed oligopoly in the presence of foreign private firms. *Canadian Journal of Economics*, 737-743. https://doi.org/10.2307/136260

Giovanni, D. F., & Flavio, D. (1990). Game theoretic models of mixed oligopoly. *Journal of Economic Surveys*, *4*(1), 1-17. https://doi.org/10.1111/j.1467-6419.1990.tb00077.x

Harris, R. G., & Wiens, E. G. (1980). Government enterprise: An instrument for the internal regulation of industry. *The Canadian Journal of Economics/Revue Canadienne d'Economique*, *13*(1), 125-132. https://doi.org/10.2307/134624

Helmuth, C., Maurice, M., & Jacques-François, T. (1991). Mixed oligopoly with differentiated products. *International Journal of Industrial Organization,* *9*(1), 43-53. https://doi.org/10.1016/0167-7187(91)90004-5

Heywood, J. S., & Ye, G. (2009). Privatisation And Timing In A Mixed Oligopoly With Both Foreign And Domestic Firms. *Australian Economic Papers*, *48*(4), 320-332. https://doi.org/10.1111/j.1467-8454.2009.00379.x

Matsumura, T., & Kanda, O. (2005). Mixed oligopoly at free entry markets.*Journal of Economics*, *84*(1), 27-48. https://doi.org/10.1007/s00712-004-0098-z

Merrill, W., & Schneider, N. (1966). Government firms in oligopoly industries: A short-run analysis. *Quarterly Journal of Economics*, *80*(3), 400-412. https://doi.org/10.2307/1880727

Myles, G. (2002). Mixed oligopoly, subsidization and the order of firms' moves: An irrelevance result for the general case. *Economics Bulletin*, *12*(1), 1-6.

Nilssen, T., & Sørgard, L. (2002). A public firm challenged by entry: Duplication or diversity? *Regional Science and Urban Economics*, *32*(2), 259-274. https://doi.org/10.1016/S0166-0462(01)00079-5

Pal, D., & White, M. D. (2003). Intra-industry trade and strategic policy police in the presence of public firms. *International Economic Journal*, *17*(4), 29-41.

Poyago-Theotoky, J. (2001). Mixed oligopoly, subsidization and the order of firms' moves: An irrelevance result. *Economics Bulletin*, *12*(3), 1-5.

Sertel, M. R. (1988). Regulation by participation. *Journal of Economics*, *48*(2), 111-134. https://doi.org/10.1007/BF01234606

White, M. D. (1996). Mixed oligopoly, privatization, and subsidization. *Economics Letters*, *53*(2), 189-195. https://doi.org/10.1016/S0165-1765(96)00916-0

9

Impact of Electronic Banking Services on Bank Transactions

Najah Hassan Salamah[1]

[1] Department of Marketing, Faculty of Economic and Administration, King Abdul-Aziz University, Saudi Arabia

Correspondence: Najah Hassan Salamah, Assistant Professor, Department of Marketing, Faculty of Economic and Administration, King Abdul-Aziz University, Saudi Arabia. E-mail: nsalamah@kau.edu.sa, almdnm@yahoo.com

Abstract

The objective of the research was to evaluate the significance of electronic system integrated in the banking sector for providing convenience services to their clients and the overall impact caused by electronic services on bank transaction. The research has applied analytical descriptive methodology to analyze the impact of electronic banking services on the bank transactions. The total sample size taken for the study was 150 and the questionnaires were distributed among the clients and bank officials to collect the data. The analysis revealed that electronic services have contributed to increase both the financial activity of the bank as well as number of its clients. In the banking sector, professional training can be given to banking officials, so that they can effectively work on the electronic system. The satisfaction has covertly impact a customer inclination towards electronic banking and electronic banking has positively influenced the banking transaction.

Keywords: electronic system, service, officials, clients, transaction

1. Introduction

1.1 Introduction to the Problem

Since the inception, banks have passed through a number of stages and have witnessed many developments in diverse fields. These developments included administrative fields, where services are rendered by these banks to their clients, whether in provision of service aspects, presenting of finance or giving of loans. It benefited the banks with number of advantages that made many people choose to deal with them for managing their funds and investments. Furthermore, the fierce competition among the banks compelled many banks to route for creation and development for achieving competency in businesses activities transactions so, as to gain a large possible number of clients. To improve the management and position of a bank, electronic banking would ply significant role and reduces the cost of operations (Ben-Jadeed & Molina, 2004, pp. 90-106). Additionally, a research reported that the customer perception of service is greatly impacted by the level of convenience they found in the service they encounter (Bahia & Nantel, 2000, pp. 84-91). Moreover, the regulation of technology to an extent has provided security in various profession likewise in financial sectors also has incorporated system to reduce threats and chances of manipulation (Rose & Hudgins, 2006).

As a result of the huge developments in technology, the electronic banking services have emerged with a view of securing competency and quality in transactions (Ito, Hiroya, & Hitachi, 2000). Since, Internet has become a possession of all people, the big banks have entered internet usage into its systems and commenced to use and present it to their clients to attract more clients. A research study examined that clients can be encouraged by integrating the electronic system and build customer relationship (Rexha, Kingshott, & Shang, 2003, pp. 53-67). There are many processes in banks that required electronic systems for making the processes effective and reduce the level of work manually performed by the employees or personnel. Moreover, the engagement of customer in transaction is greatly influenced by the electronic systems in banks, where they get the access to perform transaction (Hoffman, Pare Jr, & Lee, 2002).

1.2 Merits of Using Internet in Bank Accounts

There is a general agreement that electronic banks achieve a number of merits for their clients and the following are the most significant ones:

- To make financial services available to clients for 24 hours a day.
- To present latest information or data to clients about their accounts.

- To help clients obtain required services via Internet and receive financial advice from the bank.

In addition to the above merits, these banks save for the individuals (clients) the time they need to take to go personally to bank sites. Astonishingly, the client can go to the bank dealing with by mere pressing a particular button (Gerrard & Barton, 2003, pp. 16-28). These services include for example presentation of projects that secure for clients huge profits as well as many other similar services (Al-Janbeehi, 2005).

1.3 Objectives

The paper consisted of the following objectives:

1) To project the significance of the electronic banking system in a manner that serves the objectives of both banks and clients.

2) To highlight the significant advantages rendered by banks via the electronic services for clients.

3) To shed light on the distinctive experiment of certain Saudi banks such as Saudi Credit Bank, Saudi American Bank, Riyadh Bank and Arab National Bank regarding the electronic services as well as to know the impact of the electronic services in the efficiency and good quality of transactions, satisfaction of clients and reduction of work pressure on the employees.

1.4 Problem Statement

The problem of this research paper is to investigate the impact of electronic services rendered by the Saudi banks in the fields of quality and efficiency that is pertinent to the work provided by these banks to clients as well as the extent to which clients are satisfied with services and impact of electronic services on the smooth running of the work as perceived by the officials of these banks.

1.5 Research Questions

Below are the mentioned questions of the research paper:

1) To what extent do electronic services affect the efficiency and quality of the services rendered by the Saudi banks?

2) To what extent do electronic services rendered by Saudi banks affect the satisfaction of clients?

3) To what extent do electronic services rendered by Saudi banks reduce work pressures for officials?

1.6 Assumption

The first assumption is the usage of electronic services by Saudi banks leads to quality and efficiency of the services provided to the clients along with satisfaction to clients. Moreover, electronic services also lead to an increase in the percentage of clients. Additionally, another assumption is a reduction in the work pressure of bank officials is also obtained from the usage of electronic services by Saudi Banks.

2. Method

The study has relied on the analytical descriptive methodology for achieving the limited objectives of the research. This methodology aims to analyze and describe the problem in question as well as extract its various aspects and dimensions and the extent of its impact on the level of bank services. The data sources, which are represented in primary and secondary sources (ones), comprised the following:

2.1 Theoretical Study

Regarding the secondary data obtained by the female researcher was from reading of academic books, periodicals, proceedings as well as recommendations of symposiums, seminar and relevant reports, in addition to certain previous academic dissertations, research papers and studies as well as other sources.

2.2 Means

For collecting primary data, questionnaire technique was employed for obtaining primary data and for testing assumptions. In the design of the questionnaire, preciseness and relation between the problem, objectives and assumptions were carefully taken into account.

2.3 Applied Studies

Regarding the applied studies, the researcher has depended on the data collected via questionnaire, which was distributed among the sample members to know their opinion concerning the impact of electronic services on bank services.

2.4 Population and Sample

The population comprises of certain clients of the Saudi banks as well as some bank officials, who occupy various occupations. Since, the population is very large, the researcher applied sample to be random one as, this will represent faithfully the original population.

3. Limits & Dimensions

The research was applied during 1436H (2015AD). The geographical dimension was applied in Jeddah Province, because the female researcher is resident of the city of Jeddah and it was easy to move to different sites of the members' sample, visit personally their respective work places and obtain effective results.

Human dimension represents those who are in charge of the electronic services in certain Saudi banks via taking their views about the experiment of their banks in the field of electronic services. It also covers a random sample of the clients of the Saudi banks to know their personal views or perspectives regarding the question of the electronic services rendered by the bank and the benefit that is gained by the bank, the officials for adopting the policy of electronic services.

The female researcher has designed (2) questionnaires. The objective of the first questionnaire was to know the extent of the efficiency of the electronic services of the Saudi banks as well as to measure the extent of satisfaction of clients over such provided electronic services. Moreover, the objective of the second questionnaire was to know the extent of work efficiency through the employment of electronic services from the perspective of certain officials of the Saudi banks as well as to know the extent of the impact of application of electronic services in alleviating the work pressure on the bank officials.

4. Results

The copies of the two questionnaires were distributed over certain officials of the Saudi banks as well as over some clients of these banks. After return and examination of questionnaires, it has become evident that there were (150) questionnaires, which were useful for study. However, the female researcher has excluded certain number of questionnaires due to incomplete answers. The (150) questionnaires that were useful for study have been divided as follows:

1) (110) Questionnaires for bank clients officials.
2) (40) Questionnaires for bank officials.

The 5-grade likert scale was used in the design of these questionnaires.

4.1 Analysis of the First Assumptions

In the first assumption, the researcher assumed that the usage of electronic services by the Saudi banks leads to the efficiency and quality of the services provided to clients, increment of the percentage of clients and increasing their satisfaction over the services provided by the bank. To verify the correctness of this assumption, I have carried out the analysis for the expressions forming the assumption for both the clients and officials. The results are as follows:

Table 1. Attitude of sample (bank clients) towards the expressions of the first assumption

Expression	I strongly agree	I agree	I am neutral	I don't agree	I strongly don't agree	
	Percentage	Percentage	Percentage	Percentage	Percentage	
The usage of electronics services contributes to the reduction of the percentage of mistakes in work	16.7	3.3	1.7	3.3	0	
The electronic services contributed to the national economy	15.0	6.7	3.3	0.0	0	
Conduct of financial transaction at the bank is done through the network of the electronic services	13.3	5.0	5.0	1.7	0	
The electronic dealing at the bank is easy and rapid advanced and highly efficient	20.0	1.7	1.7	0.0	1.6	
Total	60	16.7	11.67	5.0	1,6	100

From the above Table 1, it is remarked that there is a high degree of agreement over the expressions that constitute the first assumption by the category of clients. The percentage of that agreement was (65%) of the total responses forming up the assumption. This attitude is supported by the agreement response, which were

(16.7). From the answer with (I am neutral), whose percentage was (11.7%), and it is observed that this confirms the correctness of the first assumption. This indicates the following:

1) The usage of electronic services in the Saudi banks contributed to the reduction in the percentage of mistakes in work.

2) The electronic services contributed to the economy.

3) The procedures of financial transactions in the banks via the Network of the electronic services are preferred.

4) The electronic dealings in the bank is easy, rapid, advanced and with high efficiency.

Table 2. Attitude of sample (bank officials) towards the expressions of the first assumption

Expression	I strongly agree	I agree	I am neutral	I don't agree	I strongly don't agree	
	Percentage	Percentage	Percentage	Percentage	Percentage	
The electronics services contributed to the increase of the financial activity at the bank.	16.3	4.3	3.3	1.1	0.0	
The electronic services contributed to the increase of the number of the bank clients	21.7	1.1	1.1	0.0	1.1	
The usage of electronic services attracted a number of clients to the Saudi banks.	18.5	2.2	1.1	2.2	1.1	
The electronic services contributed to the increase of quality of work presented by the bank	18.5	2.2	1.1	2.2	1.1	
Total	75	9.8	6.5	5.4	3.3	100

The above Table 2, displays the response of the sample members (officials of Saudi banks) towards the expressions of the first assumption, which stipulates that the usage of the Saudi banks for electronic services system leads to efficiency of services offered to clients, increase the percentage of clients and their satisfaction over the services provided by the bank. The percentage of those who responded to the expressions of the assumption with (I strongly agree) was (75%) of the total responses. This attitude is supported by the agreement response, which was (9.8), followed by that (percentage) of those who answered with (I am neutral), which was (6.5). However, the response of those who said (I strongly do not agree) or (I do not agree) was small and quite insignificant. This indicates the following:

1) The electronics services contributed to the increase of the financial activity at the bank.

2) The electronic services contributed to the increase of the number of the bank clients.

3) The usage of electronic services attracted a number of clients to the Saudi banks.

4) The electronic services contributed to the increase of quality of work presented by the bank.

This indicates that the usage of the Saudi banks for electronic services system contributed to the efficiency of services offered to clients; increase the percentage of clients and their satisfaction over the services provided by the bank. Thus, the results of the first assumption were correct as indicated by both the two categories; the officials of the Saudi banks and the clients of the Saudi banks.

Table 3. Attitude of sample (bank officials) towards the first expression of the first assumption

Expression	I strongly agree	I agree	I am neutral	I don't agree	I strongly don't agree	
	Percentage	Percentage	Percentage	Percentage	Percentage	
The usage of the electronics services contributed to the increase of the level of services.	24.4	4.4	2.2	2.2	0.0	
The electronic services contributed to the increase of the satisfaction of clients over the services offered by the bank.	17.8	6.7	6.7	0.0	2.2	
The electronic services contributed in securing an opportunity for clients to easily complete transactions, an act that increased the satisfaction of the clients of those banks.	26.7	4.4	2.2	0.0	0.0	
Total	68.9	15.6	11.11	2.2	2.2	100

Through the above expressions, which represent Table 3, the researcher has sought to know the extent to which clients achieve a degree of satisfaction as a result of using electronic services. All the expressions were presented to the sample, which represent client's category.

The percentage of those who responded to the expressions of the assumption with (I strongly agree) was (68.9%) of the total responses. This attitude is supported by the agreement response, which were (15.6). However, the percentage of the response of those who said (I am neutral) was (11.11%). As regards the attitude rejecting the expressions of the assumption found that the percentage of those who responded with (I strongly do not agree) was (2.2) and that of those who responded with (I do not agree) was also (2.2%), and this percentage is very small. This is evidence that the second expression of the assumption is correct, especially in connection to the fact that it confirmed the achievement of the satisfaction of clients as a result of electronic services provided by the Saudi banks. This indicates the following:

1) The usage of the electronics services contributed to the increase of the level of services.

2) The electronic services contributed to the increase of the satisfaction of clients over the services offered by the bank.

3) The electronic services contributed in securing an opportunity for clients to easily complete transactions, an act that increased the satisfaction of the clients of those banks.

4.2 Analysis of the Second Assumption

In the second assumption, the researcher has assumed that the usage of electronic services by the Saudi banks leads to the reduction of work pressure on the officials of the banks. To verify the correctness of this assumption, the researcher has formulated a number of expressions that she addressed to the officials of the Saudi banks. The response of the sample members for the expressions composing the assumption were as bellow in this Table 4:

Table 4. Attitude of sample (bank officials) towards the expressions of the second assumption

Expression	I strongly agree	I agree	I am neutral	I don't agree	I strongly don't agree	
	Percentage	Percentage	Percentage	Percentage	Percentage	
The electronics services contributed to the reduction of the percentage of the transactions that are undertaken by the official daily (or during any work day)	21.7	1.1	1.1	1.1	0.0	
The electronic services contributed to the reduction of the reception of the financial transactions that pertain to the payment of bills such as bills of electricity, water supply or mobile etc, which were paid in the past by cashiers.	25.0	0.0	0.0	0.0	0.0	
The electronic services contributed to the reduction of the cash deposits and withdrawals transactions performed daily by clients.	20.7	2.2	2.2	1.1	0.0	
The electronic services contributed to alleviating the burden of work for officials of the banks as work discharge is undertaken electronically at the end of each work day.	19.6	1.1	1.1	1.1	1.1	
Total	87	4.3	4.3	3.3	1.1	100

The above Table 4 shows the opinions of the sample members (bank officials) towards the expressions forming the second assumptions.

The percentage of those who responded to the expressions of the assumption with (I strongly agree) was (87%) of the total responses. We notice here that the agreement percentage for the expression was very high. This attitude is supported by the agreement response (I agree) which was (4.3%), and it equalized with that (percentage) of those who answered with (I am neutral). However, the percentage of the response of those who said (I do not agree) was (3.3%) and that (percentage) of those who said (I strongly do not agree) was only (1.1%). This indicates that the second assumption of the study is correct; and that the usage of electronic services at work has contributed to the reduction of work pressures suffered by bank officials. The above confirms the following:

1) The electronics services contributed to the reduction of the percentage of the transactions that are

undertaken by the official daily (or during any work day).

2) The electronic services contributed to the reduction of the reception of the financial transactions that pertain to the payment of bills such as bills of electricity, water supply or mobile etc., which were paid in the past by cashiers.

3) The electronic services contributed to the reduction of the cash deposits and withdrawals transactions performed daily by clients.

4) The electronic services contributed to alleviating the burden of work for officials of the banks as work discharge is undertaken electronically at the end of each work day.

Table 5. Personal data of the female bank clients

Statement	Percentage
18 and less than 30 years	10%
30 and less than 40 years	20%
40 and less than 50 years	60%
50 and more years	10%
Total	100%

From the above Table 5, it is conspicuous that the age bracket of 60% of the total female members of the sample is between 40 and 50 years; and that the age bracket of 20% of them is less than 40 years, followed by 10% for those whose age is either less than 30 years or above 50 years. This indicates that 60% of the sample belongs to the age bracket between 40 to less than 40 and the responses of those members are objective.

Table 6. Personal data of the female bank clients

Statement	Percentage
Secondary education	30%
University Education	50%
Postgraduate Education	20%
Total	100%

From the above table 6, it is clear that 50% of the total female members of the sample hold university education certificates, and this is followed by that holding secondary education certificate with 30%, followed by those having postgraduate university certificates with 20%. This indicates that 70% of the sample members hold university education certificates (50% hold university education degrees and 20% postgraduate education degrees).

Table 7. Occupation

Statement	Frequency	Percentage
Housewives	6	20%
officials	6	20%
Businesswomen	18	60%
Total	30	100%

From the above Table 7, it is conspicuous that the distribution of the questionnaire was according to the occupations of the sample members was that 60% of the sample members practices the occupations of businesswomen, and this was followed by 20% working as officials and an equal 20% with the occupations of housewives. This indicates that 60% of the sample was businesswomen, who are visit banks more frequently; and that they benefit more than other women practicing different occupations in the usage of Internet for bank transactions.

Table 8. Monthly income (salary)

Statement	Percentage
Less than 3000 S R	20%
Between (3000-9000) S R	50%
More than 9000 S R	30%
Total	100%

From the above Table 8, it is clear that the age bracket of 50% of the total female members of the sample receive a monthly salaries between (3000-9000), and this is followed by 30% of the sample whose monthly salaries were than 9000 and more, and this was followed lastly by 20% of sample members receiving monthly salaries less 3000 Saudi Riyals.

Table 9. Personal data of the female bank officials

Statement	Percentage
18 and less than 30 years	20%
30 and less than 40 years	40%
40 and less than 50 years	30%
50 and more years	10%
Total	100%

From the above Table 9, it is conspicuous that the age bracket of 60% of the total female members of the sample is between 30 and 50 years; and that the age bracket of 20% of them is less than 30 years, followed by 10% for those whose age is either less than 30 years ,and 10% above 50 years. This indicates that 70% of the sample belongs to the age bracket between 30 to less than 50 and the responses of those members are objective.

Table 10. Educational qualification

Statement	Percentage
Secondary education	2%
University Education	79%
Postgraduate Education	19%
Total	100%

From the above Table 10, it is clear that 79% of the total female bank officials of the sample hold university education certificates, and this is followed by those holding postgraduate education certificate with 19%, followed by those having secondary education certificates with 2%. This indicates that 98% of the sample female bank officials hold university education certificates- (79% hold university education degrees and 19% postgraduate education degrees).

Table 11. Monthly Income

Statement	Percentage
Less than 3000 S R	0%
Between (3000-9000) S R	76%
More than 9000 S R	24%
Total	100%

From the above Table 11, it is clear that the age bracket of 76% of the total female members of the sample receive a monthly salaries between (3000-9000), and this is followed by 24% of the sample whose monthly salaries were than 9000 and more, and this was followed by 0% of sample members receiving monthly salaries less 3000 Saudi Riyals.

Table 12. Year of experience

Statement	Percentage
Less than 5 years	40%
5 and less than 10 years	35%
10 years and less 15 years	20%
15 years and more	5%
Total	100%

From the above Table 12, it is conspicuous that the year of experience bracket of 75% of the total female members of the sample is between Less than 5 years and 10 years; and that the year of experience bracket of 20% of them is 10 years and less 15 years, followed by 5% for those whose year of experience is 15 years and more.

This indicates that 55% of the sample belongs to the year of experience bracket between 5 to less than 15 years and the responses of those members are objective.

6. Discussion

Through the previous analysis of data pertaining to the two assumptions of the study, the female researcher was able to reach a number of results and included that the usage of electronic services in the Saudi banks contributed to the reduction of the percentage of mistakes at work and this leads to achieve competency at work. Additionally, the results indicated that electronic services has contributed to economy of time, because many bank transactions are now performed directly through Automatic Teller Machine (ATM). It was found that the bank clients preferred the conduct of financial transactions in the banks via the network of electronic services. This contributed for achieving quality and efficiency in the services offered by the bank. The electronic form of banking provides the ease to customers as well as officials to get through the process by electronic delivery channel and give certain benefits in terms of satisfaction, loyalty, and convenient usage (Aladwani, 2001, pp. 213-225).

A study stated major's problems in the traditional banking systems, which leads to waste of time, pending transfer of money, people waiting in queue to be facilitated and errors in collecting and storing the data (ASIA, 2015). As per this problem, banking institutions took the privilege of technology and integrated electronic system in banking services. Furthermore, a reduction in the reception of financial transactions that pertain to payment of various utilities bills as well as cash deposit and withdrawal transactions was also observed (Yousafzai, Pallister, & Foxall, 2003, pp. 847-860). Also, that the integration of technology in the banking sector has been usefully employed and electronic services have reduced the burden of officials performing accounts auditing as the electronic system does effectively on their behalf. High customer satisfaction would enable long term relationship with their clients that it would build trust towards the services provided by banks. Banks are striving to allocate the transactions from the telephones to the Internet and now from the internet to the different forms of electronic bankings (Cunningham & Fröschl, 2013; Burton & Brown, 2014). Bank are in serious competitions with each other and offers their clients with more convenient products with acceptable levels of costs (Agwu & Carter, 2014).

The integration of electronic system in banks has impacted positively on the bank transaction process and increases the efficiency of rendering convenient services to the employees. Customer satisfaction has also impacted positively and the development of trust has influenced the corporate client's propensity for use the electronic banking system. Therefore, it can be concluded that satisfaction has covertly impact a customer inclination towards electronic banking. The impact that risk might exert on Information Technology adoption has established limited consideration (Martins et al., 2014; Yoon & Stege, 2013).

The research has attained some important recommendations that entails considering to disseminate the culture of electronic dealing through banking services among clients. It is suggested that proper training should be given to the bank officials on detecting and addressing electronic mistakes as well as giving suitable solutions and remedies for such mistakes. Moreover, to urge those concerned to participate in symposiums and workshops that seek to achieve competency in modern technologies that focus on electronic bank services. It is also recommended that number of field studies and researches should be conducted to know the opinions of clients on electronic services needed by the Saudi banks.

Acknowledgments

The author is very thankful to all the associated personnel in any reference that contributed in/for the purpose of this research. Further, this research holds no conflict of interest and is not funded through any source.

References

Agwu, M. E., & Carter, A. L. (2014). Mobile phone banking in Nigeria: Benefits, problems and prospects. *International Journal of Business and Commerce*, *3*(6), 50-70.

Aladwani, A. M. (2001). Online banking: a field study of drivers, development challenges, and expectations. *International Journal of Information Management*, *21*(3), 213-225. http://dx.doi.org/10.1016/S0268-4012(01)00011-1

ASIA, N. M. (2015). *Electronic Banking and Financial Performance of Commercial Banks in Rwanda: A Case Study of Bank of Kigali* (Doctoral dissertation, Jomo Kenyatta University of Agriculture and Technology).

Bahia, K., & Nantel, J. (2000). A reliable and valid measurement scale for the perceived service quality of banks. *International Journal of Bank Marketing*, *18*(2), 84-91. http://dx.doi.org/10.1108/02652320010322994

Ben-Jadeed, M., & Molina, A. (2004). The emergence and evolution of e-banking in Saudi Arabia: The case of samba financial group. *Frontiers of E-Business Research*, *1*, 90-106.

Burton, M., & Brown, B. (2014). *The financial system and the economy: Principles of money and banking*. Routledge.

Cunningham, P., & Fröschl, F. (2013). *Electronic business revolution: Opportunities and challenges in the 21st century*. Springer Science & Business Media.

Gerrard, P., & Barton Cunningham, J. (2003). The diffusion of internet banking among Singapore consumers. *International journal of bank marketing*, *21*(1), 16-28. http://dx.doi.org/10.1108/02652320310457776

Hoffman, N., Pare Jr, D. F., & Lee, J. A. (2002). *U.S. Patent No. 6,366,682*. Washington, DC: U.S. Patent and Trademark Office.

Ito, A., & Hiroya, M. (2000). *U.S. Patent No. 6,039,250*. Washington, DC: U.S. Patent and Trademark Office.

Martins, C., Oliveira, T., & Popovič, A. (2014). Understanding the Internet banking adoption: A unified theory of acceptance and use of technology and perceived risk application. *International Journal of Information Management*, *34*(1), 1-13. http://dx.doi.org/10.1016/j.ijinfomgt.2013.06.002

Rexha, N., Kingshott, R. P. J., & Shang, Aw, A. (2003). The impact of the relational plan on adoption of electronic banking. *Journal of Services Marketing*, *17*(1), 53-67. http://dx.doi.org/10.1108/08876040310461273

Rose, P., & Hudgins, S. (2006). *Bank management and financial services*. The McGraw– Hill.

Yoon, H. S., & Steege, L. M. B. (2013). Development of a quantitative model of the impact of customers' personality and perceptions on Internet banking use. *Computers in Human Behavior*, *29*(3), 1133-1141. http://dx.doi.org/10.1016/j.chb.2012.10.005

Yousafzai, S. Y., Pallister, J. G., & Foxall, G. R. (2003). A proposed model of e-trust for electronic banking. *Technovation*, *23*(11), 847-860. http://dx.doi.org/10.1016/S0166-4972(03)00130-5

Appendix

Appendix A

Questionnaire directed to the female clients of the Saudi banks

Pleas fill in the blank space of this questionnaire you think appropriate to your opinion:

Expression	I strongly agree	I agree	I am neutral	I don't agree	I strongly don't agree
The usage of electronics services at banks reduces the percentage of mistakes at work					
The electronic services have contributed in the economy of time.					
The clients of the bank prefer the conduct of financial transactions at banks via the network of electronic services.					
The electronic dealing is easy, rapid and with high efficiency work day.					
The usage of electronics services at banks has contributed to improving the level of services.					
The electronics services have contributed to increasing your satisfaction with the bank.					
Your ability to complete your financial transactions via electronic services with ease increased your satisfaction.					

Put ( ) against the appropriate expression

Personal data:

(1) Age

- 18 and less than 30 years
- 30 and less than 40
- 40 and less than 50
- 50 years and more

(2) Educational Level

- Secondary School Certificate
- Bachelor's degree
- Postgraduate Degree

(3) Occupation

- Official
- Businesswoman
- housewife
- Other (Specify------------)

(4) Monthly Salary

- less than 3000 SR
- From 3000 to less than 9000SR
- From 9000 SR and more

Appendix B

Questionnaire directed to the female officials of the Saudi banks

Pleas fill in the blank space of this questionnaire you think appropriate to your opinion:

Expression	I strongly agree	I agree	I am neutral	I don't agree	I strongly don't agree
1-The electronics services have contributed to the increase of financial activity at the bank.					
2-The electronic services have contributed to increasing the number of clients at the bank.					
3-The electronic services have attracted a number of clients to the bank.					
4-The electronic service have increased the quality of work offered by the bank.					
5-The electronics services have contributed to reducing the percentage of the daily financial transactionsperformed by the banks.					
6-The electronics services have contributed to reducing the receipt of financial transactions pertaining to payment of bills.					
7-The electronic services have contributed to reducing cash deposit and withdrawal transactions.					
8-The electronic services have contributed to lessening the burden of account auditing undertaken by bank officials.					

Put ( ) against the appropriate expression

Personal data:

(1) Age

- 18 and less than 30 years
- 30 and less than 40
- 40 and less than 50
- 50 years and more

(2) Educational Level

- Secondary School certificate
- Bachelor's degree
- Postgraduate degree

(3) Monthly salary

- Less than 3000 Saudi Riyals
- From 3000 to less than9000 Saudi Riyals

- From 9000 Saudi Riyals and more

(4) Year of Experience

- Less than 5 years
- 5 and less than 10 years
- 10 years and less 15 years
- 15 years and more

10

Random Walk in Emerging Asian Stock Markets

Muneer Shaik[1] & S. Maheswaran[2]

[1] Research Scholar, Institute for Financial Management and Research, India

[2] Senior Professor, Institute for Financial Management and Research, India

Correspondence: Muneer Shaik, Research Scholar, Institute for Financial Management and Research, # 24, Kothari Road, Nungambakkam, Chennai-600 034, India. E-mail: muneer.shaik@ifmr.ac.in

Abstract

The random walk hypothesis is an important area of research in finance and many tools have been proposed to investigate the behaviour of the fluctuations in stock prices. However, a detail study on emerging Asian stock markets which employ the various unit root tests has not been done. In this paper, we employ six different unit root tests such as the Augmented Dickey and Fuller test (1979), Phillips and Perron test (1988), Kwiatkowski-Phillips-Schmidt-Shin test(1992), Dickey-Fuller GLS (ERS) test (1996), Elliot-Rothenberg-Stock Point-Optimal test (1996) and Ng and Perron (2001) unit root tests on 10 emerging Asian stock markets to detect for the presence of a random walk in stock prices. We have conducted the unit root tests during different sub-sample time periods of global financial crisis to check for robustness. To be specific, we have found that during the overall sample period (2001-2015) 8 out of 10 Asian stock markets and during the pre-crisis period (2001-2007) all the 10 Asian stock market prices do follow random walk according to the unit root tests under consideration. However, during the crisis & post-crisis period (2008-2015) we have found only 5 out of 10 Asian markets follow the random walk movement based on unit root tests.

Keywords: unit root tests, random walk, weak-form efficiency, stock indices, emerging asian markets, global financial crisis

1. Introduction

The random walk hypothesis has been an important area of research in the academic literature and is well known that stock prices move uncertainly in an efficient market. The origins of efficient market can be traced back to the pioneering work of Bachelier (1900) and the empirical research work of Cowles (1933). In an efficient market, the prices will completely reflect all the available information. Fama (1970) classified the markets into three categories namely weak form, semi-strong form and strong form of market efficiency. In weak form market efficiency, the information set consists of only the history of past prices. In semi-strong form, the information set consists of all publicly available data whereas in strong form market efficiency, the information set incorporates all private data i.e. it includes all information known to any market participant.

The tests on market efficiency have important implications on trading strategies and in the development phase of the market. Hence it is very much essential for the investors and the policy makers to understand the efficiency of the stock markets. In a weak form efficient market, stock prices do follow random walks due to which it becomes impossible to predict the future stock prices based on the past stock price information set due to which no individual can outperform the market.

First, we contribute to the existing literature on detecting the presence of random walks in the movement of stock prices in the most important emerging Asian stock markets. Most of the studies have dealt on few Asian markets but in this paper we do an extensive empirical analysis by undertaking 10 emerging Asian stock markets namely {India, China, Hong Kong, Taiwan, Malaysia, Thailand, Pakistan, Srilanka, Indonesia & Philippines}. Second, we employ six different unit root tests such as the Augmented Dickey-Fuller test (1979), Phillips-Perron test (1988), Kwiatkowski-Phillips-Schmidt-Shin (1992) test, Dickey-Fuller GLS (ERS) test, Elliot-Rothenberg-Stock Point-Optimal test (1996) and Ng and Perron (2001) unit root tests to detect for the presence of a random walk in stock prices. We conducted the tests by considering the intercept and also by including trend & intercept in the test equation for 10 emerging Asian stock markets. Third, in order to check for robustness, we have also implemented the unit root tests for the emerging Asian stock markets during different sub-sample time periods.

We have performed the analysis during pre-crisis period (2001-2007), crisis & post-crisis period (2008-2015) and overall sample period (2001-2015). The period of study is most relevant to understand the impact of Asian stock markets with regards to the global financial crisis 2008.

The remainder of the paper is discussed as follows. Section 2 contains the literature review on the efficiency of the major Asian stock markets. Section 3 provides a description of the data and Section 4 discusses the methodology used in our paper. The results are dealt with in Section 5. The paper ends with some concluding remarks in Section 6.

2. Literature Review

We find an extensive literature on the study of random walk hypothesis or tests for weak form efficiency in the major developed markets. However, the available literature on the movement of random walk in the emerging Asian stock markets is scarce. Most of the studies have concentrated on a single Asian market than performing tests on the overall emerging markets as a whole. Chaudhuri (1991) finds Indian market does not seem to be efficient even in its weak form by undertaking serial correlation, Runs test for the period 1988-1990. Poshakwale (1996) studies Indian market from the period 1987-1994 by performing serial correlation, Runs test, KS test and found evidence of weak form efficiency. Laurence et al. (1997) studied China Market for the period 1993-1996 and found evidence of weak form efficiency by conducting the unit root tests.

Balkiz (2003) investigates Kuala Lumpur stock market weak-form efficient and finds that the market is not efficient in a weak form. Ashutosh (2005) finds evidence of weak form efficiency in the Indian market during the period 1996-2001 by doing serial correlation test. Worthington & Higgs (2006) for both developed and Asian markets by using serial correlation, Runs test, Unit root tests (ADF, PP & KPSS) and multiple variance ratio tests. Cooray et al. (2007) studied SAARC countries namely India, Srilanka, Pakistan and Bangladesh by using the unit root tests for the period 1996-2005 and supports weak form efficiency by ADF & PP unit root tests while DF-GLS and ERS tests do not support. Islam et al. (2007) examine Thailand Stock market with data from 1975 to 2001 and find that the market is not efficient. Asma *et.al* (2008) conducted studies on Bangladesh market for the period 1988-2000 by autocorrelation test and indicates that daily returns are not random.

Gupta and Basu (2007) performed ADF, PP and KPSS unit root tests on Indian stock markets and results found that market is not weak form efficient for the period from 1991-2006. Mishra (2009) used ADF, PP unit root tests on Indian stock market for the period from 2001-2009 and find weak form inefficiency. Hamid et al. (2010) performed analysis on Asia-Pacific markets for the period from 2004-2009 and found that monthly prices do not follow random walks in all the markets. Nisar et al. (2012) studied four South Asian markets and found that none of the markets follow random-walk and hence are not weak form efficient for the period 1997-2011. Mishra (2012) performed analysis on five South Asian markets for the period 2005-2010 by using ADF, PP unit root tests and provide evidence that these markets are not weak form efficient. Paulo (2013) studied 9 Asian markets by using the daily data and performed unit root tests like ADF, PP and KPSS along with variance ratio test and finds evidence that the analyzed markets are not weak form efficient. Amer et al. (2014) studied 3 south Asian markets for the period from 2003-2011 on monthly & weekly return indices and finds evidence that the markets are not weak form efficient by using ADF, PP unit root tests.

3. Data Description

The study is conducted empirically by using the daily data of stock market prices of major Asian stock indexes namely India, China, Hongkong, Malaysia, Taiwan, Thailand, Pakistan, Srilanka, Indonesia and Philippines. The closing prices of the daily stock market index data is collected from the source Bloomberg for three different sample period's i.e. the overall period (Jan2001-Mar2015), the pre-crisis period (Jan2001-Dec2007) and the crisis & post-crisis period (Jan2008-Mar2015). The continuously compounded annual rate of return is measured using, $r_t = \ln(p_t/p_{t-1})$ where r_t the return, ln is is the natural log, p_t is the current price and p_{t-1} is the previous price.

Figure 1 displays the time plots of the return and price series for 10 emerging Asian stock markets. Table 1, Panel A: shows the results for the overall sample period from Jan 2001 to Mar 2015. During this period, we find the lowest mean returns are in Hongkong (0.0001), whereas the highest mean returns are in Pakistan (0.0009). The lowest minimum returns are in Thailand (-0.1723), as are the highest maximum returns in Srilanka (0.1829). The standard deviations of returns range from 0.0080 (Malaysia) to 0.0164 (China). We find the returns in Taiwan, Pakistan and China are the least volatile, with Srilanka, Philippines and Malaysia being the most volatile. Finally, The Jarque-Bera statistic and the corresponding p-values reject the null hypothesis that the daily distributions of 10 Asian market returns are normally distributed.

Table 1, Panel B: shows the results for the sub-sample pre-crisis period from Jan 2001 to Dec 2007. During the pre-crisis period, we find the lowest mean returns are in Taiwan (0.0003), whereas the highest mean returns are for Pakistan (0.0013). The standard deviations of returns range from 0.0084 (Malaysia) to 0.0152 (China). We find Taiwan, Pakistan and Hongkong to be least volatile, with Srilanka, Philippines and Thailand being the most volatile. The Jarque-Bera statistic and the corresponding p-values reject the null hypothesis that the daily distributions of 10 Asian market returns are normally distributed.

Table 1, Panel C: shows the results for the sub-sample crisis & post-crisis period from Jan 2008 to Mar 2015. During this period, we find the lowest mean returns are in China (-0.0002), whereas the highest mean returns are for Srilanka (0.0006). The standard deviations of returns range from 0.0076 (Malaysia) to 0.0174 (China). We find the returns in Taiwan, China and Pakistan are the least volatile, with Malaysia, India and Philippines being the most volatile. The Jarque-Bera statistic and the corresponding p-values reject the null hypothesis that the daily distributions of 10 Asian market returns are normally distributed.

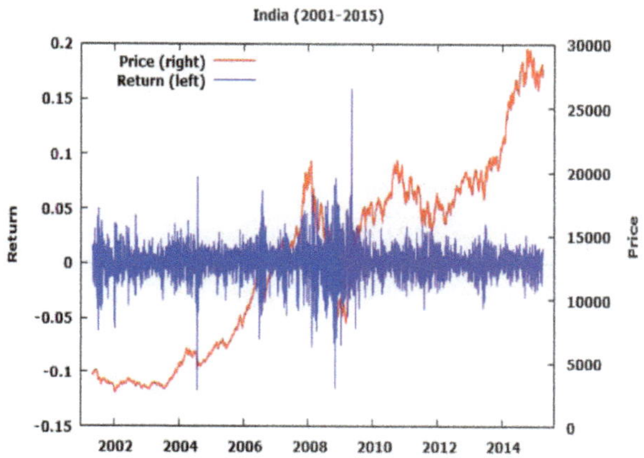

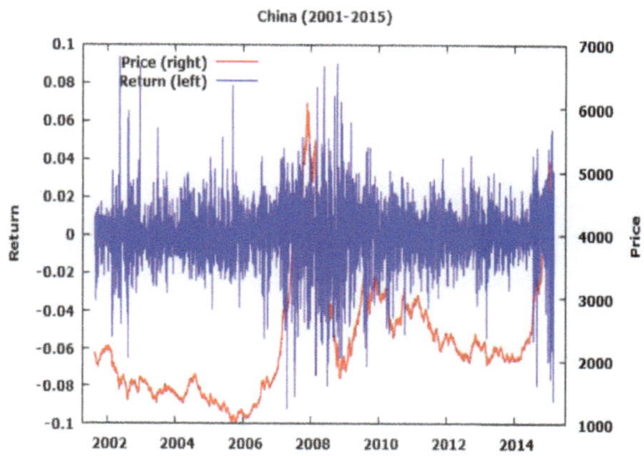

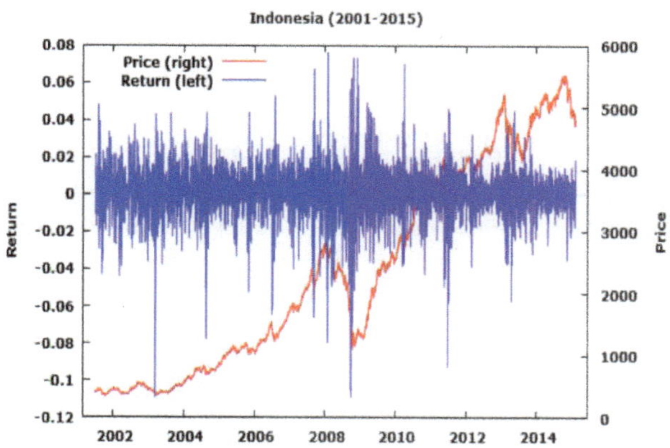

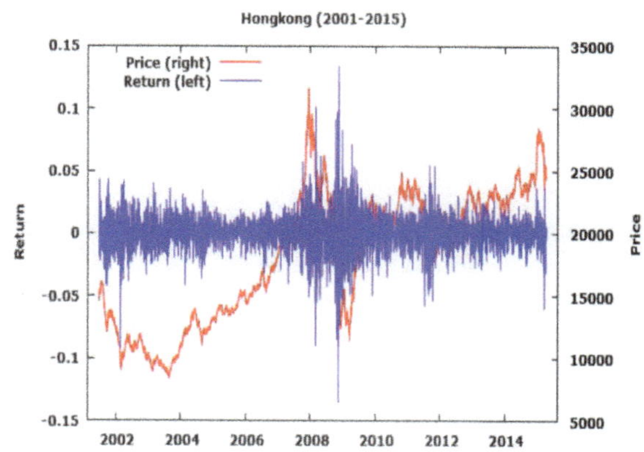

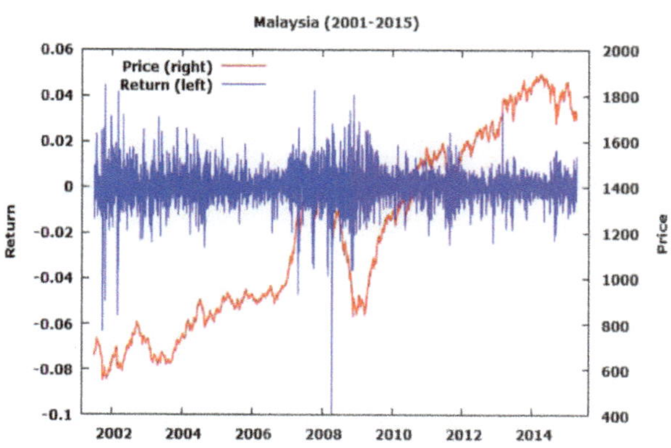

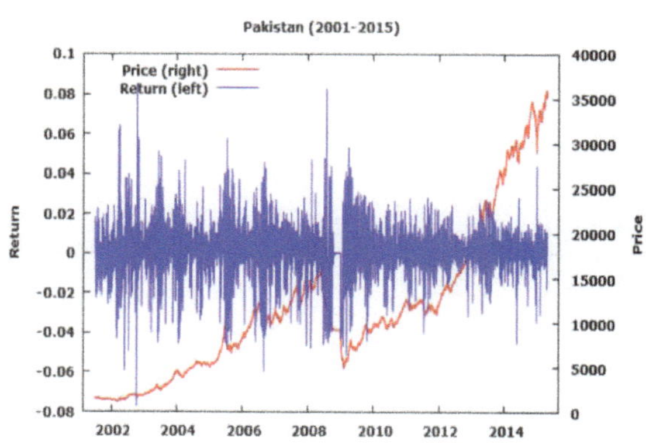

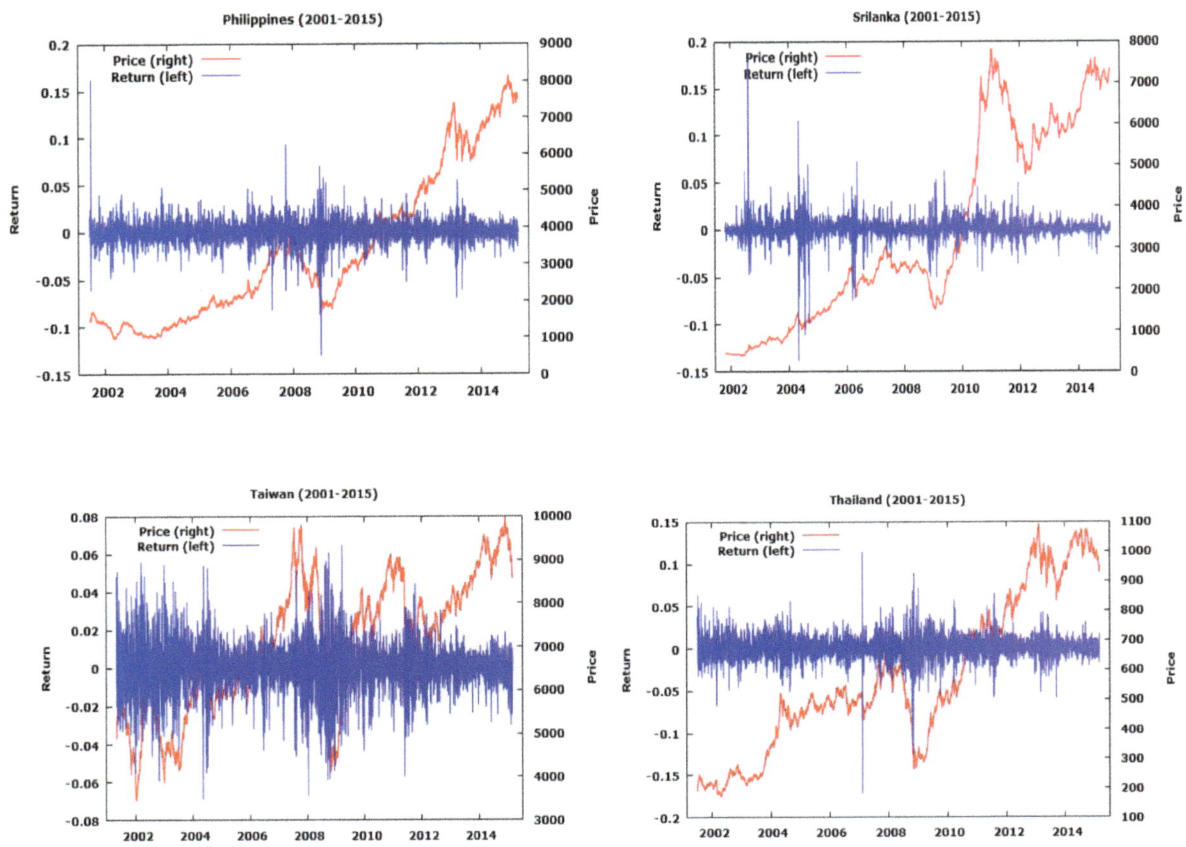

Figure 1. Time plot for return & price series of Asian stock indices

Table 1. Descriptive statistics of Asian stock market index returns

Panel A: Overall Sample Period (2001-2015)

	India	China	Hongkong	Taiwan	Malaysia	Thailand	Pakistan	Srilanka	Indonesia	Philippines
Mean	0.0005	0.0002	0.0001	0.0002	0.0003	0.0005	0.0009	0.0008	0.0007	0.0005
Median	0.0010	0.0006	0.0004	0.0005	0.0005	0.0005	0.0013	0.0005	0.0013	0.0005
Maximum	0.1599	0.0940	0.1341	0.0652	0.0450	0.1143	0.0851	0.1829	0.0762	0.1618
Minimum	-0.1181	-0.0926	-0.1358	-0.0691	-0.0998	-0.1723	-0.0774	-0.1390	-0.1095	-0.1309
Std. Dev.	0.0151	0.0164	0.0151	0.0136	0.0080	0.0152	0.0136	0.0121	0.0141	0.0131
Skewness	-0.1252	-0.2532	-0.0209	-0.1917	-0.9700	-0.5779	-0.3001	0.3211	-0.6807	-0.0424
Kurtosis	11.0044	7.1818	11.8501	5.6657	15.1137	12.7316	6.3845	32.6616	9.6916	15.6079
Jarque-Bera	9713.56	2609.14	11735.90	1091.59	22531.93	14262.08	1773.19	127375.80	6899.46	23666.14
Probability	0.0000*	0.0000*	0.0000*	0.0000*	0.0000*	0.0000*	0.0000*	0.0000*	0.0000*	0.0000*
Observations	3635	3529	3596	3612	3593	3564	3602	3473	3551	3573

Panel B: Pre Crisis Period (2001-2007)

	India	China	Hongkong	Taiwan	Malaysia	Thailand	Pakistan	Srilanka	Indonesia	Philippines
Mean	0.0009	0.0005	0.0004	0.0003	0.0004	0.0007	0.0013	0.0010	0.0011	0.0005
Median	0.0016	0.0006	0.0005	0.0002	0.0006	0.0003	0.0022	0.0008	0.0015	0.0001
Maximum	0.0793	0.0940	0.0576	0.0561	0.0450	0.1143	0.0851	0.1829	0.0673	0.1618
Minimum	-0.1181	-0.0926	-0.0929	-0.0691	-0.0634	-0.1723	-0.0774	-0.1390	-0.1093	-0.0825
Std. Dev.	0.0143	0.0152	0.0125	0.0144	0.0084	0.0152	0.0151	0.0144	0.0136	0.0132
Skewness	-0.6293	-0.0060	-0.2436	-0.0982	-0.6588	-0.6253	-0.3542	0.2936	-0.6994	0.9409
Kurtosis	8.0635	7.4860	6.2006	4.9292	10.0258	15.2525	5.6689	32.3722	8.0642	18.7767
Jarque-Bera	1991.85	1412.89	753.77	271.38	3672.69	10832.92	547.42	59623.65	1959.75	18123.40
Probability	0.0000*	0.0000*	0.0000*	0.0000*	0.0000*	0.0000*	0.0000*	0.0000*	0.0000*	0.0000*
Observations	1756	1685	1726	1732	1725	1714	1723	1658	1704	1723

Panel C: In & Post Crisis Period (2008-2015)

	India	China	Hongkong	Taiwan	Malaysia	Thailand	Pakistan	Srilanka	Indonesia	Philippines
Mean	0.0002	-0.0002	-0.0001	0.0000	0.0001	0.0002	0.0005	0.0006	0.0003	0.0004
Median	0.0005	0.0005	0.0003	0.0007	0.0003	0.0005	0.0005	0.0003	0.0011	0.0010
Maximum	0.1599	0.0903	0.1341	0.0652	0.0406	0.0892	0.0825	0.0626	0.0762	0.0706
Minimum	-0.1160	-0.0886	-0.1358	-0.0674	-0.0998	-0.1256	-0.0513	-0.0511	-0.1095	-0.1309
Std. Dev.	0.0158	0.0174	0.0172	0.0128	0.0076	0.0151	0.0119	0.0095	0.0146	0.0130
Skewness	0.2375	-0.3852	0.0748	-0.3217	-1.3684	-0.5358	-0.2379	0.2460	-0.6560	-1.0038
Kurtosis	12.7525	6.7950	12.0300	6.5671	21.7726	10.3959	7.0758	8.5125	10.7473	12.4082
Jarque-Bera	7460.10	1151.54	6351.72	1028.62	27997.29	4302.63	1317.62	2315.09	4749.00	7129.74
Probability	0.0000*	0.0000*	0.0000*	0.0000*	0.0000*	0.0000*	0.0000*	0.0000*	0.0000*	0.0000*
Observations	1878	1843	1869	1879	1867	1849	1878	1814	1846	1849

* means significant at 1% level of significance**Source:**Developed by authors

4. Methodology

In a stationary time series, the mean and auto-covariance are independent of time. However, for a non-stationary time series, the variance increases over time. *Random walk* is the common example of a non-stationary time series where,

$$z_t = z_{t-1} + \varepsilon_t \tag{1}$$

where 'ε' is a stationary random error term. The random walk is a difference stationary series since the first difference of y is stationary:

$$z_t - z_{t-1} = (1 - L)z_t = \varepsilon_t \tag{2}$$

A difference stationary series is a random walk and is said to be *integrated* and is represented as I(d) where *d* is the order of integration or the number of unit roots present to make the series stationary. For example, I (0) represent a stationary series with no unit root. I (1) represent stationary series with 1 unit root. Hence unit root is used as a standard method to check the stationary of a time series.

Now let us look at a simple Auto Regressive AR (1) process mentioned as below,

$$z_t = \rho z_{t-1} + y_t'\delta + \varepsilon_t \tag{3}$$

Where ρ and δ are parameters to be estimated, ε_t is random disturbance term and y_t is the independent term which can have a constant, a trend or both constant and a trend. A series *z* is said to be non-stationary if the absolute value of the estimated parameter ρ is greater than or equal to 1. The variance of the non-stationary time series increases with time and nears infinity. Whereas, a series is said to be (trend) stationary, if the absolute value of the estimated parameter ρ is strictly less than 1.

4.1 The Augmented Dickey-Fuller (ADF) Test

In this test, the AR(1) process mentioned in equation (3) is estimated by removing z_{t-1} from both sides of the equation as below.

$$\Delta z_t = \alpha z_{t-1} + y_t'\delta + \varepsilon_t \tag{4}$$

where $\alpha = \rho - 1$. We define the null and alternative hypotheses as,

$$H_O: \alpha = 0,\ H_1: \alpha < 0 \tag{5}$$

and t-ratio for α is measured as:

$$t_\alpha = \hat{\alpha} / (se(\hat{\alpha})) \tag{6}$$

Where $\hat{\alpha}$ is the estimated parameter of α, and $se(\hat{\alpha})$ is the coefficient standard error.

Suppose, if the time series *y* follows an AR (p) process then we test the below regression:

$$\Delta z_t = \alpha z_{t-1} + y_t'\delta + \beta_1 \Delta z_{t-1} + \beta_2 \Delta z_{t-2} + \cdots + \beta_p \Delta z_{t-p} + \vartheta_t \tag{7}$$

4.2 Dickey-Fuller Test with GLS Detrending (DFGLS)

The quasi-difference of z_t conditional on the value of 'a' is defined as:

$$d(z_t|\, a) = \begin{cases} z_t & if\ t = 1 \\ z_t - a z_{t-1} & if\ t > 1 \end{cases} \tag{8}$$

The OLS regression of the quasi-differenced data $d(z_t|\, a)$ on the quasi-differenced $d(y_t|\, a)$ is defined as below:

$$d(z_t| a) = d(y_t| a)'\delta(a) + \eta_t \quad (9)$$

Elliot, Rothenberg, and Stock (ERS) (1996) recommend the value of a to be equal to $\bar{a}$ where:

$$\bar{a} = \begin{cases} 1 - \frac{7}{T} & if\ y_t = \{1\} \\ 1 - \frac{13.5}{T} & if\ y_t = \{1, t\} \end{cases} \quad (10)$$

Now the *GLS detrended data,* z_t^d can be defined as :

$$z_t^d = z_t - y_t^{'}\hat{\delta}(\bar{a}) \quad (11)$$

In Dickey Fuller GLS test we substitute the y_t^d for the original y_t as mentioned in equation (7) to get,

$$\Delta z_t^d = \alpha z_{t-1}^d + \beta_1 \Delta z_{t-1}^d + \cdots + \beta_p \Delta z_{t-p}^d + \vartheta_t \quad (12)$$

We further consider the t-ratio for $\widehat{\alpha}$ as mentioned in ADF test.

4.3 The Phillips-Perron (PP) Test

The Phillips and Perron (1988) method estimates the equation (4) of the Dickey Fuller test and is based on the test statistic as shown below:

$$\tilde{t}_\alpha = t_\alpha (\frac{\gamma_0}{f_0})^{\frac{1}{2}} - \frac{T(f_0 - \gamma_0)(se(\hat{\alpha}))}{2 f_0^{\frac{1}{2}} s} \quad (13)$$

where $\hat{\alpha}$ is the estimate, and t_α the t-ratio of α, $se(\hat{\alpha})$ is coefficient standard error, and s is the standard error of the test regression. In addition, γ_0 is a estimate of the error variance and f_0, is a residual estimator. It is important to note that the asymptotic distribution of the Phillips-Perron modified t-ratio is the same as that of the ADF statistic.

4.4 The Kwiatkowski, Phillips, Schmidt, and Shin (KPSS) Test

The Kwiatkowski et al. (1992) test assumes the series z_t to be (trend-) stationary under the null. The KPSS statistic is defined based on the regression:

$$z_t = y_t^{'}\delta + u_t \quad (14)$$

The LM statistic is defined as:

$$LM = \textstyle\sum_t S(t)^2 / (T^2 f_0) \quad (15)$$

where f_0, is an estimator of the residual spectrum at frequency zero and S(t) is a cumulative residual function:

$$S(t) = \textstyle\sum_{r=1}^{t} \hat{u}_r \quad (16)$$

based on the residuals $\hat{u}_t = z_t - y_t'\hat{\delta}(0)$.

4.5 Elliot, Rothenberg, and Stock Point Optimal (ERS) Test

The ERS test is based on the quasi-differencing regression as mentioned in equation (9) in which the residuals are defined as $\hat{\eta}_t = d(z_t| a) - d(y_t| a)'\hat{\delta}(a)$, and let $SSR(a) = \sum \hat{\eta}_t{}^2(a)$ be the sum-of-squared residuals function. The ERS test statistic of the null that $\alpha = 1$ against the alternative that $\alpha = \bar{a}$, is then defined as:

$$P_T = (SSR(\bar{a}) - \bar{a}SSR(1))/f_0 \quad (17)$$

Where f_0, is an estimator of the residual spectrum at frequency zero.

4.6 Ng and Perron (NP) Tests

Ng and Perron (2001) construct four test statistics that depend upon the GLS detrended data. These test statistics are different forms of Phillips and Perron Z_α and Z_t statistics, the R_1 statistic, and the ERS statistic. First, define the term:

$$k = \textstyle\sum_{t=2}^{T} (z_{t-1}^d)^2 / T^2 \quad (18)$$

The modified statistics may then be written as,

$$MZ_\alpha^d = (T^{-1}(z_T^d)^2 - f_0)/(2k)$$

$$MZ_t^d = MZ_\alpha * MSB$$

$$MSB = (^k/_{f_0})^{\frac{1}{2}}$$

$$MP_T^d = \begin{cases} (\bar{c}^2k - \bar{c}T^{-1}(z_T^d)^2)/f_0, & if\ y_t = \{1\} \\ (\bar{c}^2k + (1-\bar{c})T^{-1}(z_T^d)^2)/f_0, & if\ y_t = \{1,t\} \end{cases} \tag{19}$$

where:

$$\bar{c} = \begin{cases} -7, & if\ y_t = \{1\} \\ -13.5, & if\ y_t = \{1,t\} \end{cases} \tag{20}$$

The NP tests require a specification for y_t and a choice of method for estimating f_0.

5. Empirical Results

In this section, we discuss the empirical results of the six different unit root tests that were employed in our paper to detect the random walk behaviour of the stock prices in the 10 emerging Asian stock markets under study. We also check the robustness of the unit root results by conducting the empirical tests during different sub sample periods. We perform the empirical analysis during the pre-crisis (2001-2007), crisis & post crisis (2008-2015) and also during the overall sample period (2001-2015).

5.1 Overall Sample Period (Jan 2001-Mar 2015)

Table 2, Panel A: provides us with the 5 different unit root test results in sections with only Intercept and also with both Trend & Intercept forms. First the Augmented Dickey-Fuller (ADF) Unit root test results shows that the t-test statistic is greater than the critical value at 1% level of significance at intercept level as well as both trend & intercept forms due to which we fail to the reject the null hypothesis of Unit root in the 10 emerging Asian stock markets. Second, we conduct the Phillips & Perron Unit root tests by including only Intercept and also both Trend & Intercept in the test equation. We say that the logarithm of the daily stock prices do follow random walk during overall sample period by employing PP Unit root as we observe the Adjusted t –stat is more than the critical value at 1% level of significance due to which we fail to reject the null hypothesis of Unit root. Third, we employ the Kwiatkowski-Phillips-Schmidt-Shin (KPSS) Unit root test by including only Intercept and also both Trend & Intercept in the test equation. In both the cases we observe that the Lagrange Multiplier (LM) test statistic is more than the critical values due to which we reject the null hypothesis of stationary and conclude that these series are unit root non stationary except the Malaysian market. We find the series in Malaysian market is stationary at 1% level of significance when we include both trend & Intercept in the test equation. Fourth, we have conducted Dickey-Fuller GLS (ERS) test and find that t-stat is more than the asymptotic critical values at 1% and hence we fail to reject the null hypothesis of unit root for all the stock markets except Taiwan market in Trend & Intercept form. We find the series in Taiwan market has no unit root and hence it is stationary at 5% level of significance in the Trend & Intercept form. Fifth, we have performed Elliot-Rothenberg-Stock Point-Optimal (ERSPO) test and find that the calculated P-stat is more than the critical values at 1% level of significance and hence we fail to reject the null hypothesis of unit root for all the Asian stock market series except for Taiwan Market in Trend & Intercept form. We find Taiwan market to be stationary at 5% level of significance in trend& Intercept form by way of ERSPO unit root test similar to the findings of Dickey-Fuller GLS (ERS) unit root test. Table 3, Panel A: shows the Ng-Perron Unit root test results for the overall sample period (2001-2015) and we find that the four MZ_a, MZ_t, MSB, MPT test statistics to be more than the asymptotic critical values at 1% level of significance. We accept the null hypothesis that the series has unit root for all Asian stock markets except for Taiwan Stock market where we find that the series has no unit root at 5% level of significance in Trend & Intercept form. Table 4 & 5 presents the critical values of different unit root tests at 1%, 5% and 10% level of significance.

Hence during the overall sample period (2001-2015), we empirically find that the emerging Asian stock market series has unit root in both the intercept only and trend & intercept forms by six different Unit root tests employed in our analysis except for Malaysian market (KPSS Test in Trend & Intercept form) and Taiwan market (Dickey-Fuller GLS (ERS) test, Elliot-Rothenberg-Stock Point-Optimal test and Ng-Perron unit root in trend & Intercept forms) where we find no unit root. Hence except for Malaysia and Taiwan stock markets, we say that logarithm of daily Asian stock market prices follow random walk and hence are weak form efficient.

5.2 Pre-Crisis Period (Jan 2001- Dec 2007)

Table 2, Panel B: provides us with the 5 different unit root test results in sections with only Intercept and also with both Trend & Intercept forms during pre-crisis period. First we employ the Augmented Dickey-Fuller (ADF) Unit root test result, we find that the t-test statistic is greater than the critical value at 1% level of significance due to which we fail to the reject the null hypothesis of Unit root when we include only Intercept and both trend & intercept unit root test equation. We observe that the series has unit root and hence logarithm of stock prices follow random walk in all emerging Asian stock market under consideration as per ADF test. Second, we conduct the Phillips & Perron Unit root tests by including only Intercept and also both Trend & Intercept in the test equation. We say that the logarithm of the daily stock prices do follow random walk during sub sample pre-crisis period by employing PP Unit root as we observe the Adjusted t –stat is more than the critical value at 1% level of significance due to which we fail to reject the null hypothesis of Unit root. We also find the p-values to be insignificant for each Asian stock market under consideration. Third, we employ the Kwiatkowski-Phillips-Schmidt-Shin (KPSS) Unit root test by including only Intercept and also both Trend & Intercept in the test equation. In both the cases we observe that the Lagrange Multiplier (LM) test statistic is more than the critical values due to which we reject the null hypothesis of stationary and conclude that these series are unit root non stationary. Fourth, we have conducted Dickey-Fuller GLS (ERS) test and find that t-stat is more than the asymptotic critical values at 1% and hence we fail to reject the null hypothesis of unit root for all the stock markets. Fifth, we have performed Elliot-Rothenberg-Stock Point-Optimal (ERSPO) test and find that the calculated P-stat is more than the critical values at 1% level of significance and hence we fail to reject the null hypothesis of unit root for all the Asian stock markets. Table 3, Panel B: shows the Ng-Perron Unit root test results for the sub-sample pre-crisis period (2001-2007) and we find the four MZ_a, MZ_t, MSB, MPT test statistics to be more than the asymptotic critical values at 1% level of significance. Hence we accept the null hypothesis that the series has unit root for all Asian stock markets. Table 4 & 5 presents the critical values of unit root tests.

Hence during the sub-sample pre-crisis period (2001-2007), we empirically find that the emerging Asian stock market series has unit root in both the intercept only and trend & intercept forms unanimously by six different Unit root tests employed in our analysis. Our test results show that during pre-crisis period all the Asian stock market prices follow random walk.

5.3 Crisis & Post-Crisis Period (Jan 2008- Mar 2015)

Table 2, Panel C: provides us with the unit root test results in sections with only Intercept and also with both Trend & Intercept forms for crisis & post-crisis period. First, during this sub-sample period, we find that China & Hongkong stock markets do not follow random walk in the Intercept form at 10% level of significance whereas India, Hongkong and Philippines do not follow random walk at 10%, 5%, 5% respectively in Trend & Intercept form of the Augmented Dickey-Fuller (ADF) Unit root test. The rest of the Asian stock markets do follow random walk when we employ the ADF unit root test. Second, we conduct the Phillips & Perron Unit root tests by including only Intercept and also both Trend & Intercept in the test equation. Our test results show that China & Hongkong stock markets do not follow random walk as the series has no unit root at 10% level of significance in Intercept form. Also we find that India, Hongkong and Philippines stock market series has no unit root and hence do not follow random walk at 10%, 5% and 5% level of significance respectively in both Trend& Intercept form. Third, we employ the Kwiatkowski-Phillips-Schmidt-Shin (KPSS) Unit root test by including only Intercept and also both Trend & Intercept in the test equation. In both the cases we observe that the Lagrange Multiplier (LM) test statistic is more than the critical values due to which we reject the null hypothesis of stationary and conclude that these series are unit root non stationary and follow random walks except for China market in Intercept form and Hongkong & Taiwan market in trend & intercept forms where we find series to be stationary at 1% level of significance .Fourth, we have conducted Dickey-Fuller GLS (ERS) test and find that t-stat is more than the asymptotic critical values at 1% and hence we fail to reject the null hypothesis of unit root for all the Asian stock markets. Fifth, we have performed Elliot-Rothenberg-Stock Point-Optimal (ERSPO) test and find that the calculated P-stat is more than the critical values at 1% level of significance and hence we fail to reject the null hypothesis of unit root for all the Asian stock markets. Table 3, Panel C: shows the Ng-Perron Unit root test results for the sub-sample pre-crisis period (2008-2015) and we find the four MZ_a, MZ_t, MSB, MPT test statistics to be more than the asymptotic critical values at 1% level of significance. Hence we accept the null hypothesis that the series has unit root for all Asian stock markets. Table 4 & 5 presents the critical values of different unit root tests at 1%, 5% and 10% level of significance.

Hence during the sub-sample period (2008-2015), we empirically find that the emerging Asian stock market series has unit root in both the intercept only and trend & intercept forms by six different Unit root tests employed in our analysis except for China market (ADF,PP,KPSS Test in Intercept form), Hongkong market (ADF test and PP test in Intercept and both trend & intercept forms, KPSS in Trend & Intercept form), Indian market (ADF test and PP test in trend & intercept form), Philippines market (ADF test and PP test in trend & intercept form) and Taiwan market (KPSS in Trend & Intercept form) where we find no unit root. Hence except for China, Hongkong, India, Philippines and Taiwan, we say that logarithm of daily Asian stock markets under consideration do follow random walk and hence are weak form efficient during the sub-sample period

(2008-2015).

Table 2. Unit root test results of Asian stock market indices

	INTERCEPT FORM					TREND & INTERCEPT FORM				
	ADF (t stat)	PP (Adj t stat)	KPSS (LM stat)	ERS DF GLS (t stat)	ERSPO (P stat)	ADF (t stat)	PP (Adj t stat)	KPSS (LM stat)	ERS DF GLS (t stat)	ERSPO (P stat)
Panel A: Overall Sample Period (2001-2015)										
India	-0.6686	-0.7071	6.9499	1.2911	113.7101	-1.8303	-1.8075	1.1774	-1.7523	14.7139
China	-0.9057	-1.0096	2.6586	-0.8728	9.6323	-1.6067	-1.6951	0.5044	-1.2379	26.245
Hongkong	-1.2632	-1.2070	5.7984	-0.9068	9.3296	-2.8669	-2.7956	0.5988	-1.9762	11.7412
Taiwan	-2.0373	-2.0101	4.9117	-0.6371	13.2982	-2.9991	-2.9902	0.2477	*-2.9876* **	*5.1345***
Malaysia	-1.0598	-1.0275	7.2341	0.8187	80.9415	-2.4511	-2.5064	0.1821*	-2.4352	7.6952
Thailand	-1.5985	-1.6109	6.2809	0.8731	94.2809	-2.2521	-2.3584	0.4808	-1.8106	13.2938
Pakistan	-1.0775	-1.0857	6.3058	2.5605	296.6413	-1.4316	-1.5834	1.0752	-1.1257	35.5287
Srilanka	-1.7693	-1.7411	6.8613	2.2276	344.1819	-1.5177	-1.5875	0.6859	-0.9962	31.2771
Indonesia	-1.1549	-1.1398	7.4272	1.6192	200.4015	-1.7051	-1.5779	0.8607	-1.8387	12.1544
Philippines	-0.1966	-0.1034	7.2028	1.226	74.0855	-2.8192	-2.6829	0.2911	-1.7256	15.0223
Panel B: Pre-Crisis Period (2001-2007)										
India	1.3665	1.2655	4.9426	2.6597	122.2662	-2.6494	-2.5425	0.8097	-0.4897	60.4641
China	1.5859	1.5129	1.4039	0.8276	39.7701	0.2784	0.2912	0.9649	0.6143	121.9516
Hongkong	0.7569	0.7221	3.8917	0.4105	25.7995	-2.2281	-2.2311	0.8667	-0.2629	68.5145
Taiwan	-1.1062	-1.2441	3.8062	-0.2091	16.3461	-2.6149	-2.8317	0.3352	-2.3165	8.5275
Malaysia	0.2093	0.3388	4.5508	1.4335	51.7996	-2.1837	-2.1554	0.4318	-1.4979	16.3092
Thailand	-1.0997	-1.1217	4.7145	1.0679	94.8652	-2.0929	-2.1149	0.6739	-2.0504	10.7944
Pakistan	-0.4247	-0.4759	5.2247	2.5974	317.2606	-1.9935	-2.3062	0.7419	-1.5666	18.0582
Srilanka	-1.2592	-1.2627	4.9515	1.6571	227.7765	-1.5525	-1.5651	0.7854	-1.7428	12.5173
Indonesia	0.7979	0.9348	5.0576	2.7781	164.3472	-2.3554	-2.3088	0.6012	-1.1072	26.1121
Philippines	0.3263	0.3891	4.4711	0.9305	39.77405	-2.2741	-2.2296	0.8598	-0.8822	39.3624
Panel C: Crisis & Post-Crisis Period (2008-2015)										
India	-0.9656	-0.8323	3.6066	-1.0576	8.4014	*-3.2937* ***	*-3.1556****	0.2448	-1.1815	27.9071
China	*-2.8335* ***	*-2.8595****	*0.6298* *	-0.4077	48.7051	-2.4511	-2.4789	0.3851	-0.378	59.5483
Hongkong	*-2.5903* ***	*-2.5779****	1.5141	-1.2283	8.1276	*-3.4782***	*-3.4367***	*0.1539* *	-1.5045	19.3395
Taiwan	-1.6753	-1.6063	2.0622	-1.5903	4.8405	-2.4105	-2.3798	*0.1731**	-1.6018	17.8068
Malaysia	-0.6948	-0.6997	4.4943	-0.6494	18.0261	-2.6114	-2.601	0.3382	-1.0235	44.2122
Thailand	-0.7369	-0.7563	4.533	-0.4931	19.4243	-2.3861	-2.4124	0.3344	-1.2115	31.5152
Pakistan	0.6317	0.4397	4.6636	0.8334	45.9403	-2.5826	-2.7011	0.7641	-0.4842	83.1065
Srilanka	-0.9854	-0.9353	3.7741	0.8509	105.8695	-0.9325	-1.0413	0.7996	-0.9916	42.2566
Indonesia	-0.7814	-0.7003	4.5384	-0.2899	23.9136	-2.2325	-2.1275	0.4437	-1.3656	24.4906
Philippines	-0.2898	-0.1035	5.158	0.1913	33.0413	*-3.5848***	*-3.6846* **	0.2799	-1.1307	35.3803

ADF -Augmented Dickey-Fuller test, PP-Phillips-Perron test, KPSS-Kwiatkowski-Phillips-Schmidt-Shin test, ERS DF GLS - Dickey-Fuller GLS (ERS) test, ERSPO - Elliot-Rothenberg-Stock Point-Optimal test. * means significant at 1 %, ** means significant at 5%, *** means significant at 10%. **Source:**Developed by authors.

Table 3. Ng Perron unit root test results of Asian stock market indices

	INTERCEPT FORM				TREND & INTERCEPT FORM			
Panel A: Overall Sample Period (2001-2015)								
	MZa	MZt	MSB	MPT	MZa	MZt	MSB	MPT
India	1.0000	1.2929	1.2929	112.3080	-6.1922	-1.7526	0.2830	14.7142
China	-2.2508	-0.8727	0.3877	9.6283	-3.3450	-1.2375	0.3700	26.1663
Hongkong	-2.3757	-0.9067	0.3816	9.2919	-7.8143	-1.9744	0.2527	11.6679
Taiwan	-1.3946	-0.6376	0.4572	13.1596	-17.933 **	-2.985 **	0.166 **	5.137 **
Malaysia	0.7332	0.8134	1.1094	79.9309	-12.2027	-2.4294	0.1991	7.6974
Thailand	0.7244	0.8735	1.2059	92.9983	-6.9159	-1.8092	0.2616	13.2467
Pakistan	1.2385	2.5659	2.0717	291.7130	-2.5582	-1.1263	0.4403	35.4456
Srilanka	0.9751	2.2341	2.2911	335.8510	-2.5508	-0.9980	0.3913	31.0746
Indonesia	0.9228	1.6178	1.7533	197.3220	-7.7115	-1.8355	0.2380	12.1549
Philippines	1.2239	1.2262	1.0018	73.3691	-6.1017	-1.7265	0.2830	14.9242
Panel B: Pre-Crisis Period (2001-2007)								
India	2.2608	2.6803	1.1856	120.3320	-0.9180	-0.4880	0.5316	58.4678
China	1.1711	0.8282	0.7072	39.6949	0.8620	0.6151	0.7136	120.0310
Hongkong	0.7291	0.4108	0.5634	25.7888	-0.4707	-0.2623	0.5573	66.8664
Taiwan	-0.4531	-0.2090	0.4613	16.0729	-10.9057	-2.3098	0.2118	8.4881
Malaysia	1.8929	1.4440	0.7628	50.9221	-5.5295	-1.4970	0.2707	16.1031
Thailand	0.9085	1.0691	1.1768	92.4558	-8.4783	-2.0459	0.2413	10.7952
Pakistan	1.2143	2.6000	2.1412	309.5420	-5.0541	-1.5647	0.3096	17.9194
Srilanka	0.8958	1.6640	1.8576	219.3190	-7.5837	-1.7494	0.2307	12.4934
Indonesia	1.9707	2.7940	1.4178	160.9240	-3.1648	-1.1092	0.3505	25.6123
Philippines	1.3589	0.9375	0.6899	39.3655	-2.0024	-0.8808	0.4399	38.5241
Panel C: Crisis & Post-Crisis Period (2008-2015)								
India	-2.8017	-1.0605	0.3785	8.4001	-3.1522	-1.1831	0.3753	27.2940
China	-0.4215	-0.4075	0.9667	47.2739	-0.7253	-0.3775	0.5205	58.1713
Hongkong	-3.0756	-1.2276	0.3991	7.9465	-4.7579	-1.5027	0.3158	18.9156
Taiwan	-5.0816	-1.5900	0.3129	4.8323	-5.1644	-1.6020	0.3102	17.6256
Malaysia	-1.1342	-0.6542	0.5768	18.0165	-2.0976	-1.0239	0.4882	43.4345
Thailand	-0.8544	-0.4931	0.5772	19.3366	-2.9342	-1.2107	0.4126	31.0398
Pakistan	1.0775	0.8369	0.7767	45.6502	-0.7562	-0.4848	0.6411	80.3886
Srilanka	0.6649	0.8513	1.2804	102.5770	-2.0753	-0.9892	0.4767	42.2352
Indonesia	-0.4698	-0.2946	0.6272	23.6836	-3.7523	-1.3659	0.3640	24.2308
Philippines	0.2758	0.1926	0.6982	32.7648	-2.6105	-1.1303	0.4330	34.4741

* means significant at 1 %, ** means significant at 5%, *** means significant at 10% . **Source:** Developed by authors.

Table 4. Critical values of ADF, PP, KPSS, ERS DF GLS, ERSPO Unit tests during different sub sample periods

		INTERCEPT FORM					TREND & INTERCEPT FORM				
		ADF (t stat)	PP (Adj t stat)	KPSS (LM stat)	ERS DF GLS (t stat)	ERSPO (P stat)	ADF (t stat)	PP (Adj t stat)	KPSS (LM stat)	ERS DF GLS (t stat)	ERSPO (P stat)
Overall Sample Period (2001-2015)	**1% level**	-3.431	-3.433	0.739	-2.565	1.990	-3.960	-3.960	0.216	-3.480	3.960
	5% level	-2.862	-2.862	0.463	-1.940	3.260	-3.411	-3.411	0.146	-2.890	5.620
	10% level	-2.567	-2.567	0.347	-1.616	4.480	-3.127	-3.127	0.119	-2.570	6.890
Pre-Crisis Period (2001-2007)	**1% level**	-3.433	-3.433	0.739	-2.566	1.990	-3.963	-3.963	0.216	-3.480	3.960
	5% level	-2.862	-2.862	0.463	-1.941	3.260	-3.412	-3.412	0.146	-2.890	5.620
	10% level	-2.567	-2.567	0.347	-1.616	4.480	-3.128	-3.128	0.119	-2.570	6.890
Crisis & Post-Crisis Period (2008-2015)	**1% level**	-3.433	-3.433	0.739	-2.566	1.990	-3.962	-3.962	0.216	-3.480	3.960
	5% level	-2.862	-2.862	0.463	-1.940	3.260	-3.412	-3.412	0.146	-2.890	5.620
	10% level	-2.567	-2.567	0.347	-1.616	4.480	-3.128	-3.128	0.119	-2.570	6.890

ADF -Augmented Dickey-Fuller test , PP-Phillips-Perron test, KPSS-Kwiatkowski-Phillips-Schmidt-Shin test, ERS DF GLS - Dickey-Fuller GLS (ERS) test, ERSPO - Elliot-Rothenberg-Stock Point-Optimal test.
Source: Developed by authors.

Table 5. Asymptotic critical values of MZa, MZt,MSB,MPT tests of Ng-Perron unit root tests

	INTERCEPT FORM	TREND & INTERCEPT FORM
During all Sample Periods	1% -13.8000, -2.58000, 0.17400, 1.78000	1% -23.8000, -3.42000, 0.14300, 4.03000
	5% -8.10000,-1.98000, 0.23300, 3.17000	5% -17.3000, -2.91000, 0.16800, 5.48000
	10% -5.70000, -1.62000, 0.27500, 4.45000	10% -14.2000, -2.62000, 0.18500, 6.67000

Source: Developed by authors.

6. Conclusion

This paper examines empirically on whether the important emerging Asian stock markets follow random walk or not. A market will be weak form efficient if the stock markets follow random walk. We performed six different unit root tests in intercept as well as trend & intercept forms of unit root equations on 10 emerging Asian stock markets for different time periods to carry out the robustness check in our analysis. The analysis of random walk tests at different time periods before and after the global financial crisis 2008 is particularly relevant to understand how the Asian stock markets movements have been impacted by the crisis.

Our empirical findings show that firstly, during the overall sample period (2001-2015) except for Malaysia and Taiwan stock markets, the test results find the evidence of unit root i.e. random walk movement in 8 Asian stock markets. Hence 8 out of 10 Asian stock markets are weak form efficient during the period 2001-2015. Secondly, during the sub-sample pre-crisis period (2001-2007), our test results show that all the 10 Asian stock markets has unit root in the series. Hence we find all the 10 Asian stock markets are weak form efficient and follow random walk. Thirdly, during the crisis & post-crisis period (2008-2015) except for China, Hongkong, India, Philippines and Taiwan, we find the presence of unit root for the rest of the markets. Hence only 5 out of 10 Asian stock markets are weak form efficient and follow random walk. Thus in our analysis we find evidence that global financial crisis does had an impact on the movement of important Asian stock market prices.

References

Amer, S., Ghulam, M., Qamar, H., & Azeem, M. (2014). Efficiency of South Asian capital markets: An empirical analysis. *European Journal of Business and Management, 6*(11), 30-33.

Ashutosh, V. (2005). The study of the weak form informational efficiency in Bombay Stock Market. *Finance India, 19*(4), 1421-1424.

Asma, M., Mollah, A. S., & Bhuyan, R. (2008). Market Efficiency in Emerging Stock Market: Evidence from Bangladesh. *Journal of Emerging Market Finance,* 7(1), 17-41. https://doi.org/10.1177/097265270700700102

Bachelier, L. (1900). Theorie de la Speculation. *Annales Scientifiques de l'Ecole Normale Superieure, 3*(17), 21-86.

Balkiz, O. (2003). Testing Informational Market Efficiency on Kuala Lumpur Stock Exchange. *Jurnal Ekonomi Malaysia, 37*, 3-20.

Chaudhuri. S. K. (1991). Short-run Share Price Behaviour: New Evidence on Weak Form of Market Efficiency. *Vikalpa, 16*(4), 17-21. https://doi.org/10.1177/0256090919910402

Cooray, A. V., & Wickremasinghe, G. (2007). Efficiency of Emerging Stock Markets: Some Empirical Evidence from the South Asian Region. *Journal of Developing Areas,* 41(1), 171-183. https://doi.org/10.1353/jda.2008.0030

Cowles, A. (1933). Can stock market forecasters forecast? *Econometrica, 1*(3), 309-324. https://doi.org/10.2307/1907042

Dickey, D., & Fuller, W. A. (1979). Distribution of the estimates for autoregressive time series with a unit root. *Journal of the American Statistical Association, 74*(366), 427-431. https://doi.org/10.2307/2286348

Elliot, G., Rothenberg, T. J., & Stock, J. H. (1996). Efficient Tests for an Autoregressive Unit Root. *Econometrica, 64*(4), 813-836. https://doi.org/10.2307/2171846

Fama, E. F. (1970). Efficient capital markets: A review of theory and empirical work. *Journal of Finance, 25*(2), 383-417. https://doi.org/10.2307/2325486

Gupta, R., & Basu, P. (2007). Weak-Form Efficiency In Indian Stock Markets. *International Business and Economic Research Journal, 6*(3), 57-64.

Hamid, K., Suleman, M. T., Ali, S. S. Z., & Akash, R. S. (2010). Testing the weak form of efficient market hypothesis: Empirical evidence from Asia-pacific markets. *International Research Journal of Finance and Economics, 58,* 121-133.

Islam, S., Watanapalachaikul, S., & Clark, C. (2007). Some Tests of the Efficiency of the Emerging Financial Markets: An Analysis of the Thai Stock Market. *Journal of Emerging Market Finance, 6*(3), 291-302. https://doi.org/10.1177/097265270700600304

Kwiatkowski, D., Phillips, P. C. B., Schmidt, P., & Shin, Y. (1992). Testing the null hypothesis of stationarity against the alternative of a unit root. *Journal of Econometrics, 54*(1-3), 159-178. https://doi.org/10.1016/0304-4076(92)90104-Y

Laurence, M., Francisc, C., & Sun, Q. (1997). Weak-Form Market efficiency and Causality Test in Chinese Stock Markets. *Multinational Finance Journal, 1*(4), 291-307. https://doi.org/10.17578/1-4-3

Malkiel, B. (1992). Efficient market hypothesis. In P. Newman, M. Milgate, & J. Eatwell (Eds.), *New Palgrave Dictionary of Money and Finance*. Macmillan,London.

Mishra, P. K. (2009). Capital Market Efficiency and Financial Innovation – A Perspective Analysis. *The Research Network, 4*(1), 1-4.

Mishra, P. K. (2012). Efficiency of South Asian capital markets. *Pakistan Journal of Commerce and Social Sciences, 6*(1), 27-34.

Ng, S., & Perron, P. (2001). Lag Length Selection and the Construction of Unit Root Tests with Good Size and Power. *Econometrica, 69*(6), 1519-1554. https://doi.org/10.1111/1468-0262.00256

Nisar, S., & Muhammed, H. (2012). Testing weak form of efficient market hypothesis: Empirical evidence from South-Asia. *World Applied Sciences Journal, 17*(4), 414-427.

Paulo, V. (2013). The Efficiency of Asian Stock Markets: A Weak-Form Efficiency analysis. *IJER, 10*(1), 117-136.

Phillips, P. C. B., & Perron, P. (1988). Testing for a Unit Root in Time Series Regression. *Biometrika, 75*(2), 335-346. https://doi.org/10.1093/biomet/75.2.335

Poshakwale, S. (1996). Evidence on Weak Form Efficiency and Day of the Week Effect in the Indian Stock Market. *Finance India, 10*(3), 605-616.

Worthington, A. C., & Higgs, H. (2004). Random Walks and Market Efficiency in European Equity Markets. *Global Journal of Finance and Economics, 1*(1), 59-78.

11

Foreign Direct Investment and Economic Growth in the Arab Region: The Case of Knowledge Spillover Effects

Nayef Al-Shammari[1] & Huda Al-Rashid[1]

[1] Department of Economics, College of Business Administration, Kuwait University, Kuwait

Correspondence: Nayef Al-Shammari, Department of Economics, College of Business Administration, Kuwait University, Kuwait. E-mail: alshammari@cba.edu.kw or alshammari2000@gmail.com

Abstract

This research aims to focus on how institutional barriers in the Arab region may account for losses in FDI inflows along with their potential technology spillover effects, as well as to show how the deficiency of absorptive capacities serve as an important factor for attracting inflows. The analysis relies on endogenous growth models at an aggregate regional level and a microeconomic firm-level. Findings based on linear OLS regressions, reveal a positive correlation between improved institutional factors and potential FDI spillovers, with significance varying in certain countries. Policy implications involve having targeted FDI policies to enhance absorptive capacities, improving information asymmetry to reduce corruption, and enhancing the labor market regulatory framework to improve human capital development as an incentive for FDI inflows.

Keywords: economic growth, endogenous growth theories, foreign direct investment, spillovers

1. Introduction

Foreign direct investment is key contributor to economic growth, both explicitly and implicitly. Investment is a major factor to boost economic growth, however, with FDIs also lead to positive externalities that additionally increase growth levels through their technology spillover effects. When FDIs flow inwards towards a host economy, they also transmit their knowledge and technology; for example, the presence of US-based transnational corporations like Apple Inc. in its manufacturing bases not only adds to the economic growth of the host country by increasing the cumulative gross domestic product (by increasing production and sales), but also boosts economic development by transmitting the technology associated with its products and by providing extensive training to local employees.

This therefore boosts GDP levels as well as human capital development, and may induce further local innovation. These externalities (that the literature most often refers to as "spillovers") emphasize the importance of giving enough recognition to the potential of FDIs as sources of economic growth. This research investigates how institutional factors in the Arab region may act as a hindrance towards FDI spillovers from reaching their full potential. In order to do that, we must first ask, what is the current state of foreign investment in the Arab region? Figure 1, illustrates a recent decline in FDI levels in the Arab region especially after the 2008 economic crisis. The trend is continuously declining and clearly illustrates the detrimental aftermath of the global crisis on the investment levels as a whole. However, it is important to examine whether FDI levels are low because of the recession or due to other factors? Figure 2 illustrates a trend comparison between the Arab region and other developed economies such as the United States and United Kingdom, the European Union, and other high-income economic groups.

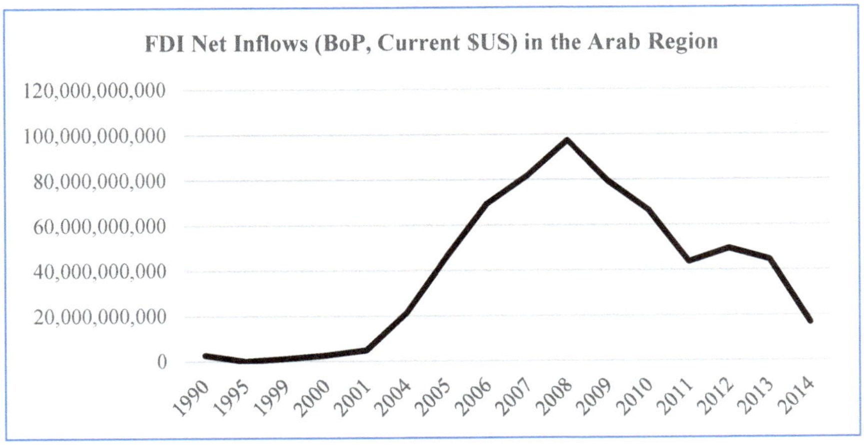

Figure 1. FDI net inflows in the Arab world 1990-2014 (World development indicators, 2015)

The trend line is consistent with FDIs in the Arab region, whereby inflows have decline severely after the 2008 crisis. However, high income OECD countries and the European Union have a substantially larger amount of FDI inflows than the Arab region. It is true that other advanced economies such as the US and UK have similar low levels of inflows, but trend lines in the Arab world seem to have an *overall* lower level than other economic "groups" such as the high income OECD countries as a *whole*. Thus, the decline in FDI inflows in the region are most likely due to the effects of the economic recession, as in the trend lines in other economic groups, however, there must be an explanation underlying the overall *amount* or stock of inflows, that is substantially lower than that of high income OECD countries; this highlights the topic of focus, which is to look at the institutional framework as a major underlying determinant of FDI inflows.

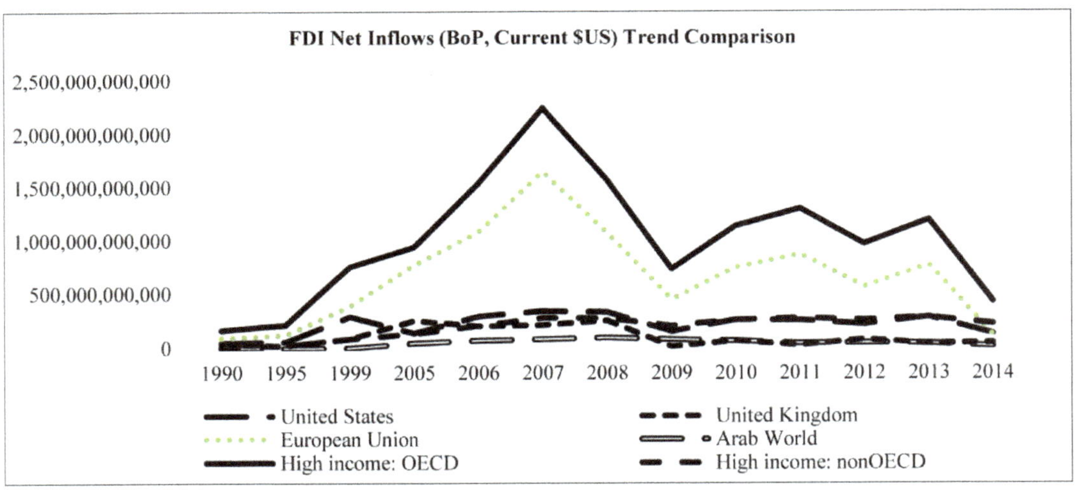

Figure 2. FDI net inflows trend comparison 1990-2014 (World development indicators 2015)

Specifically, the investment climate acts as an important indicator got the institutional framework in the region; Figure 3 illustrates the "ease of doing business" in different Arab countries, while comparing the overall trend in the region with more advanced economies (Note 1). The data indicates that in most Arab countries, the procedures to conduct business is often very difficult; some countries are better off than others such as the UAE, Bahrain and Qatar. However, when comparing even the most effective Arab countries in terms of doing business, the data still falls short when looking at developed economies such as the US, UK, Germany and Singapore with a perfect score of 1 indicating a perfectly easy environment for business startups. Thus, although the overall trend in the region is quite low, it is important to look at a sample of firms from each country, to account for differences within the region, which is what the microeconomic firm-level analysis aims to examine the business environments for a selection of Arab countries.

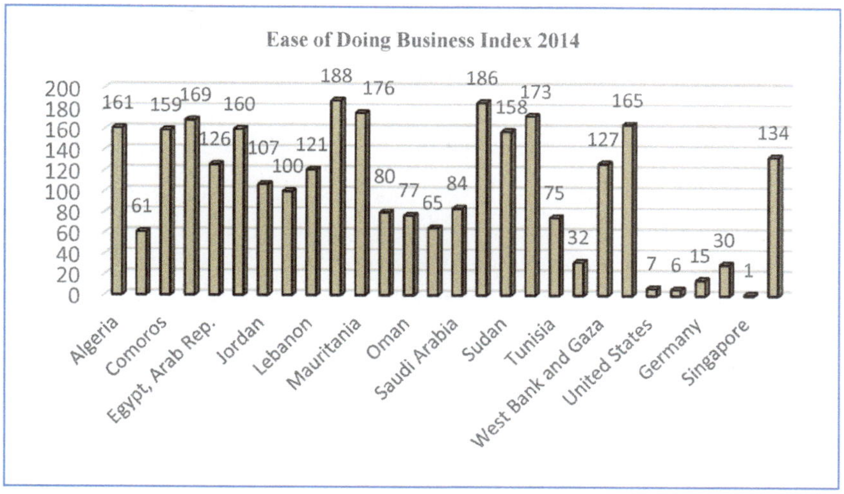

Figure 3. Ease of doing business in the Arab region (World Bank, doing business database 2015)

Another crucial element of the institutional framework is the quality of governance. The Heritage Foundation indices on economic freedom (Note 2) are important indicators to evaluate the level of government effectiveness in the region. Figure 4 indicates that the results are mixed within the region. Some countries such as Algeria, Comoros, Mauritania and Yemen for instance have lower economic freedom indices. Other countries such as UAE, Bahrain and Qatar have indices closely matching those of other developed economies such as the US and Germany. However, when looking at the subcomponents making up the overall economic freedom score, results may differ; for example, it seems that the majority of the Arab region is falling behind when it comes to the degree of "business freedom" and "freedom from corruption" (Appendix I).

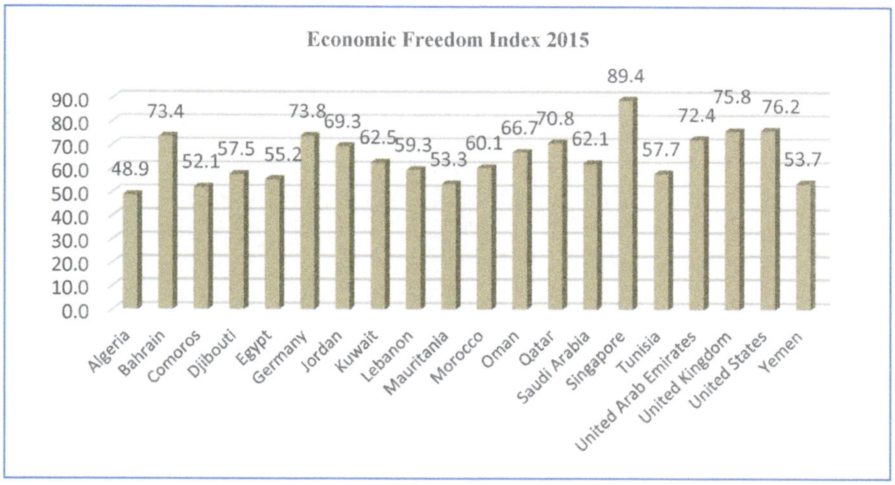

Figure 4. Economic freedom index 2015 (The Heritage foundation, 2015)

This result is consistent with the World Bank ease of doing business data presented above. Therefore, with these statistics in mind, it is evident that although varying in significance within the Arab region, corruption issues along with inflexible investment climates are a major problem. These are major determinants towards incentivizing the inflows of FDIs into the region, and thus deserve to be focused on in this research. Furthermore, our analysis will include both aggregate and firm-level data in order to account for differences within the region pertaining to analyzing FDI spillovers, which is something that has not yet been done in the literature.

Following this overview of the state of FDI inflows and institutional barriers in the Arab region, it is now crucial to link all these elements together and present a comprehensive research illustrating how institutional constraints can hinder not only FDI inflow levels, but also reduce the effectiveness of potential spillovers. Section II presents a selection of the literature clarifying the relationship between growth and FDIs as well as how institutional factors affect spillovers. Section III will explain the theoretical background and data methodology approaches using endogenous growth models. Section IV will briefly present a description of the regional and firm-level data used in the analysis. Section V will include the empirical data analysis for both aggregate regional data, and firm-level data. Finally, Sections VI, VII, and VIII will cover concluding remarks, a selection of policy implications and short notes regarding further research in this area.

2. Literature Review

This section will present a selection of the literature that will first clarify the relationship between foreign direct investment (FDI) and economic growth. Second, the notion of associated "spillover" effects with recipients of FDIs is highlighted. Third, how the investment climate might act as a factor affecting the growth potentials of FDIs is presented. Fourth, a presentation of literature exploring different models to measure technology spillovers from FDIs will be analyzed. Finally, the review will examine how this relationship between FDIs, spillover effects, and economic growth has been explored within the Arab region.

2.1 Foreign Direct Investment (FDI) and Economic Growth

Foreign direct investment has been linked to economic growth, especially in terms of the "positive externalities" that are associated with its presence. The impact of FDIs on economic growth had first taken focus in new endogenous growth models, focusing on the works of Romer, Lucas, and others, following the "neoclassical" theories supported by Solow, and Cobb-Douglas, which didn't fully recognize the effect of FDIs on technology; these models and their techniques will be examined further below. Upon the introduction of these endogenous growth models, many studies have begun to examine the relationship between growth and FDIs. For example, a study examining the impact of FDIs on the economic growth trends in Indian and Chinese economies found a positive impact that contributed to an increase in per capita income (Iqbal et al., 2013). Moreover, the World Bank indicated the importance of FDIs in contributing to the development of Sub-Saharan African countries (Farole & Winkler, 2014). Al-Shammari and Al-Saran (2012) examine the main determinants of FDI across developing Asia. They find that main factors determining FDI in Asian developing countries are market size, development in the infrastructure, trade openness, financial developing, economic growth and labor. In addition to many other studies that support this relationship in various economies, there has been an emphasis on *how* FDIs might contribute to economic growth. In other words, having seen how FDIs increased per capita income, it is important to ask, *what factor* contributed to the positive effect of FDIs on economic growth?

The answer to this question lies in analyzing the impact of FDIs on "technology" which can also be represented as a proxy for human capital (skills, or "knowledge"). This idea takes is linked to the new endogenous growth theories discussed above. Following Solow and Cobb-Douglas models (neoclassical) that focus on capital accumulation as the main contributor to economic growth (Romer, 2012), it is necessary to refer to models that recognize an *underlying* factor contributing to growth, i.e. exploring the element of technology or knowledge. The endogenous growth theories therefore can be relied on to explain the impact of FDIs on the element of knowledge and hence, on economic growth (Romer, 2012).

2.2 FDIs and Spillover Effects: Analyzing Technology Spillovers

After recognizing the important relationship between FDIs and economic growth, the next step is to now build upon the arguments brought about by these new endogenous growth theories, and investigate how FDIs may lead to economic growth through the element of technology. Based on a survey of the literature, studies have indicated a "spillover effect" or a positive externality on host countries from FDI inflows. This spillover effect has been in the form of technology transfer. For example, referring back to the study by the World Bank, results show that FDIs in developing countries serve as valuable sources of knowledge and technology that assist in developing local economic units (Farole & Winkler, 2014, p. 247). Furthermore, when examining a study on FDI impacts on Mexico and Costa Rica, FDIs have a positive impact "at the macro level through increases in investment, employment, foreign exchange, and tax revenue, and at the micro level through positive spillovers that will advance the host country's knowledge-based assets" (Paus & Gallagher, 2007, p. 54). A study by Amann and Virmani (2015) ensures the impact of FDI on productivity growth across OECD countries. A theoretical paper by Perri and Peruffo (2016) argues that the model of FDI knowledge spillover should include the macro- level as well as micro –level aspects of spillovers. A study by Wang, Ning, Li. and Prevezer (2016) finds positive influence of FDI on technological spillovers in China. The later result is also consistent with Wang, Liu, Cao, and Wang (2016) where technology spillover is found across varies industrial sectors in China.

Additional studies by De Mello (1999), Obwona (2001) and Borensztein et al. (1998), all emphasize the potential of FDIs on contributing to the transfer of technology to host countries, and even suggest that this contribution may account for growth more than domestic investment would (Hussien, 2009). Again, in making this argument, the endogenous growth models were used to examine FDI impacts on knowledge spillovers. Thus, based on these findings, it can be concluded that one of the ways in which FDIs lead to economic growth is through the transfer in technology (which support the ideas in the endogenous growth theories). The next step is to examine the *extent* in which FDIs can lead to these positive externalities, and what factors would affect the *magnitude* of these spillovers.

2.3 Analyzing the Relationship between FDIs and Institutional Capacities

When analyzing the impact of FDIs on economic growth, it is clear that some *shortages* might occur in terms of how much FDIs contribute to knowledge spillovers. Thus, under what conditions would FDIs lead to positive technology spillover effects? According to the World Bank's report on FDI spillovers in Sub-Saharan Africa, there exist constraints that categorize into: foreign firm characteristics, domestic firm characteristics, transmission channels (supply chains, labor turnover, market restructuring), host country factors and institutional frameworks (Farole & Winkler, 2014). Specifically, in chapter three and four of this report, Farole and Winkler (2014) uses an empirical approach to evaluate which absorptive capacities facilitate FDI linkages, by using simple regressions to clarify the impact of this factor on FDI spillovers (pp. 71, 97). Having clarified these important factors, it is apparent that the "absorptive institutional capacity" in the host country is a major factor towards fully realizing FDI positive externalities. This factor has been emphasized in a research by the OECD investigating the potentials of FDIs in China; by using a simple production function (measuring FDI as an exogenous variable impacting the endogenous variable, output), the study concluded that the quality of FDI inflows along with the *complementary assets in host regions* are main determinants of knowledge-based externalities (Fu, 2008).

Furthermore, another study by Paus and Gallagher (2001) investigates the missing link found in FDIs in Costa Rica and Mexico; the results indicate that the missing links involve poor government strategy to direct the potentials of FDIs into their governing and economic system, as well as the failure of local institutions to provide supportive inputs that meet the standards of inflowing transnational corporations (TNCs). This again emphasized the role of institutional variables in contributing to the host country's "absorptive capacity" which will in turn lead to positive FDI spillovers (2001, p. 58). Moreover, another study investigates investment climates by using the World Bank's "ease of doing business" indicators, and focusing on a selection of developing countries (Bayraktar, 2013). The methodology used was a simple correlation matrix, which would examine the effects of "ease of doing business" indicators on FDI levels; results indicated that countries with less constraints towards doing business tend to attract more FDI inflows (2013).

This concept has also been emphasized in a study examining FDIs in China and India; results indicated that economic activity, infrastructure, political system, and the business environment of the host country were major factors affecting FDI levels (Iqbal et al., 2013). Therefore, when looking at all of these studies, it is clear that there is an important correlation between institutional capacities and the potential of positive FDI spillovers, or externalities. This in turn makes it worthwhile to consider this factor when analyzing FDI spillovers for the case of the Arab Region.

2.4 FDIs, Spillovers Effects and Economic Growth: The Case of the Economies of the Arab Region

The literature also covers research in this topic pertaining to the cases in the Arab region. A study examining the effects of FDIs on GCC economies using a heterogeneous panel analysis, results in findings that align with the propositions of the endogenous growth theories (Al-Iriani, 2007). Furthermore, supporting the arguments about institutional capacities, this paper also states that GCC countries can further benefit from FDIs improving their transparency, policies, legal systems, and institutions (Al-Iriani, 2007). Furthermore, a study examining the effects of FDIs on 16 Arab countries using a dynamic panel analysis, concludes that the current impact of FDIs is limited or negligible; however, it also mentions that findings indicate factors that are hindering the positive potential benefits that FDIs offer these countries such as financial development, trade openness, human capital and infrastructure quality (El- Wassal, 2012).

Another study by Al-shammari, Al-halaq, and shammari (2016) investigates determinants of FDI inflow for Kuwait. they find that macroeconomic factors such as of market size, economic development, financial deepening, infrastructure development, openness are in the long and short runs related to FDI inflows in Kuwait. Other studies in the MENA region also indicate that institutional variables such as property rights for example, are one of the key determinants of FDI inflows in the region (Mohamed & Sidiropoulos, 2010). Moreover, according to an Economic Update Report published by the National Bank of Kuwait (2014), the GCC region has been aiming to improve their business environments especially in terms of enhancing the ease of doing business factors (starting business, obtaining credit, enforcing contracts etc.) in order to encourage FDI inflows into the region. This further supports the relevance of this research in terms of focusing on institutional factors such as investment climates in examining the full potential of FDIs on the Arab economies.

Thus, this literature review has presented a background supporting a positive relationship between FDI and economic growth, through its ability to provide technology spillover effects. Furthermore, institutional capacities act as major factors impacting the full potentials of FDI knowledge spillover effects. These relationships were then supported by taking a look at new endogenous growth theory models and some international trade theory models. Finally, the implications of these relationships and concepts in the context of the Arab region were examined. Now that these factors, relationships, and concepts have been identified, it is time to apply a selected methodology to investigate FDIs and knowledge spillovers taking into consideration institutional capacities as a major barrier, for the case of the Arab region.

3. Methodology

The main approach in analyzing the impact of institutional factors on FDI spillovers is to divide the analysis into two levels; an aggregate, macroeconomic regional-level analysis, and a microeconomic firm-level analysis. This will provide a holistic analysis of the performance of FDIs in the region given the environmental (institutional) factors that may differ from one country to another. Models will be based on the concepts explored in new endogenous growth theories to compute the spillover effects at the firm-level and regional-level starting off with the general production function as a base,

$$Y = AL^{\beta}K^{\alpha} \tag{1}$$

in which Y (output) is a function of A (technology), L (labor), and K (capital) (Note 3). Building on this basic production function, the general form of the endogenous growth model can be derived,

$$\dot{A}(t) = B[a_k K(t)]^{\beta}[a_L L(t)]^{\gamma} A(t)^{\theta} \text{ such that } B > 0 \;\; \beta \geq 0 \;\; \gamma \geq 0 \tag{2}$$

in which the growth of technology or knowledge $\dot{A}(t)$ is a function of the stock of capital, labor, and technology (Romer, 2012). Thus, it is "endogenous" since the *stock* of knowledge $A(t)^{\theta}$ is a variable affecting the *growth* of knowledge $\dot{A}(t)$. In using this concept, it is possible to analyze the impact of the stock of FDI inflows (representing the stock of knowledge $A(t)^{\theta}$) on FDI spillovers (representing the growth of knowledge $\dot{A}(t)$) while considering control variables as well as variables representing institutional factors. For the regional analysis, adapting the same concept of the general endogenous growth model, the industry value added as a percentage of GDP $IndVA$ serves as a proxy for FDI spillovers. Control variables affecting spillovers include gross capital formation as a percentage of GDP GCF, labor productivity LP (or GDP per person employed as reported by the World Bank), trade openness $Trade$ (or trade as a percentage of GDP), and economic growth GR (or annual percentage growth rate of GDP at market prices based on constant local currency). The stock of FDI inflows FDI (net inflows in current US dollars) as well as proxies for institutional factors that might affect FDI spillovers $InstF$ will also be included within the model. The regional-level model is expressed below,

$$IndVA = \alpha + FDI + GR + LP + GCF + Trade + InstF + \varepsilon \tag{3}$$

For the cross-country firm level analysis, the endogenous model will take the following form (Note 4),

$$NS_{ij} = \alpha + FDI_{ij} + LP_{ij} + FC_{ij} + InstF_{ij} + \varepsilon \tag{4}$$

The dependent variable NS_{ij} represents net annual sales (total sales minus the total cost incurred, which reflects the "value added" for the firm) for time period *i* and industry *j*. For the case of the independent variables, FDI_{ij} represents the ownership share of private foreign individuals, companies or organizations, LP_{ij} refers to labor productivity (effective labor) which is quantified by using values for the education level of the firm's employees and managers. Moreover, FC_{ij} represents capital formation within the firm quantified as the net value of assets after depreciation for land and buildings, and $InstF_{ij}$ represents institutional factors facing the firms.

4. Data Description

For the regional model, the selected variables are all extracted from the World Bank's World Development Indicators 2015 database, with proxies for institutional barriers extracted from the World Bank's Worldwide Governance Indicators database. This regional panel dataset is comprised of 12 Arab countries (Note 5), with time series ranging from 1996 till 2014; data gaps do exist according to the availability of data for each country (Note 6). For this microeconomic analysis, data is obtained from the World Bank Enterprise Surveys for five Arab countries (Note 7) for years 2013 or 2014, depending on the latest survey datasets available for each country. Variables used as proxies reflecting institutional factors are based on survey responses by firms on how severe a certain obstacle is in hindering their performance. These five countries are also included in the regional, aggregate analysis, and will therefore provide clearer idea of differing trends *within* the region in terms of the potential of FDI spillovers.

5. Empirical Results and Analysis

Having set the aggregate regional and firm-level endogenous models, it is now important to direct the analysis towards a linear ordinary least squares (OLS) regression analysis, which will identify the impact of selected institutional factors on the potential *magnitude* of FDI spillovers.

5.1 FDI Spillovers in the Arab Region: An Aggregate Regional Analysis

Starting off with the regional endogenous growth model, the results below indicate findings corresponding to what the literature has reported. FDI inflows are significantly positively correlated with the industry value added variable. This supports the notion of the endogenous growth theory in which the stock of technology is an important factor affecting the growth of technology (or spillovers). Having this finding be consistent with the theoretical base, it is possible to look at how other factors affect FDI *spillovers*. The most surprising result is having one of the control variables, trade openness, be significantly negative to the industry value added. This result could be explained by the fact that the majority of the data sample countries are importers; a deficiency in an economy's trade balance usually negatively affects growth or output, which is the case in this model. Labor productivity measured as GDP per person employed serves as a factor significantly and positively affecting spillovers which is consistent with the theoretical model.

Table 1. Aggregate regional analysis of FDI spillovers

IndVA	Coef.	Std. Err.	t	P>t	[95% Conf.	Interval]
FDI	2.90E-10	1.13E-10	2.57	0.012	6.58E-11	5.14E-10
GR	0.2081814	0.2555394	0.81	0.417	-0.2994161	0.715779
GCF	0.0281398	0.1518185	0.19	0.853	-0.2734289	0.3297085
Trade	-0.2765657	0.0391606	-7.06	0.000	-0.3543534	-0.198778
LP	0.00151	0.0001397	10.81	0.000	0.0012325	0.0017875
Regulatory Quality	0.3911266	0.0645759	6.06	0.000	0.2628545	0.5193986
Constant	13.12441	3.937303	3.33	0.001	5.303443	20.94538

Looking at the variable of interest, the value of "regulatory quality perception" is selected as a proxy for institutional factors (extracted from the Worldwide Governance Indicators database). In this case it is clear that as regulatory quality is enhanced, FDI spillovers will increase (because of the positive and significant relationship between the variables). Similar results were obtained when looking at other governance variables such as "government effectiveness," "control of corruption," "law perception" and "voice accountability" (results in Appendix III). Therefore, based on these aggregate empirical results, institutional quality is a major factor in determining the effective magnitude of FDI spillovers on the economies of the Arab region. Hence, these results are consistent with the major propositions of the endogenous growth model. This empirical model reported to have a 76.9% adjusted R-squared value, indicating a strong model with exogenous variables effectively explaining their effects on the endogenous variable.

5.2 FDI Spillovers in Arab Businesses: A Firm-Level Analysis

The firm-level analysis will focus on the impact of legislative or institutional constraints on the performance of a sample of firms, in terms of accounting for the percentage of firms with international ownership. For the case of this analysis, it is important to see the extent in which FDIs are an important part of the performance of the firm or not, for each Arab country. Starting off with Jordan (2013), the results below (Note 8) indicate that the presence of foreign ownership in local firms have a significantly positive effect on business' net sales, which supports the endogenous growth theory whereby FDI spillovers lead to greater productivity and growth (here demonstrated at a firm-level by increased sales). Moreover, there are positive significant relationships between other control variables such as capital stocks, and direct exports (a proxy for trade openness from our general endogenous model). When looking at the variables of interest, the only significant institutional factor that affects net sales in businesses in Jordan is corruption; this infers that local enterprises face corruption as a major obstacle towards their growth (based on their survey response), and that higher corruption weight thus transcends into lower sales (explaining the negative coefficient). Hence, results in Jordan support this paper's hypothesis and are consistent with the aggregate regression model.

Table 2. Jordan (2013) firm-level analysis

Net Sales	Coef.	Std. Err.	t	P>t	[95% Conf.	Interval]
Foreign Ownership Share	66719.09	19803.79	3.37	0.001	27777.32	105660.8
Capital: Land and Buildings	1.54161	0.182214	8.46	0.000	1.183309	1.899911
Direct Exports	55221.18	16287.3	3.39	0.001	23194.19	87248.18
Business Licensing Obstacles	-19466.91	374439.2	-0.05	0.959	-755756.1	716822.3
Political Instability Obstacle	285041.7	322069.5	0.89	0.377	-348269	918352.4
Corruption Obstacle	-409094.6	188012	-2.18	0.03	-778797.3	-39391.8
Regulatory Policy Uncertainty Obstacle	466874.9	244111.9	1.91	0.057	-13141.57	946891.3
Labor Regulations Obstacle	-620964.3	471061.7	-1.32	0.188	-1547250	305321.6
Constant	356072.9	767480.4	0.46	0.643	-1153084	1865230

Moving on to the case of Egypt (2013), the results are more ambiguous, especially in terms of the significance of the presence of foreign shares (FDIs) to the total sales (Note 9) outcomes of local firms. This can be explained by the politically unstable environment in Egypt, especially after the Arab Spring movement. Thus, FDI inflows may not be an important factor in determining the direction of sales in local firms because of its lack of presence. The estimated correlation index between sales and foreign ownership shares is 0.043, which indicates a positive but insignificant relationship. Similar findings were obtained when analyzing Tunisia (2013), with a correlation index of 0.013 between sales and foreign ownership.

For the case of Lebanon (2013), the regression results (Note 10) show significant relationships between our control variables (foreign ownership, capital stock, and direct exports) and total annual sales, however, the significance of the institutional variables of interest are absent. Although variables such as informal competition, business licensing, corruption and labor regulations are negatively related to the performance of businesses (i.e. negatively affecting the potentials of FDI spillovers), there are not significant. Thus, in this case, factors *other* than institutional constraints explain hindrances towards FDI spillover performance.

Table 3. Lebanon (2013) firm-level analysis

Total Annual Sales	Coef.	Std. Err.	t	P>t	[95% Conf.	Interval]
Foreign Ownership Share	3.03E+08	1.31E+08	2.33	0.021	4.62E+07	5.61E+08
Capital: Land and Buildings	1.995297	0.267278	7.47	0.000	1.468489	2.522105
Direct Exports	1.12E+08	5.45E+07	2.06	0.040	4953821	2.20E+08
Employees' Education Level	7.93E+07	1.98E+08	0.4	0.689	-3.11E+08	4.70E+08
Customs/Trade Regulations Obstacle	4.14E+08	6.94E+08	0.6	0.551	-9.53E+08	1.78E+09
Informal Competition Obstacle	-3.05E+08	5.03E+08	-0.61	0.545	-1.30E+09	6.86E+08
Business Licensing Obstacles	-3.90E+08	8.36E+08	-0.47	0.641	-2.04E+09	1.26E+09
Political Instability Obstacle	2.51E+08	1.86E+09	0.13	0.893	-3.42E+09	3.92E+09
Corruption Obstacle	-3.08E+08	1.05E+09	-0.29	0.769	-2.37E+09	1.76E+09
Labor Regulations Obstacle	-1.64E+09	1.49E+09	-1.1	0.273	-4.57E+09	1.30E+09
Regulatory Policy Uncertainty Obstacle	3.43E+08	5.20E+08	0.66	0.511	-6.83E+08	1.37E+09
Constant	3.76E+09	6.32E+09	0.6	0.552	-8.70E+09	1.62E+10

Mauritania (2014) exhibited results (Note 11) similar to Lebanon, with significant contributions of FDIs to total annual sales (spillovers), however, the only significant variable of interest is access to finance as an obstacle. Thus, institutional framework may not be as important in affecting FDI performance, in comparison to financial resources. However, institutional and financial constraints are interrelated; therefore, even though institutional variables of interest below don't exhibit significant relationships, this doesn't completely negate their importance. Having a stable institutional environment can help relieve financial obstacles within the economy.

Table 4. Mauritania (2014) firm-level analysis

Total Annual Sales	Coef.	Std. Err.	t	P>t	[95% Conf.	Interval]
Foreign Ownership Share	2.95E+07	1.10E+07	2.67	0.011	7217315	5.18E+07
Capital: Land and Buildings	4.061968	3.943557	1.03	0.309	-3.902208	12.02614
Employees' Education Level	-3.40E+07	2.53E+07	-1.34	0.187	-8.50E+07	1.71E+07
Business Licensing Obstacles	1.16E+08	2.08E+08	0.56	0.580	-3.05E+08	5.37E+08
Political Instability	1.58E+08	2.46E+08	0.64	0.525	-3.39E+08	6.55E+08
Corruption Obstacle	-2.01E+08	1.96E+08	-1.03	0.310	-5.97E+08	1.94E+08
Access to Land Obstacle	2.26E+08	2.02E+08	1.12	0.270	-1.82E+08	6.34E+08
Access to Finance Obstacle	-9.23E+08	3.22E+08	-2.86	0.007	-1.57E+09	-2.72E+08
Constant	2.27E+09	7.69E+08	2.96	0.005	7.22E+08	3.83E+09

6. Conclusions

According to endogenous growth theory models and empirical case studies, FDIs are important contributors to economic growth especially in terms of their potential knowledge spillover effects. Much of the literature has pinpointed institutional constraints as major obstacles affecting the positive externalities of FDIs on growth, especially in terms of the host economy's "absorptive capacity" or its ability to handle advanced, incoming investment from abroad. When analyzing the case of the Arab region, there is a recent decline in the inflows of FDIs, and this research aims to analyze why this decline might have occurred, by focusing on the investment climate as a determining factor of incentivizing foreign investment. The analysis showed that both at a regional and firm-level perspective, institutional constraints are in fact major factors to consider when analyzing their impact in attracting FDIs; variances in *significance* differ from one country to another usually depending on the political nature of the country or its economic framework.

Based on the firm-level analysis, for some Arab countries within the region, FDIs play an important role in increasing firm-level performances, as shown by increased total or net sales; these highlight the potential of knowledge spillover effects that the endogenous growth model supports. However, these spillovers are less significant in some countries especially those with recent political instabilities arising from the Arab Spring aftermath, due to the fact that the actual FDI stocks may be significantly lower than other countries. Furthermore, some countries account for factors other than institutional barriers to affect the performance of their FDI spillovers, but as mentioned above, it is important to note that different categories of barriers are closely related and are often interdependent, thus not completely considering institutional constraints as negligible.

7. Policy Recommendations

Based on the obtained results, the institutional framework is an important barrier towards the potential of positive FDI spillovers on the economies of the Arab region (especially in terms of the quality of governance), even though it may be less significant in certain Arab countries. Thus, it is crucial to examine potential policy proposals aiming to relieve these institutional barriers to FDI spillovers. This paper's findings are generally consistent with the literature, hence emphasizing the need to focus on the "absorptive capacity" of these economies, as clarified in the World Bank report on FDIs in the sub-Saharan African region (Farole & Winkler, 2014).

A crucial approach to improving the absorptive capacities is to have *targeted* FDI policy actions, whereby incentives are enhanced for inward FDI flows, while simultaneously attracting their spillovers towards the region's economic growth. The importance of having such targeted policies is accentuated in economic theory as well as within the literature covering this topic; FDIs are an important contributor to holistic economic growth and development, and targeted policies aiming to improve their performance, can be especially beneficial for economies in the region that need a *diversified* source of growth (such as oil-exporting GCC countries).

As demonstrated by the endogenous growth model, the technology spillovers arising from FDI inflows has an implicit impact of growth through the transfer of "knowledge." This can in turn enhance human capital levels, innovation, and other forms of development. Having this can of diversified source of growth (even though it is indirect or implicit), can be extremely beneficial for non-diversified economies of the GCC region for instance. In determining how to set the preferred set of targeted policies, we must first examine the different components that make up an economy's "absorptive capacity;" these components are comprised of many different factors that are interdependently related (Farole & Winkler, 2014). Specifically, the absorptive capacity links the institutional framework as well as firm-level characteristics into ultimately affecting the outcome of FDI spillovers. Policies to tackle the subcomponents under these two broad categories include emphasizing the government's role in institutional development.

For example, the government should work to develop "an *environment* that supports the growth and dissemination of innovative technologies for and by SMEs to take advantage of the knowledge-based economy" (Emine, 2012, p. 28). Moreover, government policy plans should "maintaining close integration" between the policies pertaining to private sector businesses and to that of general economic policy; this consistency within general economic policies would create a more stable environment for these businesses to further develop within the scope of the general economy (Alasarg, 2006, p.11); more developed businesses will in turn enhance the absorptive capacity, thus attracting more FDIs. Attracted FDIs would eventually lead to even further growth through the transmission of positive externalities. Other targeted policies should also ease institutional constraints and enhance investment climates; for example, in the region, the "ease of doing business" as shown above, ranks well below the average levels, thus dampening the potentials of FDI inflows and spillovers. Targeted policies aiming to enhance regulations for startups are an essential component of an economy's absorptive capacity, in order to attract FDIs.

Other major factors pertaining to the Region's absorptive capacity relates to the problem of information asymmetry. Research has noted that transparency issues are important impediments towards businesses in the Arab world; thus, policies aiming to maintain stability and transparency within institutions in the economy must be considered. Certain studies also recommended the creation of a line of communication between various organizations and bodies responsible for the development of local enterprises (Alasarg, 2006, p.13). This communication should be inter-sectoral between businesses, government institutions (like public funds, ministries, etc.), and even financial intermediaries. Having a clear correspondence between these different sectors can help reduce information gaps, thus creating a more attractive investment climate for FDIs. Furthermore, this is also related to corruption; policies directed towards eliminating or reducing corruption levels are important for the effectiveness of FDI spillovers in the Region, as revealed in the empirical results. Policies that reduce information asymmetry will in turn reduce corruption levels, since illicit actions will be transparent, thus incentivizing each sectors to act within the rule of law.

Another important policy area to consider is in terms of enhancing human capital levels in the region. Human capital serves to be an important component of the absorptive capacity framework (Farole & Winkler, 2014). According to the data from the World Bank's World Enterprise Surveys, underdeveloped skills, education, and experience (which are tenets of human capital development) seem to be the most important managerial obstacles cited in the Arab world; undereducated workers can not only contribute to lower revenues, but can also contribute to lower employment contributions as a consequence of lower sales. Foreign investment would not flow inwards towards economies with a shortage of human capital, since these economies would not be able to "absorb" the advanced level of these investments. Policies to enhance human capital skills is a vast area which includes many subcategories; for instance, policies may be as broad as improving the education system in the region, the school-to-work transition, and as narrow as improving at-work training programs for employees.

Since this research pertains to handling the institutional framework aiming to improve the absorptive capacity, policies can include improving regulations in the labor market that ease school-to-work transitions for fresh graduates. The labor market structure is facing severe problems in terms of having correct "signaling" between the supply (graduates from universities) and demand (businesses in the labor market) elements in the region (Faour, 2015); thus, enhancing institutional factors such as solving problems of meritocracy deficits in the labor market, is necessary to ensure the optimal human capital development, therefore enabling foreign investments to benefit from local talent and skills. Another policy direction would be improve financial resources for businesses by having cooperation between public and private educational and research institutions as that would increase the educational and technological capabilities of SMEs (Emine, 2012, p. 28). This cooperation between the two sectors would be essential to overcoming managerial barriers faced by local businesses; certain cooperative decisions may include working on creating efficient training programs in areas that employees need the most for instance. All in all, these policy implications will enhance the business climate to allow the local businesses to thrive in the region, while simultaneously multiplying the potential for growth by attracting FDIs with their growth-promoting spillovers.

7. Further Research

Although this research has provided sufficient evidence on the importance of improving the institutional framework in the Arab region, there are many shortages that may be taken into consideration in attempting future work in this research area. Further studies would include a larger sample size, a wider selection of variables of interest (especially proxies for determining factors of FDI spillover performance such as R&D investments in the Arab region), and may even include analyzing other dimensions aside from institutional quality, such as foreign firm characteristics, or the labor market supply and demand channels. Furthermore, additional analyses on comparing intra-industry data results within selected Arab economies may provide interesting insights as to which industry or sector would most benefit from FDI spillovers.

References

Alasarg, H. (2006). Enhancing Competitiveness for SMEs in the Arab Countries. *Ministry of Trade and Industry.* 1-20.

Al-Irani, M. (2007). Foreign Direct Investment and Economic Growth in the GCC Countries: A Causality Investigation Using Heterogeneous Panel Analysis. *Topics in Middle Eastern and North African Economies*. 9.

Al-Shammari, N. N., & Al-Sarhan, A. A. (2012). Foreign Direct Investment in Developing Asia according to the

Location Advantage Hypothesis. *Arab Journal of Administrative Sciences, 19*(3).

Al-Shammari, N., Al-Halaq, S., & Al-Shammari, D. (2016). Testing The FDI Hypothesis Of Location Advantage In The Case Of Kuwait. *Journal of Applied Business Research, 32*(2), 597. https://doi.org/10.19030/jabr.v32i2.9598

Amann, E., & Virmani, S. (2015). Foreign direct investment and reverse technology spillovers. *OECD Journal: Economic Studies, 2014*(1), 129-153. https://doi.org/10.1787/eco_studies-2014-5jxx56vcxn0n

Bayraktar, N. (2013). Foreign Direct investment and Investment Climate. *Procedia Economics and Finance*, 83-92. https://doi.org/10.1016/S2212-5671(13)00013-0

Borensztein, E., De Gregorio, J., & Lee, J. W. (1998). How does foreign direct investment affect economic growth? *Journal of International Economics, 45*(1), 115-135. https://doi.org/10.1016/S0022-1996(97)00033-0

DeMello, L. R., Jr. (1999). Foreign direct investment-led growth: Evidence from time series and panel data. *Oxford Economic Papers, 51*(1), 133-151. https://doi.org/10.1093/oep/51.1.133

El-Nakib, O. (2014, August 5). Economic Update: GCC: FDI down for fifth year in a row; Kuwait the top Arab investor. *NBK Economic Research.*

El-Wassal, K. (2012, December). Foreign Direct Investment and Economic Growth in Arab Countries (1970-2008): An Inquiry into Determinants of Growth Benefits. *Journal of Economic Development, 37*(4), 79-100.

Emine, D. (2012). Financial challenges that impede increasing the productivity of smes in arab region. *Journal of Contemporary Management*, 17-32.

Faour, M. (2015). Enhancing Employability: The Double Transition from Education to Work in the Arab World Proceedings of the Third Arab Development Symposium. *The International Bank for Reconstruction and Development, World Bank and the Arab Fund for Economic and Social Development*, 1-31.

Farole, T., & Winkler, D. (2014). Making Foreign Direct Investment Work for Sub-Saharan Africa: Local Spillovers and Competitiveness in Global Value Chains. *World Bank – Directions in Development*, 1-279.

Fu, X. (2008, March 27-28). Foreign Direct Investment, Absorptive Capacity and Regional Innovation Capabilities: Evidence from China. *OECD Global Forum on International Investment*.

Garcia-Bolivar, O. (2006). *Informal Economy: Is It A Problem, A Solution, or Both? The Perspectives of the Informal Business* (pp. 1-26). Northwestern University School of Law – Law and Economics Papers.

Hale, G., & Long, C. (2007, February). Are there Productivity Spillovers from Foreign Direct Investment in China? (pp. 1-33). *Federal Reserve Bank of San Francisco*.

Hussein, M. (2009, April). Impacts of Foreign Direct Investment on Economic Growth in the Gulf Cooperation Council (GCC) Countries. *International Review of Business Research Papers, 5*(3), 362-376.

Iqbal, Z., Masood, I., & Ramzan, M. (2013). Foreign Direct Investment and Economic Growth: Comparative Positon of Chinese and Indian Economies. *Journal of Business Studies Quarterly, 4*(3), 52-61.

Kinda, T. (2010). Investment Climate and FDI in Developing Countries: Firm-Level Evidence. *World Development, 38*(4), 498-513. https://doi.org/10.1016/j.worlddev.2009.12.001

Leamer, E. (1995). The Heckscher Ohlin Model in Theory and Practice. *Princeton Studies in International Finance, 77*, 1-50.

Mohamed, S. E., & Sidiropouls, M. G. (2010). Another Look at the Determinants of Foreign Direct Investment in MENA Countries: An Empirical Investigation. *Journal of Economic Development, 35*(2), 75-95.

Obwona, M. (2001). Determinants of FDI and their impact on economic growth in Uganda. *African Development Review, 13*, 46-81. https://doi.org/10.1111/1467-8268.00030

Paus, E., & Gallagher, K. (2007). Missing Links: Foreign Direct Investment and Industrial Development in Costa Rica and Mexico. *St Comp Int Dev., 43*, 53-80. https://doi.org/10.1007/s12116-007-9016-2

Perri, A., & Peruffo, E. (2016). Knowledge Spillovers from FDI: A Critical Review from the International Business Perspective. *International Journal of Management Reviews, 18*, 3-27. https://doi.org/10.1111/ijmr.12054

Romer, D. (2012). *Advanced macroeconomics* (4th ed.). New York: McGraw-Hill Companies.

Wang, H., Liu, H., Cao, Z., & Wang, B. (2016). FDI technology spillover and threshold effect of the technology gap: regional differences in the Chinese industrial sector. *SpringerPlus, 5*(1), 1. https://doi.org/10.1186/s40064-016-1962-6

Wang, Y., Ning, L., Li, J., & Prevezer, M. (2016). Foreign direct investment spillovers and the geography of innovation in Chinese regions: the role of regional industrial specialization and diversity. *Regional Studies, 50*(5), 805-822. https://doi.org/10.1080/00343404.2014.933800

Notes

Note 1. Data for the "ease of doing business" index is extracted from the World Bank's Doing Business Database. The index is based on rankings ranging from 1-189, with 1=easiest, 189=most difficult.

Note 2. The Economic Freedom overall index and ranking has many subcomponents that make up the final score. Detailed data on each of these subcomponents are in Appendix I.

Note 3. Growth models may be "labor-augmenting" with technology directly affecting labor, "capital-augmenting" with technology directly affecting capital, or "Hicks-neutral" with technological progress not affecting the balance of labor and capital in the production function (Romer, 2012, p. 10). For this research, we will be looking at general effects of technological progress not limited to affecting a specific input (i.e. Hicks-neutral).

Note 4. This firm-level empirical model is influenced by the methodology used by Hale and Long (2007).

Note 5. Arab countries included in the aggregate panel dataset are: Comoros, Djibouti, Egypt, Jordan, Lebanon, Mauritania, Morocco, Oman, Palestine, Saudi Arabia, Sudan and Tunisia (a total of 12 countries with the time series 1996-2014).

Note 6. Given the limited availability of data for the Arab region, we have selected 12 countries with data from 1996 till 2014, in order to present the most complete dataset, considering the variables of choice.

Note 7. Arab countries included in the firm-level analysis are: Egypt, Jordan, Lebanon, Mauritania and Tunisia.

Note 8. Estimated model adjusted R-squared value = 23.9%

Note 9. Total annual sales are used in some cases instead of net sales based on the availability of sufficient data.

Note 10. Estimated model adjusted R-squared value = 21.7%

Note 11. Estimated model adjusted R-squared value = 20.6%

Appendix A

Detailed Data on Institutional Constraints

Table A1. Components of the economic freedom index (Heritage Foundation, 2015)

Country Name	World Rank	2015 Score	Freedom Indices									
			Property Rights	Corruption	Fiscal	Government Spending	Business	Labor	Monetary	Trade	Investment	Financial
Algeria	157	48.9	30.0	36.0	80.0	38.7	66.6	50.5	71.2	60.8	25.0	30.0
Bahrain	18	73.4	60.0	48.0	99.9	73.1	72.5	83.1	74.2	78.6	65.0	80.0
Comoros	142	52.1	30.0	28.0	64.5	78.8	47.3	52.0	77.9	73.0	40.0	30.0
Djibouti	112	57.5	25.0	36.0	81.2	57.1	55.4	66.6	78.9	54.8	70.0	50.0
Egypt	124	55.2	20.0	32.0	85.8	68.0	65.4	53.6	67.4	70.0	50.0	40.0
Germany	16	73.8	90.0	78.0	60.8	40.1	88.2	51.2	81.5	88.0	90.0	70.0
Jordan	38	69.3	60.0	45.0	93.7	70.7	59.1	74.4	80.6	79.6	70.0	60.0
Kuwait	74	62.5	45.0	43.0	97.7	61.1	58.6	64.2	74.0	76.2	55.0	50.0
Lebanon	94	59.3	20.0	28.0	91.3	70.6	54.7	60.7	72.0	75.8	60.0	60.0
Mauritania	135	53.3	25.0	30.0	80.2	59.8	50.5	52.1	76.6	69.0	50.0	40.0
Morocco	89	60.1	40.0	37.0	70.9	61.0	68.8	33.4	81.9	78.2	70.0	60.0
Oman	56	66.7	55.0	47.0	98.5	44.2	68.4	76.1	76.2	76.8	65.0	60.0
Qatar	32	70.8	70.0	68.0	99.7	71.9	70.5	71.2	79.7	81.8	45.0	50.0
Saudi Arabia	77	62.1	40.0	46.0	99.7	61.9	65.8	72.7	68.4	76.4	40.0	50.0
Singapore	2	89.4	90.0	86.0	91.2	93.8	96.9	96.9	83.7	90.0	85.0	80.0
Tunisia	107	57.7	40.0	41.0	74.3	70.8	81.2	69.1	74.8	61.2	35.0	30.0

United Arab Emirates	25	72.4	55.0	69.0	99.5	85.8	74.7	83.8	83.8	82.4	40.0	50.0
United Kingdom	13	75.8	90.0	76.0	62.9	30.3	91.1	75.6	74.4	88.0	90.0	80.0
United States	12	76.2	80.0	73.0	66.2	51.8	88.8	98.5	76.6	87.0	70.0	70.0
Yemen	133	53.7	30.0	18.0	91.5	59.9	54.0	57.1	68.5	77.6	50.0	30.0

Appendix B

Extended Regional Aggregate Regression Results

Table B1. Interest variable: Government effectiveness perception; Adjusted R-Squared = 73.2%

IndVA	Coef.	Std. Err.	t	P>t	[95% Conf.	Interval]
FDI	2.97E-10	1.22E-10	2.43	0.017	5.43E-11	5.39E-10
GR	0.202432	0.276591	0.73	0.466	-0.3469822	0.7518471
GCF	0.11899	0.165189	0.72	0.473	-0.2091377	0.4471181
Trade	-0.2515	0.043562	-5.77	0.000	-0.3380264	-0.1649662
LP	0.001759	0.000142	12.4	0.000	0.0014774	0.0020411
Government Effectiveness	0.252465	0.058707	4.3	0.000	0.13585	0.369079
Constant	10.54104	4.398901	2.4	0.019	1.803168	19.27892

Table B2. Interest variable: Control of corruption; Adjusted R-Squared = 72.7%

IndVA	Coef.	Std. Err.	t	P>t	[95% Conf.	Interval]
FDI	2.89E-10	1.23E-10	2.36	0.020	4.57E-11	5.33E-10
GR	0.2046751	0.278436	0.74	0.464	-0.3484047	0.757755
GCF	0.0827088	0.165388	0.5	0.618	-0.2458136	0.411231
Trade	-0.2362001	0.042078	-5.61	0.000	-0.3197836	-0.15262
LP	0.001708	0.000144	11.84	0.000	0.0014215	0.001994
Control of Corruption	0.2310492	0.055737	4.15	0.000	0.1203348	0.341764
Constant	12.51077	4.324169	2.89	0.005	3.921342	21.10021

Table B3. Interest variable: Law perception; Adjusted R-Squared = 74.5%

IndVA	Coef.	Std. Err.	t	P>t	[95% Conf.	Interval]
FDI	2.41E-10	1.18E-10	2.04	0.044	6.44E-12	4.76E-10
GR	0.1953408	0.268384	0.73	0.469	-0.3377702	0.728452
GCF	0.2017705	0.162978	1.24	0.219	-0.1219653	0.525506
Trade	-0.2457661	0.039789	-6.18	0.000	-0.324802	-0.16673
LP	0.0016041	0.000143	11.2	0.000	0.0013196	0.001889
Perception of Law	0.2929845	0.058766	4.99	0.000	0.1762533	0.409716
Constant	8.727032	4.345944	2.01	0.048	0.0943488	17.35972

Table B4. Interest variable: Voice accountability perception; Adjusted R-Squared = 69.7%

IndVA	Coef.	Std. Err.	t	P>t	[95% Conf.	Interval]
FDI	3.55E-10	1.35E-10	2.63	0.010	8.72E-11	6.22E-10
GR	0.1726332	0.293934	0.59	0.558	-0.4112301	0.756496
GCF	0.0560898	0.173907	0.32	0.748	-0.2893558	0.401535
Trade	-0.2074419	0.046146	-4.5	0.000	-0.2991043	-0.11578
LP	0.0020156	0.000171	11.77	0.000	0.0016753	0.002356
Voice Accountability	0.2566349	0.09995	2.57	0.012	0.0580962	0.455174
Constant	11.6389	4.760816	2.44	0.016	2.182126	21.09568

12

Research on Quantitative Trading Strategy Based on Neural Network Algorithm and Fisher Linear Discriminant

Zi-Yu Li[1], Yuan-Biao Zhang[1,2], Jia-Yu Zhong[1], Xiao-Xu Yan[1] & Xin-Guang Lv[2]

[1] Innovation Practice Base of Mathematical Modeling, Electrical and Information College of Jinan University, Zhuhai, China

[2] Key Laboratory of Product Packaging and Logistics of Guangdong Higher Education Institutes, Jinan University, Zhuhai, China

Correspondence: Yuan-Biao Zhang, Innovation Practice Base of Mathematical Modeling, Electrical and Information College of Jinan University, Zhuhai 519070, China. E-mail: zybt@jnu.edu.cn

Abstract

Based on the trend background of financial development in China in recent years, and statistical analysis of trend line, this paper establishes the quantitative trading strategy through the BP Neural Network Algorithm and the Fisher Linear Discriminant. Firstly, the data is linearly regressed into equal-length trend lines and the slope is fuzzified to build the matrix of upward trend and downward trend. And then use BP Neural Network Algorithm and Fisher Linear Discriminant to carry on the price forecast respectively and take transaction behavior, and correspondingly we take Shanghai and Shenzhen 300 stock index futures as an example to carry on the back test. The result shows that, firstly, the initial price trend is well retained by fitting; secondly, the profitability and risk control ability of the trading system are improved through the training optimization of Neural Network and Fisher Linear Discriminant.

Keywords: neural network algorithm, fisher linear discriminant, quantitative trading

1. Introduction

1.1 Background Description

Quantitative trading strategy is an innovative analytical method combining mathematical theory with financial data, on which, with the aid of the swift operation of the computer, subjective judgment of individuals in the market can be avoided. They break through human's limit in time and space and control the risk accurately and effectively. These incomparable advantages have made it develop along with the rapid development of the global economy and the continuous integration, making it a major trading model with great potential.

Quantitative investing, fundamental analysis and technical analysis are the most important methods so that they are widely used in overseas investment markets. More and more people begin to accept and try a variety of strategies, making it favorable in China's market prospects.

In the early history of quantitative trading, statistical model once took a dominant position. It shows the volatility of prices by exploring and analyzing financial data. Various technical indexes were also applied to assess risks, identify trends and measure volatility and other aspects. However, because the selected indicators are simple and the setup model is too subjective, there was some inaccuracy in the back test. Later the emergence of a series of intelligent algorithm promoted the development of quantitative trading. Intelligent algorithm can be learned and heavily trained to explore the non-linear relationship between the variables, thus price forecast can be possible. It is very meaningful to construct the quantitative strategy.

1.2 Relevant Scholarship

Quantitative investment develops with the development of quantitative finance. Sharper (1964) developed Capital Asset Pricing Model in 1964. Then it serves as the basic theory in the financial world; Malkiel and MaFama (1970) put forward the famous Efficient Markets Hypothesis in 1970, that is, if asset prices complete reflect the available information in a stock market, then the market is efficient. It divides the market into three types: weakly efficient, semi-strong and strong effective. In weak form market, it is meaningless to analyze the technical index which is based on historical data. Fama and Blume (1966), Jensen and Benington (1970) verified the moving average and relative strength in American stock market, but didn't get more returns than that obtained via buy- and – hold strategy. With the financial innovation, Black and Scholes built the Option Pricing Model of derivative commodities in 1973. Ross (1976) established Arbitrage Pricing Theory, and Multi-factor Asset Pricing for choosing shares can be a typical theory of APT.

In the 1990s financial economists focused more on controlling financial risk. Efficient Markets Hypothesis was queried by more people. Using the Dow Jones index, Brock (1992) tested the moving average (MA) and the trading price range model without considering trading costs. The periodic rising trend was captured and there came returns. Burgess (1999) raised the covariate arbitrage, that is, open a position when the price spread (residual of co-integration equation) of a stock deviates to a degree. Buy in an undervalued stock and sell an overvalued stock; close position with gains when the price spread returns to normalcy. Madhavan (2002) developed VMA strategy, which synthesizes price prediction, mean-reversion and trend tracker to forecast the short-term trend of a subject matter with the help of information about volumes. Stefano Fiorenzani (2006) systematically expounded the risk control in quantitative trading. He argued that risk, with advanced mathematical and statistical methods involved, could be controlled.

The birth of intelligent algorithm is progress for constructing quantitative trading strategy. Franklin Allen (1999) achieved the best trading rules based on Genetic Algorithm; Tak-chung Fu (2013) found the best stock portfolio among many technical indexes. Having compared FF three factor linear model and the predicting capacity of neural network, Cao and others (2005) proved the latter is better; Liao and Wang (2010) built Neural Network Model on the basis of valid function at random time and Brownian Movement. The input variables are trading prices and volumes, then the volatility of A-share index, B-share index of Shanghai Stock Exchange and four overseas stock indexes are studied and forecast. The data-fitting is ideal. Youngohc Yoon (1993) analyzed and compared Artificial Neural Network and Fisher Linear Discriminant. Fisher Linear Discriminant is more applied to hereditary and image recognition. This paper attempts to apply this feature extraction method to quantitative trading strategy.

1.3 Research Design

In this paper, we will build a quantitative trading strategy dominated by intelligent algorithm, combined with statistical methods. Take Shanghai and Shenzhen 300 stock index futures data as an example, the K-line data is linear regression fitted to make it become an equal-length trend line. Then the slope of the trend lines is encoded based on fuzzy process, and next, according to a trade rule, an uptrend matrix or a downtrend matrix is constructed by sliding window method to analyze the features of K lines before rising and declining. Then Neural Network Algorithm and Fisher Linear Discriminate were introduced to predict the price trend of stock index futures and form trading rules. This paper consists of five parts: the first part is introduction; the second part focuses on the idea and principle of quantitative trading strategy construction, as well as BP Neural Network Algorithm and Fisher Linear Discriminant method for training optimization; the third part is about the prediction and empirical test about Shanghai and Shenzhen 300 stock index futures based on the quantitative trading strategy; the fourth part is discussion about the results; the fifth part is conclusion.

2. Method

This paper takes advantage of statistical analysis of trend line and respectively base on the BP Neural Network Algorithm and the Fisher Linear Discriminant to establish the quantitative trading strategy to do a guide for the stock index futures trading.

2.1 Model Introduction

The following two methods BP Neural Network Algorithm and Fisher Linear Discriminant will be introduced respectively.

2.1.1 BP Neural Network Algorithm

Artificial Neural Network (ANNs) is an artificial intelligence method with a powerful learning ability of a strong approximation to nonlinear continuous function. It is successfully applied in economic and financial field (Pao, 2006). It consists of a series of inter-connected neurons, each of which performs two calculations and makes linear combination of variables at the input. At the output the results of the non-linear computation is given and connected to next neuron, on the basis of which the connecting weight between neurons needs to be determined. Back-propagation algorithm is a commonly used optimizing algorithm that operates connecting weights. Training samples are fit through multiple iterations to obtain the smallest prediction standard error (Zhong-Zhi, 2009).

2.1.2 Fisher Linear Discriminant

Fisher Linear Discriminant is a classic pattern recognition algorithm. It was introduced into pattern recognition and artificial intelligence by Belhumeur in 1996. His basic idea is: projecting high dimensional pattern samples over optimal discriminant vectors space to extract classified information and reduce the dimensions of eigenspace. After being projected, the maximum inter-class distance and the minimum in-class distance in the subspace, and therefore it is an effective feature extraction method (Zhao-Qi & Xue-Gong, 2000). The specific process is as follows (Fisher, 1936):

First, we establish the mapping of the dimension space d to the 1-dimensional space: for the samples $X_1, X_2, \ldots, X_n$, in the d-dimension sample space X, there is a class n_1 that belongs to the class W_1 and forms a subset Y_1; a class n_2 that belongs to the class W_2 and forms a subset Y_2. Then:

$$y_i = \omega^T X_k \quad k = 1, 2, \cdots, n; i = 1, 2$$

Several basic parameters are then defined:

(a)Parameters in the d-dimension sample space X. The mean vector of each sample is defined as:

$$m_i = \frac{1}{n_i} \sum_{x_k \in Y_i} X_k \quad i = 1, 2$$

The in-class sample scatter matrix S_i and total in-class scatter matrix S_w are:

$$S_i = \sum_{x_k \in Y_i} (X_k - m_i)(X_k - m_i)^T \quad i = 1, 2$$

$$S_w = S_1 + S_2$$

The inter-class sample scatter matrix S_b is:

$$S_b = (m_1 - m_2)(m_1 - m_2)^T$$

(b)Parameters in the 1-dimension sample space Y. The mean vector of each sample is defined as:

$$\tilde{m}_i = \frac{1}{n_i} \sum_{x_k \in Y_i} y \quad i = 1, 2$$

The in-class sample dispersion and total intra-class dispersion are:

$$\tilde{S}_i^2 = \sum_{x_k \in Y_i} (y - \tilde{m}_i)^2 \quad i = 1, 2$$

$$\tilde{S}_w = S_1^2 + S_2^2$$

In summary, the definition of Fisher Discriminant criteria function is:

$$J_F(\omega) = \frac{(\tilde{m}_1 - \tilde{m}_2)^2}{\tilde{S}_1^2 + \tilde{S}_2^2}$$

So look for the maximum value, in other words, the numerator is as large as possible and the denominator is as small as possible. In fact, it can be obtained:

$$\omega^* = S_\omega^{-1}(m_1 - m_2)$$

Because of the prior probability:

$$p_1 = p_2 = \frac{1}{2}$$

The threshold is chosen to be:

$$y_0 = \frac{(\tilde{m}_1 + \tilde{m}_2)}{2}$$

For any given unknown eigenvector X, the projection point is calculated in

$$y = \omega^{*T} X$$

When $y > y_0$, $X \in W_1$, the stock index futures belong to class A, which is up trend;

When $y < y_0$, $X \in W_2$, the stock index futures belong to class B, which is falling trend.

2.2 Description of the Principle

Because K-line data is random, massive and changeable, statistical method is introduced to fit the data, making it a combination of isometric trend line. Thus the data of K-line can be characterized. The angle range of the processed trend line is between -90° and 90°, then the scope is encoded in a fuzzy process. With a specific level to divide the slope of the isometric trend line and according to a rule using the sliding window method, an uptrend matrix and a downtrend are built, on the basis of which the changing trend of price in a period before stock index futures rise or decline can be found, therefore the potential rules of rising and falling are analyzed. Finally, BP Neural Network and Fisher Linear Discriminant are used to study and train the statistical data. Based on this, the price trend forecast of stock index futures is carried out. The process of building Quantitative Trading Strategy is as follows:

2.2.1 Linear Regression Fitting

MATLAB programming software applied, The K-line data is constructed by linear regression fitting every m time units (minutes), the first n time units are taken for fitting to build trend line combination, the trend line combination total number is:

$$\lambda = \frac{m}{n}$$

The number of the i trend line is:

$$x_i = x_{i-1} + 1 \qquad i = 1, 2, \cdots, \lambda$$

2.2.2 Fuzzy Encoding

After being fitted, the angle range of the trend line is between -90° and 90°, the uptrend scope's angle range is (0,90°), the downtrend scope's angle range is (-90°,0). The rules for fuzzy code is shown in Table 1.

Table 1. Fuzzy encoding rules

Rank code	Uptrend 1	Uptrend 2	...	Uptrend R	Downtrend R+1	Downtrend R+2	...
Angle range	$0 \sim \theta_1$	$\theta_1 \sim \theta_2$	...	$\theta_r \sim 90°$	$90° \sim \theta_{r+1}$	$\theta_{r+1} \sim \theta_{r+2}$	...
Slope range	$0 \sim \tan\theta_1$	$\tan\theta_1 \sim \tan\theta_2$	...	$\tan\theta_r \sim +\infty$	$-\infty \sim \tan\theta_{r+!}$	$\tan\theta_{r+1} \sim \tan\theta_{r+2}$	...

2.2.3 Statistics

With a sliding window method, starting from the first x_i trend line, we count the preceding trend line code of section k. Automatically slide backwards, from the first x_{i+1} trend line with the trend line of section k before is encoded, and so on to build the matrix X, namely:

$$X = \begin{bmatrix} x_1 & x_2 & \cdots & x_k \\ x_2 & x_3 & \cdots & x_{k+1} \\ \vdots & \vdots & \cdots & \vdots \\ x_{\lambda-k+1} & x_{\lambda-k+2} & \cdots & x_\lambda \end{bmatrix}$$

If the first x_i trend line is larger than the specified rising level, we count the preceding trend line code of section k and then the upward trend coding matrix is constructed as the input layer which judges the rising trend;

If the first x_i trend line is smaller than the specified falling level, we count the preceding trend line code of section k and then the downward trend coding matrix is constructed as the input layer which judges the falling trend.

2.2.4 Study and Training

(a) Training based on BP Neural Network

With MATLAB software, setting parameters of neural network and the training can be realized. For the rising matrix, the output layer corresponds to the value of 1, and for the declining matrix, the output layer corresponds to the value is 0, that is, 1 indicates upward trend, 0 indicates the downward trend.

(b) Training based on Fisher Linear Discriminant

The encoded "uptrend" matrix and "downtrend" matrix determine the category: the upward trend is type 1, and the downward trend is type 0. They can serve as the basis for the guidance of trading operations.

3. Empirical Study

Then this paper will use CSI 300 stock index futures to do a case study to verify the correctness of the quantitative trading strategy.

3.1 Data Description

The research focuses on one-minute K-line data of CFFE 300 stock index futures, which are standard and processed financial data. They were from the Second Guangdong College Students Financial Modeling Competition and Guangdong Shanghai Friendship Competition. The interval of the data was from April 16th, 2010 to December 31st, 2013. The fee is charged bilaterally (Open and close positions) by 1.5%.

With MATLAB programming software, a price chart for per minute in three years of stock index futures that had low frequency trading is made, as is shown in Figure 1. It clearly shows that there are many inflection points and trends.

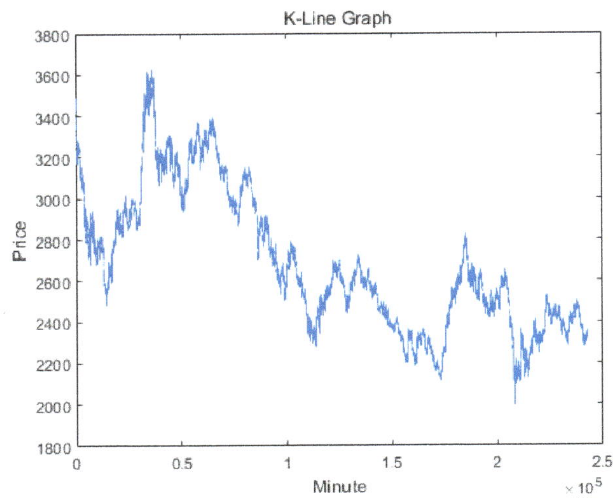

Figure 1. The K-line of stock index futures

3.2 Parameters Determination

MATLAB programming software applied, the K-line data of per 40 time units (minute) is fitted in linear regression. Then the first 160000 time units (minutes) are fitted. The fitting results for the first 4000 time units are shown in Figure 2.

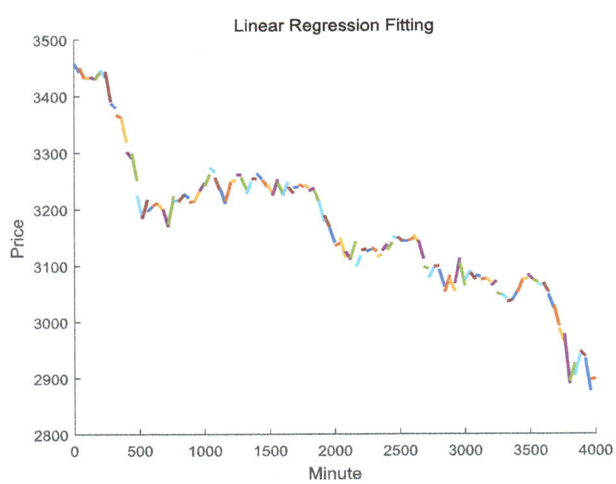

Figure 2. Linear regression of trend line fitting

In Figure 2, the price trend well fits the K-line of stock index futures with times developing, both reflect that with time going, the K-line of stock index futures is on a downward trend. Therefore it is practical to characterize the trend of stock index futures with an isometric line segment of linear regression.

The slope code grade of the isometric trend line combination is divided into uptrend 1 (0~0.536), uptrend 2 (0.536~1.732), uptrend 3 (1.732~+∞), downtrend 4 (-∞~-1.732), downtrend 5 (-1.732~-0.536), downtrend 6 (-0.536~0). With a sliding window method and from the first 11 trend line, if the code grade of trend-line is larger than rising level of uptrend 1, we count the preceding trend line code of section 10 and then the upward trend coding matrix is constructed; Similarly, if the code grade of trend-line is smaller than falling level of downtrend 6, we count the preceding trend line code of section 10 and then the downward trend coding matrix is constructed.

3.3 Conservatism Test

The K- line data following 160000 time units (minute) for the 1-minute, 5-minute, 10-minute, 50-minute, and 100-minute periods trading are respectively taken as an interval to test the robustness of quantitative trading strategy.

- 1-minute trading profit results are shown in Figure 3:

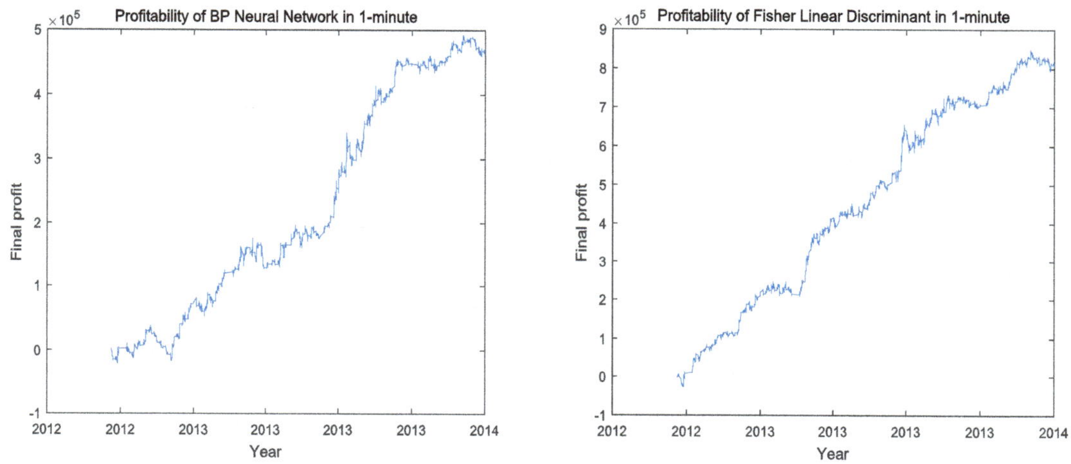

(a) Returns on BP (b) Returns on Fisher

Figure 3. Final profit of BP Neural Network and Fisher Linear Discriminant at 1-minute interval

- 5-minute trading profit results are shown in Figure 4:

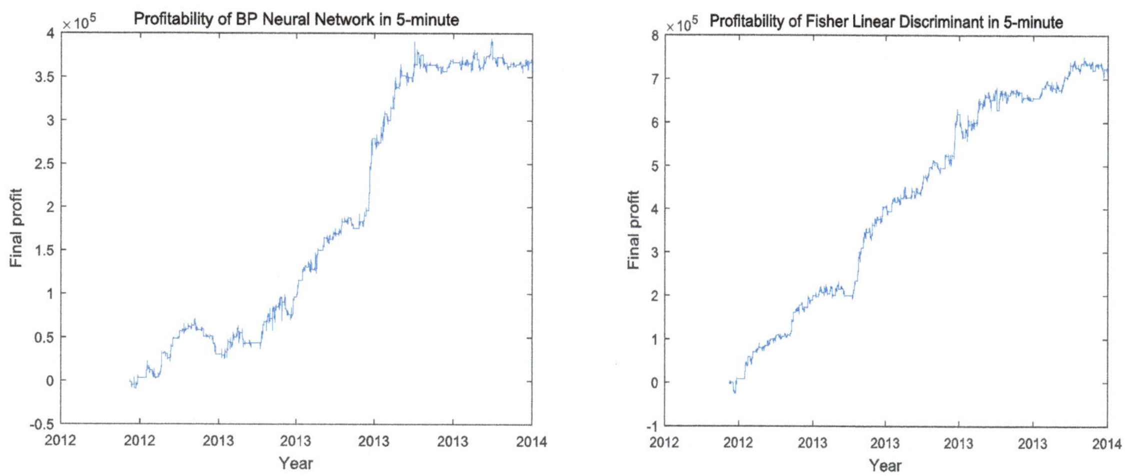

(a) Returns on BP (b) Returns on Fisher

Figure 4. Final profit of BP neural network and fisher linear discriminant at 5-minute interval

- 10-minute trading profit results are shown in Figure 5:

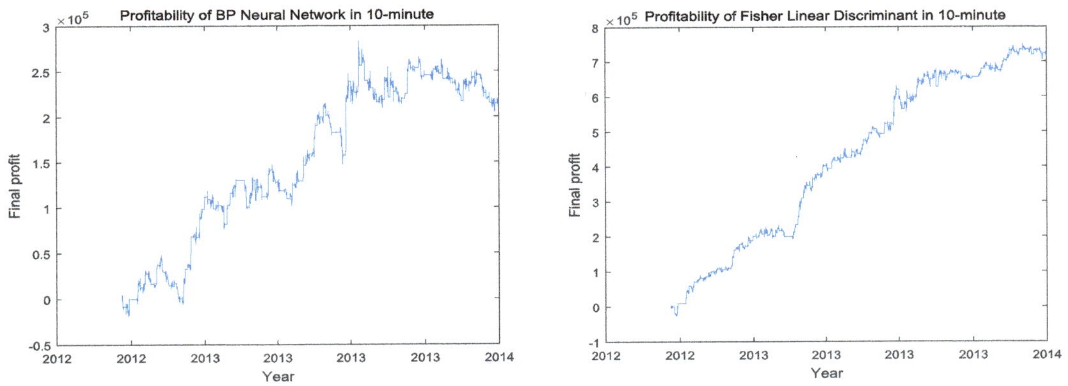

(a) Returns on BP (b) Returns on Fisher

Figure 5. Final profit of BP neural network and fisher linear discriminant at 10-minute interval

- 30-minute trading profit results are shown in Figure 6:

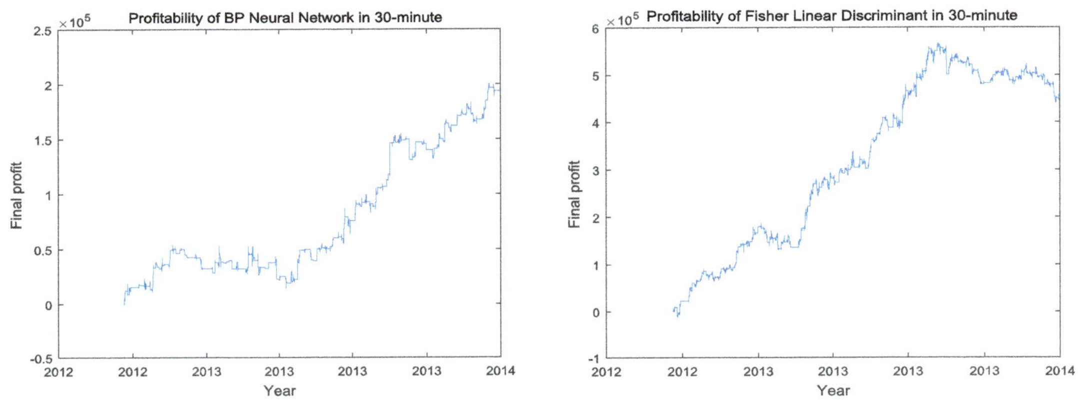

(a) Returns on BP (b) Returns on Fisher

Figure 6. Final profit of BP neural network and fisher linear discriminant at 30-minute interval

- 60-minute trading profit results are shown in Figure 7:

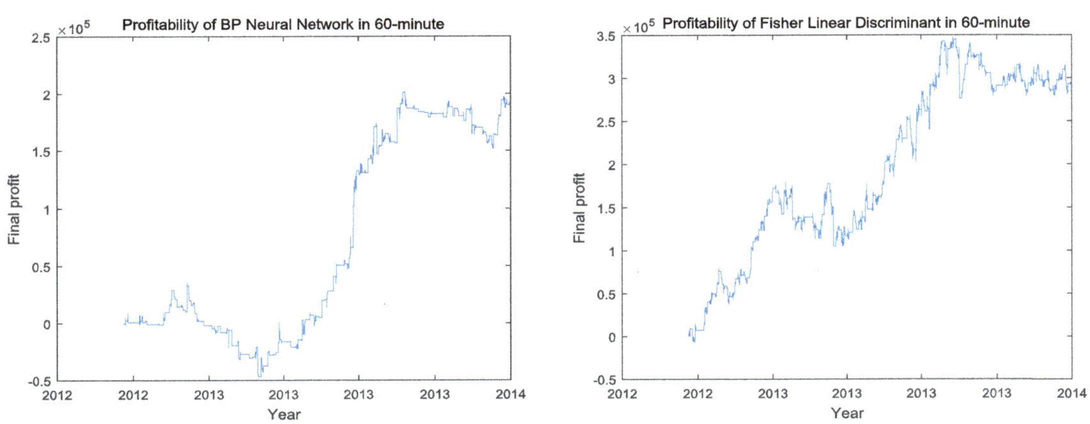

(a) Returns on BP (b) Returns on Fisher

Figure 7. Final profit of BP neural network and fisher linear discriminant at 60-minute interval

It can be seen from the Figure 3, 4, 5, 6, 7 that, in general, the BP Neural Network strategy and the Fisher Linear Discriminant strategy all have an increasing trend with time, which indicates that the strategy has a certain robustness. And as the trading time period gradually increases, the rising trend of the profit situation also increases gradually, and the instability increases.

Because of the randomness of the BP Neural Network algorithm, the profit graph of the BP Neural Network is different at different time, and the Fisher Linear Discriminant method avoids the randomness, and has the characteristics of high income and low risk. The result is superior to the BP Neural Network strategy.

4. Discussion

The results from the comparison between the BP Neural Network Strategy and the Fisher Linear Discriminant strategy for the 1-minute, 5-minute, 10-minute, 30-minute, and 60-minute periods trading are respectively shown in the following Table 2:

Table 2. The comparison between BP neural network algorithm and fisher linear discriminant

Trading time period		Maximum retracement rate	Income to risk ratio	Transactions	Final profit
1-minute	BP	11.88%	1.97	309	469620
	Fisher	8.96%	2.62	920	803620
5-minute	BP	12.93%	1.81	382	358370
	Fisher	11.22%	2.26	920	714400
10-minute	BP	35.88%	0.65	192	217790
	Fisher	10.31%	2.27	920	714220
30-minute	BP	21.12%	1.11	177	191570
	Fisher	28.18%	0.83	920	453140
60-minute	BP	42.96%	0.55	145	192010
	Fisher	25.66%	0.91	677	289370

As is shown in Table 2 in general, the BP Neural Network Algorithm has higher risk and less stable income in different trading time periods, the Fisher Linear Discriminant has the relative characteristics of high returns and low risk, then more trades can be made, hence the returns are better.

BP Neural Network strategy to deal with different time periods respectively, the randomness is strong, and the income risk is unstable, in practice, the operation is weak. The Fisher Linear Discriminant strategy is relatively more regular and stable performance, when it trades within a period of 10-minute, the number of transactions is more and the income risk ratio is greater than 2, and the profit performance is good. After a period of 10-minute in the back of the test performance is slightly weaker than 10 minutes, but its profitability and transaction number are considerable, that is to prove that this strategy has a certain degree of robustness.

5. Conclusion

Based on statistical analysis, having BP Neural Network Algorithm and Fisher linear Discriminate involved, quantitative trading strategy is constructed. It carries on the back test of Shanghai and Shenzhen 300 stock index futures and can well predicts the changing price trend of stock index futures. During the process of the statistical analysis, the data are linear regression fitted, making it a combination of isometric trend line to characterize the characteristics of K-line data, and the slope range is fuzzified to encode it. With a certain level, The slope range and the level of division can be adjusted several parameters, which can be built up and down trend encoding matrix.

As the intelligent algorithm has a strong learning and training capacity, finally, the BP Neural Network and the Fisher Linear Discriminant are used to analyze the potential characteristics of the stock index futures before and after the rise or fall. In the empirical study, it is proved that the model has strong robustness. Based on the transaction cost, the Fisher Linear Discriminant strategy is relatively more objective returns.

Currently financial innovation in Chinese capital market is developing quickly. With more and more stock index futures and a short selling mechanism entering the stock market, the trading ideas and techniques of investors will change too. Quantitative trading strategy will play a vital part and various trading strategies will be established. Quantitative trading strategy presented in this paper can discover the declining trend of stock index futures by introducing a short selling mechanism, and can avoid the problem of overfitting and reduce the waste of time and cost. Its profitability and risk control can be ensured. In the following study, macroeconomic index and company's financial index can be included in stock pricing forecast to further optimize setting a stop-loss and stop-profit point, making the strategy more practical.

Acknowledgments

Thanks to my teacher Yuan-Biao Zhang and my classmates Jia-Yu Zhong, Xiao-Xu Yang for their support and help, and acknowledge the encouragement by my good friend Dong-Mei Liu. In the preparation of the manuscript, I encountered many problems, but tried to solve it with the help of them and learned a lot of things. I hope to work together with my friends and teachers to achieve better results.

References

Allen, F., & Karjalainen, R. (1999). Using Genetic Algorithms to Find Technical Trading Rules (Revision of 20-93) (Vol. 51, pp. 245-271). Wharton School Rodney L. White Center for Financial Research.

Black, F., & Scholes, M. (1973). The pricing of options and corporate liabilities. *Journal of Political Economy, 81*(3), 637-54. https://doi.org/10.1086/260062

Brock, W., Lakonishok, J., & Lebaron, B. (1992). Simple technical trading rules and the stochastic properties of stock returns. *The Journal of Finance, 47*(5), 1731-1764. https://doi.org/10.1111/j.1540-6261.1992.tb04681.x

Cao, Q., Leggio, K. B., & Schniederjans, M. J. (2005). A comparison between fama and french's model and artificial neural networks in predicting the chinese stock market. *Computers & Operations Research, 32*(10), 2499-2512. http://dx.doi.org/10.1016/j.cor.2004.03.015

Fama, E. F., & Blume, M. E. (1965). Filter rules and stock-market trading. *Journal of Business, 39*(S1), 226. https://doi.org/10.1086/294849

Fiorenzani, S. (2006). *Quantitative methods for electricity trading and risk management: Advanced mathematical and statistical methods for energy finance.* Palgrave Macmillan. https://doi.org/10.1057/9780230598348

Fisher, R. A. (1936). The use of multiple measurements in taxonomic problems. *Annals of Human Genetics, 7*(2), 179-188. http://dx.doi.org/10.1111/j.1469-1809.1936.tb02137.x

Fu, T. C., Chung, C. P., & Chung, F. L. (2013). Adopting genetic algorithms for technical analysis and portfolio management. *Computers & Mathematics with Applications, 66*(10), 1743-1757. http://dx.doi.org/10.1016/j.camwa.2013.08.012

Madhavan, A. N. (2002). VWAP strategies. *Trading, 2002*(1), 32-39.

Malkiel, B. G., & Fama, E. F. (1970). Efficient capital markets: A review of theory and empirical work. *The Journal of Finance, 25*(2), 383-417. https://doi.org/10.1111/j.1540-6261.1970.tb00518.x

Pao, H. T. (2006). Comparing linear and nonlinear forecasts for taiwan's electricity consumption. *Energy, 31*(12), 2129-2141. http://dx.doi.org/10.1016/j.energy.2005.08.010

Ross, S. A. (1976). *The arbitrage theory of capital asset pricing* (Vol. 13, pp. 341-360). Wharton School Rodney L. White Center for Financial Research. https://doi.org/10.1016/0022-0531(76)90046-6

Sharpe, W. F. (1964). Capital asset prices: A theory of market equilibrium under conditions of risk. *The Journal of Finance, 19*(3), 425-442. https://doi.org/10.1515/jbvela-2013-0019. https://doi.org/10.1111/j.1540-6261.1964.tb02865.x

Vassar, R., Bennett, B. D., Babukhan, S., Kahn, S., Mendiaz, E. A., & Denis, P. et al. (1999). Secretase cleavage of alzheimer's amyloid precursor protein by the transmembrane. *Science, 286*(5440), 735-41. https://doi.org/10.1126/science.286.5440.735

Xuan-Cheng, W. (2014). Construct Intelligent Quantitative Trading Systems Based on LASSO and ANNs-A Case Study of CSI300 Futures. *Investment Research,* (9), 23-39.

Yoon, Y., Swales, G., & Margavio, T. M. (1993). A comparison of discriminant analysis versus artificial neural networks. *Journal of the Operational Research Society, 44*(1), 51-60. http://dx.doi.org/10.1057/jors.1993.6

Zhao-Qi, B., & Xue-Gong, Z. (2000). *Pattern Recognition.* Tsinghua University Press.

Zhe, L., & Wang, J. (2010). Forecasting model of global stock index by stochastic time effective neural network. *Expert Systems with Applications, 37*(1), 834-841. http://dx.doi.org/10.1016/j.eswa.2009.05.086

Zhong-Zhi, S. (2009). Neural Network.

13

Improvement and Test of Stock Index Futures Trading Model Based on Bollinger Bands

Xiao-Xu Yan[1], Yuan-Biao Zhang[1, 2], Xin-Kun Lv[1] & Zi-Yu Li[1]

[1] Innovation Practice Base of Mathematical Modeling, Electrical and Information College of Jinan University, Zhuhai, China

[2] Key Laboratory of Product Packaging and Logistics of Guangdong Higher Education Institutes, Jinan University, Zhuhai, China

Correspondence: Yuan-Biao Zhang, Innovation Practice Base of Mathematical Modeling, Electrical and Information College of Jinan University, Zhuhai 519070, China. E-mail: zybt@jnu.edu.cn

Abstract

Bollinger Bands trading model is an important strategy in program trading. But in practice, the trade model based on the traditional Bollinger Bands theory has great flaws such as "over-sensitive" flaw, incomplete transaction stop-loss, and the adaptability of the model's basic parameters is poor. In this paper, the empirical research method is used to analyze the shortcomings of the traditional Bollinger Bands transaction model and put forward improved methods. Accordingly, we introduce the price speed, improve the stop-loss rules, and adjust the basic parameters to improve the model. The improved trading model is tested with the data of Shanghai and Shenzhen stock index futures. The result showed that the modified Bollinger Bands transaction model has strong profitability and low risk, which is instructive to the practice of stock index futures.

Keywords: bollinger bands, stock index futures, program trading, flaws, improved methods

1. Introduction

1.1 Introduce the Problem

Stock index futures refers to the stock index as the subject matter of standardized futures contracts, the two sides agree upon a specific date in the future and follow the pre-determined size of the stock price index for the sale of the underlying index. Since Kansas Futures Exchange has developed a value index futures contract in February 1982, Stock index futures have been increasingly valued by all kinds of investors, the scale of the transaction has been expanding rapidly and the variety of trading has been increasing. At present, the stock index futures have become the world's largest futures trading varieties. Shanghai and Shenzhen 300 stock index futures (CSI300) market has been running in China for more than six years. It is active during these years and provides researchers with lots of real and valuable market data.

With the rise and gradual development of the stock index futures market, in order to obtain greater profits and hedging, the major trading institutions and investors began to conduct in-depth research and focus on discovering more complex trading strategies. However, the implementation of most trading strategies must rely on the implementation of programmatic transactions. In foreign markets, as the main trading mode in the securities market, programmatic transactions have gradually replaced ordinary artificial trading. Due to the backward development of China's financial market, there is a certain gap on the development of program trading between America and European countries. Development of programming trading can not only help to achieve the risk management and optimize investment combination, but make full use of the advantages of speed in the process of trading to improve the market efficiency.

According to the transaction mechanism, the programmed trading strategy model is divided into technical indicator model and forecasting model. The technical indicator model has wider application because of its high accuracy. Among them, the Bollinger Bands model has become one of the most widely used trading models in the capital market because of its flexibility and adaptability. It plays an important role in the practice of Chineese and international securities exchange market.The Bollinger Bands model has beed widely ued for about 30 years. However, in the practice of different markets, some defects of traditonal model appeared gradually. Traditional

Bollinger Bands model needs to be improved to adapt to different markets.

1.2 Describe Relevant Scholarship

At present, the research on Bollinger Bands trading model is relatively mature in the world . Bollinger Bands theory was first proposed by John Bollingerin the 1980s to measure the level of stock prices (John, 2001). Then the research on Bollinger Bands has become popular around the world, and the research scope is very extensive.After comparing the profitability of the moving average and Bollinger Bands model were compared, Joseph Man-Joe Leung and TerenceTai-Leung Chong finds that Bollinger Bands model is more capable to capture sudden price fluctuations, but the profitability is lower than the moving average model (Joseph & Terence, 2003). According to OD Williams (2006), Bollinger Bands could capture the abrupt fluctuation of the price level and profits level of the model could be affected by the adjustment of its input. According to Lento (2007), by testing the profitability of the Bollinger Bands model, she found that the profitability of the Bollinger Bands model might not be as good as the strategy of buying and holding when the transaction costs were adjusted. Then, Bollinger Bands model was put forward to be applied to forecast stock price trend widely and its application value was proved (K. Senthamarai, 2010). Basing on the previous research, some scholars began to propose the strategy to improve the traditional model. Bouble-Bollinger Bands theory compensated the defects of the traditional Bollinger Bands model and could more accurately judge the running trend of the security price (Kathy, 2015).

The research on Bollinger trading model is few in China, scholars mainly analyzed the theory framework of the Bollinger Bands and put forward the use of this index in China's securities market.The scientific rigor of the Bollinger Bands its use limitations in China's securities market were first explained in 2001 (Deng, 2001). According to Shenjun, Qing and Yunbo (2011), the K line and Bollinger Bands could be used as the basic tool to determine and predicte the Xiamen real estate cycle fluctuations and price trends. As the Chinese markets are quite different from the foreign, some scholars attempted to evaluate the validity of the Bollinger Bands based on the Shanghai Composite Index.The results shows that the Bollinger Bands model is effective in Chinese market (Jusheng, Yixuan, & Wei, 2014). As we can see, the domestic and foreign scholars mainly pay attention to the profitability of Bollinger Bands theory and its application research. The study on the improvement of Bollinger trading model and the application of Bollinger Bands trading model in stock index futures are few.

1.3 Frame of Paper

This paper first builds the Bollinger Bands transaction model based on the traditional Bollinger Bands theory, then analyzes its shortcomings and finds out the improvement strategy. Finally, we use the one-minute K-line data of CSI300 market from 2010 to 2013 to test the improved Bollinger Bands model and put forward the rationalization suggestion according to the practice of China's stock index futures market.

2. Bollinger Bands Model and Its Shortcomings

2.1 Theory of Bollinger Bands

Bollinger Bands was first designed by the stock analyst John Bollinger in USA in the actual transaction based on statistical principles. It is one of the technical indicators commonly used in the capital market. Bollinger Bands is put forward according to the philosophy of relativity, Bollinger argued that stock prices were relative rather than absolute, so he set a "channel" (consisting of upper, middle and lower tracks), which the price of stock fluctuates around. He hoped that through this "channel" on the stock price, relatively high and low of the prices could be defined. That is to say when the stock traverses the trajectory, the stock price is relatively high. On the contrary, when the stock price fell below the trajectory, the stock price is relative low. Therefore, the rationality of "channel" design rationality is the key to the rationality of the design of Bollinger bands.

Weighted moving average, moving Average, and exponential smoothing average line, etc. can be used as the trajectory of Bollinger Bands. Bollinger validated these different methods through statistical methods. The results show that the weighted average line and the exponential smoothing average line are more complex, but their promotion to grasp the price trends is not obvious. So, the trajectory of the Bollinger Bands is generally defined by the moving average. The main line of traditional Bollinger Bands is decided by the 20-day moving average. Of course, investors in the practical application can change the time parameter according to the actual situation. The width of the Bollinger "channel" is determined by the standard deviation. The upper trajectory is a multiple of the standard deviation of the stock price, and the lower trajectory is the same multiple of the standard deviation of the stock price minus the trajectory. From a statistical point of view, when the multiples of 2, the probability of the stock price between the upper and lower trajectory is more than 95%. In other words, when the stock price is outside the trajectory, we believe that the corresponding high or low stock price is reasonable. This shows that the design of Bollinger "channel" is reasonable. The relationship between Bandwidth and statistical probability is shown in Table 1.

Table 1. Relationship between bandwidth and statistical probability

width of Bollinger Bands	statistical probability
1.7 times the standard deviation	More than 90%
2 times the standard deviation	More than 95%
2.3 times the standard deviation	More than 97%

2.2 Basic Indicators of Bollinger Bands

Calculation of N-minute moving average:

$$MA = \frac{\sum_{i=1}^{N} c_i}{N} \tag{1}$$

Where, N is the period of the moving average, C_i is the closing price of the *i-th* minute.

Calculation of N-minute of standard deviation of the price.

$$SD = \sqrt{\frac{\sum_{i=1}^{N} (c_i - MA)^2}{N}} \tag{2}$$

Calculation of the trajectory,

$$\begin{aligned} ML &= MA \\ UP &= MB + K \times SD \\ LW &= MB - K \times SD \end{aligned} \tag{3}$$

Where, ML is the main line or the middle trajectory, UP is the upper bands, LW is the lower bands, SD is standard deviation of the price, K represents bands will be K standard deviations above or below the main line.

2.3 Design of Trading Strategy of Traditional Bollinger Bands Model

2.3.1 Admission Rules

Sell and open a position: When Price breaks the upper line, it indicates stock index futures prices are overvalued and have more possibility of correction. In order to avoid risks and gain profits, we will sell and open a position.

Buy and open a position: When Price breaks the lower line, it indicates stock index futures prices are undervalued and have more possibility of rebounding. In order to avoid risks and gain profits, we will buy and open a position.

2.3.2 Departure Rules

Buy and close a position: when the price fall down to the main line from the peak, it indicates the stock index futures prices have more possibility of rising. In order to avoid risks and gain profits, we will buy and close a position.

Sell and close a position: when the price rises up to the main line from the bottom, it indicates the stock index futures prices have more possibility of falling. In order to avoid risks and gain profits, we will sell and close a position.

2.3.3 Scaling Rules

To simplify the transaction process and explain the basic principles of transactions, this article does not consider the scaling rules. In the study, the transactions are single-handed transactions, that is, when you open a position, you have to close the position before a new trade.

2.3.4 Principles of Profits

When stock index futures price rise to the upper line, we have the bearish outlook, sell the contract and open a position. We will buy the contract and close a position when price falls down to the main line. Therefore, we could gain the profits because of the difference in price.Just like that, we can also buy the contract and open a position when stock index futures price fall to the lower line, and then sell the contract and close a position when a correction sent prices is up to the main line.

2.4 Traditional Bollinger Bands Model Analysis of Traditional Bollinger Bands Transaction Model's Defects

With MATLAB software, we wrote a program and used the traditional Bollinger Bands model to have a back test to find its shortcomings. The date was1 minute K-line transaction data in CSI 300 index market from 2010-2013. In this quantitative strategy operation, the closing price of the stock index futures transaction was taken every 1 minute. We took the 20-cycleclosing price to calculate the average price as a point of the main line. As the cycle shifts one unit, we would get a new point, and connect these points to get moving average line, that is, the main line. Upper bands would be 2 times standard deviations above the main line, and the lower would be below. The test results are shown in Figure 1 and Table 2 below.

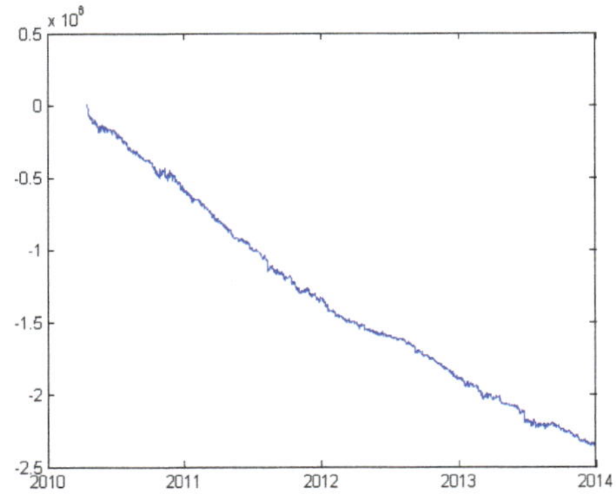

Figure 1. The cumulative profits curve of the traditional Bollinger bands model

Table 2. Test results of traditional Bollinger bands model

Statistical indicators	Results
Final profits	-2356400 Yuan
Accumulated maximum profits	625.1460 Yuan
Winning rate	0.4439
Maximum retracement	2361600 Yuan
Transaction number	9129
benefit-to-risk ratio	-0.2339

Figure 1 shows that the model only gains profits at the beginning of the transaction and then have a substantial decline, the transactions are at a loss. Table 2 shows the number of transactions is up to 9129 times, the ultimate loss of is up to 2.35 million Yuan, and the maximum retracement of is up to 2.36 million Yuan, while the cumulative maximum profits are only 625.1460 Yuan. Though the winning rate is relative high, the final income is negative, indicating that the amount of transactions to achieve profitability is very small. The benefit-to-risk ratio is negative indicates the trade losses are serious. It shows that the traditional Bollinger Bands model fails in the test and has serious flaws. It is found that the defects of the traditional Bollinger Bands transaction model are mainly embodied in several aspects, such as "over-sensitive" and transaction stop-loss, and the adaptability of the model's basic parameters is poor.

2.4.1 Over-Sensitive Defects

As shown in Figure 2, we extract the test process from 36034 minutes to 36054 minutes for a total of 20 minutes and get the Bollinger Bands plot. In accordance with the traditional Bollinger band trading strategies, at the point A, when the stock price rises to the upper band, we will sell the contract and open a position and then buy the contract back and close a position when a correction sent prices down to the main line. Through the transaction, we will gain profits. However, according to Figure 2,we can see the price still rise above point A to point B. In practice, we sell the contract and open a position at point A and have a bearish outlook, resulting in a large loss. Actually, the time when price is at the point B or close to the point B, it is the best opportunity to deal. At this time we can lead to smaller losses and obtain higher profits.

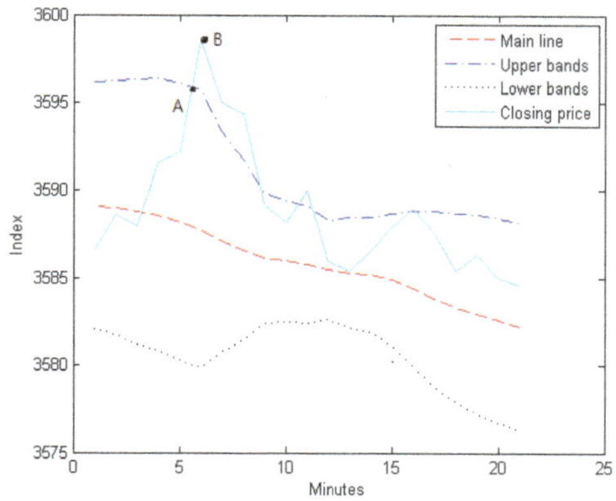

Figure 2. 20-minute trading of traditional Bollinger bands model

The above analysis shows that the traditional Bollinger Bands trading strategy has the problem that the model transaction is excessively sensitive and does not take the influence of price trend into account. When the stock price breaks main line, upper bands, or lower bands, the stock price may still continue to run along the original trend. At this time, if we open a position, it will reduce the profits and even close out the open positions at a loss to stop the loss .In order to solve this problem, it is necessary to confirm whether the original trend has ended when the stock price breaks the bands. We believe that, in most cases, before changing the original trend, stock prices will still run in accordance with the original trend for some time. Stock prices will eventually reverse until the failure of the original trend. We call this nature of stock price "inertia of stock price." Therefore, according to the traditional trading strategy, we define the original trend is about to reverse when the stock price break. This does not meet the logic of the stock price movement --- "stock price inertia."

2.4.2 Stop-Loss Deficiencies

Stop loss is one of the basic concepts of investment. The setting of stop-loss during a programmed trading is called "the soul of a programmed transaction". Some stop-loss strategies such as Time stop-loss, spreads stop-loss, tracking stop-loss and limit stop-loss are common in practice. Futures trading have the delivery date and a leverage effect because of the characteristics of its margin trading. If the loss can't be stopped in time, we will face the risk being forced to cut positions and lead to serious losses. Traditional Bollinger Bands trading strategy stops loss mainly rely on the breakout of the main line to select the time to close a position, which has great limitations in the volatile, frequent changes market. As shown in Figure 3, we extract the test process from 712minutes to 812 minutes for a total of 100 minutes and get the Bollinger Bands graph.

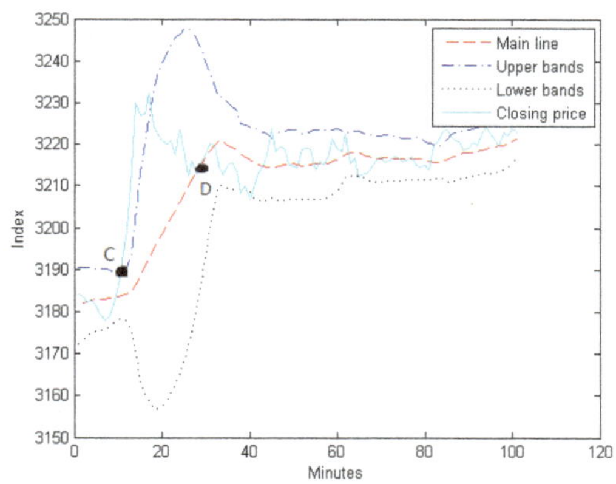

Figure 3. 100-minute trading of traditional Bollinger bands model

As shown in Figure 3, In accordance with the traditional Bollinger Bands trading model, the program will sell and open a position at point C when the price rises to the upper line. At this point, the CSI is 3192 points. In traditional Bollinger Bands model, if you do not set a stop-loss point properly, you need to carry until the price fall to the intersection of the price line and the main line at point D. You won't buy and close a position until the point D. However, according to the transaction rules in Stock index futures market, you will suffer catastrophic losses. Therefore, in addition to taking into account the "stock price inertia", choose the right time to trade, we also need to set a reasonable stop-loss strategy to avoid trading risk caused by the excessive price fluctuations.

2.4.3 Lack of Basic Parameters' Applicability

Because of the complexity, variability and periodic characteristics of the stock index futures market, thebasic parameters of the traditional Bollinger Bands model are difficult to adapt to the changing market.

In practice, it is necessary to adjust the basic parameters of the Bollinger Bands model according to the different types of stages of the transactions to design different trading strategies, which are more in line with the actual transactions.

3. Improvements of Bollinger Bands Model

3.1 Improvement of Over-Sensitive Defects

The above analysis of defects has pointed out that when the stock price breaks through the Bollinger Bands, we determine the original trend is about to reverse, which does not meet the stock index price logic —— "stock price inertia". Taking into account this situation into account, we set rules that when the stock price breaks the Bollinger Bands, the program will not make reverse transactions immediately, but determine whether the original trend has changed through a series of conditions. When the change in the trend is confirmed, the program will open or close a position.

Referring to the results of previous research (Ting, 2013) on the stock index futures price trend, this paper uses the price index of stock index futures to judge the price trend. (y_t, $t=1, 2\ldots$) are regarded as price series of stock index futures. That means y_t represents the t time of the stock index futures price $t=1$ is regarded the as the first minute stock index futures closing price. Price series econometric model are established as follows.

$$Y = \alpha_t X + \beta_t + \varepsilon \tag{4}$$

Where, Y is the closing price in recent N minutes, ε is an error term with a independent identically distributed variance σ^2 and mean 0.

$$Y = \begin{bmatrix} y_{t-N+1} \\ y_{t-N+2} \\ \vdots \\ y_t \end{bmatrix}, \quad X = \begin{bmatrix} 1 \\ 2 \\ \vdots \\ N \end{bmatrix}, \quad \varepsilon = \begin{bmatrix} \varepsilon_1 \\ \varepsilon_2 \\ \vdots \\ \varepsilon_N \end{bmatrix} \tag{5}$$

$$Y_i = y_{t-N+i}, X_i = i \tag{6}$$

The coefficients of the regression model are estimated using the least squares estimator:

$$\alpha_t = \frac{\sum_{i=1}^{N} (X_i - \bar{x})(Y_i - \bar{y})}{\sum_{i=1}^{N} (X_i - \bar{x})^2} \tag{7}$$

$\bar{x}$ and $\bar{y}$ are defined as follows

$$\bar{x} = \frac{1}{N}\sum_{i=1}^{N} X_i = \frac{N+1}{2}, \quad \bar{y} = \frac{1}{N}\sum_{i=1}^{N} Y_i = \frac{1}{N}\sum_{t-N+1}^{t} y_i \tag{8}$$

Substituting into the calculation, we can get the result.

$$\omega_{i,t} = \frac{12i - 12t + 6N}{N^3 + 2N} \tag{9}$$

Where, S_t is defined the price speed at the t minute.

$$s_t = \alpha_t = \sum_{i=t-N+1}^{t} \omega_{i,t}(y_i - \bar{y}) \tag{10}$$

Where, $S_t>0$ means futures prices have rising trend, $S_t<0$ means futures prices have downward trend. $S_t=0$ means the prices were flat.As seen from the formula of price speed, the speed can be defined as the weighted average of stock price centering. For a certain time t and a fixed number of observations N, the weight increases with the increase of the price. That is, the closer to time t, the greater the weight of the price. The principle is consistent with the view that the actual price is strongly influenced by the recent price. When the futures price breaks the bands and $S_t>0$, there is a big possibility to keep the rising trend. When $S_t=0$, there is a big possibility that the original upward trend is over. Making transactions at this time can increase revenue a lot. In general, the probability of events that price rise to the upper bands and fall to the lower bands are small. Though it happens, the futures prices are very high or very low and the trends are not stable. At this point the misjudgment of the timing of transactions will result in huge losses. In order to accurately determine the timing of the transaction without causing too much loss, when the price of the price changes in the range of [*-a, a*], futures prices are in a flat state and close to the peak point. The best trading opportunity is in this period of time. This paper tested and found that when *a* is between 0-0.1, the effect of transaction is better. In practice, it can be adjusted according to transaction needs. Prices close to the main line are in the middle and fluctuant. When the price of the price changes in the range of [*-b, b*], futures prices are in a relative flat state and close to the peak point. The best trading opportunity is in this period of time. We tested and found that when *b* is between 0.1-0.2, the effect of transaction is better. Also, in practice, the parameters can be adjusted.

3.2 Improvement of the Trading Stop Defect

From the analysis of the stop-loss trade, it is necessary to set the stop-loss in the process of trading. Stop-loss strategies such as time stops, spreads stops, tracking stop-loss and limit stops are common and widely applied. This article draws on the view of Lai Xiangqun (2008), and uses the method of limit stop to set stop-loss rules. Assuming the principal is one unit, after the transaction of *n* times, the previous (*n-1*) times are at a loss, the last time we get profits, then at this time our amount of money can be expressed by the following formula.

$$Rn = (1-\beta)^{n-1} \times (1+x\beta) \ (n \geq 2) \tag{11}$$

From the above formula, the profits and loss of the transaction are determined by a single time stop loss β, profits and loss ratio x and the winning rate v. Due to the prevailing winning rate in the existing procedural trading model is about 1/3, setting a single stop loss of 0-5% is appropriate. In practice, according to the needs of the transaction, it can be adjusted. The optimal stop loss is a mathematical concept that has important reference value, it helps to achieve the lowest possible risk to obtain the maximum profits in the transaction. Stock index futures investment is an art, the program trading model need to set the necessary transaction profits and loss ratio and stop loss and resolutely implement.

So for the above defects, we make the following improvements. When the closing price breaks through the upper bands, we may choose a time to open and sell positions. At the same time, we set γ times the price as a stop-loss point. When the closing price in the future does not reach the right time to buy open, and the closing price has reached the γ times as much as the open price, the program immediately buy and close a position to prevent greater losses.

Similarly, when the closing price breaks through the lower price, we may choose a time to open and buy positions. At the same time, we set ω times the price as a stop-loss point. When the closing price in the future does not reach the right time to open and sell a position, and the closing price ω times below the open price of buying times, the program immediately sell and close a position to prevent greater losses. And the value γ and ω can be adjusted according to trading practices.

3.3 Adjustment of Basic Parameters

The trading model should be designed according to the different transaction types and trading phases. The adjustment of the basic parameters of the Bollinger Bands model is more in line with the actual transaction, thus reducing the risk and gaining more profits.

4. Empirical Testing

We improve the design of trading strategy according to the above principles and test the improved model with 1 minute K-line transaction data in CSI 300 market from 2010-2013 again.

4.1 Design of Improved Bollinger Bands Model

4.1.1 Basic Parameters

The parameters of the Bollinger Bands in actual transaction can be set according to different actual conditions. Considering the model applied to China's stock index futures market has its particularity, we make some adjustments to the basic parameters. After lots of tests, we find that when $N=14$ and $k=17$, the transaction indicators of the model are ideal. In the following, the specific parameters in the trading rules are also adjusted.

4.1.2 Admission Rules

Sell and open a position: When Price breaks the upper bands, it indicates stock index futures prices are overvalued and have more possibility of correction. At the same time, the price speed S_{t1} changes in [-0.0547, 0.0547], futures prices are in a relative flat state and close to the peak point. The best trading opportunity is in this period of time.

Buy and open a position: When Price breaks the lower bands, it indicates stock index futures prices are undervalued and have more possibility of rebounding. At the same time, the price speed S_{t1} changes in [-0.0547, 0.0547], futures prices are in a relative flat state and close to the peak point. Then, we will buy and open a position to gain profits.

4.1.3 Departure Rules

Buy and close a position: when the price fall down to the main line from the peak, it indicates the stock index futures prices have more possibility of rising. At the same time, the price speed S_{t2} changes in [-0.1785, 0.1785], futures prices are in a relative flat state and close to the peak point. Then, we will buy and close a position to gain profits.

Sell and close a position: when the price rise up to the main line from the bottom, it indicates the stock index futures prices have more possibility of falling. At the same time, the price speed S_{t2} changes in [-0.1785, 0.1785], futures prices are in a relative flat state and close to the peak point. Then, we will sell and close a position to gain profits.

4.1.4 Stop-Loss Rules

When the price breaks through the upper bands, we may choose a time to open and sell positions. We may choose a time to open and buy positions. At the same time, the program will choose the point that is 2.11% higher than the price of CSI 300 as a stop-loss point. When the closing price in the future does not reach the price of buying, and the closing price has reached a point which is 2.11% higher than the selling price, the program will immediately buy and open a position to prevent greater losses. Similarly, when the price breaks through the lower bands, we may choose a time to open and buy a position. At the same time, the program will choose the point that is 2.11% lower than the price of CSI 300 index as a stop-loss point. When the closing price in the future does not reach the price of selling, and the price falls to the 98.74% of the buying price, the program will immediately sell and close a position to prevent greater losses.

4.2 Analysis of the Test Results

There are lots of data of the results, the main performance results are shown in Table 3 and Figure 4.

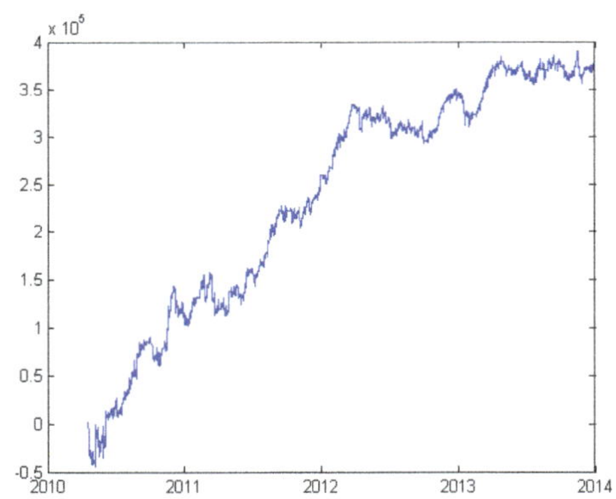

Figure 4. Profits curve of improved Bollinger bands

Table 3. Test results of improved Bollinger bands model

Statistical indicators	Results
Final profits	374800Yuan
Accumulated maximum profits	390500 Yuan
Winning rate	0.4364
Maximum retracement	45600 Yuan
Transaction number	3510
Benefit-to-risk ratio	2.1658

Figure 4 shows that the model at the beginning of the transaction is at a loss, and then after the cumulative profits with the transaction, the total profits curve volatility rises, finally turnaround and achieves a higher level of profitability. Table 3 shows the number of transactions is 3510 times, compared with the trading model before the improvement, there is a significant reduction in the number of transactions. That means the transaction costs will be greatly reduced, and there is more profits margins. We can see that the "transaction over-sensitive" defects have improved. The maximum retracement is 45,600 Yuan, which is about 1/60 of the traditional trading strategy model. Therefore, the risk of improved model declined dramatically. We can see the "over-sensitive" and trading stop defects have improved a lot. For winning rate, it is similar to the traditional model. The profitability of the improved model unit transaction is greatly improved, the final income reaches 374,800 Yuan, and the profits-to-risk ratio is up to 2.1658. Generally speaking, when profits-to-risk ratio is greater than 2, we believe that the model has practical value. Therefore, the improved model can be applied to actual market operation and is highly likely to be profitable. This improvement method is scientific and feasible.

5. Conclusions and Recommendations

The traditional Bollinger Bands model has serious flaws. In this paper, we make a series of improvements to the existing defects.

Firstly, the traditional Bollinger Bands model does not take into account the "stock price inertia", which generally exists in the stock index futures market. Before changing the original trend, stock prices will still run in accordance with the original trend for some time. Stock prices will eventually reverse until the failure of the original trend. This article creatively introduces the price speed to judge whether the original trend has changed. When the price speed is close to zero, the change of the trend can be confirmed and it is the proper time to open or close a position.

Secondly, the set of the stop-loss rules in traditional Bollinger Bands model is not perfect. In the improved model, when the price rise is up to the upper bands, the program will choose a proper time to sell and open a position while setting γ times the price of the CSI 300 as a stop point. When the price fall down to the lower bands, the program will choose a proper time to buy and open a position while setting ω times the price of the CSI 300 as a stop point. Improved stop-loss settings reduce losses due to trend misjudgments a lot.

Thirdly, basic parameters of Bollinger Bands model should be adjusted according to the transaction type and the trading stage to meet the actual transaction, thereby reducing the risk and get more benefits.

In this paper, based on the review of the Bollinger Bands model at home and abroad, the paper first builds the traditional Bollinger Bands transaction model, and then analyzes its "excess sensitivity", "stop loss" and "basic parameter adaptability "defects. Next, we improve the model by introducing price speed to judge the price trend, improving the stop rules and adjusting the basic parameters. Finally, we use the one-minute K-line data of CSI 300 market from 2010 to 2013 to test the improved Bollinger Bands model. The empirical results show that the modified Bollinger Bands transaction model has higher profitability and lower risk. This article is of great significance to the practice of stock index futures market.

In addition, the improved Bollinger Bands trading model can be applied not only to the stock index futures market, but also a wider range of trading varieties by learning the basic ideas and adjusting the basic parameters.

Acknowledgments

While remaining responsible for any errors in this paper, the authors would like to thank guidance and advice from Tongzi Lin who studies in School of Electrical and Information Engineering in Jinan University on choosing topics and programming.

References

Bollinger, J. (2002). *Bollinger on Bollinger Bands.* New York: McGraw Hill.

Chuanhai, D. (2001). Bollinger principle and its application. *Statistics and Decision*, (3), 25-26.

Joseph, M. J. L., & Terence, T. L. C. (2003). An empirical comparison of moving average envelopes and Bollinger Bands. *Applied Economics Letters*, 106. http://dx.doi.org/10.1080/1350485022000041032

Jusheng, S., Yixuan, H., & Wei, Z. (2014). Study on the Effectiveness of Boolean Line. *Statistics and Decision,* (17), 168-171.

K. Senthamarai, K., P. Sailapathi, S., & M. Mohamed, P. (2010). Arumugam. Financial Stock Market Forecast using Data Mining Techniques. *Lecture Notes in Engineering and Computer Science*, 21801.

Kathy, L. (2015). Technical Strategy: Trading with Double Bollinger Bands. *Day Trading and Swing Trading the Currency Market*, 2015.

Lento, C., Gradojevic, N., & Wright, C. S. (2007). Investment information content in Bollinger Bands? *Applied*

Financial Economics Letters, 34. http://dx.doi.org/10.1080/17446540701206576

Shenjun, Q., Qing, W., & Yuanbo, Z. (2011). Market Trend Forecasting of Real Estate Base on K-line Theory and Bollinger Bands. *Journal of Wuhan University of Technology (Information & Management Engineering),* (4), 622-625.

Ting, N. (2013). Study of the Stock Index FuturesProgram Trading Investment Strategy. *South China University of Technology,* 23-24.

Williams, O. D. (2006). *Empirical optimization of Bollinger Bands for profitsability*. Available at SSRN 2321140, 2006. http://dx.doi.org/10.2139/ssrn.2321140

Xiangqun, L. (2008). Try to comment on the stop-loss settings. *Special Zone Economy*, (3), 114-115.

The Determinants of Chinese Property Prices

Ming Qi[1]

[1] School of Business Administration, China University of Petroleum (Beijing), China

Correspondence: Ming Qi, School of Business Administration, China University of Petroleum (Beijing), China. E-mail: qiming@cup.edu.cn

Abstract

In this paper, the determinants the housing prices boom in China are investigated. We extend the original model of Yuan and Xiao and Zhou (2006) by involving banks, in order to investigate the behavior of the money lender. A sample of 28 Chinese domestic commercial banks during the period between 2003 and 2009 are used for the empirical test. The results suggest that the mortgage loan has a significant impact on the property prices. Their effects on both condominium and residential prices are positive. However, the prices of High_Grade and Economical Houses have shown an entirely different response to the movement of mortgage credits.

Keywords: mortgage, house price, banks, interest rate, CPI

1. Introduction

The past decade has witnessed an overall boom of home price growth in both new and existing markets with first- and selected second-tier cities in China. The soaring property prices have been extensively documented in China. China provides a representative figure of emerging property market which experienced the soaring property prices. Figure 1 illustrates the movements of mortgage loans and property prices. In a recent survey of 70 cities by the National Bureau of Statistics (NBS), 51 reported price gains in new houses. The surge of property prices can be attributed to both monetary and financial policies in China (Yu 2010). House stock is also regarded as the response to the land-use regulation through the elasticity of new housing supply. (Quigley & Raphael, 2005).

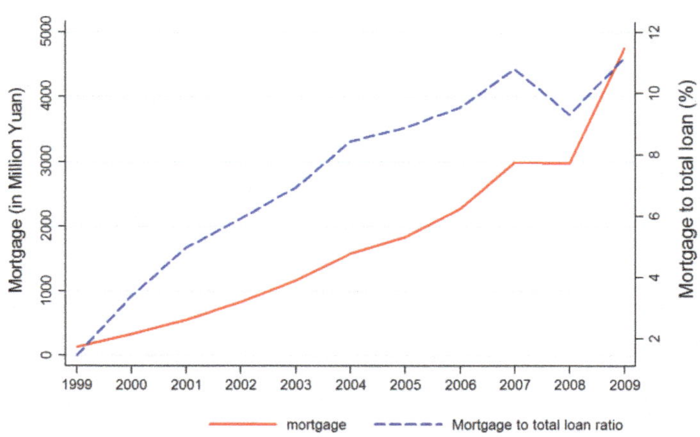

Figure 1. Mortgage outstanding and average property prices

The government authorized all the commercial banks to issue household mortgage in 1998. Commercial banks also recognize the residential mortgage credits as health assets in their portfolio given the lower default rate of loans to individual mortgagors than that to state-owned entrepreneurs. (Deng & Fei, 2008). The mortgage boom has significantly contributed to the property price surge in China. (Zhang, 2000) In this paper we investigate what determinants the housing prices boom in China. National disposable income is the primary factor which has significant impact on the property prices (McQuinn & O'Reilly, 2007, Hill & Gan, 2008). On the other hand,

China has witnessed a dramatic urbanization and industrialization process during the past decades (Zheng et al., 2007). More and more internal immigrants choose to settle down in cities. Their demand on houses is another significant accelerator to the housing prices surge. We test to what extend the bank's behaviors and monetary policies have impacts on the property sector. The interest rate is a typical indicator of monetary policy in estimating the property market. Real interest rate is more closely associated with property prices than with bank lending. Hofmann (2003), Wolswijk (2006) and Égertand and Mihaljek (2007) find the negative effect of interest rate on housing prices. A declining interest rate is benefit to the increasing demand for property investments. (Green & Shoven, 1986; Kearl, 1979; Tsatsaronis & Zhu, 2004; Wolswijk, 2006; Égertand & Mihaljek, 2007). Figure 2 shows the movements of Required Reserve Ratio for banks and mortgage rates.

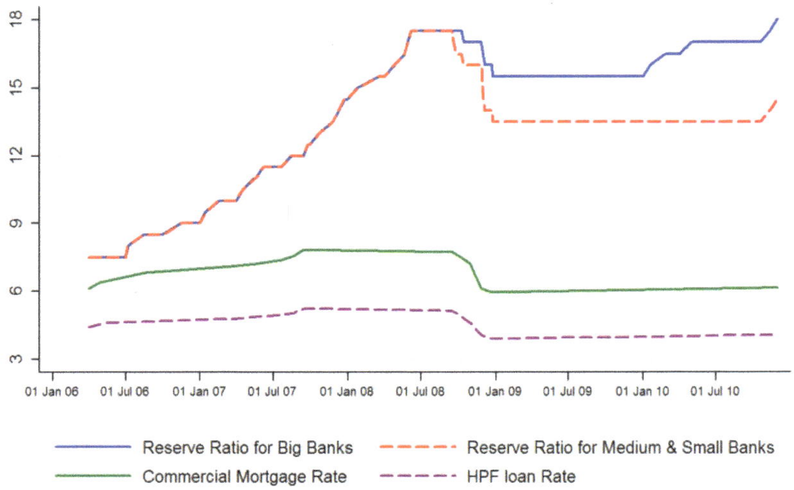

Data source: The People's Bank of China.
Note: Big banks refer to five State-Owned banks and the Postal saving bank.

Figure 2. Movements of required reserve ratio for and mortgage rates

In terms of the property prices, we use four different housing prices to capture the dynamic of property market in China. They are condominium price, which is the average housing price; residential price, which is the index of solo residential market; high_grade houses price, which represents the luxury and high-end real estate market; and last economic houses price, which is the price of affordable houses. Figure 3 illustrates the movements of property prices in four separate real estate market. The paper is organized as follows. Section 2 reviews the literature on Chinese property market. Section 3 describes the data and methodology. The empirical results are presented in section 4. Section 5 concludes this paper.

Data source: Nationa Bureau of Statistics of China.
Note: Property prices are in real term.

Figure 3. Movements of property prices

2. Literature Review

Various theoretical models and empirical frameworks have been proposed to explain what determines the property price movements in China. Wu et al. (2016) investigates the Chinese property market from the perspective of supply and demand conditions. The results imply that there is strong positive trend in house price and land value in China. Zhang et al. (2015) introduces the house searching model with down-payment constraints. They find strong Granger relationship in coastal cities where house prices are high with speculation, but weak relationship in inland cities where speculative activity is relatively weak. Market intervention have some impacts but cannot affects the market power as a whole. On the other hand, several cross-country evidence have indicated that the property have close relationship with mortgage lending (Égert & Mihaljek, 2007; Lacoviello & Minetti, 2008; Goodhart & Hofmann, 2008; Davis & Zhu, 2010). Capozza et al. (2002), Gimeno and Martinez-Carrascal (2006); and Fitzpatrick and McQuinn (2007) investigate the case of USA, Spain and Irland respectively and reach the same conclusion. Liang and Cao (2007) find a unidirectional causality from bank lending, interest rate and income to property prices in China. Some researches also confirm the significant impact of household income on housing prices (Jud & Winkler, 2002; Gimeno & Martinez-Carrascal, 2006; Bourassa et al., 2006). Nevertheless, some researches find little impact of household income on housing prices. (Tsatsaronis & Zhu, 2004) Zhang et al. (2012) use the Nonlinear Auto Regressive Moving Average with eXogenous inputs (NARMAX) to investigate determinants of housing prices in China. The findings suggest that mortgage rate, producer price, broad money supply and real effective exchange rate and price variables can be used to explain the housing price dynamics in China. Two alternative models have been proposed to explain the housing prices movements in the literature. Muellbauer and Murphy (1997 and Meen (2002) suggest the inverted demand model which involves the housing supply and credit conditioning. The alternative one is house price-to-rent model, which is proposed by Ayuso and Restoy (2006). In this model, the arbitrage between owned and rental houses are investigated. Wu et al. (2014) suggests that the simple average method cannot explain the substantial complex-level dynamics in Chinese housing market. They apply a hedonic method to 35 major newly-built housing markets and provide the first multi-city constant-quality house price index in China.

3. Data Description and Methodology

3.1 Methodology

We firstly propose a theoretical model to understand both borrowers' and banks' behavior. This model is an extension of Yuan and Xiao (2003) and Zhou (2006). The bank is involved in this modified model, in order to investigate the behavior of the money lender.

3.1.1 Borrower's Behavior

Assume there are two kinds of goods in the market - the house occupation and a composite consumption good. We use Cobb-Douglas utility function to analyze borrower's behavior:

$$U = X^{\alpha} \cdot Y^{1-\alpha} \tag{1}$$

Where U denotes the utility of a borrower, X is the consumption of a composite good; Y is the house occupation of the household and α is the indicator of house purchase intension. Considering the monotonicity of utility function, we take logarithmic transformation of the utility function.

$$\log U = \alpha \cdot \log X + (1-\alpha) \cdot \log Y \tag{2}$$

Suppose the households use mortgage loans to finance the house occupation, and then use the dispensable income to support the consumption of house service and the composite good. We can maximize the borrower's utility under the constraint of dispensable income.

$$\max_{X,Y} \log U = \alpha \cdot \log X + (1-\alpha) \cdot \log Y \tag{3}$$

$$\text{s.t. } X + [1 + (r - i)] \cdot M = I \tag{4}$$

$$M = P \cdot Y \tag{5}$$

Where I represent the dispensable income of borrowers, r is the real interest rate of individual banks, i denote the inflation rate, M is the total mortgage loans, *and* P is the house price. Optimal allocation is solved through the Lagrange function:

$$L = \alpha \cdot \log X + (1-\alpha) \cdot \log Y - \lambda[X + (1 + r - i) \cdot P \cdot Y - I] \tag{6}$$

Thesis of the Lagrange function is shown as follows:

$$\begin{cases} \frac{\partial L}{\partial X} = \frac{\alpha}{X} - \lambda = 0 \\ \frac{\partial L}{\partial Y} = \frac{1-\alpha}{Y} - \lambda \cdot (1+r-i) \cdot P = 0 \\ \frac{\partial L}{\partial \lambda} = X + (1+r-i) \cdot P \cdot Y - I = 0 \end{cases} \tag{7}$$

By solving the linear equation system above with three unknowns, which are P, M, and λ respectively, we get:

$$M = P \cdot Y = \frac{(1-\alpha) \cdot I}{(1+r-i)} \tag{8}$$

It implies that the mortgage demand increases with borrower's income and house price, but decreases with the house purchase intension and the interest rate. In addition, the inflation rate has a positive impact on the mortgage demanding.

3.1.2 Bank's Behavior

We assume the whole deposits of banks are interest-bearing assets. They allocate a proportion of total deposits on the mortgage market. The total mortgage lending is denoted as *Y*, which is equal to consumers' demand of mortgage loans. The Loan_To_Deposit ratio is θ. Then the mortgage lending can be rewritten as $Y = \theta \cdot D$. An individual bank earns the interest rate r on its mortgage loans and pays out the interest rate r^d for customers' deposits. The lending business incurs a cost *C*, which is a quadratic function of total mortgage loans, i.e. $C(Y) = c(1+Y^2)$. The individual bank aims to maximize its total profits, which is denoted as π. Then the maximization function of banks is proposed as follows:

$$\max \pi = r \cdot M - N \cdot c[1+Y^2] - r^d \cdot D \tag{9}$$

$$\text{s.t. } M = N \cdot P \cdot Y \tag{10}$$

$$M = \theta \cdot D \tag{11}$$

If we plug *M* and *D* into our target function, we get:

$$\max_M \pi = r \cdot M - N \cdot c[1+(\frac{M}{N \cdot P})^2] - r^d \cdot \frac{M}{\theta} \tag{12}$$

$$\Leftrightarrow \frac{\partial \pi}{\partial M} = (r - \frac{r^d}{\theta}) - \frac{2cN \cdot M}{(N \cdot P)^2} = 0 \tag{13}$$

$$M = \frac{(r - r^d / \theta) \cdot N \cdot P^2}{2c} \tag{14}$$

then we replace the loan to deposit ratio θ by Y / D and get:

$$M = \frac{(r - \frac{r^d}{M/D}) \cdot N \cdot P^2}{2c} = \frac{(r - \frac{r^d \cdot D}{M}) \cdot N \cdot P^2}{2c} = \frac{(r \cdot M - r^d \cdot D) \cdot N \cdot P^2}{2cM} = \frac{\frac{r \cdot M - r^d \cdot D}{D} \cdot N \cdot P^2}{2c \frac{M}{D}} \tag{15}$$

Now, we can find that $\frac{r \cdot M - r^d \cdot D}{D}$ is the net interest margin (NIM) of the individual bank, and the denominator is $2cM / D = 2c \cdot \theta$. The optimal mortgage supply provided by the bank increases with its NIM, the number of mortgagers (*N*), housing price (*P*) but decrease with the Loan_To_Deposit ratio (θ).

3.1.3 Econometric Approach

Previous research also indicates that House price is rather an endogenous variable and driven by market factors including credit/mortgage rationing. We employ a simplified Inverted demand model, which was introduced by Muellbauer and Murphy (1997), to estimate the movements of housing price (Note 1).

$$HS / Pop = f(I, \mu, D) \tag{16}$$

$$\mu = P(r + \delta - \dot{P}^e / P) \tag{17}$$

Where μ is the real user cost of housing service; *P* is the housing price and P^e/P is the expected appreciation rate of housing price (Note 2). Muellbauer and Murphy (1997) pointed out that a proxy of mortgage rationing is often included in measuring the housing price. By substituting the user cost into the housing stock function and involving the proxy of credit conditions, we get the invert demand function to estimate the housing price.

$$P = f(HS, \dot{P}^e / P, I, credit\_rationing) \quad (18)$$

Where HS, P^e/P and I represent the housing stock, housing price appreciation rate and the Income respectively. We employ the ratio of house price to house rental index as the measure of housing appreciation rate in our estimation. Although the down payment ratio is a good and popular index of credit rationing, the house financing system in China has not experienced a significant change of this ratio. However, the change of Mortgage can partially reflect the bank's credit rationing. The increase of mortgage loans is associated with loosened credit criteria and lower interest rate. Therefore, we employ the change of mortgage to measure banks' credit rationing. Taking into account the estimation of mortgage lending, we then form a simultaneous equation system to estimate the movements of mortgage loans and housing prices as follows. Considering the bank-level mortgage data, the panel data approach and two-stage least squares/Instrument variable method are employed for the estimation.

$$House\ Price_{it} = \beta_0 + \beta_1 Housing\ Stock_{it} + \beta_2 Mortgage_{it} + \beta_3 Interest\ Rate_{it} + \beta_4 CPI_{it} + \beta_5 Housing\ Appriciation_{it-1} + \beta_6 Required\ Reserves_{it-1} + \varepsilon_{it} \quad (19)$$

3.2 Data Description

We carefully select explanatory variables for the empirical analysis so as to ensure our estimation is robust to omitted variables. The macro data which is collected from the People's Bank of China and National Bureau of Statistics of China. Mortgage loans, bank specific variables and house prices are collected from ALMANAC OF CHINA'S FINANCE AND BANKING. The number of house sales is used to estimate the housing stocks. The ratio of house price index to rental index is used to measure the house prices appreciation, which reflects consumers' purchase intention. In order to capture the heterogeneity among banks, we use the ratio of the interest revenues over total interest bearing assets to estimate the interest rates for each individual bank. We use four different categories of housing prices: condominium price, residential price, high_grade price and economic price. Table 1 lists the summary statistics of variables.

Table 1. Summary statistics of variables

Variable	Mean	Std. Dev	Min	Max
Income(log)	9.58	0.32	8.60	10.27
Interest (log)	1.65	0.25	0.44	2.14
Mortgage(log)	10.13	2.17	4.59	13.68
Condominium price(log)	8.31	0.37	7.63	9.53
Residential price(log)	8.26	0.38	7.53	9.49
High grade price(log)	8.91	0.32	8.06	10.00
Economical price(log)	7.58	0.27	6.94	8.38

4. Results

The determinants of housing prices are illustrated in Table 2. We find that the mortgage loan has a significant impact on the property prices. Their effects on both condominium and residential prices are positive. It implies the procyclical behavior of credits boom and condominium prices as a general. However, the prices of High_Grade and Economical Houses have shown an entirely different response to the movement of mortgage credits. The economic house in China is also referred to as the capped-price house. Its price is more administrative interference, rather not market-oriented. And the market of High_Grade houses is featured by the high demand rigidity. The movements of these two special property markets cannot meet the boom of mortgage credits. In spite of the little effect of raising reserve ratio, the interest rate moves negative to the condominium prices and plays an active role in restraining the housing prices. We do not find significant impact of Housing Stock, expected appreciation rate of housing price or inflation rate on the movements of housing prices.

Table 2. Determinants of housing prices

	(1) Condominium	(2) Residencial	(3) High_Grade	(4) Economical
Mortgage	0.814*	0.744**	-1.608*	-0.361***
	(1.92)	(2.54)	(-1.92)	(-3.43)
Income	0.554	0.414	2.154**	1.016***
	(0.97)	(0.81)	(2.09)	(4.33)
Intere rate	-0.417*	-0.394**	0.602	0.153**
	(-1.84)	(-2.22)	(1.38)	(2.25)
CPI	1.085	1.065	-6.148*	-2.812***
	(0.66)	(0.79)	(-1.88)	(-4.04)
Housing	0.351	0.120	-2.223	-1.273*
appreciation	(0.35)	(0.14)	(-1.31)	(-1.73)
Required	-0.199	-0.129	0.285	-0.0122
reserves	(-0.95)	(-0.75)	(0.80)	(-0.23)
Housing Stock	-0.469	-	-	-
Condominium	(-1.35)	-	-	-
Housing Stock	-	-0.347	-	-
Residencial	-	(-1.45)	-	-
Housing Stock	-	-	0.651	-
High_Grade	-	-	(1.63)	-
Housing Stock	-	-	-	-0.0817
Economical	-	-	-	(-1.21)
N	78	78	78	73

Note. *t* statistics in parentheses: * p<0.10, ** p<0.05, *** p<0.01.

5. Conclusion

China's property market has experienced dynamic change during the past decades. In this paper, we extend Yuan and Xiao (2003) and Zhou (2006)'s model to involve the role of banks. The theoretical model implies that the mortgage demand increases with borrower's income and house price, but decreases with the house purchase intension and the interest rate. The inflation rate has a positive impact on the mortgage demanding. On the other hand, The optimal mortgage supply provided by the bank increases with its NIM, the number of mortgagers, housing price, but decrease with the Loan_To_Deposit ratio. Following Muellbauer and Murphy (1997)'s invert demand model, we propose the empirical framework. The results show that the mortgage lending has significant contributions to the housing price surge. The procyclical behavior of credits boom and condominium prices are documented in China. But the situation for High_Grade and Economical housing market is quite different. The interest rate moves negative to the condominium prices and plays an active role in restraining the housing prices. Therefore, the interest rate is the most useful monetary tool for policy makers to restrain the rocketing property prices in China.

Acknowledgement

This work was supported by Beijing Natural Science Foundation under Grant (9164034); Humanity and Social Science Youth Foundation of Ministry of Education in China (Project No. 13YJC790112); Science Foundation of China University of Petroleum, Beijing under Grant 2462013YJRC009.

References

Ayuso, J., & Restoy, F. (2006). House prices and rents: An equilibrium asset pricing approach. *Journal of Empirical Finance, 13*, 371-388. https://doi.org/10.1016/j.jempfin.2005.10.004

Bourassa, S. C., Hoesli, M., & Sun, J. (2006). A simple alternative house price index method. *Journal of Housing Economics, 15*, 80-97. https://doi.org/10.1016/j.jhe.2006.03.001

Capozza, D., Hendershott, P., Mack, C., & Mayer, C. (2002). Determinants of Real House Price Dynamics. *NBER Working Paper* No. W9262. https://doi.org/10.3386/w9262

Davis, E. P., & Zhu, H. (2010). Bank lending and commercial property cycles: Somecross-country evidence. *Journal of International Money and Finance, 30*, 1-21. https://doi.org/10.1016/j.jimonfin.2010.06.005

Deng, Y., & Fei, P. (2008). The Emerging Mortgage Markets in China. In D. Ben-Shahar, C. K. Y. Leung, & S. E. Ong (Eds), *Mortgage Markets Worldwide* (pp. 1-33). Oxford, UK: Blackwell Publishing Ltd. https://doi.org/10.1002/9781444302301.ch1

Égert, B., & Mihaljek, D. (2007). Determinants of house prices in central and eastern Europe. *Comparative Economic Studies, 49*, 367-388. https://doi.org/10.1057/palgrave.ces.8100221

Fitzpatrick, T., & McQuinn, K. (2007). House prices and mortgage credit: Empirical evidence for Ireland. *Manchester School, 75*, 82-103. https://doi.org/10.1111/j.1467-9957.2007.01004.x

Gimeno, R., & Martinez-Carrascal, C. (2006). The Interaction between House Prices and Loans for House Purchase: The Spanish Case. *Banco de Espana Research Paper,* No. WP-0605. https://doi.org/10.2139/ssrn.901145

Goodhart, C., & Hofmann, B. (2008). House prices, money, credit, and the macroeconomy. *Oxford Review of Economic Policy, 24*, 180-205. https://doi.org/10.1093/oxrep/grn009

Green, J., & Shoven, J. (1986). The Effects of Interest Rates on Mortgage Prepayments. *Journal of Money, Credit and Banking, 18*, 41-59. https://doi.org/10.2307/1992319

Hill, R. J., & Gan, Q. (2008). A New Perspective on the Relationship Between House Prices and Income. *UNSW Australian School of Business Research Paper* No. 2008 ECON 13. https://doi.org/10.2139/ssrn.1313073

Hofmann, B. (2003). Bank Lending and Property Prices: Some International Evidence. *HKIMR Working Paper* No. 22/2003. https://doi.org/10.2139/ssrn.1009079

Jud, G., Winkler, D., & Sirmans, S. (2002). The impact of information technology on real estate licensee income. *Journal of Real Estate Practice and Education, 5*, 1-16.

Kearl, J. R. (1979). Inflation, Mortgage, and Housing. *The Journal of Political Economy, 87*, 1115-1138. https://doi.org/10.1086/260815

Lacoviello, M., & Minetti, R. (2008). The credit channel of monetary policy: Evidence from the housing market. *Journal of Macroeconomics, 30*, 69-96. https://doi.org/10.1016/j.jmacro.2006.12.001

Liang, Q., & Cao, H. (2007). Property prices and bank lending in China. *Journal of Asian Economics, 18*, 63-75. https://doi.org/10.1016/j.asieco.2006.12.013

McQuinn, K., & O'Reilly, G. (2007). A Model of Cross-Country House Prices. *Research Technical Papers from Central Bank & Financial Services Authority of Ireland (CBFSAI),* No 5/RT/07.

Meen, G. (2002). The time series behavior of house prices: A transatlantic divide? *Journal of Housing Economics, 11*, 1-23. https://doi.org/10.1006/jhec.2001.0307

Muellbauer, J., & Murphy, A. (1997). Booms and Busts in the UK Housing Market. *The Economic Journal, 107*, 1701-1727. https://doi.org/10.1111/j.1468-0297.1997.tb00076.x

Quigley, J., & Raphael, S. (2005). Regulation and the High Cost of Housing in California. *The American Economic Review, 95*, 323-328. https://doi.org/10.1257/000282805774670293

Tsatsaronis, K., & Zhu, H. (2004). What drives housing price dynamics: cross country evidence. *BIS Quarterly Review*, March.

Wolswijk, G. (2006). Determinants of Mortgage Debt Growth in EU Countries. *European Journal of Housing Policy, 6*, 131-149. https://doi.org/10.1080/14616710600787627

Wu, J., Deng, Y., & Liu, H. (2014). House price index construction in the nascent housing market: The case of China. *The Journal of Real Estate Finance and Economics, 48*(3), 522-545. https://doi.org/10.1007/s11146-013-9416-1

Wu, J., Gyourko, J., & Deng, Y. (2016). Evaluating the risk of Chinese housing markets: What we know and what we need to know. *China Economic Review, 39*, 91-114. https://doi.org/10.1016/j.chieco.2016.03.008

Yu, H. (2010). China's house price: Affected by economic fundamentals or real estate policy? *Frontiers of Economics in China, 5*, 25-51. https://doi.org/10.1007/s11459-010-0002-7

Yuan, Z., & Xiao, X. (2003). An Analysis of Rational Bubbles in the Real Asset Market. *Economic Research Journal, 3*, 34-43.

Zhang, L., Hui, E. C. M., & Wen, H. (2015). Housing price–volume dynamics under the regulation policy: Difference between Chinese coastal and inland cities. *Habitat International, 47,* 29-40. https://doi.org/10.1016/j.habitatint.2015.01.003

Zhang, X. Q. (2000): The Restructuring of the Housing Finance System in Urban China. *Cities, 17,* 339-348. https://doi.org/10.1016/S0264-2751(00)00030-5

Zhang, Y., Hua, X., & Zhao, L. (2012). Exploring determinants of housing prices: A case study of Chinese experience in 1999-2010. *Economic Modelling, 29*(6), 2349-2361. https://doi.org/10.1016/j.econmod.2012.06.025

Zheng , L., Huang, Q., Lu, T., & Zhou, W. (2007): The Process and Problems of Industrialization and Urbanization in China: The Status of the Tenth Five-Year Plan and Recommendations for the Eleventh Five-Year Plan. *Chinese Economy, 40*, 6-30. https://doi.org/10.2753/CES1097-1475400101

Zhou, J. (2006). Forming and Evolvement of Real Estate Bubble —An Explanation of Hypothesis Financial Supportive Excess. *Finance & Trade Economics, 5*, 3-10.

Notes

Note 1. Dougherty and Order investigate the measurement of the housing cost through two alternative approaches. They deduct the capital cost by maximizing household utility or implicit rent of the landlord and come up with the same results.

Note 2. Murphy also pointed that the long-run price-to-rent ratio can be estimated by real user cost and loan-to-value ratio.

15

The Effect of Promotion Strategy in the Jordanian Islamic Banks on a Number of Customers

Bader Mustafa Al-Sharif[1], Amjad Qwader[1] & Zaher Abdel Fattah Al-Slehat[1]

[1] Faculty of Business, Tafila Technical University, At-Tafila, Jordan

Correspondence: Bader Mustafa Al-Sharif, Faculty of Business, Tafila Technical University, AT-Tafila, P.O. Box 179, Tafila, 66110, Jordan. E-mail: bader.alsharif99@gmail.com

Abstract

This study aimed at recognizing the effect of promotion strategy in the Jordanian Islamic banks on a number of customers. To accomplish the objective of this study, the researcher designed a questionnaire composed of three parts. The first part designed to collect data about the sample, while the second part was designed to collect information about the attitude to deal with Islamic banks. The questionnaire was distributed for a sample of 100 dealers with Islamic banks. The researcher recovered 95% of the distributed questionnaires. The collected questionnaires were entered to statistical software (SPSS) and analyzed. The results showed that the advertisement is the most important field in promotion that should be concerned by banks to increase its customers. The study concluded that the marketing strategy in Islamic banks is practiced randomly and not concentrated on that Muslims prefer the deal with Islamic banks.

Keywords: promotion strategy, Islamic banks

1. Introduction

Promotion is considered as one of the means used in order to spread and to increase the market share of the organization by increasing its competition against similar organizations in the market, as well as it is considered as the only means by which the product offers the advantages of the goods provided to final consumer.

Promotion became an essential part of the organization's policy, which is the only means used by the organization in light of the intense competition with other organizations. It is also as a means that enables the organization to reach its target consumers in order to create customer's desire, and here it is necessary to develop firm integrated promotional strategies that contribute to achieving the organization's strategic objectives (Assuhn, 1997).

Competition increased in the Islamic banks sector as a result of increasing orientation towards these banks, the existence of Arab Islamic banks at the Jordanian market, which makes it imperative for these banks to improve their promotion strategies with the intensification of the competition, and at the same time the measurement of the conformity of promotion strategies with the provisions of Islamic law which are consistent with the obligations of individual in the Islamic Community.

This study aims at identifying the effect of promotion strategy in the Jordanian Islamic banks on a number of customers, and how these strategies work on documenting the adherence of these banks to the provisions of Islamic Sharia in their work.

2. Theoretical Framework

2.1 Defining Promotion Strategy

Promotion is a marketing effort involves a persuasive communication regarding a product or service (Armstrong & Kotler, 1996).

Promotion is used to inform and remind the customer and to influence its feelings, behavior and beliefs towards the promoted product or service (Stanton, 1997).

Promotion is an integrated communication system based on the delivery of information about the product or service in a persuasive manner to targeted customers in order to make the individuals accept the product or the promoted service (Kincaid, 2003).

2.2 Promotion Tools

1) Advertisement: it is a non-personal communication process to promote products and services such as television, newspapers, and radio for a fee in order to influence the behavior of the people to deal with the banks (Assuhn, 1997).

2) Personal selling: it is a personal communication process aimed at promoting a product or a service; this method of promotion requires a high level of skills, training and the ability to supply and persuasion and the good appearance of the salesman (McCarthy & Perreault, 2004).

3) Sales promotion: this involves any marketing or non-marketing activity which is used at a specific time to increase the demand for goods and services, such as price discounts and free subscriptions (Abu, 1996).

4) Publicity: this involves any news published about a product or service through the media (television, newspapers, etc. ...) by official authorities. This is a free of charge service such as the raising awareness of the harmful effects of smoking on television by the Ministry of Health (Fzaz, 2014).

5) Public Relations: this process involves the employment of media to build a good image of the bank and the pursuit of satisfaction among the target customers, also through the bank's support of the social, sports, environmental and health activities in the community (Edlayme, 2005).

2.3 The Importance of Promotion

2.3.1 As for the Customers of the Banks

1) Promotion makes customers know the benefits of banks and the specifications, prices, locations, and times of the products or services provided to them. Promotion provides an environment of entertainment among customers through the sights and poignant expressions accompanying the advertisement process (Alaq & Rbaba'a, 1998).

2) Promotion reminds customers of their desires and needs through several means including publicity and advertisement (Rachman, 1988).

2.3.2 As for the Marketing Staff

1) The increment of the sales size through the interaction of sales staff, distributors and various means of sales promotion (Mualla, 1996).

2) Overcoming the problem of low sales size which usually occurs during Slump in sales stage through promotion (Hurb, 1999).

3) Overcoming the far distance between the bank and customers using the Internet to provide services and products. Promotion increases competition among banks in order to increase demand for sales and services in spite of similar quality and prices (Alaq, Bashir, Abdali, & Ghalib, 1999).

3. Literature Review

Otoum, F.,This study aimed at identifying the impact of banking promotion on the increment of savings accounts at banks operating in Jordan and to determine the best means of promotion. This study has used descriptive analytical approach using a questionnaire distributed to 506 employees working at banks where 357 questionnaires were retrieved. SPSS software was used to perform statistical tests needed to find out the significance between variables. The results of the study showed that advertisements have a significant impact on the increment of savings accounts in banks, followed by public relations through offering prizes to the owners of savings accounts at banks operating in Jordan (Otoum, 2010).

Marji, A., This study aimed at identifying the impact of the use of Internet and cell phone in the promotion by the banks operating in Jordan on the market share of banks. The study has used descriptive analytical approach using a questionnaire distributed to 120 employees working in banks. 100 was questionnaires were retrieved, and then percentages, means, standard deviations were analyzed in order to describe the sample, and statistical tests were used to identify the significance between variables. The results of the study showed that public relations have a significant impact on the increment of market share, and that the e-promotion does not require significant financial resources, despite the scarcity of e-promotion skilled staff, and that 87% believe that electronic advertisements increase the competitiveness of the bank, and 64% of respondents emphasized that e-promotion is credible (Marji, 2008).

Edhmour and Shraideh, The study aimed to identify the impact of promotional mix elements (advertisement, publicity and public relations, personal selling, and means of sales promotion) on the Jordanian consumer decisions to use cell phone service .In order to achieve the objectives of the study and to test its hypotheses, a questionnaire was designed and distributed to a simple sample of (600) respondents from the study population (494) questionnaires were retrieved with a retrieving percentage of (82.33%). The study has used descriptive and analytical approach, and then the percentages, means, standard deviations were analyzed to describe the sample, and statistical tests were used to identify the significance between variables. The study found that a strong impact of promotional mix elements on the Jordanian consumer decisions to use cell phone service (Edhmour & Shraideh, 2008).

Grankvist, Kollberg, and Person., The study aimed to get a clear understanding of the promotional strategies in the international retail banking in Estonia. Descriptive approach was used. The study showed that personal selling is the most important promotional tool in the retail banking followed by advertisements. Also, the results showed that a strong brand attracts customers, and the study found that market segmentation is essential for the success of the promotion process (Grankvist, Kollberg, & Person, 2004).

Pitt, Berthon, and Waston., This study aimed at providing a theoretical framework to identify the impact of "the world wide web as an advertising medium descriptive analytical approach was used. The study found a model that consists of six stages, where the model has addressed the problem of recipients of advertising message on the World Wide Web through two groups; one group is interested in the advertising organization and the other group is not interested in the advertising organization. This study has demonstrated that the organization attractiveness (as an advertising tool) for clients depends on the number of members interested in the advertising organization (Pitt, Berthon, & Waston, 1996).

4. Methodology

Islamic banks are characterized by private nature as their principles are derived from Islamic law. The public has a desire to deal with Islamic banks, but because there are some misconceptions about the Islamic transactions, a group of customers are turning to deal with commercial banks; hence the problem of the study is to identify the impact of promotion in the Islamic banks to attract customers.

The study of the impact of promotion strategy on the number of customers of Islamic banks in Jordan is a good outset. In order to enable Islamic banks to increase the bank's ability to compete and spread and then to achieve financial and economic requirements, the study provides information on the level of promotion in Islamic banks and then straightening the bank's path to improve the level of promotion for subsequent periods of time.

Based on this context, the following hypotheses are proposed:

Ho1: There is no statistically significant impact at the level of significance ($\alpha \leq 0.05$) for the promotion strategy followed by the Jordan Islamic banks (advertisement) on the number of customers of the Islamic banks.

Ho2: There is no statistically significant impact at the level of significance ($\alpha \leq 0.05$) for the promotion strategy followed by the Jordan Islamic banks (personal selling) on the number of customers of the Islamic banks.

Ho3: There is no statistically significant impact at the level of significance ($\alpha \leq 0.05$) for the promotion strategy followed by the Jordan Islamic banks (sales promotion) on the number of customers of the Islamic banks.

Ho4: There is no statistically significant impact at the level of significance ($\alpha \leq 0.05$) for the promotion strategy followed by the Jordan Islamic banks (publicity) on the number of customers of the Islamic banks.

Ho5: There is no statistically significant impact at the level of significance ($\alpha \leq 0.05$) for the promotion strategy followed by the Jordan Islamic banks (Public relations) on the number of customers of the Islamic banks.

4.1 Scope of the Study

The study population consisted of the customers of Islamic banks and due to the difficulty of access to all members of population, the researcher distributed (100) questionnaires on the employees working at Islamic banks, and retrieved (95) with retrieving percentage of 95%. The researcher has entered these questionnaires on a computer in preparation for analysis.

4.2 The Study Tool

The study tool consisted of three parts, and the parts were designed as follows:

Part I: this part is dedicated for gathering data of the demographic characteristics of the study sample, which consisted of the following questions:

Gender: This includes (male/female) choice.

Age: The age distribution included 5 categories.

Academic qualifications: The academic qualifications included (high school and less/ diploma/bachelor's degree/MA/PhD).

Part II: This part consisted of the independent variable in the study which is (the component of promotion strategy) as this variable was measured using 5-point Likert scale which included:

Advertisement: measured through three statements.

Personal selling: measured through three statements.

Sales promotion: measured through three statements.

Publicity: measured through three statements.

Public Relations: measured through three statements.

Part III: This part included statements relating to the measurement of demand for Islamic banks and 5-point Likert scale has been used for data collection on this part, where this part included the following fields:

The demand for deposit in Islamic banks: it has included three statements.

Commitment to the religious dimension: measured through three statements.

Advantage of Islamic banks over other banks: measured through three statements.

4.3 Multivariate Analysis – Probit Model

In order to access the results of the study, the researcher has used the following statistical methods:

Descriptive statistics: the researcher used the frequencies and percentages in order to identify the personal characteristics of the individuals of the sample, while he used means and standard deviations in order to identify the trends of the sample in the study variables.

Statistical inference: The researcher has used simple and multiple regressions for the purpose of measuring the impact of the components of promotion strategy on the demand for Islamic banking and thus test of hypotheses.

4.4 Validity & Reliability of Study Tool

The study tool (questionnaire) was subjected to Validity and Reliability tests in order to ensure the achievement of the objectives of the study as Cronbach's Alpha was used in order to verify the reliability of the current study. The results in Table (1) show reliability in the respondents' responses, because the standard value of Cronbach's Alpha is more than 60%, which is the accepted percentage in management research (Sekaran, 2008).

Table.1. Reliability test of the results of the study tool (Cronbach's alpha)

Field	Cronbach's alpha
Components of promotion strategy	0.931
Advertisement	0.933
Personal selling	0.853
Sales promotion	0.881
Publicity	0.943
Public relations	0.865
The demand for deposit in Islamic banks	0.842
Commitment to the religious dimension	0.921
Advantage of Islamic banks over other banks	0.897
Demand for Islamic banks	0.921
The tool as a whole	0.958

Source: Authors.

5. Analysis

5.1 Sample Attitudes towards the Promotion Strategy of Islamic Banking

It is noted from the results that sample attitudes towards the promotion strategy of Islamic banking was average, where "advertisement "was rated "very good" where the mean was 3.7 and the standard deviation was 0.59, and the consent of the statements of "advertisement" was average.

State the results showed a decline in personal selling as compared to advertisement in Islamic banks, where the mean was 3.4 as compared to 3.7 for advertisement, and this refers to the decline in personal selling operations in Islamic banks.

Evaluation of sales promotion, publicity and public relations was average where the mean of each of them was

3.4, 3.3 and 3.4 which is an average value and the answer all the statements of promotion, publicity and public relations was average.

Table 2. Means, standard deviations for the sample's evaluation of promotion strategy in the Islamic banks

Statement	Mean	standard deviation
Advertisement		
Islamic banks offer their advertisements that commensurate with the nature of their work	3.80	0.61
Islamic bank advertisements Promote Islamic orientation of the bank	3.70	0.51
Advertisement helps in determining the choice of Islamic banks in preference to commercial ones	3.60	0.81
Average	3.70	0.59
Personal selling		
Employees working in the Islamic bank give a clearer conceive of Islamic banking transactions	3.50	0.63
Employees working in the Islamic bank clarifies the advantages of Islamic banks over the commercial ones	3.40	0.52
Employees working in the Islamic bank comprehensiveness of service at the Islamic bank	3.40	0.41
Average	3.40	0.42
Sales promotion		
Islamic banks encourage customers to deal with them	3.50	0.32
The bank contributes to improve its image	3.40	0.51
The Bank provides an image of its activities and transactions	3.30	0.33
Average	3.40	0.41
Publicity		
Publicity provided by the bank envisages the promotion strategies	3.40	0.41
Publicity contributes to explain the Islamic banking strategies and transactions	3.20	0.32
Bank works to embed positive aspects of the application of Sharia in its advertisements	3.20	0.42
Average	3.30	0.39
Public relations		
Public Relations spread the application of Sharia	3.50	0.33
public relations spread the advantage of Islamic banks over other banks	3.40	0.35
Public relations contribute to improving the image of Islamic banks	3.40	0.61
Average	3.40	0.41

Source: Authors.

5.2 Sample's Attitudes towards the Demand for Islamic Banks

The evaluation of the demand for deposit in Islamic banks, the commitment to the religious dimension and showing the advantage of Islamic bank over other banks was average where the mean was 3.4, 3.4 and 3.3 respectively. The results showed that the answer to all statements in the areas of demand for deposit in Islamic banks, commitment to the religious dimension and showing the advantage of the bank over other banks was average.

Table 3. Means, standard deviations to evaluate the demand for Islamic banking

Statement	Mean	standard deviation
The demand for deposit in Islamic banks		
The bank attract customers to deposit in Islamic banks	3.50	0.31
The bank contributes to provide advantages for Innovation in Islamic banks	3.40	0.33
Bank works to explain the deposit transactions in accordance with Islamic Sharia	3.30	0.33
Average	3.40	0.33
Commitment to the religious dimension		
Islamic bank complies with all Islamic instruction in all banking transactions	3.40	0.12
Bank refuses to perform transactions conflicting with Islamic law	3.40	0.33
The bank takes into account the facilities provided to its customers	3.30	0.34
Average	3.40	0.31
Showing the advantage of the bank over other banks		
Strategic plan of the bank highlight the positive aspects of Islamic Bank	3.40	0.41
The Bank shows its advantages over for commercial banks	3.30	0.42
The Bank offers its advantages according to the requirements of Islamic law	3.30	0.46
Average	3.30	0.39

Source: Authors.

6. Appropriate Model Test

Ho1: There is no statistically significant impact at the level of significance ($\alpha \leq 0.05$) for the promotion strategy followed by the Jordan Islamic banks (advertisement) on the number of customers of the Islamic banks.

Table 4. Regression and t-test of the effect of advertisement on demand for Islamic bank

R	R2	Calculated t value	Significance
0.582	0.339	11.554	0.001

Source: Authors.

The results showed that advertisements contribute to 33.9% of the demand for Islamic banks. The results showed the presence of statistically significant effect for advertising on demand for Islamic banks as the value of t was (11.554) and the significance level was 0.001, which is less than the level of significance ($\alpha \leq 0.05$).

Ho2: There is no statistically significant impact at the level of significance ($\alpha \leq 0.05$) for the promotion strategy followed by the Jordan Islamic banks (Personal selling) on the number of customers of the Islamic banks.

Table 5. Regression and t-test of the effect of personal selling on demand for Islamic bank

R	R2	Calculated t value	Significance
0.655	0.429	13.984	0.001

Source: Authors.

The results showed that Personal selling contribute to 42.9% of the demand for Islamic banks. The results showed the presence of statistically significant effect for Personal selling on demand for Islamic banks as the value of t was (13.984) and the significance level was 0.001, which is less than the level of significance ($\alpha \leq 0.05$).

Ho3: There is no statistically significant impact at the level of significance ($\alpha \leq 0.05$) for the promotion strategy followed by the Jordan Islamic banks (Sales promotion) on the number of customers of the Islamic banks.

Table 6. Regression and t-test of the effect of Sales promotion on demand for Islamic bank

R	R2	Calculated t value	Significance
0.593	0.352	11.871	0.001

Source: Authors.

The results showed that Sales promotion contribute to 35.2% of the demand for Islamic banks. The results showed the presence of statistically significant effect for Sales promotion on demand for Islamic banks as the value of t was (11.871) and the significance level was 0.001, which is less than the level of significance ($\alpha \leq 0.05$).

Ho4: There is no statistically significant impact at the level of significance ($\alpha \leq 0.05$) for the promotion strategy followed by the Jordan Islamic banks (Publicity) on the number of customers of the Islamic banks.

Table 7. Regression and t-test of the effect of publicity on demand for Islamic bank

R	R2	Calculated t value	Significance
0.727	0.529	17.073	0.001

Source: Authors.

The results showed that Publicity contribute to 52.9% of the demand for Islamic banks. The results showed the presence of statistically significant effect for Publicity on demand for Islamic banks as the value of t was (17.073) and the significance level was 0.001, which is less than the level of significance ($\alpha \leq 0.05$).

Ho5: There is no statistically significant impact at the level of significance ($\alpha \leq 0.05$) for the promotion strategy followed by the Jordan Islamic banks (Public relations) on the number of customers of the Islamic banks.

Table 8. Regression and t-test of the effect of public relations on demand for Islamic bank

R	R2	Calculated t value	Significance
0.642	0.413	15.032	0.001

Source: Authors.

The results showed that Public relations contribute to 41.3% of the demand for Islamic banks. The results showed the presence of statistically significant effect for Public relations on demand for Islamic banks as the value of t was (15.032) and the significance level was 0.001, which is less than the level of significance ($\alpha \leq 0.05$).

7. Conclusions and Recommendations

7.1 Conclusions

The current study found the following results:

1) There are deficiencies in Islamic banks marketing strategies and the reason is that these strategies have not been able to attract a large segment of the Muslims to deal with Islamic banks.

2) The components of promotion strategy in the field of advertising, publicity and the field of personal selling, public relations are still immature and the reason is the absence of clear strategies targeting the largest segment of the customers or who are interested in dealing with Islamic banks.

3) The results showed that advertising has the greatest impact on the demand for deposit in Islamic banks.

4) The effect of the other items on the demand for deposit in Islamic banks was average.

7.2 Recommendations

Through previous conclusions, we can formulate a set of recommendations as follows:

1) Setting clear policies and strategies with specific targets in Islamic banks and which target a different segments of society.

2) The development of the banking sector to meet the required expectations of these banks and meet the needs of the community.

3) Banks shall avoid circumvention of Islamic law in order to make a profit in order to build a stronger trust with the Muslim.

4) Expand the access to promotion strategies to reach a broad category of citizens who desire to deal with Islamic banks.

References

Abu, Q., & Abdul, S. (1996). *Lectures in the Declaration Engineering.* Alexandria, Egypt: Dar Aljamay'a for Printing and Publishing.

Alaq, B., & Rbaba'a, A. M. (1998). *Promotion and advertising*. Integrated Approach, Dar scientific Yazouri, Amman, Jordan.

Alaq, B., Abdali, Q., & Ghalib, S. (1999). *The marketing strategy*. Dar Zahran for Publishing and Distribution, Amman, Jordan

Armstrong, G., & Kotler, P. (1996). *Principles of Marketing*. Prentice Hall.

Asshun, M. F. (1997). *Advertising.* Alexandria, Egypt: Dar Aljamay'a for Printing and Publishing.

Edhmour, H. H., & Shraideh, M. T. (2008). The impact of promotional mix elements of the Jordanian consumer in the use of cellular phone service decisions. *Jordanian Business Management Journal*, University of Jordan, Amman, Jordan.

Edlayme, A. R. M. (2005). *The public relations in the application*. Amman, Jordan: Dar Greer for Publishing and Distribution.

Fzaz, K. (2014). *The impact of e-marketing on promotion mix in the economic institution*. Unpublished Master Thesis, University of Mohamed KHIDER-Biskra, Algeria.

Grankvist, A., Kollberg, C., & Person, A. (2004). *Promotion Strategies for Banking Services*. Retrieved from http://www.smartbize. com/article/view440

Hurb, B. H. (1999). *Principles of Marketing.* Warraq Foundation, Amman, Jordan.

Kincaid, M., Jr. (2003). *Promotion, Product, Service and Ideas* (6th ed.). Columbus, Hoi, Bell 7, Howell Co.

Lovelock, C., & Wirtz, J. (2004). *Service Marketing* (4th ed., pp. 37-38). Pearson, UK.

Marji, A. M. (2008). *The impact of electronic promotion market share in the operating banks in Jordan*. Unpublished Master Thesis, Al al-Bayt University, Mafraq, Jordan.

McCarthy, J., & W. D. Perreault, Jr. (2013). *Basic Marketing* (5th ed., pp. 37-38). Irwin.

Mualla, N. (1996). *The scientific assets of commercial promotion and advertising*. The University of Jordan, Jordan.

Otoum, F. R. (2010). *The impact of the banking promotion to increase savings accounts at banks operating in Jordan.* Unpublished Master Thesis, Yarmouk University, Irbid, Jordan.

Pitt, L., Berthon, P., & Waston, R. (1996). The World Wide Web as an Advertising Medium: Toward an Understanding of Conversion Efficiency. *Journal of Advertising Research*, 43-54.

Rachman, D. J. (1988). *The Marketing Today* (2nd ed.). Rinehart & Winston, Inc.

Sekaran, U. (2008). *Research Methods for Business: A Skill Building Approach*. New York: John Wiley and Sons.

Stanton, W. (1997). *Fundamental of Marketing* (6th ed.). McGraw-Hill, Co.

16

The Effects of Celebrity Endorsement on Customer's Attitude toward Brand and Purchase Intention

Nguyen Minh Ha[1] & Nguyen Hung Lam[1]

[1] Graduate School, Ho Chi Minh City Open University, Vietnam

Correspondence: Nguyen Minh Ha, Graduate School, Ho Chi Minh City Open University, 97 Vo Van Tan Street, District 3, Ho Chi Minh City, Vietnam. E-mail: ha.nm@ou.edu.vn or ngmiha2014@gmail.com

Abstract

Celebrity endorsement has become a popular choice in advertising due to the its originality and the celebrity's attractiveness that make a big impact on brand awareness and customer behavior. This study analyzes the effect of celebrity endorsement on customer's attitude toward brand as well as the effect of customer's attitude toward brand on customer's purchase intention in Vietnam. A survey was conducted with 306 individuals in Vietnam. After conducting the explanatory factor analysis (EFA), and multi-variable regression analysis, results indicate that customer's attitude toward brand is positively affected by 03 factors: celebrity match-up congruence with the brand/product, celebrity trustworthiness, and celebrity expertise. Attitude toward brand also has a positive impact on customer's purchase intention.

Keywords: celebrity endorsement, customer's attitude toward brand, purchase intention

1. Introduction

In recent years, the development of commercial communication and of rise-up of live TV shows has attracted lots of attention from the public, especially young generation. Marketing strategies of companies focus mostly on promoting products to the market with core objectives as to persuade their customers; since the customers have got a lot of knowledge, references, and choices before making a purchase decision, competition has also became more severely. There are a number of ways to promote brands, but employing celebrity as an aid to the brand has become popular in all over the world (Friedman et al., 1979; Kamins, 1989). This is because advertisements in which celebrity appears are generating effective outcomes in making the brand identity and retaining customers' attention, that is the mandatory objective of any commerce (Erdogan, 1999; Kamins & Gupta, 1994; Kaikati, 1987; Patti & Frazer, 1988). Belch and Belch (2004, p. 174) showed that "in today's television viewing environment and the "stopping power" of celebrity endorsed commercials are more remarkable". However, if they later make up a negative image of themselves, brand image will also be affected. Therefore, it is very important to select appropriate celebrity to represent a brand.

There have been a lot of studies in the world on the effect of celebrity on brand promotion activities, but this field hasn't been addressed adequately in Vietnam. The questions are that which factors of celebrity endorsement will have effect on customer's attitude toward brand and how is the relationship between customer's attitude toward brand and purchase intention in Vietnam?

2. Literature Review

There are a lot of definitions of celebrity. According to Young and Pinsky (2006, p. 464) "individuals who have achieved a significant level of fame that makes them well known in society". The celebrity has rose to become a powerful force in the 21st century and hold an important role in the contemporary culture (Koernig & Boyd, 2009; Lord & Putrevu, 2009). A celebrity is a person whose name can attract public attention, ignite public interest, and create individual values from the public (Kotler, Keller, & Jha, 2007). However, perhaps the most impressive and widely referenced definition is Daniel Boorstin's (1982, p. 49), in which he defined: as "The celebrity is a person who is known for his well-knownness".

Early definition of celebrity endorsement is mentioned by Freiden (1984). According to him, celebrity endorsement means celebrity in direct connection to an advertised product. According to McCracken (1989, p.

310): "An individual who enjoys public recognition and who uses this recognition on behalf of a customer good by appearing with it in an advertisement". According to Kotler et al. (2007), celebrity endorsement is one of communication channels that are used by celebrity as a means of expressing their words to promote the brand on basis of their fame and personalities.

2.1 Meaning Transfer Model

According to McCracken (1989), this model is developed to illustrate celebrity endorsement process. Advertising is one of means to transfer individual meaning to the brands. This model is divided into three stages. First stage is the development of celebrity image and description of cultural meaning of the society. In this stage, it is assessed whether subject, people and context are suitable to the celebrity. The second stage is relevant to the celebrity's transfer of meanings from brand endorsement to the product. In the final stage, brand image is transferred to the customers.

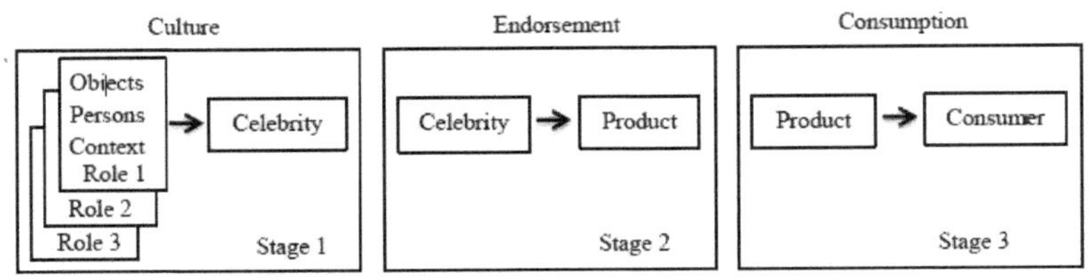

Figure 1. Meaning transfer model

Note. ➔ Path of meaning movement. □ Stage of meaning movement.

Source: McCracken, 1989, p. 45.

2.2 Customer's Attitude Toward Brand

Customer's attitude toward brand is predisposition that focuses on favorable or unfavorable impact on a specific brand after watching an advertisement on that brand (Phelps & Hoy, 1996). According to Lutz et al. (1983), customer's attitude toward brand is the customer's emotional reaction toward a brand advertisement. It is associated with the customer's feeling if his/her purchase intention toward the brand is positive or negative, favorable or unfavorable.

2.3 The Elaboration Likelihood Model (ELM)

Elaboration Likelihood Model (ELM) is a model that consists of two phases of response toward advertising incentive. It explains how attitudes are formed on basis of the degree of participation. Current attitude may be changed and it is assumed that when a customer receives a message, he starts processing it. There are two possible directions: Central route used for persuasion if customer participation is high, or peripheral route used for persuasion if customer participation is low. The model has two fundamental factors, motivation and ability to process communication. Motivation means the customer's readiness, participation, and needs. Ability means the knowledge, qualification, and capacity to process information (Petty et al., 1983).

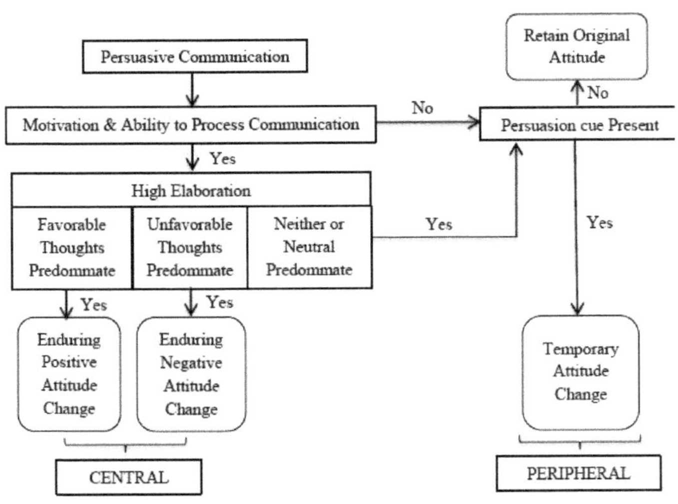

Figure 2. Elaboration Likelihood Model (ELM)

Source: Petty et al., 1983.

2.4 The Relation between Source Credibility Model and Customer's Attitude toward Brand

Hovland & Weiss (1953) introduced a source credibility model, which is further studied by Ohanian (1990) (cited by Armando, 2014). According to source credibility model, "the effectiveness of a message depends on the apparent level of expertise and trustworthiness of the endorser" (Hovland & Weiss, 1953, p. 20)

2.4.1 Celebrity Trustworthiness

Trustworthiness refers to "the honesty, integrity and believability of an endorser" (Erdogan et al., 2001, p. 40). A celebrity is considered as trustworthy (Goldsmith et al., 2000) and his/her trustworthiness is described as a summary of values that create positive features and increase the acceptance of the message (Erdogan, 1999). Trustworthiness is the most useful and effective tool to make the customer be more confident and reliable on the brand (Ohanian, 1990). A hypothesis is provided:

Hypothesis 1 (H1): The more celebrity trustworthiness is perceived by the customer, the more positive customer's attitude toward brand will be.

2.4.2 Celebrity Expertise

Hovland et al. (1953) defines expertise as the level of knowledge and experience that a person may obtain in a specific field that is acknowledged as valid. The more persuasive a celebrity's expertise is (Aaker, 1997), the more purchase decisions will be generated (Ohanian, 1991). Speck, Schumann, and Thompson (1988) affirms that celebrity is considered as an expert in a specific field, resulting in a higher brand endorsement than a celebrity without expertise (Hoekman & Bosmans, 2010). Following hypothesis is provided:

Hypothesis 2 (H2): The more celebrity expertise is perceived by the customer, the more positive customer's attitude toward brand will be.

2.5 The Relation between Source Attractiveness Model and Customer's Attitude toward Brand

Source attractiveness model is developed by McGuire (1985), he holds that an individual message is accepted and affected by the similarity between the receiver and the sender together with the familiarity and likeliness. The meaning of source attractiveness model is referenced to be a famous philosopher, Aristotle: "beauty is a greater recommendation than any letter of introduction". Aristotle wants to emphasize that the most importance is beauty and attractiveness (Hoekman & Bosmans, 2010).

2.5.1 Celebrity Attractiveness

Physical attractiveness transited via a person's weight, height, and facial beauty is the very first expressions perceived by another (Bardia et al., 2011). This concept does not only means physical attractiveness. It also requires mental skills, personality, lifestyle, and art talents (Erdogan, 1999). A celebrity is attractive because he/she has built up a popular image among the public. His/her attractiveness increases the persuasiveness toward the customers as they want to be like the celebrity that they love (Cohen & Golden, 1972). A hypothesis is given

Hypothesis 3 (H3): The more celebrity attractiveness is perceived by the customer, the more positive customer's attitude toward brand will be.

2.5.2 Celebrity Similarity

Similarity is described as "a supposed resemblance between the source and the receiver of the message" (McGuire, 1985). In other words, a customer may similarize himself with the endorser. People will be more easily influenced when they find the similarity between them and the endorser. If the celebrity and the customers share popular factors, such as similar interest or lifestyle, a better association will be formed (Erdogan, 1999). Following hypothesis is provided:

Hypothesis 4 (H4): The more celebrity similarity is perceived by the customer, the more positive customer's attitude toward brand will be.

2.5.3 Celebrity Liking

Likeability is the "affection for the source as a result of the source's physical appearance and behaviour" (McGuire, 1985, p. 239). In addition, McGuire also holds that when customers like a celebrity, they will like brands associated with the celebrity. A hypothesis is provided:

Hypothesis 5 (H5): The more celebrity liking is perceived by the customer, the more positive customer's attitude toward brand will be.

2.5.4 Celebrity Familiarity

Familiarity means the feeling of similarity by means of emotions and contact with a celebrity (Erdogan, 1999;

Belch & Belch, 2004). Celebrity familiarity will have a more positive impact when the customer himself finds that he/she is similar to the celebrity. This is called the mere exposure effect (Zajonc, 1968). When the customers have short contacts with the celebrity and contact interval becomes longer, the effects of familiarity will improve customer's attitude toward brand. On the contrary, the effect is negative when they have long contacts and contact interval becomes shorter (Bornstein, 1989). A hypothesis is given by:

Hypothesis 6 (H6): The more celebrity familiarity is perceived by the customer, the more positive customer's attitude toward brand will be.

2.6 The Relationship between Brand/Product Match – up Hypothesis Model and Customer's Attitude toward Brand

According to Forkan (1980); Kamins (1989), brand/product match – up hypothesis model means that celebrity image and product message must be similar and matched up in order for the advertisement to be effective.

2.6.1 Celebrity Match-up Congruence With The Brand/Product

A number of studies conducted by Cooper (1984) and Forkan (1980) indicate that celebrity match-up congruence with the brand/product has a significant play. When a product is advertised by a celebrity with suitable image that is highly relevant to the product, the confidence will be higher on the advertisement and the celebrity compared to a product image promoted by a less famous, less relevant person (Kotler, 1997). A hypothesis is given:

Hypothesis 7 (H7): The more celebrity match-up congruence with the brand/product is perceived by the customer, the more positive customer's attitude toward brand will be.

2.6.2 The Relationship between Customer's Attitude toward Brand and Purchase Intention

Customer's purchase intention addresses the predisposition to purchase a certain brand or product (Belch & Belch, 2004). Purchase intention also tells about the possibility that a person will purchase a product (Phelps & Hoy, 1996). Amos, et al. (2008) hold that the customer's positive attitude toward celebrity endorsement will improve his/her purchase intention. Many studies also indicate that customer's attitude toward brand has a positive and significant impact on purchase intention (Mitchell & Olson, 1981; Gresham & Shimp, 1985; Batra & Ray, 1986; Phelps & Hoy, 1996). A hypothesis is provided:

Hypothesis 8 (H8): The more positive customer's attitude toward brand is, the more positive purchase intention will be.

3. Methodology and Research Model

3.1 Methodology

This study is conducted in two major stages. A qualitative study is conducted by face-to-face direct interview on 04 marketing experts and a group discussion is carried out among 12 customers of 18 years old or more, which is intended to modify, supplement, and complete the measurement scale. A quantitative study is carried out to collect data by using a questionnaire survey based on Likert rating scale with 5 options, including "1-Totally Disagree", "2-Disagree", "3-Neutral", "4-Agree", "5-Totally Agree", used to measure observation variables for each factor.

3.2 Proposed Research Model

From theories and previous studies, an analysis is conducted on the effect of the celebrity endorsement consisting of 07 factors, which are: celebrity trustworthiness, celebrity attractiveness, celebrity expertise, celebrity similarity, celebrity liking, celebrity familiarity, celebrity match-up congruence with the brand/product are independent varieties. Customer's attitude toward brand means temporary variable. Purchase intention means dependent variable.

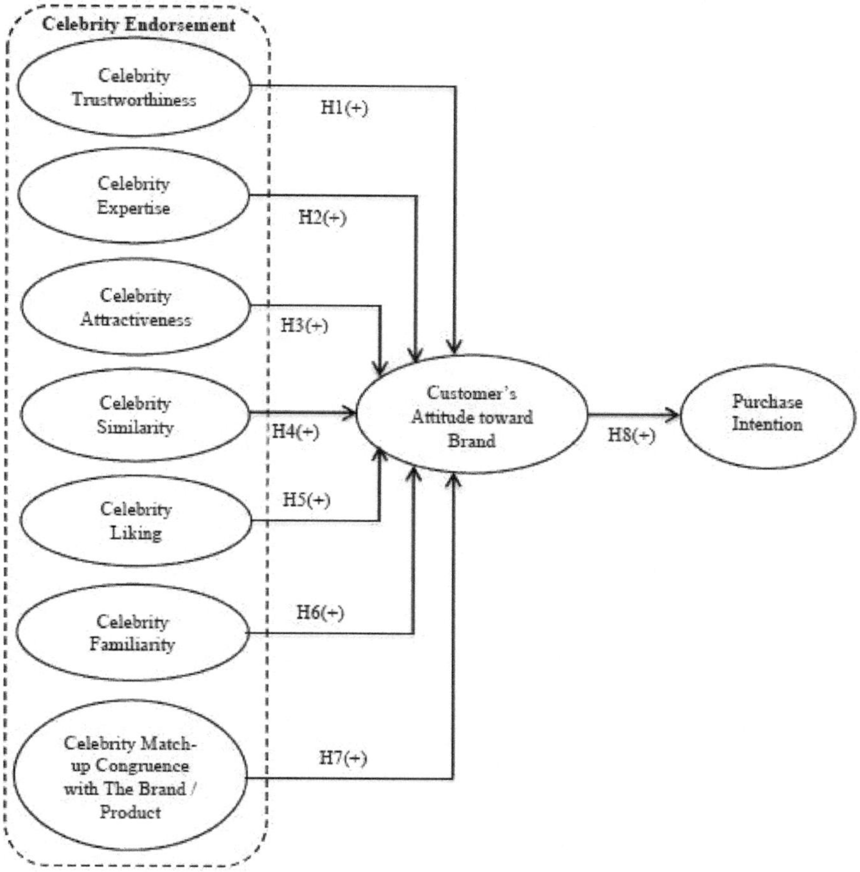

Figure 3. Proposed research model

3.3 Research Data

A total of 534 questionnaire sheets were directly distributed to the customers of 18 years old or more in Vietnam or via online method. A total of 392 sheets were returned and, after being screened, 306 sheets were valid for data analysis, achieving a ratio of 78.06% compared to actual data.

4. Research Results

4.1 Descritptive Statistics by Characteristics

For gender, there are 184 female and 122 male respondents, accounting for 60.1% and 39.9%, respectively, of which 61.4% are single, 38.6% are married. For age, respondents of 18–25 years old account for 28.1%, of 26–35 years old account for 58.5%, 36–45 years old account for 7.5%, and of more than 45 years old account for 5.9%. For education, university respondents account for 45.1%, post-graduate ones account for 28.4%, primary school ones account for 2.6%, secondary school ones account for 7.2%, high school ones account for 8.5%, and college-intermediary school ones account for 8.2%.

4.2 Descriptive Statistics of Model Variables

Table 1. Descriptive statistic of quantitative variables

	Content	Min	Max	Mean	Standard Deviation
Celebrity Trustworthiness					
CT1	You believe in celebrity's brand choice.	1	5	3.15	0.904
CT2	You think that the celebrity is an honest person.	1	5	2.92	0.866
CT3	You think that the celebrity provides reliable source of information.	1	5	2.94	0.878
CT4	You think that the celebrity is a sincere person.	1	5	2.93	0.875
CT5	You think that the celebrity is a trustworthy person.	1	5	2.96	0.892
Celebrity Expertise					
CE1	You think that the celebrity is an expert in the field that he/she represents.	1	5	2.60	0.964
CE2	You think that the celebrity has experience in using the brand.	1	5	3.02	0.887

CE3	You think that the celebrity has a lot of knowledge about this brand.	1	5	2.92	0.884
CE4	You think that the celebrity has got high professional qualification.	1	5	2.77	0.908
CE5	You think that the celebrity has skilled this brand.	1	5	3.01	0.905
Celebrity Attractiveness					
CA1	You think that the celebrity has got a strong attractiveness.	1	5	4.01	0.696
CA2	You think that the celebrity is a very classy.	1	5	3.36	0.881
CA3	You think that the celebrity has a very pretty face.	1	5	3.81	0.831
CA4	You think that the celebrity has a very elegant fashion style.	2	5	3.87	0.801
CA5	You think that the celebrity has a very attractive appearance.	1	5	3.82	0.864
CA6	You think that the celebrity has a very persuasive voice.	1	5	3.46	0.846
CA7	You think that the celebrity has a very professional manner.	2	5	3.81	0.778
Celebrity Similarity					
CS1	You think that the celebrity and you share the same culture.	1	5	3.01	0.861
CS2	You think that the celebrity and you share similar lifestyle.	1	5	2.56	0.817
CS3	You think that the celebrity and you share similar interests.	1	5	2.89	0.873
CS4	You think that the celebrity and you share similar perspectives.	1	5	2.60	0.771
CS5	You think that the celebrity and you share similar likings.	1	5	2.67	0.886
Celebrity Liking					
CL1	You like the celebrity's behaviors.	1	5	3.36	0.757
CL2	You like the celebrity's appearance.	1	5	3.75	0.762
CL3	You think that the celebrity is very popular.	1	5	4.07	0.721
CL4	You like the celebrity's voice.	1	5	3.34	0.800
CL5	You like the celebrity's fashion style.	1	5	3.64	0.818
CL6	You like the celebrity's professional manner.	1	5	3.71	0.799
CL7	Overall, you like the celebrity.	1	5	3.66	0.806
Celebrity Familiarity					
CF1	You often see the celebrity on the TV.	1	5	4.15	0.625
CF2	You often see the celebrity on the stage or in the cinema.	1	5	3.31	0.950
CF3	You often see the celebrity at events or festivals.	1	5	3.52	0.877
CF4	You often see the celebrity on the advertising boards.	2	5	4.06	0.627
CF5	You often see the celebrity on the newspapers.	1	5	4.10	0.609
CF6	You often see the celebrity in person.	1	5	2.57	0.994
CF7	You often see the celebrity on the Internet.	1	5	4.15	0.672
CF8	You often listen to the celebrity over the radio.	1	5	3.07	0.989
Celebrity Match-up Congruence with The Brand / Product					
CM1	You often see the celebrity in the advertisements of this brand.	1	5	3.93	0.694
CM2	You think that celebrity image suits this brand.	1	5	3.74	0.736
CM3	You think that this brand is totally suitable for the celebrity to represent.	1	5	3.67	0.779
CM4	You think that the celebrity that represents this brand is trustworthy.	1	5	3.43	0.787
CM5	You believe that the celebrity is using this brand.	1	5	3.05	0.943
Customer's Attitude toward Brand					
AB1	You believe that this brand is a good one.	1	5	3.54	0.724
AB2	You think that this brand is very interesting.	1	5	3.50	0.712
AB3	You like this brand.	1	5	3.44	0.763
AB4	You think that this brand has a good quality.	2	5	3.46	0.751
AB5	You are satisfied with this brand.	1	5	3.46	0.734
AB6	You are confident in this brand.	1	5	3.42	0.766
Purchase Intention					
PI1	You will seek more information on this product.	1	5	3.59	0.806
PI2	You will actively seek for this product.	1	5	3.41	0.857
PI3	You will try this product when you see it.	1	5	3.68	0.762
PI4	You will purchase this product.	1	5	3.34	0.823
PI5	Celebrity appearance in the advertisement has motivated you to purchase this product.	1	5	3.21	1.009

Celebrity trustworthiness: CT1 has the highest mean value (3.15), while CT2 has the lowest mean value (2.92). So, the customers are confident on celebrity's brand choice, but they don't think that the celebrity is honest.

Celebrity expertise: CE2 has the highest mean value (3.02), while CE1 has the lowest mean value (2.60). Hence, the customers think that the celebrity has a lot of experience in using this brand, but they don't think that the celebrity is an expert in the field that he/she represents.

Celebrity attractiveness: CA1 has the highest mean value (4.01), while CA2 has the lowest mean value (3.36). Hence, the customers think that the celebrity has got a strong attractiveness, but they don't think that the celebrity is a very skilled elite.

Celebrity similarity: CS1 has the highest mean value (3.01), while CS2 has the lowest mean value (2.56). Hence, the customers think that the celebrity and they share the same culture, but they don't think that the celebrity and them share similar lifestyle.

Celebrity liking: CL3 has the highest mean value (4.07), while CL4 has the lowest mean value (3.34). Hence, the customers think that the celebrity is very popular, but they don't like his/her voice.

Celebrity familiarity: CF1 and CF7 has the highest mean value (4.15), while CF6 has the lowest mean value (2.57). Hence, the customers agree that they often see the celebrity on the TV and Internet, but they don't agree that they often see the celebrity in person.

Celebrity match-up congruence with the brand / product: CM1 has the highest mean value (3.93), while has the lowest mean value (3.05). Hence, the customers often see the celebrity in brand advertisements, but they don't believe that the celebrity is using this product.

Customer's attitude toward brand: AB1 has the highest mean value (3.54), while AB6 has the lowest mean value (3.42). Hence, the customers believe that the brand represented by the celebrity is a good one, but they don't believe in this brand.

Purchase intention: PI3 has the highest mean value (3.68), while PI5 has the lowest mean value (3.21). Hence, the customers agree that they will try this product when they see it, but they don't think that celebrity appearance in the advertisement has motivated them to purchase the product.

4.3 Testing the Cronbach's Alpha

Celebrity trustworthiness: Removing CT1 has the Cronbach's Alpha if item deleted is 0.908 larger than the Cronbach's Alpha coefficient of the 1st scale test value of 0.907. In the 2nd test, the Cronbach's Alpha coefficient is 0.908, and item-total correlation for all variables are satisfied (higher than 0.3). Therefore, remaining 4 observation variables are included in factor analysis (EFA).

Celebrity expertise: The Cronbach's Alpha coefficient is 0.817, and item-total correlation for all variables are satisfied (higher than 0.3). Therefore, the 5 observation variables are included in EFA.

Celebrity attractiveness: The Cronbach's Alpha coefficient is 0.810, and item-total correlation for all variables are satisfied (higher than 0.3). Therefore, the 7 observation variables are included in EFA.

Celebrity similarity: removing CS1 has the Cronbach's Alpha if item deleted is 0.867 larger than the Cronbach's Alpha coefficient of the 1st scale test value of 0.851. In the 2nd test, the Cronbach's Alpha coefficient is 0.867, and item-total correlation for all variables are satisfied (higher than 0.3). Therefore, remaining 4 observation variables are included in factor analysis (EFA).

Celebrity liking: The Cronbach's Alpha coefficient is 0.833, and item-total correlation for all variables are satisfied (higher than 0.3). Therefore, the 7 observation variables are included in EFA.

Celebrity familiarity: 3 varieties which are eliminated because the correlation coefficients of item-total is not satisfied (lower than 0.3) include CF1(0.273), CF6 (0.243), and CF8 (0.297). After eliminating such varieties, the Cronbach's Alpha coefficient has been increased. Hence, the 2nd test shall be conducted, the Cronbach's Alpha coefficient is 0.684, and the item-total correlation for all variables are satisfied (higher than 0.3). Therefore, remaining 5 observation variables are included in EFA.

Celebrity match-up congruence with the brand / product: CM1 and CM5 are eliminated because they have the Cronbach's Alpha if item deleted are 0.787 and 0.801 respectively, and higher than the Cronbach's Alpha coefficient of the 1st test scale of 0.784. In the 2nd test, CM4 is eliminated because it has the Cronbach's Alpha if item deleted is 0.863 higher than the Cronbach's Alpha coefficient of the 2nd scale test value of 0.822. In the 3rd test, the Cronbach's Alpha coefficient is 0.863, and item-total correlation for all variables are satisfied (higher than 0.3). Therefore, remaining 2 observation variables are included in EFA

Customer's attitude toward brand: AB2 is eliminated because it has the Cronbach's Alpha if item deleted is 0.930, which is higher than the 1st scale test value of 0.923. In the 2nd test, AB1 is eliminated because it has the Cronbach's Alpha if item deleted is 0.931, which is higher than the Cronbach's Alpha coefficient of the 2nd scale test value of 0.930. In the 3rd test, the Cronbach's Alpha coefficient is 0.931, and item-total correlation for all variables are satisfied (higher than 0.3). Therefore, remaining 4 observation variables are included in EFA.

Purchase intention: PI5 is eliminated because it has the Cronbach's Alpha if item deleted is 0.865, which is higher than the Cronbach's Alpha coefficient of the 1st scale test value of 0.860. In the 2nd test, the Cronbach's Alpha coefficient is 0.865, and item-total correlation for all variables are satisfied (higher than 0.3). Therefore, remaining 4 observation variables are included in EFA.

Table 2. The Cronbach's Alpha coefficient of the variables in the model

Variable	Corrected Item-Total Correlation	Cronbach's Alpha if Item Deleted	Cronbach's Alpha
Celebrity Trustworthiness			
CT2	0.803	0.877	
CT3	0.734	0.901	0.908
CT4	0.828	0.868	
CT5	0.803	0.877	
Celebrity Expertise			
CE1	0.546	0.800	
CE2	0.612	0.779	
CE3	0.706	0.752	0.817
CE4	0.563	0.794	
CE5	0.616	0.778	
Celebrity Attractiveness			
CA1	0.462	0.798	
CA2	0.469	0.800	
CA3	0.661	0.764	
CA4	0.656	0.765	0.810
CA5	0.582	0.778	
CA6	0.488	0.795	
CA7	0.513	0.790	
Celebrity Similarity			
CS2	0.705	0.836	
CS3	0.696	0.840	0.867
CS4	0.784	0.807	
CS5	0.697	0.840	
Celebrity Liking			
CL1	0.523	0.819	
CL2	0.578	0.811	
CL3	0.533	0.818	
CL4	0.562	0.814	0.833
CL5	0.602	0.807	
CL6	0.604	0.807	
CL7	0.666	0.796	
Celebrity Familiarity			
CF2	0.389	0.671	
CF3	0.430	0.641	
CF4	0.513	0.610	0.684
CF5	0.503	0.616	
CF7	0.436	0.636	
Celebrity Match-up Congruence with The Brand / Product			
CM2	0.760		0.863
CM3	0.760		
Customer's Attitude toward Brand			
AB3	0.817	0.917	
AB4	0.814	0.918	0.931
AB5	0.867	0.901	
AB6	0.857	0.904	
Purchase Intention			
PI1	0.733	0.820	
PI2	0.778	0.800	0.865
PI3	0.631	0.860	
PI4	0.719	0.826	

4.4 Explanatory Factor Analysis (EFA)

Explanatory factor analysis is conducted on whether celebrity endorsement has an impact on customer's attitude toward brand. After the 1st analysis, CA1, CA2, CL1, CL3 CL7, CL2, CL5, CE1, CF4, CL6, CL4 are eliminated. After the 2nd analysis, CA6, CA7, CE4 are eliminated. After 3nd analysis, CF5 and CF7 are eliminated. After 4th analysis, factor loading values are satisfactory with KMO coefficient of 0.844 with significance level of the Bartlett test of 0.000.

Table 3. Results of the Explanatory Factor Analysis (EFA)

Conducting times	**Eliminating the variable**	**KMO coefficient**	**Significance of Bartlett test**
1st time	CA1, CA2, CL1, CL3, CL7, CL2, CL5, CE1, CF4, CL6, CL4	0.883	0.000
2nd time	CA6, CA7, CE4	0.848	0.000
3rd time	CF5, CF7	0.834	0.000
4th time		0.844	0.000

Composition		**Component**					
		1	**2**	**3**	**4**	**5**	**6**
Celebrity Trustworthiness	CT4	0.874					
	CT5	0.856					
	CT2	0.852					
	CT3	0.789					
Celebrity Similarity	CS4		0.860				
	CS2		0.802				
	CS5		0.758				
	CS3		0.757				
Celebrity Attractiveness	CA5			0.863			
	CA4			0.860			
	CA3			0.847			
Celebrity Expertise	CE2				0.815		
	CE3				0.799		
	CE5				0.769		
Celebrity Match-up Congruence with The Brand / Product	CM2					0.905	
	CM3					0.879	
Celebrity Familiarity	CF3						0.850
	CF2						0.823
Eigenvalues		5.791	2.416	1.705	1.512	1.234	1.108
% of Variance		32.172	13.422	9.472	8.403	6.857	6.156
% Cumulative		32.172	45.594	55.066	63.469	70.326	76.482

Based on results presented in Table 3, 18 observation variables are satisfactory and divided into 6 factor groups. Factors are unchanged from original ones. However, "celebrity liking" factor is eliminated and hypotheses and research model are corrected as follows:

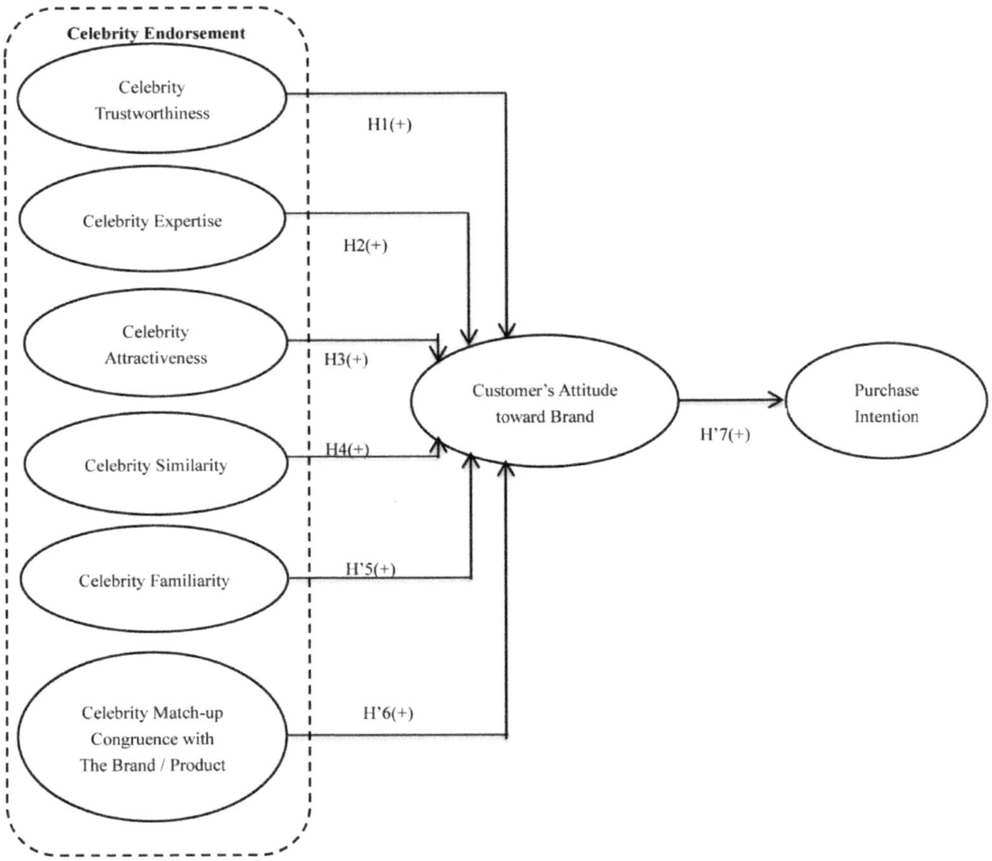

Figure 4. Research model correction

4.5 Regression Analysis

According to results in Table 4, Analysis of the fitness of the regression model on customer's attitude toward brand, Adjusted R^2 get value is 0.273, which is varied by 27.3% in term of "customer's attitude toward brand", it can be explained by independent factors in the model. F = 20.058 with significant level of 0.000. Therefore, the regression model is considered as overall fit.

Table 4. Results of regression analysis the model of customers' attitude towards brand

Model	Unstandardized Coefficients (B)	Standardized Coefficients (β)	t	Sig.	VIF
(Constant)	1.126		4.210	0.000	
Celebrity Trustworthiness	0.182***	0.206	3.491	0.001	1.455
Celebrity Expertise	0.165***	0.181	3.148	0.002	1.385
Celebrity Similarity	0.050	0.052	0.856	0.393	1.548
Celebrity Attractiveness	0.036	0.038	0.717	0.474	1.197
Celebrity Match-up Congruence with The Brand/Product	0.278***	0.288	5.223	0.000	1.275
Celebrity Familiarity	-0.002	-0.003	-0.055	0.956	1.034
R	0.536				
R^2	0.287				
Adjusted R^2	0.273				
F (Anova)	20.058				
Sig. (Anova)	0.000				
Durbin - Watson	2.069				

Note. Dependent variable: Customer's attitude toward brand. ***: Results at the significance level of 1%.

According to the Table 5, the match-up congruence of the regression model of purchase intention, Adjusted R^2 get value is 0.483, means 48.3% upon the variability of the purchase intention can be explained by the customers' attitude towards brand. F = 285.814 with significant level of 0.000; therefore, the regression model is considered as overall fit.

Table 5. Results of regression analysis the model of purchase intention

Model	Unstandardized Coefficients (B)	Standardized Coefficients (β)	t	Sig.	VIF
(Constant)	1.106		7.646	0.000	
Customers' attitude towards brand	0.696***	0.696	16.906	0.000	1.000
R	0.696				
R^2	0.485				
Adjusted R^2	0.483				
F (Anova)	285.814				
Sig. (Anova)	0.000				
Durbin - Watson	1.973				

Note. Dependent variable: Purchase intention. ***: Results at the significance level of 1%.

4.6 Discussion of Results

4.6.1 Celebrity Trustworthiness

This variable is statistically significant at 1%, with value $\beta = 0.206 > 0$, this means that H1 hypothesis is supported. Trustworthiness refers to "the honesty, integrity and believability of an endorser" (Erdogan et al., 2001). The celebrity is considered as a trustworthy person (Goldsmith et al., 2000). A study by Pham & Nguyen (2015) indicates that "celebrity trustworthiness" has a positive impact on "customer's attitude toward the advertisement". Results of this study also find positive impact of "celebrity trustworthiness" on "customer's attitude toward brand". This can be explained as follows: celebrity appearance in commerces in Vietnam has become popular because the celebrity can influence the public. However, "scandals" in their personal lives have caused the public wonder and lose trusts in the celebrity's ethics. Only a few celebrities are acknowledged for their talents and ethics, and they are respected and relied upon by most of the public and colleagues. Therefore, celebrity endorsement will have more impact on the customers than non-celebrity trustworthy.

4.6.2 Celebrity Expertise

This factor is statistically significant at 1%, with value $\beta = 0.181 > 0$, this means that H2 hypothesis is supported. The expertise mentions the level of knowledge and experience that a person may obtain in a specific field that is acknowledged as valid (Hovland et al., 1953). The more persuasive a celebrity's expertise is (Aaker, 1997), the more purchase decisions will be generated (Ohanian, 1991). A study by Pham and Nguyen (2015) indicates that "*celebrity expertise*" has a positive impact on "customer's attitude toward the advertisement". Results of this study also find positive impact of "celebrity expertise" on "customer's attitude toward brand". This can be explained as follows: With their attractiveness and influencing ability, celebrities are highly paid for their appearance in advertisements although the brand is not related to their expertises. Therefore, customers feel that they are not assured, and their confidence in the brand is wondered. So, enterprises need to select the celebrities that have expertises related to the brand to be advertised so that customers will be more confident and accept it more positively.

4.6.3 Celebrity Attractiveness

This variable is statistically significant at 5%, with value $\beta = 0.038$, this means that H3 hypothesis is not supported. A study by Pham & Nguyen (2015) indicates that "*celebrity attractiveness*" has a positive impact on "customer's attitude toward the advertisement". However, this study only considers the "customers' attitude towards brand" and the its results indicate no positive effect of the "celebrity attractiveness" factor on the "customer's attitude toward brand". This can be explained as follows: Most of today's celebrities have pretty, attractive and ideal appearance to make their advertisements more impressive. Therefore, celebrity attractiveness will generate attention toward the customers and make advertisements more attractive, however, attractiveness has no impact on customer's attitude toward brand.

4.6.4 Celebrity Similarity

This factor is statistically significant at 5%, with value $\beta = 0.052$, this means that H4 hypothesis is not supported. A study by Pham and Nguyen (2015) indicates that "celebrity similarity" has a positive impact on "customer's attitude toward the advertisement". However, this study only considers the "customers' attitude towards brand"

and the its results indicate no positive effect of the "celebrity similarity" factor on the "customer's attitude toward brand". This can be explained as follows: Celebrities have ideal appearance and outstanding talents. All fans want to become like the ones that they like, from their lifestyle, likings, fashion style, etc. They learn after celebrities and think that they share similar values, to a certain extent, with celebrities. However, similarity only makes advertisements with celebrity endorsement receive more attention and be remembered, but it does not affect customer's attitude toward brand.

4.6.5 Celebrity Familiarity

This variable is statistically significant at 5%, with value $\beta = 0.003$, meaning that H'5 hypothesis is not supported. The study by Pham and Nguyen (2015) does not consider "celebrity familiarity" factor. A study by Shahrokh and Arefi (2013) indicates that there is a positive impact of "celebrity familiarity" on "source attractiveness model", and thereby resulting in a positive impact on "the effectiveness of celebrity endorsement". However, this study only considers the "customers' attitude towards brand" and the its results indicate no positive effect of the "celebrity familiarity" factor on the "customer's attitude toward brand". This can be explained as follows: This celebrity will be covered everywhere so that customers can easily see the ones they love just by clicking or navigating a remote control. It is celebrity familiarity that will help the customers easily memorize and be impressed at the advertisements with celebrity endorsement, but familiarity has no impact on customer's attitude toward brand.

4.6.6 Celebrity Match-up Congruence with The Brand/Product

This factor is statistically significant at 1%, with value $\beta = 0.288 > 0$, meaning that H'6 hypothesis is not supported. Celebrity match-up congruence with the brand / product may create the absolute confidence through the homogeneous process (Langmeyer & Walker, 1991), and cause positive effect on the customers' attitude towards advertisment, brand / product and purchase intention (Kirmani & Shiv, 1998). A study by Pham and Nguyen (2015) indicates that "celebrity match-up congruence with the brand / product" has a positive impact on "customer's attitude toward the advertisement". Results of this study also find positive impact of "celebrity match-up congruence with the brand / product" on "customer's attitude toward brand". This can be explained as follows: everyday, customers can watch a lots of advertisements with celebrity, even the same one in different advertisements. When a brand / product is advertised by a celebrity with suitable image that is highly relevant to the brand / product, the confidence will be higher on the advertisement and the celebrity compared to a brand / product image promoted by a less famous, less relevant person.

4.6.7 Customer's Attitude toward Brand

This variable is statistically significant at 1%, with value $\beta = 0.696 > 0$, meaning that H'7 hypothesis is not supported. Customer's attitude toward brand is predisposition that focuses on favorable or unfavorable impact on a specific brand after watching an advertisement on that brand (Phelps & Hoy, 1996). The study by Pham and Nguyen (2015) does not consider the effect of "customer's attitude toward brand" factor on the "purchase intention". Studies of Qurat and Mahira (2012), Aycha and Kaouther (2010) and Mazzini et al. (2014) indicate the positive effect of "customer's attitude toward brand" factor on the "purchase intention". Results of this study also affirm the correctness of previous studies. This impact is positive and considerable in Vietnamese market. Attitude is used as factor to forecast customer's intention and behavior (Fishbien & Ajzen, 1975; Ajzen, 1991). When customers have more positive attitude toward brand, they will more likely intend to purchase the products.

5. Conclusions and Recommendations

5.1 Conclusions

The final study model includes 7 factors of celebrity endorsement with impact on customer's attitude toward brand. Also, factors of attitude toward brand have impacts on customer's purchase intention. After testing the reliability of the measurement scale and conducting explanatory factor analysis, results are that celebrity liking factor is eliminated while other factors are retained, resulting in a correction of study model hypotheses. Results of the multi-variable regression analysis indicate that customer's attitude toward brand in Vietnam is positively affected by 03 factors: celebrity match-up congruence with the brand / product, celebrity trustworthiness, and celebrity expertises. Results also indicate that purchase intention is strongly and positively impacted by customer's attitude toward brand.

5.2 Suggestions of Policy Implications

Based on findings, the study suggests some policy implications as follows:

Firstly, enterprises should pay careful attention to selecting celebrities for promoting the brand. If the celebrity has made any dispute statement, improper behavior, and a negative scandal, it will negatively affect the brand and reputation of the enterprises. Therefore, it is necessary to select a trustworthy celebrity that is trusted by the public.

Secondly, not every celebrity endorses a brand that is within his/her expertise. Therefore, customers usually wonder that celebrity endorsement is just intended to make the ads attractive, but product quality is not persuasive because it is beyond his/her expertise. Thus, if an enterprise luckily chooses a celebrity that is an expert in the brand that it wants to promote, the persuasiveness and customer's attitude toward brand will be more positively impacted.

Thirdly, when enterprises can formulate a meaningful message that is suitable to the celebrity and brand, this will have a positive impact on customer's attitude toward brand. So, enterprises need to select a suitable celebrity for their brand images and advertising message that they want to transfer, so that customers have better perception of the advertisements and positive attitude toward the brand.

References

Amos, C., Holmes, G., & Strutton, D. (2008). Exploring The Relationship between Celebrity Endorser Effects and Advertising Effectiveness. A Quantitative Synthesis of Effect Size. *International Journal of Advertising, 27*(2), 209-234. http://dx.doi.org/10.1080/02650487.2008.11073052

Aycha, M. G., & Kaouther, S. B. R. (2010). The Persuasive Effectiveness of Famous and Non Famous Endorsers in Advertising. *IBIMA Business Review*, 14. http://dx.doi.org/10.5171/2010.474771

Broostin, D. (1982). The Image: A Guide to Pseudo-Events in America. *New York: Athenneum*, 49.

Erdogan, B. Z. (1999). Celebrity endorsement: A literature review. *Journal of Marketing Management, 14*, 291-314. http://dx.doi.org/10.1362/026725799784870379

Freiden, J. B. (1984). Advertising Spokesperson Effects: An Examination of Endorser Type and Gender on Two Audiences. *Journal of Advertising Research, 24*(5), 33-41.

Friedman, H., Termini, S., & Washington, R. (1976). The Effectiveness of Advertisements Utilizing Four Types of Endorsers. *Journal of Advertising, 5*(3), 22-24. http://dx.doi.org/10.1080/00913367.1976.10672647

Goldsmith, R., Lafferty, B., & Newell, S. (2000). The Impact of Corporate Credibility and Celebrity Credibility on Consumer Reaction to Advertisements and Brands. *Journal of Advertising, 29*(3), 43-54. http://dx.doi.org/10.1080/00913367.2000.10673616

Gresham, L. G., & Shimp, T. A. (1985). Attitude toward The Advertisement and Brand Attitudes: A Classical Conditioning Perspective. *Journal of Advertising, 14*(1), 10-18. http://dx.doi.org/10.1080/00913367.1985.10672924

Hoekman, M. L. L., & Bosmans, A. M. M. (2010). *Celebrity Endorsement. How Does Celebrity Endorsement Influence The Attitude towards The Brand and How Does Negative Publicity Affect This Relationship?* Bachelor Thesis, ANR. 343396, Tilburg University, Netherlands.

Hovland, C. I., & Weiss, W. (1953). The Influence of Source Credibility on Communication Effectiveness. *Public Opinion Quarterly, 15*, 635-650. http://dx.doi.org/10.1086/266350

Kaikati, J. G. (1987). Celebrity Advertising: A Review and Synthesis. *International Journal of Advertising*, (6), 99-105. http://dx.doi.org/10.1080/02650487.1987.11107007?src=recsys

Kamins, M. A., & Gupta, K. (1994). Congruence between Spokesperson and Product Type: A Matchup Hypothesis Perspective. *Psychology and Marketing, 11*(6), 569-586. http://dx.doi.org/10.1002/mar.4220110605

Kotler, P., Keller, K., & Jha, M. (2007). Marketing Management. A South Asian perspective (12th ed.). *Pearson Education*, 340.

Mazzini, M., Musa, R., Mohamed, R. N., & Borhan, H. (2014). Celebrity Entrepreneur Endorsement and Advertising Effectiveness. *Procedia – Social and Behavioral Sciences, 130*, 11-20. http://dx.doi.org/10.1016/j.sbspro.2014.04.002

McCracken, G. (1989). Who Is The Celebrity Endorser? Cultural Foundation of The Endorsement Process. *Journal of Consumer Research, 16*, 310-321. http://dx.doi.org/10.1086/209217

McGuire, W. J. (1985). Attitudes and Attitude Change. In G. Lindzey, & E. Aronson (Eds), *Handbook of Social Psychology* (Vol. 2, pp. 233-346). New York: Random House.

Ohanian, R. (1990). Construction and Validation of A Scale to Measure Celebrity Endorsers' Perceived Expertise, Trustworthiness, and Attractiveness. *Journal of Advertising, 19*(3), 39-52. http://dx.doi.org/10.1080/00913367.1990.10673191

Ohanian, R. (1991). The Impact of Celebrity Spokesperson's Perceived Image on Consumers' Intention to Purchase. *Journal of Advertising Research, 31*(1), 46-52.

Pham, T. M. L., & Nguyen, T. V. (2015). The Effect of Celebrity Endorsement in Advertising on Consumer Attitude. *Journal of Economics and Development*, (215), 76-86.

Phelps, J. E., & Hoy, M. G. (1996). The Aad-Ab-PI Relationship in Children: The Impact of Brand Familiarity and Measurement Timing. *Psychology and Marketing, 13*(1), 77-101. http://dx.doi.org/10.1002/(SICI)1520-6793(199601)13:1<77::AID-MAR5>3.0.CO;2-M

Pornpitakpan, C. (2003). The Effect of Celebrity Endorsers' Perceived Credibility on Product Purchase Intention: The Case of Singaporeans. *Journal of International Consumer Marketing, 16*(2), 55-74. http://dx.doi.org/10.1300/J046v16n02_04

Qurat, U. A., & Mahira, R. (2012). Impact of Celebrity Advertisement on Customers' Brand Perception and Purchase Intention. *Asian Journal of Business and Management Sciences, 1*(11), 53-67.

Shahrokh, Z. D., & Arefi, A. (2013). Identify Factors Influencing on The Effectiveness of Celebrities Advertising. *Journal of Applied Environmental and Biological Sciences, 3*(12), 112-121.

17

Designing a Portfolio Based On Risk and Return of Various Asset Classes

Rashmi Soni[1]

[1] K J Somaiya Institute of Management Studies and Research, Mumbai, India

Correspondence: Rashmi Soni, K J Somaiya Institute of Management Studies and Research, Mumbai, India. E-mail: rashmi.soni@somaiya.edu

Abstract

Every investor's dream is to maximize return with minimum risk. Since this is practically impossible, the target is to optimize the risk and return. Different asset classes perform differently at different points of time. The performance is affected by the business as well as other local and global macroeconomic parameters. Crude oil, real estate, gold etc. have given very high returns previously but have turned unattractive in recent times. Equity market has over a long term returned handsome benefits but is highly volatile and hence fraught with risks. The risk free investments like fixed, on the other hand, fall in the low-risk low-return category. The purpose of this study is to analyze the returns of various asset classes and correlate these with their risk characteristics in order to verify whether there is always a positive relation between risk and return across all asset classes and to find out the portfolio mix of the various asset classes corresponding to the desired return and risk.

Keywords: portfolio, equity, gold, debt, assets class, risk, return

1. Introduction

A resource with economic value to any entity or with the potential to provide benefits in the future is an asset. An asset class is a group of financial instruments with similar characteristics. Securities in an asset class behave similarly in the marketplace and are also subject to the same laws and regulations. Equity, fixed deposits, bonds, real estate, gold, cash equivalents and alternative assets are some of the varied asset classes available to investors in India.

Equity represents ownership in a company and is also known as stock. In this paper we will consider stocks of publicly traded companies only. Investors categorize equities into growth stock and value stock. A growth stock is characterized by a price which is high compared to its current earnings and book value and is expected to reach its current price levels in eventually. A value stock on the other hand is priced lower than its actual earnings and book value and it is expected that market will soon discover its intrinsic value leading to an eventual rise in its share price.

Debt is a fixed income instrument through which an investor lends money to a corporate or government entity at a fixed or variable rate of interest. Such instruments are usually termed as bonds and are available for public trading. The rate of interest on a bond is called the coupon rate and the internal rate of return of the bond is known as yield. The bond price holds an inversely proportional relationship with its yield. For a country, the government bonds are considered risk-free and hence the yield on a government bond is assumed as the risk free rate of return. Fixed deposits are another kind of fixed income investment where the interest rate is fixed but cannot be traded. In the Indian context, fixed deposits can be issued only by banks and are considered the safest mode of investment.

In the Indian context, investments in equity and debt can also be done through mutual funds which are pool of funds collected from multiple investors for investing in stated securities. Mutual funds are of particular benefit to small investors with small capital base who get access to well diversified and professionally managed portfolios.

Another asset class providing stable income returns, besides providing partial protection against inflation, is real-estate. It has the advantage of bearing low correlation to the performance of other financial assets therefore and hence is a significant diversifier in a portfolio. For investors who do not wish to lock in their money by investing in physical real-estate, Real Estate Investments Trust (REIT) provides a highly liquid stake in real estate. REITs are professionally managed funds which are tradable in the exchanges and receive tax consideration and usually offer high dividend-yields.

Gold is another asset class which has relatively low correlation with investments in other asset classes. It has played a major role in trade historically and has been the most favor precious metal for investment purpose mainly because of its liquidity and portfolio diversifying characteristic. Gold Exchange Traded Funds (ETF) is a professionally managed fund allowing investors to gain exposure to gold without holding physical gold.

Speaking of liquidity, the most liquid asset class is the cash equivalents consisting of cash, savings account deposits and money market funds like treasury bills, certificates of deposit issue by banks, corporate commercial papers and other money market instruments. These are short term securities with have high credit quality and have a low-risk, low-return profile.

Apart from these traditional assets discussed above, some other assets available for investment are arts, antiques and collectibles. Together these non-traditional assets are classified as alternate assets. These are usually less liquid long term investments requiring comparatively larger capital base and are therefore mostly limited to high net worth individuals (HNIs). Because of no evident co-movement with other assets such as equity and debt, it can sustain market volatility and thus helps in effective portfolio diversification.

The two fundamental aspects of investment are risk and return. Return measures the gain or loss on any investment over a specified time period and is inclusive of income and capital gain or loss relative to the investment. The amount of return anticipated based on historical data while making an investment is the expected rate of return. The actual gain or loss on the investment is the actual or realized return and is also known as Ex-post return. The possibility that the actual return will different than the expected return is known as risk. It also includes the possibility that all or part of the investment will be lost. It is usually measured by calculating the standard deviation of returns. The risk which is inherent to the market as a whole is known as the systematic risk or market. Such risks contribute to the market volatility and are undiversifiable, mostly unpredictable and not completely avoidable. If the risk is specific to an issuer or security, it is known as unsystematic risk or business risk and can be diversified with the help of a well balanced portfolio. A fixed-rate debt instrument faces interest rate risk when there is a rise in interest rates and hence its value declines. It also faces a credit risk whereby the issuer defaults on the payment of interest or principal. In a declining interest rate scenario an investor faces reinvestment risk because the cash flows from the investment have to be reinvested at lower rates. Every investment also faces an inflationary risk which is the possibility that the purchasing power of the cash flow generated from the investment will decline due to future inflation. Liquidity risk arises from the possibility that the investor may not be able to buy or sell the securities in sufficient quantity as and when desired because of limited opportunities. An investment in some foreign asset or currency also bears the exchange rate risk in case of currency rate fluctuations.

Every investor's dream is to maximize return with minimum risk. Since this is practically impossible, the target is to optimize the risk and return (ICICIdirect, 2013). Different asset classes perform differently at different points of time. The performance is affected by the business cycle (Dzikevicius & Vetrov, 2012) as well as other local and global macroeconomic parameters. Crude oil, real estate, gold etc. have given very high returns previously but have turned unattractive in recent times. Equity market has over a long term returned handsome benefits but is highly volatile and hence fraught with risks. The risk free investments like fixed, on the other hand, fall in the low-risk low-return category. Standard theory predicts a positive relationship between risk and return (Han, 2013). The purpose of this study is to analyze the returns of various asset classes and correlate these with their risk characteristics in order to verify this theory and to find the other major factors which influence them.

2. Literature Review

Each asset class has its own merits and demerits. Investors evaluate each of these assets based on multiple factors. Such factors which determine the choice of an investment avenue have been the subject of study for academics since long. Dr. Rama (2015) surveyed and found that safety, returns and liquidity are the primary concerns for investors, followed by concerns about absence of entry barrier, tax efficiency and cash flow effectiveness. Allocation in each of these asset classes needs to be a well-educated decision. Dzikevicius and Vetrov (2012) combined business cycle and asset allocation theories by adding valuable information about performance of asset classes during different phases of the business cycle and demonstrated that different asset classes have different return/risk characteristics over the business cycle. They thus demonstrated how business cycle approach can be used for decision making. Thomas and Maciej (2013) compared factor-based asset allocation and asset-class-based asset allocation and addressed the issue of the alleged superiority of risk-factor-based asset allocations over the more traditional asset-class-based asset allocation. Through the use of both an idealized model, capable of precise mathematical treatment, and optimizations based on different periods of historical data, it was shown that neither approach is inherently superior to the other.

Taking the various asset classes into consideration independently we now look at the various academic researches that have been done in the past. Equity is a major investment asset-class and value stocks are seen as the most profitable in the Indian stock market. An empirical study by Jaspal Singh and Kiranpreetkaur (2014) have revealed that the portfolio selected on the basis of tangible book value rule of Benjamin Graham provided significantly positive mean market adjusted returns in maximum number of years when the holding period of the portfolio is extended from 12 months to 24 months. This valuation metric is aimed at buying the securities whose prices are lesser than the tangible book value of the assets of the company. The portfolio also showed lesser volatility than the market portfolio. Hence, it can be safely assumed that investment period and volatility are important parameters to be considered while investing. As far as Indian stock markets are concerned, return and volatility for both the index are scattered over a period of time where risk averse investors are willing to commit huge amount to high risk transactions hoping that market discounts all information and reacts immediately towards news shocks (Shanthi, Thamilselvan, & Srinivasan, 2015). Also, the presence of seasonality in the stock market makes the equity prices predictable based on past pattern, though this violates the Efficient Market Hypothesis (Ash, 2010). Stock prices are also affected by investor sentiments apart from fundamental risk factors (Saumya & Jitendra, 2013). Rajni (2015) had calculated that the Indian equity market (Sensex) had provided an average return of 16.59% as against the expected rate of 10.84% during the period of 2003-2013 with a delivered risk premium of 9.78% per annum. Such a high risk premium may be the reason why Indian equity market is able to attract the foreign investors. The risk premium is however lower than the 12.5% as calculated by Verma and Barua (2006) signaling that the Indian equity market is maturing gradually.

Debt is another significant asset class for the investors and the major debt instruments are the bonds, mostly the government securities. Bond returns depends on changes in macroeconomic factors such as expected inflation, long term interest rate, money supply, forex reserves, exchange rate and LIBOR (Thenmozhi & Karthika, 2014). The relationship between India's stock and bond markets returns has also been the subject of many academic researches. Bharat and Mahmoud (2010) have found the evidence of substitution of risky stocks for risk-free bonds in Indian markets suggesting that stock market volatility drives up bond returns through a flight-to-quality and/or cross-hedging trades of stock market risk. They were also able to establish that the covariance between foreign exchange rates changes and stock returns is empirically small, while the covariance between exchange rate changes and bond returns is much larger.

Gold as an asset class which is very famous among Indians because of reasons both cultural and financial. It has the ability to provide liquidity as well as transparent price discovery. Currently gold Exchange-Traded Funds (ETFs) and gold mutual funds provide an alternative to investment in physical gold. Analysis has shown that investment in gold has negative correlation with that in equity, and therefore, can act as a perfect instrument for hedging equity investment risk to reduce the overall portfolio risk (Mukesh, Vikrant, & Sougata, 2012). Overall, gold has been found to be a valuable asset class that can improve the risk-adjusted performance of a well-diversified portfolio of stocks while acting as a hedge against various market and macroeconomic factors (Dilip, 2014).

Another asset class which has gained prominence with the rapidly growng economy of India is real-estate. Physical property, REITS, real-estate mutual funds and real estate stocks are the avenues available for investing in real-estate in India. However, the real estate markets were found to under-perform the stock market in India over 1998-2005 although there was some improvement in their performance in more recent years (Graeme & Rajeev, 2007).

Alternative assets, such as art, antiques and collectibles, are driven by the same risk factors like that of stock and bond volatility, besides depending on changes in interest rates, cash flows, credit spreads, liquidity and other specialized factors (Niels, Sébastien, & Fei, 2014).

3. Research Methodology

3.1 Research Objective

The purpose of this study is to analyze the returns of various asset classes and correlate these with their risk characteristics in order to verify whether there is always a positive relation between risk and return across all asset classes and to find out the portfolio mix of the various asset classes corresponding to the desired return and risk.

3.2 Data Description

Secondary data corresponding to last ten quarters ending 31st March 2015 were. For equity we have considered Nifty 50, for debt 10 year G-sec yield has been taken, for fixed deposit we have taken the RBI data for term deposit rates corresponding to 1-3years maturity period and for real estate we have taken the Residex Index published by National Housing Board. Portfolios have been constructed using the variance-covariance method and

3.3 Research Design

To design a portfolio with these assets using the calculated returns and risk through simulation by Solver tool in Excel we have used the Variance-Covariance method.

4. Data Analysis

As can be seen from Figure 1, each year has seen a different winner in terms of return. Also, each asset class has different risk characteristics. It therefore becomes necessary to build a portfolio to diversify the risk in accordance with the required rate of return. However, we must study the individual risk and return characteristics of each of the asset classes before we move on to building a portfolio.

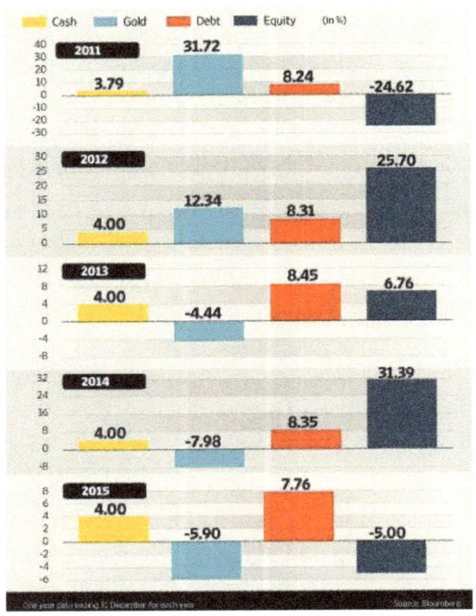

Figure 1. Year-wise returns 2011-15

Data corresponding to last ten quarters ending 31st March 2015 were collected and average annualized risk and returns were calculated. Risk has been calculated using standard deviation of returns. For equity we have considered Nifty 50, for debt 10 year G-sec yield has been taken, for fixed deposit we have taken the RBI data for term deposit rates corresponding to 1-3years maturity period and for real estate we have taken the Residex Index published by National Housing Board. By analyzing we get the following result:

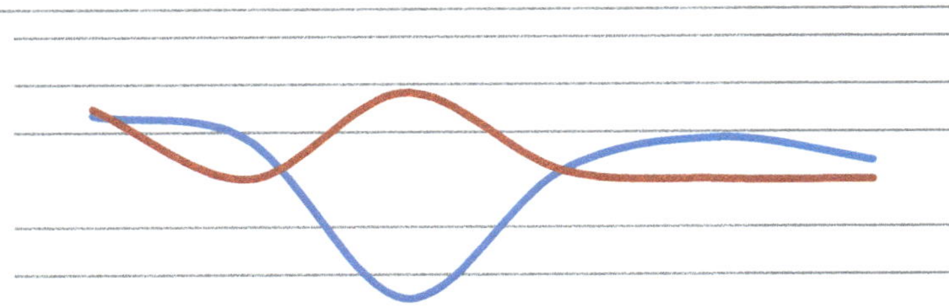

	Equity	Debt	Gold	Real Estate	FD	Cash
Annual Average Return	13.53%	8.30%	-25.07%	1.83%	8.75%	4.00%
Annual Average SD	14.90%	0.23%	18.25%	2.04%	0.13%	0.00%

Figure 2. Risk vs return January 2013 – April 2015

From the above analysis, it can be seen that for the mentioned period gold had the highest volatility, implying the highest risk, while delivering the lowest return. On the other hand, fixed income securities such as government bonds and fixed deposits had reasonably high return with very little risk. The positive relation between risk and return could be verified only for equities and cash savings and hence cannot be generalized for all individual asset classes.

We now try to design a portfolio with these assets using the calculated returns and risk through simulation by Solver tool in Excel. The Minimum Variance Portfolio is attained by minimizing the standard deviation and the Optimal Risky portfolio is attained by maximizing the Sharpe's Ratio. Sharpe's Ratio is the measure of risk adjusted return and is calculated as the average return earned in excess of the risk free rate per unit of volatility of total risk. Risk free rate has been taken as the 10 year Indian Government bond yield on 1st April 2015.

The portfolio of a person will depend on his required rate of return and his/her risk appetite. Hence various situations have been simulated by keeping a minimum of 10% allocation to cash in each case, except for the optimal risky portfolio, since this much of liquidity is always necessary. The different portfolios are as follows:

Table 1. Optimal portfolios

	Min Variance portfolio	**Optimal risky portfolio**	**Portfolio mean return 9%**	**Portfolio mean return 10%**	**Portfolio mean return 11%**	**Portfolio mean return 12%**	**Max Return Portfolio**
Expected Return	8.09%	8.75%	9.00%	10.00%	11.00%	12.00%	12.57%
SD	0.11%	0.13%	8.63%	8.95%	9.28%	11.62%	13.41%
Sharpe's Ratio	2.190	6.780	0.132	0.239	0.338	0.356	0.352
Equity	0%	0%	54%	58%	62%	78%	90%
Debt	11%	0%	1%	0%	0%	0%	0%
Gold	0%	66%	5%	3%	1%	0%	0%
Real Estate	2%	0%	2%	1%	0%	0%	0%
FD	78%	20%	28%	27%	27%	12%	0%
Cash	10%	14%	11%	11%	10%	10%	10%

From Table 1 it can be seen that the minimum risky portfolio gives a return of 8.09%, which is higher than the risk-free rate, while the maximum return possible is 12.57%, which is lower than the return of Nifty 50. The optimal risky portfolio provides a return of 8.75%. At 9% expected return, slightly above the average fixed deposit rate of return, we get a well balanced portfolio but the risk component is higher. In fact, by designing a portfolio we have been able to diversify our risk and we can see that the risk component increases as the expected rate of return increases, thereby giving us a high risk-high return scenario.

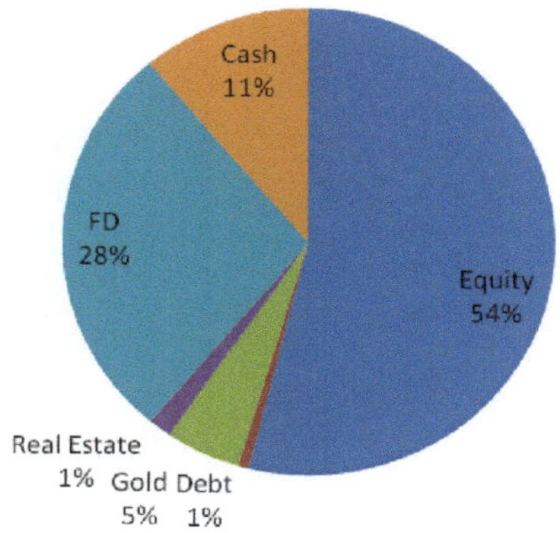

Figure 1. Portfolio for 9% return

From the above analysis we observe that real estate never forms a significant part of the portfolio. Also, cash component of portfolio depends on individual's liquidity requirement which is broadly based on one's lifestyle and life stage. Hence, we reanalyze keeping these two components aside. Also, for better accuracy we use monthly returns of equity, gold, debt and fixed deposit from last ten years ending April 2015.

By analyzing the risk and returns of these asset classes we obtain the following result:

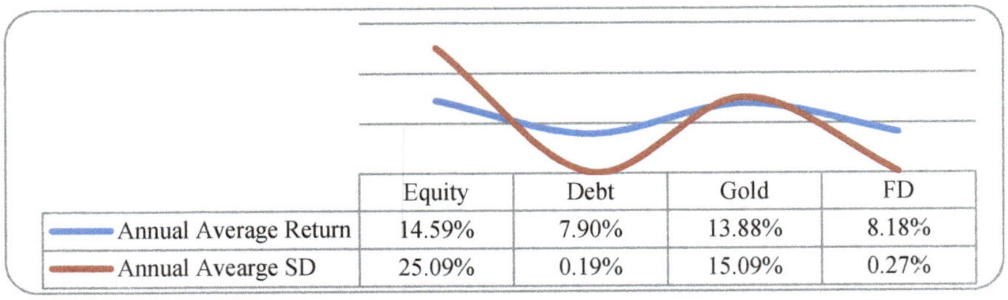

Figure 2. Risk vs return April 2005 - April 2015

From this analysis we can see that there is always a positive relationship between risk and return where equity has the highest risk and return and debt the lowest. To further analyze the relation we run a regression between the risks and return values considering return depends on risk.

From the linear regression analysis we obtain a strong positive relation with a R square value of 0.93 indicating that around 93% of variation in return can be explained by change in the risk component. The relation between risk and return can be defined by the equation:

$$y = 72.69x^3 - 30.67x^2 + 3.412x + 0.072 \quad (1)$$

where x is the average annualized return and y is the average annualized standard deviation, with fair degree accuracy where MAPE (Mean Absolute Percentage Error) is 0.006.

Table 2. Return derivation from risk

Asset Class	Annual Average SD	Calculated Return	Actual Return	Absolute % Error
Equity	25.09%	14.55%	14.59%	0.002
Debt	0.19%	7.83%	7.90%	0.009
Gold	15.09%	13.83%	13.88%	0.004
FD	0.27%	8.11%	8.18%	0.008
		Mean Absolute Percentage Error (MAPE)		0.006

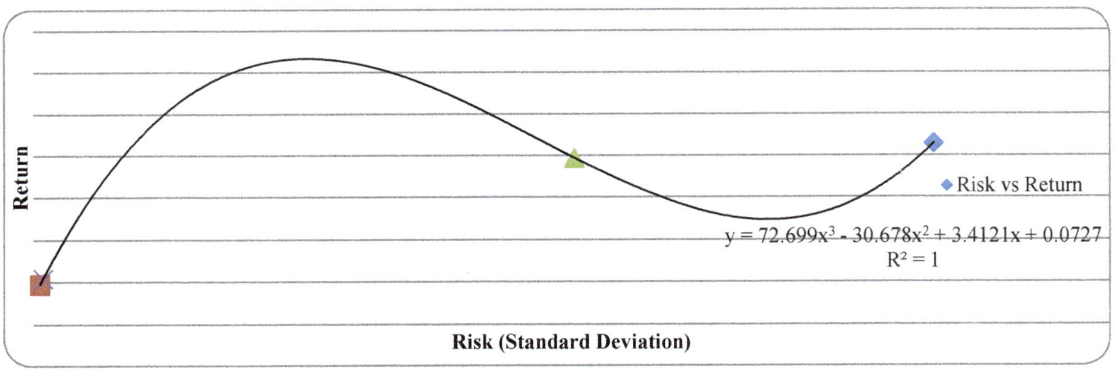

Figure 3. Regression analysis - Risk vs Return

With this background, we now try to find out the portfolios with minimum variance, optimal risk, maximum return and mean returns in the range of 9-14%. The results are as below:

Table 3. Optimal portfolios

	Min Variance portfolio	Optimal risky portfolio	Portfolio mean return						Max Return Portfolio
			9%	**10%**	**11%**	**12%**	**13%**	**14%**	
Expected Return	7.95%	8.26%	9%	10%	11%	12%	13%	14%	14.59%
SD	0.18%	0.28%	2.57%	6.55%	10.59%	14.63%	18.67%	22.72%	25.09%
Sharpe's Ratio	0.528	1.424	0.443	0.327	0.297	0.283	0.275	0.270	0.268
Equity	0%	1%	11%	27%	43%	59%	75%	91%	100%
Debt	11%	0%	43%	36%	28%	20%	12%	5%	0%
Gold	0%	1%	5%	4%	3%	2%	1%	0%	0%
FD	78%	99%	41%	34%	27%	19%	12%	4%	0%

From Table 3 it can be seen that the minimum risky portfolio gives a return of 7.95%, which is higher than the risk-free rate of 7.86%, while the maximum return possible is 14.59%, which is equal to the return of Nifty 50. The optimal risky portfolio provides a return of 8.26%.

Apart from these conventional asset classes, there are the alternate assets such as arts, antiques and collectibles which can be considered for investment but the risk and returns cannot be generalized or quantified.

4.1 Limitations of the Study

It is always preferable to take as much data for study as is available for analysis. Our first analysis was limited to quarterly data of last ten quarters ending financial year 2014-15. This is because the only index for real estate in India available is the Residex which was launched by National Housing Board from Q2 FY 2012-13 with 2007 as the base year. Hence, for comparability we had to limit our data for other asset classes to the same period. The second analysis based on 10 years data appears to be more accurate.

For equity returns we have considered the widely traded CNX Nifty 50 index. However, the result might change if some other index such as the S&P BSE Sensex is used for the study. Similarly, for debt we have considered only 10 year G-sec yield. Result might vary of other forms of debt instruments such as the corporate bonds, are included in the portfolio.

Fixed deposit rates in India vary depending of the maturity period and also from bank to bank. For simplicity purpose we have taken the 1-3 year term deposit rates published by RBI. If longer period term deposits are included the portfolios might change. The returns used above for portfolio calculation are pre-tax returns and unadjusted for inflation. An investor must also consider the different tax implications arising from various asset classes and also how much return they provide when inflation is taken into consideration.

The investor's age and life-stage is another very important factor which must be taken into consideration for designing a portfolio since the liquidity requirement, risk appetite and other parameters change through one's life.

5. Conclusion

From our study we can conclude that there is a strong positive relation between risk and return of individual asset classes. However, when a diversified portfolio of various asset classes is considered, the risk can be mitigated to a large extent and is usually higher for higher expected return. This helps in planning one's investment corresponding to his/her expected rate of return and the risk appetite. From the various portfolios it can be seen that simply keeping the whole money as cash is not desirable since almost double the savings interest can be earned at very low risk level. On the other hand, investing only in equity markets is also not desirable since risks exceed returns. Also, we can earn a higher return compared to the risk free return with a lower risk component compared to 10 year G-sec bonds. Investing in a well-diversified portfolio also helps in evening out the variations in the returns from different asset classes over the years thereby introducing an element of certainty.

References

Ash, N. S. (2010). *Stock Market Seasonality: A Study of the Indian Stock Market.* NSE India.

Bharat, K., & Mahmoud, W. (2010). *An Examination of India's Stock and Bond Markets Co-movements*. Paper Presented at the Northeast Decision Sciences Institute.

Dilip, K. (2014). Return and volatility transmission between gold and stock sectors: Application of portfolio management and hedging effectiveness. *IIMB Management Review, 26*(1).

Dzikevicius, A., & Vetrov, J. (2012). Analysis of asset classes through the business cycle. *Business, Management and Education, 10*(1), 1-10. https://doi.org/10.3846/bme.2012.01

Gopinathan, N., & Ramakoti, N. (2014). A Study on Role of Gold Portfolio Allocation. *International Journal of Applied Engineering Research, 9*(23), 19083-19088.

Graeme, N., & Rajeev, K. (2007). The Significance and Performance of Real Estate Markets in India. *Journal of Real Estate Portfolio Management, 13*(2), 161-172.

Graham, B. (1973). *The Intelligent Investor* (Revised Edition).

Han, L. (2013). Understanding the Puzzling Risk-Return Relationship for Housing. *Review of Financial Studies, 26*(4), 877-928. https://doi.org/10.1093/rfs/hhs181

ICICIdirect. (2013, August). *ICICIdirect Money manager.* Retrieved from http://content.icicidirect.com/mailimages/MM-FOMAugust.html?utm_source=email&utm_medium=email&utm_campaign=MoneyManager_August2013

Jaspal, S., & Kiranpreetkaur. (2014). Examining the Profitability of Value Stocks in Indian Stock Market – An Empirical Analysis. *The Journal of Institute of Public Enterprise, 37*(3&4).

Kavita, A. (2015). Risk-adjusted Performance Evaluation of Indian Mutual Fund Schemes. *Paradigm, 19*(1), 79-94. https://doi.org/10.1177/0971890715585203

Mukesh, K. M., Vikrant, K., & Sougata, R. (2012). Gold ETF Performance: A Comparative Analysis of Monthly Returns. *The IUP Journal of Financial Risk Management, IX*(2), 59-63.

Naresh, B., Robert, A. C., & Chris, S. (2014). The Stock-Bond Return Relation, the Term Structure's Slope, and Asset-Class Risk Dynamics. *Journal of Financial and Quantitative Analysis, 49*(3), 699-724. https://doi.org/10.1017/S0022109014000258

Pedersen, N., Page, S., & Fei, H. (2014). Asset Allocation: Risk Models for Alternative Investments. *Financial Analysts Journal, 70*(3), 34-45. https://doi.org/10.2469/faj.v70.n3.4

Rajni, K. R. (2015). Equity Risk Premium Puzzle: The Case of Indian Stock Market.

Rama, N. M. (2015). Analysis Of Investment Options. *International Journal of Research in Commerce, It & Management, 5*(5).

Saumya, R. D., & Jitendra, M. (2012). Investor sentiment, risk factors and stock return: Evidence from Indian non-financial companies. *Journal of Indian Business Research, 4*(3), 194-218. https://doi.org/10.1108/17554191211252699

Shanthi, A., Thamilselvan, R., & Srinivasan, K. (2015). The Day of the Week Effect and Conditional Volatility in Indian Stock Market: Evidence from BSE & *NSE. International Journal of Applied Engineering Research, 10*(3), 7495-7508.

Thenmozhi, M., & Nair, K. S. (2014). Impact of Changes in Macroeconomic Factors on Treasury Bond Returns: Evidence from Emerging and Developed Markets. *Amity Global Business Review, 9*, 24.

Thomas, M. I., & Maciej, K. (2013). Factor-Based Asset Allocation vs. Asset-Class-Based Asset Allocation. *Financial Analysts Journal, 69*(3).

Varma, J. R., & Barua, S. K. (2006). *A First Cut Estimate of the Equity Risk Premium in India*. WP No. 2006-06-04, IIM Ahmedabad.

18

The Overnight Return Temporal Market Anomaly

Vasiliki A. Basdekidou[1]

[1] SRFA Aristotle University of Thessaloniki, Greece

Correspondence: Vasiliki A. Basdekidou, Special Research Fund Account (ELKE), Aristotle University of Thessaloniki, Greece. E-mail: Vasiliki.Basdekidou@gmail.com

Abstract

The main goal of this paper is to introduce an innovative market anomaly relating to "time" during the overnight post-market session and therefore characterized as a *temporal* market anomaly. Anomalies in the markets appear from time to time and test the efficient market hypothesis. Many investors and traders believe that the markets follow the efficient market hypothesis. According to this theory the current price of a security (trading instrument) reflects all public and private information about that security (instrument). Changes in price are due to insider information, current news, or sudden events, which are impossible to predict. Hence, security's price action follows the path of a random walk, the hypothesis and argument of which states that current price is not dependent on past price and is normally or abnormally distributed over time. In financial and economical literature, many studies have presented approaches about what the academics call "*market anomalies*" and according to literature the anomalies are classified in three categories: *Fundamental*, *Technical*, and *Calendar-based* anomalies. In this article another class of market anomalies is introduced, that simply could be referred to as "temporal" because of the timing functionality involved. Finally, I will discuss one of these "temporal" anomalies, called the *overnight return temporal market anomaly*. The presented research shows that momentum profit accumulates entirely overnight, while profit on all other strategies occurs entirely intraday. These findings strongly reject classical theories of intraday versus overnight returns.

Keywords: market anomalies, liquidity, market timing, temporal (timing) trading functionalities (TTF), temporal market anomalies, intraday vs. overnight returns

1. Introduction

The main goal of this paper is to introduce a new market anomaly, challenging the efficient market hypotheses and relating to "time" during the overnight post-market session (Ang et al., 2006; Bali & Cakici, 2008; Basdekidou, 2015; Basdekidou, 2016b). This innovative anomaly characterized and documented as a temporal market anomaly (Basdekidou, 2017; Basdekidou & Styliadou, 2017).

1.1 Problem Introduction

In corporate finance literature, both the risk-based and the expected returns were examined in detail (Vayanos & Woolley, 2013; Campbell et al., 2014). In this domain, understanding cross-sectional variants in returns is critical for market and stock evaluation and trading purposes (Lou et al., 2016).

Trading is regarded as a temporal historical living system (Styliadis, 2007; Styliadis & Vassilakopoulos, 2005) with a number of time-based anomalies challenging the efficient market hypothesis and initiating relative trading functions. Anomalies in the markets appear from time to time and test the efficient market hypothesis. Many investors and traders believe that the markets follow the efficient market hypothesis. According to this theory the current price of a security (trading instrument) reflects all public and private information about that security (instrument). Changes in price are due to insider information, current news, or sudden events, which are impossible to predict. Hence, security's price action follows the path of a random walk, the hypothesis and argument of which states that current price is not dependent on past price and is normally (or abnormally) distributed over time (Livermore 1940/2001).

In financial and economical literature, many studies have presented approaches about what the academics call "*market anomalies*" and according to literature the anomalies are classified in three categories: *Fundamental*, *Technical*, and *Calendar-based* anomalies (Demiralp et al., 2011; Basdekidou, 2015). Current paper reasoning that there is also another class of anomalies that simply could be referred to as "*temporal*" because of the timing functionality involved. In this article I will discuss one of these "temporal" anomalies, called the overnight return temporal market anomaly. Historically, market anomalies have a great temporal (timing) trading functionality (Hovakimian & Hu, 2016; Basdekidou, 2016b), resulting in excellent profit & wealth growth opportunities.

The observed mispricing in price action, as a typical technical market anomaly, camouflaged such as trading timing and could be regarded as the result of the lack of any available temporal trading functionality (TTF) for the investors, traders, institutions and speculators, and for the embedded time-based behavioral biases dominant in securities (equities), Forex and option markets ((Ogden & Wu, 2013; Basdekidou & Styliadou, 2017). The main reason that the institutions and the long-term investors usually buy overbought shares, is explained in Edelen, Ince, and Kadlec (2015), who in their paper reasoning that long-term investors, traders and speculators prefer to build positions on shares classified as overbought (i.e. a momentum trading psychology functionality) based on a number of classical equities-trading strategies (i.e. a "trend-follow" trading, but without any TTF functionality in this case) (Basdekidou, 2016a; Choie, 2016). Financial economics approaches emphasize that disengagement of holding and domination has as a result the clash of interest between outside collaborators, stakeholders, CEOs, and governors. In this domain, the literature reasoning is that big corporate shareowners (not interested in short-term trading, nor using TTF functionalities in their trading plans) can ease and lighten such things as "conflict arguments" by observing and controlling CEOs through the SEC reports (Hartzell & Starks, 2003).

Also, in economics and finance, *timing in trading* approaches try to clarify such attitude, assuming that any trading decision (i.e. open/close positions; lot trade size, etc.) is formed for the regard of old non-speculative shareowners (investors), who adequately take profit from trading shares just as a consequence of right-timing daily trading initiatives based on short-term (intraday) time trading functionalities (intraday TTF) and not as a result of a well-designed, based on long-term TTF, trading strategy (Baker & Wurgler, 2002). The current paper agrees that the data are consistent and produce profit with such expectations, as far as the timing of the trading initiatives and executive orders (open/close position) is regarded as TTF functionality (Skyba, 2012).

1.2 The Overnight Return Anomaly Rule

Lou et al. (2016) deliver remarkable new evidences about intraday and overnight returns. According to their research, nearly 100% of the abnormal (i.e. market anomalies) returns on momentum strategies occur overnight. On the other hand, according to Lou et al., the average intraday component of momentum profit is statistically insignificant. Their findings are subject to a number of controls and risk-adjustments. So, the overnight return is bigger among large-cap stocks, 3x ETFs/ETNs (Note 1) instruments, and stocks with relatively large prices. The presented result is inconsistent with the classical theories and explanations about intraday and overnight trading return. Hence, this inconsistency could be characterized as a new market *anomaly* not belonging to well-known fundamental, technical or calendar-based *anomalies*. The rule for this new *anomaly* is defined as follows:

The Overnight Return Anomaly (ORA) rule:

Buy at the *Close* of the current daily session.

Hold position overnight.

Sell at the *Open* of the next day's session.

1.3 Problem Importance Exploration

In securities trading "timing" (stocks, options, Forex, ETF, ETN, instruments, etc.), Cesari, Espenlaub, Khurshed, and Simkovic (2012) argue and disagree on the effects of share-holding and stock liquidation on the timing transactions for open and close positions ("*buy*" in case of a short position; and "*sell*" in case of a long position), but in their paper no more details for short-term or daily and intraday TTF functionalities were given; and Demiralp, D'Mello, Schlingemann, and Subramaniam (2011), in their paper, state that old-issue share returns and passive trading, are both strongly connected with the coexisting of old-issue changes in corporate holding for a time period as long as up to 3 years after the TTF time. Obviously, this period is regarded as too big, even for the "*buy-and-hold*" investors, for nowadays swing and volatile securities markets traded on a daily and intraday bases; e.g. leveraged 3x ETFs; Gold, Silver, WTI Oil, and Natural Gas ETNs; etc.

Daytime (intraday) versus overnight returns can be studied by analyzing the differences in returns between the day's session (defined here as regular NYSE trading hours) and the overnight after-hours post- and pre-session period. In testing the returns for the day and overnight periods, I used the SPDR S&P 500 ETF (SPY) from January 1, 2010 to June 30, 2016. I define the day's return (TTF functionality) as the price difference between the day's *open* and the day's *close*. The overnight return (TTF functionality) is the difference between the day's *close* and the following morning's *open* (Basdekidou & Styliadou, 2017).

1.4 Motivation and Previous Literature

The current article, as far as the *trading timing* is concern, is relative to some other articles that investigate corporate share-holding under the prism of the *trading timing*. In this frame, some articles (Choie, 2016; Markoulis & Neofytou, 2016) targeted on the information asset and stock-taking intelligence of corporate investors, while others (Hao, 2014; Baker, Stein, & Wurgler, 2003; Gibson, Safieddine, & Sonti, 2004) targeted on the trading strategies, tactics and plans, but in both cases no TTF information was given.

Chemmanur, He, and Hu (2009) find that long-term passive-trading investors (as opposed to non-commercial short-term investors, traders, overnight and intraday speculators) are likely to experience bigger share positions in SEOs and IPOs hoping on better returns and their transactions somewhat greatly exceed a passive "*buy-and-hold*" trading strategy with no *(trading) psychological timing* (Nguyen & Tran, 2016; Basdekidou, 2016a; Hovakimian & Hu, 2016). In this article the *(trading) psychological timing* functionality is apparent and obvious but the daytime and overnight alternatives are not discussed (Livermore 1940/2001).

In accordance to the above situation, Edelen, Ince, and Kadlec (2015), examined corporate trading and securities (instruments) return divergences, and discovered that corporate firms prefer to purchase shares categorized as *overbought* and this is regarded as a non-positive association (i.e. relationship functionality) in trading timing. Also, in this article the *(trading) psychological timing* functionality is apparent and obvious but the daytime and overnight alternatives are not discussed.

In opposition to these articles that spotlight mainly on whether long-term investors and old-shareowners are better-informed (i.e. insiders functionality), rather on the *(trading) psychological timing* TTF functionality; the current research article targets on the dominant relationship between *trading* and *timing* and the underlined trading functionalities (Basdekidou, 2016b; Livermore 1940/2001).

Alti and Sulaeman (2012) also expressed a disagreement to these articles, by pointing out how new shares issuing initiatives (IPOs) are influenced by corporate and non-commercial trading. Actually, they support the position that strong securities trading returns trigger equity derivation only if it is connected with a great pre-issue corporate investor demand (supply vs. demand approach), as it is regarded to be consistent with the new corporate holdings (i.e. swing momentary traders). Alti and Sulaeman also clarify their results as logical and dependable with trading initiatives using the corporate investor supply vs. demand functionality as a gauge of the market's interest in the company's equity initiative. Also, in this article the *(trading) psychological timing* functionality is apparent and obvious but the daytime and overnight alternatives are not discussed.

In this domain, the main target of the current article is divergent. Actually, I investigate whether the overnight shareowners, as short-term investors, gain profit from the proposed overnight return temporal market anomaly. It is notable that, the results obtained does depend on the trading instrument (e.g. 3x leveraged ETF/ETN; index-based ETF; etc.) and therefore always an adaptive personalized functionality is involved ("volatility" in case of the trading instrument and "user profile" for the case of the investors, traders, and momentary speculators) in designing overnight return based trading strategies.

1.5 Paper's Structure

The rest of the article is organized as follows: Section 2 ("*Trading Data: Daytime & Overnight Returns*") describes the trading data as the daytime and overnight return variables; Section 3 ("*Analysis: The Overnight Return Temporal Market Anomaly*") documents the introduced innovative term by examining the relation between daytime and overnight timing trading, as well as the impact of the adaptive personalized instrument selection on this "timing"; Finally, Section 4 ("*Conclusions & Discussion*") summarizes the conclusions and discusses paper's innovations and contributions.

2. Trading Data: Daytime & Overnight Returns

The main difference between intraday (daytime: 09:30 am – 04:00 pm EST) and overnight periods is that much of the overnight return has earnings announcements functionality (at least for the USA stock markets) and therefore may reflect information surprises. Nearly a 25% of these overnight earnings announcements published in the first 30 minutes after market close; while the 60% published in the morning before market opening.

According to my review of the 2010-2016 data, companies tend to submit important regulatory filings just after market closing. Barclay and Hendershott (2003) find that though price action is more active and efficient during the intraday period, after-hours trading contain more information and support greater trading functionality than the daytime trading. Also, according to my research with the pre-open auctions on the NYSE and NYSE Arca, the same conclusions were documented.

For the current paper, the profit/losses trading data (2010-2016) for the UGAZ 3x leveraged Exchange-Traded Note (ETN) (VelocityShares, 2017) came from many resources. The Barron's information databases and sources, a Wall Street Journal affiliate (Barron's, 2016); the StockCharts.com initiative; the Securities & Exchange Commission/SEC notices, releases & announcements; the Commitments of Traders (CoT)/CFTC speculative net positions reports; the Yahoo! Finance insiders data feed; the SEC EDGAR database; and the Thomson Financial corporate holdings database (Nguyen & Tran, 2016; Basdekidou, 2016a; Baker & Wurgler, 2002; Barclay & Hendershott, 2003; Livermore 1940/2001).

The proposed volatility-strategy and volatility-tactical can be used in concert with stocks, leveraged instruments, ETFs, ETNs, swaps, futures, and/or options to implement risk management strategies and it is dedicated to providing individual traders and institutional investors with sophisticated solutions for portfolio and trading risk management: (i) reward to risk ratios; and (ii) stop-loss and stop-profit sell orders. The proposal's success results from delivering innovative, efficient, and intelligent functionality for a wide range of intraday traders and institutional investors.

In this paper, the above numbers were used to estimate, with an acceptable standard deviation (st. dev., σ), total corporate securities profit / loss and position changes (if applicable) and for a period from January 1st, 2010 to June 30th 2016 (Yan & Zhang, 2009). So, for each of the above thirteen (13) semesters, the traders involved parameterized as overnight and daytime returns for the UGAZ 3x leveraged ETN (VelocityShares (Note 2)) and categorized as profit or loses in following Figures 1 and 2.

The result is an unbalanced panel, covering the sample time period from January 1st (2010) to June 30th (2016), with more than 2,000 observations used in the back-testing procedure. The presentation equity curve (returns), in Figures 1 and 2, incorporates the standard deviation for a quality interpretation of both trading strategies: Overnight and Intraday (Vayanos & Woolley, 2013; Campbell et al., 2014; Lou et al., 2016; Hovakimian & Hu, 2016; Livermore 1940/2001).

Overnight Returns: Exchange-Traded Note (3x ETN) Curve Detailed – UGAZ Daily
(01/01/2010 16:00 – 30/06/2016 16:00)

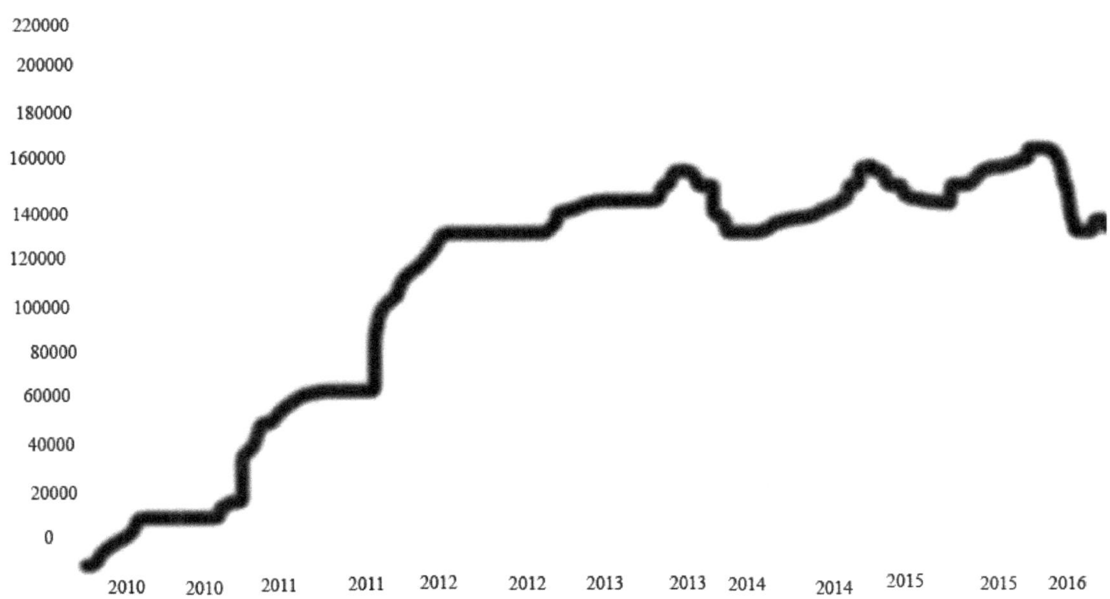

Figure 1. UGAZ 3x ETN, from 1/1/2010 to 30/06/2016

Note. The equity curve of Overnight Returns (today's open – yesterday's close) of $100,000 invested per trade is displayed. Transactions don't include commission or slippage costs.

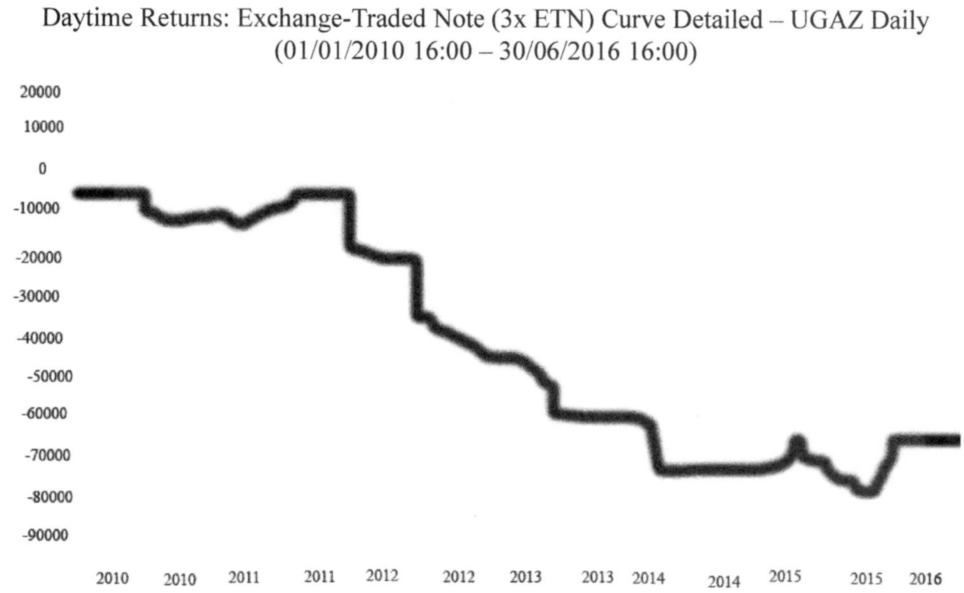

Figure 2. UGAZ 3x ETN, from 1/1/2010 to 30/06/2016

Note. The equity curve of Daytime Returns (today's close – today's open) of $100,000 invested/trade is displayed. Transactions don't include commission or slippage costs.

It is a common misinterpretation between the market participants that the majority of returns from short-term trading are extracted from the daytime (intraday), rather than from the overnight period. This would make sense, as more people are active during the normal daytime hours as opposed to the overnight period (i.e. a strong emotional relation to relative price actions in case of trading). But, as Figures 1 and 2 indicate, the opposite is true of day vs. overnight returns. Following, Figures 3 (overnight returns) and 4 (daytime returns) display the equity curve detailed for the SPY 1x ETF daily and for the period 02/02/1993 – 15/06/2011 (Skyba, 2012).

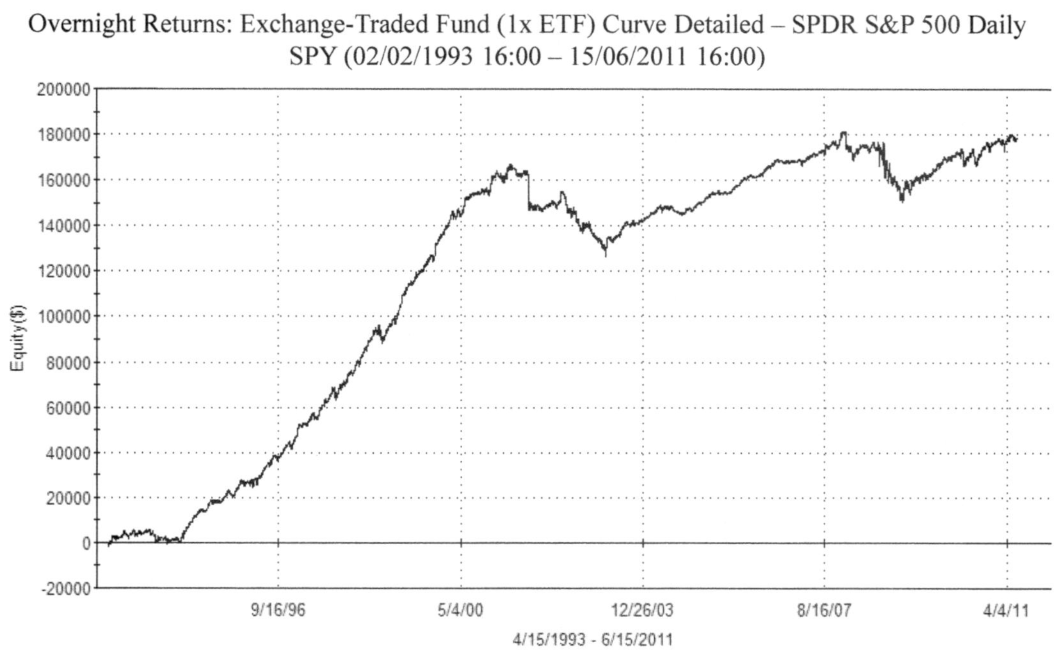

Figure 3. SPDR S&P 500 1x ETF, from 2/2/1993 to 15/6/2011

Note. The equity curve of Overnight Returns (today's open – yesterday's close) of $100,000 invested per trade is displayed. Transactions don't include commission or slippage costs.

Daytime Returns: Exchange-Traded Fund (1x ETF) Curve Detailed – SPDR S&P 500 Daily
SPY (02/02/1993 16:00 – 15/06/2011 16:00)

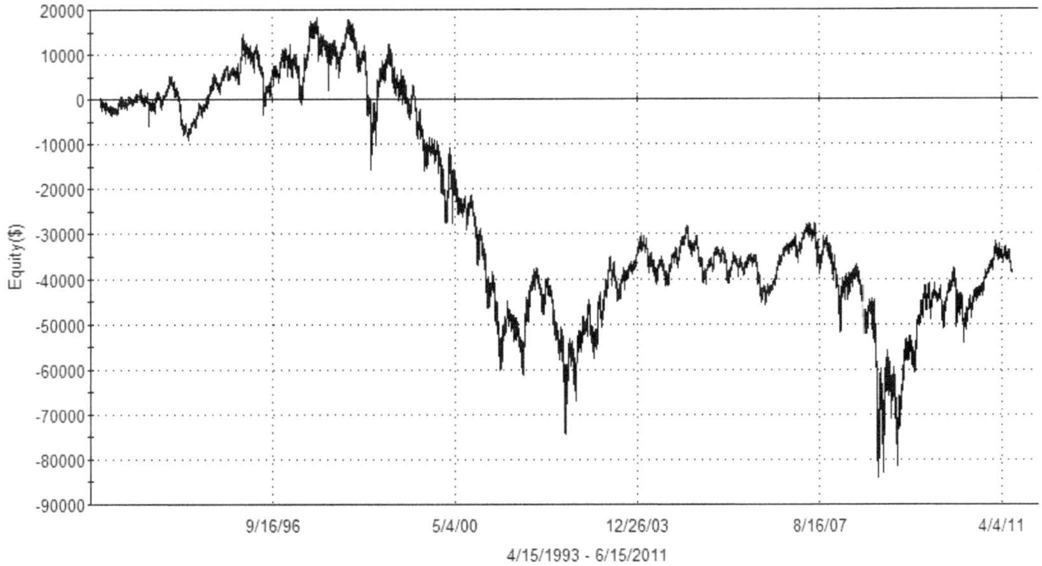

Figure 4. SPDR S&P 500 ETF, from 2/2/1993 to 15/06/2011

Note. The equity curve of Daytime Returns (today's close – today's open) of $100,000 invested/trade is displayed. Transactions don't include commission or slippage costs.

3. Analysis: The Overnight Return Temporal Market Anomaly

In this Section, the innovative term *The Overnight Return Temporal Market Anomaly* is defined, analyzed and documented. So, *The Overnight Return Temporal Market Anomaly* is defined as a two-dimension (2D) array of temporal trading functionalities (TTF), following the definition of the ORA rule (Section 1), applied both to daytime and overnight trading; and obey and restricted by stock's (instruments) price action patterns like *Gaps* ("*Windows*" in technical analysis terminology) and *Breakouts*. These TTF temporal functionalities are, for this temporal market anomaly, short-term functionalities parameterized by popular very short price action time-frames ([1-minute], [2-minute]); and they could be documented by time-targets in trading securities and instruments (stocks, options, futures, Forex, bonds, warrants, 3x ETF/ETN, etc.) as follows: executive define the *Overnight Return Temporal Market* trading strategy (open/close long/short positions) on specific time-targets. An example of an open-position time-target could be the last 5 minutes time period before the "closing bell" (i.e. 03:55-04:00 pm EST; New York time), and an example of a close-position time-target could be the first 5 minutes time period after the "opening bell" (i.e. 09:30-09:35 am EST; New York time). The TTF temporal functionalities operate as, complementary to above time-targets, warning dynamics trading signals when they are related to particular candlestick and price action pattern-targets.

Following, Tables 1-4 present, for the 3x ETN/instrument UGAZ and the 1x ETF SPY, the related trade performance distributions based on the above definition of the overnight return specific time-targets. Also, for the overnight return trading strategies, the TTF functionalities operate as warning dynamics signals (w!D signals), awaiting the final confirmation signal (e.g. candlestick *Break*; Jesse Livermore's resistance pivotal-line *Breakout*; Jesse Livermore's support pivotal-line *Breakdown*) just before the triggering (i.e. Open/Close position) during the executive overnight return period (i.e. the first/last 5 minutes during the trading session).

3.1 The Overnight versus Daytime Returns

The relation *Overnight Return vs. Daytime Return* is defined by analyzing the differences in returns between the overnight period and the trading session (NYSE: 9:30 am–4:00 pm). For volatility-strategy and volatility-tactical purposes, a back-test procedure has been applied on both, a 3x ETN instrument (UGAZ) and a 1x ETF instrument (SPY). This procedure generated, for these two instruments, 3,820 and 4,624 trades respectively.

Individual trades contain more information and trading TTF functionality after hours (overnight) than during the daily session (intraday: 09:30 am – 04:00 pm EST). Hence, because the information asymmetry declines over the intraday trading hours, price changes are larger, reflect more private information and trading functionality, and they are less noisy before the open than after the bell-clock.

Table 1 presents, in summary, the annual returns (%) after the application of the backtest procedure to the 3x instrument UGAZ, for the period: 1st January 2010 – 30th June 2016 (3,820 trades generated). I note that the UGAZ has an annual overnight return of 8.61%, while the annual daytime return is -4.90%. Additionally, a quality analysis, based on the recorded standard deviation values, says that -surprisingly- an overnight return trading strategy is less risky than a daytime return strategy, because of the lower annual std. dev. (σ) value recorded in overnight vs. daytime returns. This is why the statistical quality indicator *Sharpe Ratio* (which does not include in calculations the risk-free interest rate) for the overnight period is 0.93, compared to the -0.30 of the daytime period.

Table 1. UGAZ 3x leveraged ETN: Annual returns (%) from a backtesting procedure (3,820 trades)

	Trading Results (%)			
	Annual Return	Annual std. dev.	Sharpe Ratio	Total Return
Overnight Return Strategy	8.61%	11.92%	0.93	130.42%
Daytime Return Strategy	-4.90%	18.10%	-0.30	-67.31%

Table 2 presents, in summary, the annual returns (%) after the application of the backtest procedure to the 1x instrument SPY, for the period: 2nd February 1993 – 15th June 2011 (4,624 trades generated) (Skyba, 2012).

Table 2. SPDR S&P 500 1x leveraged ETF: Annual returns (%) from a backtesting procedure (4,624 trades)

	Trading Results (%)			
	Annual Return	Annual std. dev.	Sharpe Ratio	Total Return
Overnight Return Strategy	9.23%	10.46%	0.89	171.29%
Daytime Return Strategy	-4.33%	17.05%	-0.25	-39.36%

A comparative return analysis of 3x leveraged UGAZ and 1x leveraged SPY, if it is temporaly (daily, annualy, total period) parameterized, indicates that the 1x instrument has had better performance annualy and totally, whilst the 3x instrument achives better results in daily (if you are on the right side). This is because of the well-known in Wall Street *3x leveraged paradox*, i.e. both (long) leveraged and (short) inverse-leveraged 3x instruments, of the same underline asset or index, in the long term decline in price.

3.2 Trade Performance Analysis

Tables 3 and 4 present the trade performance analysis results after applying the backtesting procedure on both instruments. For statistical backtesting purposes, a capital of $100,000 has been invested per trade. Commission cost of $0.01 per traded share results on significant (net) profit decrease as shown in Tables 3 and 4.

Please note that in case of a commission cost of $0.02 per share, the total net profit of both overnight and daytime return strategies would be less than zero. Even worst, if we add any slippage cost in overnight return strategy. But, thanks to internet-based low-cost brokerage nowadays available, commission cost is very low ($0.005) and slippage cost is not applicable.

Table 3. UGAZ 3x leveraged ETN: Trade performance analysis from backtesting data ($100,000 invested per trade; Total period: 1/1/2010 – 30/6/2016)

	Total number of trades	Winner trades	Loser trades	Profit without commission cost	Net Profit with commission cost $0.01 per share
Overnight Return Strategy	3,820	2,112	1,670	$130,420	$49,666
Daytime Return Strategy	3,820	1,850	1,922	$-67,310	$-148,064

Table 4. SPDR S&P 500 1x leveraged ETF: Trade performance analysis from backtesting data ($100,000 invested per trade; Total period: 2/2/1993 – 15/6/2011)

	Total number of trades	Winner trades	Loser trades	Profit without commission cost	Net Profit with commission cost $0.01 per share
Overnight Return Strategy	4,624	2,480	2,112	$171,289	$73,539
Daytime Return Strategy	4,624	2,234	2,371	$-39,360	$-137,110

4. Conclusions & Discussion

Price action is more efficient and therefore more information and trading functionality is revealed per hour during the intraday session than after hours (overnight). However, the after-hours overnight low trading volume generates significant trading opportunities (albeit inefficient) and offer great price action analysis and a new market anomaly discovery.

The main goal of this paper was to introduce an innovative market anomaly relating to time during the overnight trading session and therefore characterized as a temporal market anomaly. Anomalies in the markets appear on occasion and challenge the efficient market hypothesis. Many within the financial community believe that the markets follow the efficient market hypothesis. This theory asserts that the current price of a security reflects all public and private information about that security. Changes in price are due to current news or events, which are impossible to predict. Thus, the price action follows the path of a random walk, the premise of which states that current price is not dependent on past price and it is normally distributed over time (Vayanos & Woolley, 2013; Lou et al., 2016; Livermore 1940/2001).

Individual trades contain more information and trading TTF functionality after hours (overnight) than during the daily session (intraday: 09:30 am – 04:00 pm EST). Hence, because the information asymmetry declines over the intraday trading hours, price changes are larger, reflect more private information and trading functionality, and they are less noisy before the open than after the bell-clock.

Over the years, many studies have presented data about what academics call "*market anomalies*" These anomalies appear from time to time and challenge the efficient market hypothesis. There are three common classifications: Fundamental, Technical, and Calendar-based Anomalies. There is another class of anomalies that simply could be referred to as "temporal" because of the timing functionality involved. In this article we discussed one of these "temporal" anomalies, called the *overnight return temporal market anomaly*.

The proposed volatility-strategy and volatility-tactical can be used in concert with ETFs, ETNs, swaps, futures, and/or options to implement risk management strategies and it is dedicated to providing individual traders and institutional investors with sophisticated solutions for portfolio and trading risk management. The proposal's success results from delivering innovative, efficient, and intelligent functionality for a wide range of intraday traders and institutional investors.

Paper contributes to corporate finance literature by: (a) the introduction of the new market inefficiency category "*temporal market anomalies*"; (b) the introduction, defining, analyzing and documentation of the innovative term "*the overnight return temporal market anomaly*" as a temporal market anomaly; and (c) the comparative analysis of the executive application (back-testing case study) of these new terms in two instruments, one 3x leveraged ETN and another 1x leveraged ETF.

The trade performance analysis applied on these instruments, demonstrated that in a nowadays internet-based trading with very low commission cost and none slippage cost; a well designed overnight return strategy could gain benefit at the expense of short-term and intraday non-commercial speculators.

Acknowledgments

The financial support (covering mainly the CoT/CFTC and the Barron's & WSJ.com market data expenses) from the EU/LLP Programme "EPOCHE 2013" (with Project No. 2012-1-GR-ERA10-10609) is gratefully acknowledged.

Conflict of Interests

The author has not declared any conflict of interests.

References

Alti, A., & Sulaeman, J. (2012). When do high stock returns Trigger Equity Issues? *Journal of Financial Economics, 103*, 61-87. http://dx.doi.org/10.1016/j.jfineco.2011.08.007

Ang, A., Hodrick, R. J., Xing, Y., & Zhang, X. (2006). The Cross-Section of Volatility and Expected Returns. *Journal of Finance, 61*, 259-299. Retrieved from http://web.ics.purdue.edu/~zhang654/jf2006.pdf

Baker, M., & Wurgler, J. (2002). Market Timing and Capital Structure. *The Journal of Finance, 57*, 1-32. http://dx.doi.org/10.1111/1540-6261.00414

Baker, M., Stein, J. C., & Wurgler, J. (2003). When does the Market Matter? Stock Prices and the Investment of Equity-dependent Firms. *The Quarterly Journal of Economics, 118*, 969-1005. http://dx.doi.org/10.1162/00335530360698478

Bali, T. G., & Cakici, N. (2008). Idiosyncratic Volatility and the Cross Section of Expected Stock Returns. *Journal of Financial and Quantitative Analysis 43*, 29-58. Retrieved from http://citeseerx.ist.psu.edu/viewdoc/download?doi=10.1.1.468.6852&rep=rep1&type=pdf

Barclay, M. J., & Hendershott, T. (2003). Price Discovery and Trading After Hours. *The Review of Financial Studies, 16*(4), 1041-1073. http://dx.doi.org/10.1093/rfs/hhg030

Barron's Financial Investment News and Market Data. (2016). Retrieved from http://www.barrons.com/data; and http://www.wsj.com; and http://www.wsj.com/europe

Basdekidou, V. A. (2015). *Functionality, Returns and Efficiency before and after the Debt Crisis: An Empirical Analysis of the Greek Stock Market* (Unpublished doctoral dissertation). Bulgarian Academy of Sciences –Economic Research Institute, Bulgaria.

Basdekidou, V. A. (2016a). IPO Trading with Short-term and Intraday Temporal Functionalities. *Business and Economics Journal, 7*(4). http://dx.doi.org/10.4172/2151-6219.1000257

Basdekidou, V. A. (2016b). Personalized Temporal Trading Functionalities Engaged in Calendar Market Anomalies: Empirical Evidences from the 2007 and 2009 Financial Crises. *Journal of Business & Financial Affairs, 5*(4). http://dx.doi.org/10.4172/2167-0234.1000225

Basdekidou, V. A. (2017). Seasoned Equity Offerings as Technical Market Anomalies: Long-Term Temporal Trading Functionalities. *International Journal of Economics and Finance, 9*(1), 96-105. http://dx.doi.org/10.5539/ijef.v9n1p96

Basdekidou, V. A., & Styliadou, A. A. (2017). Technical Market Anomalies: Leveraged ETF Trading with Daily and Intraday Temporal Functionalities. *Business and Economics Journal, 8*(1). http://dx.doi.org/10.4172/2151-6219.1000275

Campbell, J. Y., Giglio, S., Polk, C., & Turley, R. (2014). *An Intertemporal CAPM with Stochastic Volatility*. London School of Economics and Political Siences working paper, LSE London, UK. Retrieved from https://pdfs.semanticscholar.org/0044/748cabfc0ee3f7fdeea1992ce8efd7aaaa5f.pdf

Cesari, A. D., Espenlaub, S., Khurshed, A., & Simkovic, M. (2012). The Effects of Ownership and Stock Liquidity on the Timing of Repurchase Transactions. *Journal of Corporate Finance, 18*, 1023-1050. http://dx.doi.org/10.1016/j.jcorpfin.2012.06.004

Chemmanur, T. J., He, S., & Hu, G. (2009). The role of Iinstitutional Investors in Seasoned Equity Offerings. *Journal of Financial Economics, 94*, 384-411. http://dx.doi.org/10.1016/j.jfineco.2008.12.011

Chen, X., Harford, J., & Li, K. (2007). Monitoring: Which institutions matter? *Journal of Financial Economics, 86*, 279-305. http://dx.doi.org/10.1016/j.jfineco.2006.09.005

Choie, K. S. (2016). Factors of IPO Underpricing. *International Journal of Economics and Finance, 8*(2), 107-114. http://dx.doi.org/10.5539/ijef.v8n2p107

Demiralp, I., D'Mello, R., Schlingemann, F. P., & Subram Aniam, V. (2011). Are there Monitoring Benefits to Institutional Ownership? Evidence from Seasoned Equity Offerings. *Journal of Corporate Finance, 17*, 1340-1359. http://dx.doi.org/10.1016/j.jcorpfin.2011.07.002

Edelen, R. M., Ince, O., & Kadlec, G. B. (2015). Institutional Investors and Stock Return Anomalies. *E- Journal SSRN*. http://dx.doi.org/10.2139/ssrn.2359744

Gaspar, J. M., Massa, M., & Matos, P. (2005). Shareholder Investment Horizons and the Market for Corporate Control. *Journal of Financial Economics, 76*, 135-165. http://dx.doi.org/10.1016/j.jfineco.2004.10.002

Gibson, S., Safieddine, A., & Sonti, R. (2004). Smart investments by smart money: Evidence from seasoned equity offerings. *Journal of Financial Economics, 72*, 581-604. http://dx.doi.org/10.1016/j.jfineco.2003.05.001

Hao, G. Q. (2014). Institutional shareholder investment horizons and seasoned equity offerings. *Financial Management, 43*, 87-111. http://dx.doi.org/10.1111/fima.12038

Hartzell, J. C., & Starks, L. T. (2003). Institutional Investors and Executive Compensation. *Journal of Finance, 58*, 2351-2374. http://dx.doi.org/10.1046/j.1540-6261.2003.00608.x

Hovakimian, A., & Hu, H. (2016). Institutional Shareholders and SEO Market Timing. *Journal of Corporate Finance, 36*, 1-14. http://dx.doi.org/10.1016/j.jcorpfin.2015.09.009

Livermore, J. (2001). *How to Trade in Stocks*. (R. Smitten, Translation). New York, NY: McGraw-Hill, 179 pages, ISBN: 0-07-146979-6. (Original work published 1940)

Lou, D., Polk, C., & Skouras, S. (2016). *A Tug of War: Overnight versus Intraday Expected Returns*. London School of Economics and Political Sciences working paper, LSE London, UK. Retrieved from http://personal.lse.ac.uk/loud/overnightmom.pdf

Markoulis, S. N., & Neofytou, N. (2016). An Empirical Analysis of the Relationship between Oil Prices and Stock Markets. *International Journal of Economics and Finance, 8*(12), 120-131. http://dx.doi.org/10.5539/ijef.v8n12p120

Nguyen, X. M., & Tran, Q. T. (2016). Dividend Smoothing and Signaling Under the Impact of the Global Financial Crisis: A Comparison of US and Southeast Asian Markets. *International Journal of Economics and Finance, 8*(11), 118-123. http://dx.doi.org/10.5539/ijef.v8n11p118

Nickerson, D. (2016). Asset Price Volatility, Credit Rationing and Rational Lending Discimination. *International Journal of Economics and Finance, 8*(10), 140-158. http://dx.doi.org/10.5539/ijef.v8n10p140

Ogden, J. P., & Wu, S. (2013). Reassessing the Effect of Growth Options on Leverage. *Journal of Corporate Finance*, *23*, 182-195. http://dx.doi.org/10.1016/j.jcorpfin.2013.08.008

Skyba, E. (2012). The Overnight Return Study. *Stocks & Commodities*, *30*(2), 34-38. Retrieved from http://technical.traders.com/archive/articlefinal.asp?file=\V30\C02\241SKYB.pdf

Styliadis, A. D. (2007). E-learning Documentation of Historical Living Systems with 3-d Modeling Functionality. *Informatica*, *18*(3), 419-446. Retrieved from http://www.mii.vu.lt/informatica/pdf/INFO686.pdf

Styliadis, A. D., & Vassilakopoulos, M. G. (2005). A Spatio-Temporal Geometry-based Model for Digital Documentation of Historical Living Systems. *Information & Management*, *42*(2), 349-359. http://dx.doi.org/10.1016/j.im.2004.01.006

Vayanos, D., & Woolley, P. (2013). An Institutional Theory of Momentum and Reversal. *Review of Financial Studies, forthcoming*. London School of Economics and Political Sciences working paper. LSE London, UK. Retrieved from http://personal.lse.ac.uk/vayanos/Papers/ITMR_RFS13.pdf

VelocityShares. (2017). Retrieved from http://www.velocitysharesetns.com/

Yan, X., & Zhang, Z. (2009). Institutional Investors and Equity Returns: Are Short-term Institutions Better Informed? *The Review of Financial Studies*, *22*, 893-924. http://dx.doi.org/10.1093/revfin/hhl046

Notes

Note 1. ETF: Exchange-Traded Funds; ETN: Exchange-Traded Notes.

Note 2. VelocityShares® is a leader in designing exchange-traded products, instruments (ETF, ETN) and sophisticated volatility strategies for institutional investors. The team is focused on developing liquid instruments that enable institutional investors to manage their risk, generate additional yield and express short-term market views. The team has significant experience across asset classes on both the buy- and sell-sides of the financial markets. Employing that combined knowledge and insight enables the development and delivery of innovative products.

19

The Operation Mechanism of Emission Right Trading and Analysis on the Operation Effect

Ding Shanshan[1] & Duan Jindong[2]

[1] Graduate of Economics and Management College, Nanjing University of Aeronautics and Astronautics, Nanjing, China

[2] Professor of Economics and Management College, Nanjing University of Aeronautics and Astronautics, Nanjing, China

Correspondence: Ding Shanshan, College of Economics and Management, Nanjing University of Aeronautics and Astronautics, Nanjing, 210000, China. E-mail: 2401151250@qq.com

Abstract

The current environment pollution problem is becoming increasingly serious in the world, many solutions are being explored. Emission right trading as a means which can promote economic development and protect the ecological environment has attracted more and more attention of international society. With China's increasing emphasis on environmental governance problem, it is important to be familiar with emission right trading and the general operation mechanism. Referring to the successful operation experience of the developed countries such as the United States, undoubtedly has important effect on promoting China's relevant management departments and enterprises in energy-saving emission reduction work.

Keywords: emission rights trading, analysis on the effect, operation mechanism

1. Introduction

The current situation of global environmental problem becomes more and more serious, especially the waste water, waste gas and waste (commonly known as the "three wastes") pollution. In order to better solve the problem of environmental pollution and as for the impact on industrial production and economic development, western countries put forward the theory of emission rights trading early in the 20th century 60 years and in 1977 the United States took the lead in the implementation of emissions rights trading system. Since then, emission rights' trading has promoted the environmental governance in the relevant countries.

Our country in recent years is full implementing the system, but many aspects of emission rights trading in our country is still a blank. It is imperative to learn from the successful experience of developed countries and finally to find out the most suitable system for China's emissions rights trading.

2. Emission Right Trading and Its Operation Mechanism

Emission trading is a positive economic trading based on the market, the government firstly determines the jurisdiction of the environmental quality objectives, and establishes a legal compliance of sewage in the sewage line according to a certain proportion of emission rights, then uses a variety of ways to make the enterprise get normal amount of sewage so as to change the government's mandatory requirements to the enterprise consciousness management. The biggest advantage is the high efficiency of controlling environmental pollution. Specifically, the main responsibilities of environmental supervision and management departments is to determine the jurisdiction of quality objectives of regional environment, and enterprises pollution control objectives turns into enterprises decision matters. That is to say, in the emission rights trading market, the enterprise could independently decide to buy or sell the emission rights according to its own situation.

2.1 The Principle of Emission Rights Trading

The connotation of Emission rights trading explicitly requires enterprises freely to choose to buy or sell emission rights trading according to their own capacity of controlling pollution in the emissions trading market and to achieve the optimal allocation of resources. The motivation of this operation is the different abilities, levels as well as costs for corporate to fight against pollution. For some enterprises with low cost of controlling pollution can obtain compensation through the sale of emission rights. And those enterprise with high cost of controlling pollution, as long as the price of purchasing emission rights is lower than the cost of controlling pollution, these enterprises can spend less money to achieve the goal of pollution control, under the premise of paying a certain price for its pollution emission, in order to protect the ecological environment with relatively lower costs compared with controlling pollution by themselves, and finally to achieve a win-win situation.

2.2 Determination of the Optimal Level of Pollution Emission Is the Fundamental of Emission Rights Trading

The principle of emissions trading is based on the price and quantity of optimal emission rights, and achieving optimal allocation of social resources under the premise of free market.

Optimal emission quantity is also called optimal pollution level Q*, it is determined by the marginal private net income MNPB (consumers obtain an extra unit of satisfaction degree through the increase of goods or services consumption) and marginal external cost MEC (due to an extra unit of a product yield increase the third persons' cost). There is inverse relationship between Marginal private net income MNPB and production scale, MNPB reducing with the expansion of the scale of production; There is positive relationship between marginal external cost MEC and the scale of production, MEC increasing with the scale of production, the relationship between both of them and the scale of production can be seen by the following figure. As shown in the figure, the area underneath the line MNPB is the total revenue and the area underneath line MEC is the total cost. When the marginal private net income MNPB is equal to the marginal external cost MEC, the difference between the total revenue and total cost is maximum, at this time, the pollution level of Q* determined by the horizontal axis is the optimal pollution level, under the optimal level of pollution, net contribution is maximum.

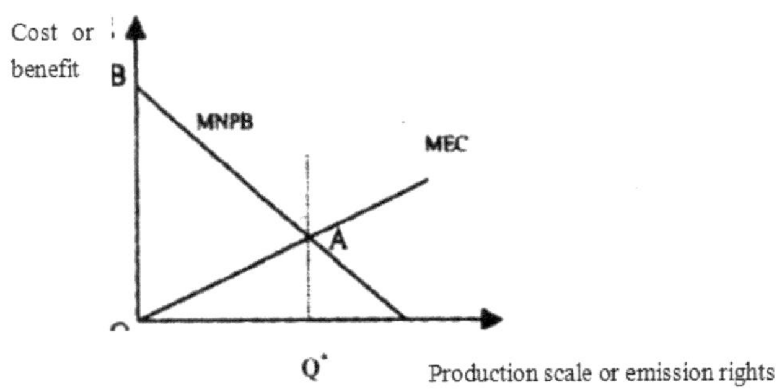

Figure 1. How to determine the optimal discharge level

2.3 The Core of the Government Management Is to Determine the Legal Emission Rights

The basis of government environmental supervision and management department to identify legal compliance emission rights and issuing emission rights licenses is the optimal pollution level Q*. Issuing emission rights license is regulated by government, obviously, the purpose of the government issuing emission rights license is to protect the ecological environment without intended profit, so the total supply curve of emission rights in the figure below is perpendicular to the horizontal axis line, it doesn't change with the price change. The p* on the vertical axis indicates the government charging when issuing every unit of emission permits to enterprises. So, for the enterprises which need to discharge waste, they need to make choices between buying emission rights and governing pollution by themselves. Sewage Demand of emission rights for these enterprises is determined by the marginal cost of fighting against pollution, so the marginal cost curve MAC can be seen as the total demand curve of emission rights. According to the supply theory, the market price of emission rights is decided by the total demand of emission rights MAC and the total supply S, the optimal price of emission rights is just the price determined by MNPB. When MAC (D1) >MNPB, then the price of emission rights P1>P*. At this time, the costs of enterprises fighting pollution on their own are too high, enterprises will choose to buy emission rights; on the contrary, when the MAC (D2) <MNPB. At this time, the price of emission rights P2<P*. Obviously, enterprises will choose to fight against pollution by themselves with lower cost, and then sell the remaining emission rights in the emission rights trading market so as to realize the maximization of personal income. This can greatly improve the consciousness of enterprises to reduce pollution and to protect ecological environment.

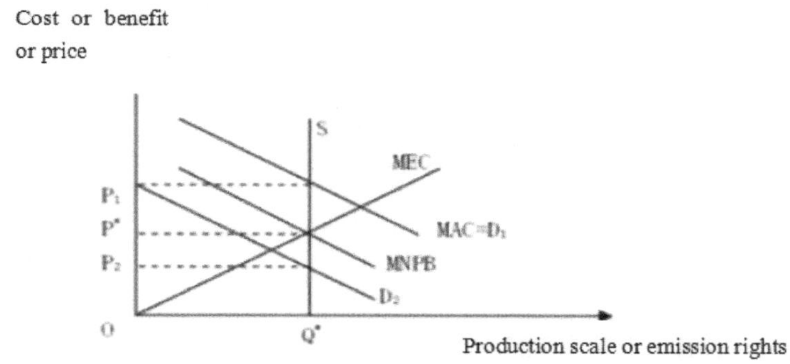

Figure 2. Principle and transaction process of emission trading

In short, environmental resource capacity (the capacity of natural ecological environment containing and digesting pollution) is regarded as a trading goods placed in the market. The perfection of the market mechanism will solve the external environment problem which has been troubled the government and the enterprise. Obviously, the emission rights trading will significantly reduce the administrative costs of the government to control and treat environmental pollution, and emission rights trading market is full of flexibility. Government as the unit of controlling the issue of emission rights licenses, the supply curve of emission rights licenses is controlled by the number of emission rights licenses issued by the government, and it can move with the change of emission rights licenses issued by the government. At the same time, the demand curve will move with the exit of older firms and the join of new enterprises. As is shown below.

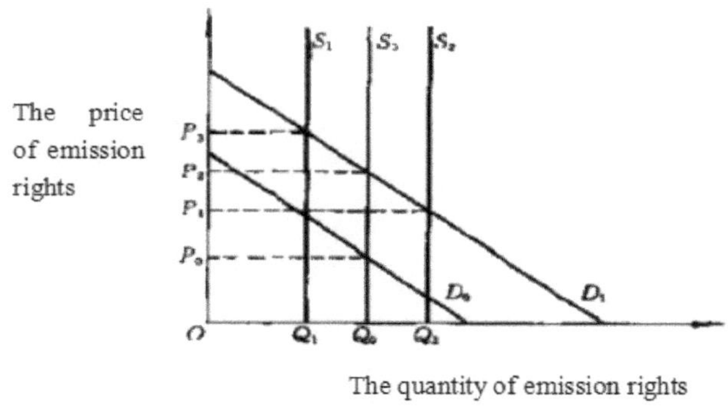

Figure 3. The change of the supply and demand of emission rights

As we can see in the figure above, when the government expands the number of emission rights licenses issued, the license number increases from Q0 to Q2, with the supply curve shifted to the right from S0 to S2, with the demand curve unchanged, the equilibrium price for emission rights decreases; on the contrary, when the government reduces the issuance of emission rights licenses, that is to say the number of licenses decreases from Q0 to Q1, at this time, the supply curve shifts from S0 to S1 to the left, if the present demand curve doesn't change, then the equilibrium price of emission rights will rise. If in the circumstance that the supply curve unchanged, the join of new enterprises will cause the increase of demand, the demand curve shifts from D0 to D1 to the right, eventually price of emission rights rises. This operation mechanism will eliminate enterprises with large amount of pollution as well as high costs for pollution control, which is advantageous to achieve the optimal allocation of resources.

3. Analysis of the Mode of American Emission Right Trading

After years of practice, American emission right trading has formed three different transaction modes which are very important for the effectiveness and efficiency of the emission right trading. The three emission right trading patterns are respectively total amount-transaction mode, non continuous cutting pollutant emission mode and standard-credit mode.

3.1 Total Amount-Transaction Mode

Many U.S. environmental protection plan use total amount-transaction mode such as grading reducing lead plan, grading reducing CFC program, the acid rain program and regional clean air incentive market plan. Due to different pollutants, total amount-transaction mode can be divided into "production permit total amount-transaction" and "emission permit total amount-transaction"."production permit total amount-transaction" specific point to producers produced products causing pollution in the use process, the issuing emission permits in this mode means hidden pollution load which is allowed to be contained in products. Relatively, "emission permit total amount-transaction" points to producers produced products causing pollution in the production process, the permit is for the emissions of pollutants produced in the production. Total amount-transaction mode is conducting emission credit transaction according to the total amount of pollutants. Environmental protection supervision department first assesses the environmental quality of a region, obtains the environmental carrying capacity of the region, so as to get the total amount of emission rights within the region, then divides the emission rights into the same parts, and distributes to the enterprises in need making emission rights disperse to the whole society. At that time, the emission right trading system was not perfect, enterprises need to make a deal by full-time agents who are responsible for the coordination between the buyers and sellers. Different subjects can purchase or sell emission rights with information on the supply and demand right in this way. In addition, the enterprises can also buy emission rights through the annual auction.

3.2 Non Continuous Cutting Pollutant Emission Mode

The highlighting characteristic of non-continuous cutting pollutant emission mode is non continuous which means the enterprise can get emission credit continuous emission reduction on many occasions in a period of time. After all, it's very hard to achieve continuous emission reduction in a continuous time owing to many affecting factors, such as economic conditions, weather and production cycle. But noncontiguous emission reduction on many occasions is relatively easy for the enterprise which means they can make their own to avoid adverse external factors interference in order to achieve emission reduction. In this way, requirement for enterprises to obtain emission credit is greatly reduced, not only can stimulate initiative of enterprises, but also make emission reduction standards more flexible. What's more, the environmental protection supervision department will be easier to implement this system. With less restrictions of this mode, it can no doubt reduce the burden of the work of the relevant departments, thereby reduce management costs and save management time.

3.3 Standard-Credit Mode

The last but not least is standard-credit mode which was first applied to the state atmosphere "emission trading scheme" proposed the United States Environmental Protection Agency. An example is given to illustrate the operation of this mode. For example, the government environmental protection supervision departments sets that under a year, total emissions sulfur dioxide from thermal power enterprises should be no more than 40 million tons, A power plant in the year up to now has discharged sulfur dioxide 10 million tons, and has been devoted to emission reduction in the remaining time of the year. Now a power plant has the right to apply for emission credit from the environmental protection supervision department which is exactly the difference of 40 million tons set by the government environmental protection supervision department and 10 million tons discharged by a power plant. In this mode, there are many needs to meet in order to obtain credit, such as emission behavior must occur within a continuous period of time, different from non continuous cutting pollutant emission mode which can be segmented several times and also the emissions of pollutants must be quantified and recognized by the public. In a word, it is the pattern to apply most early in practice with the most restricts.

4. The Choice of Operation Mode and Effect Prediction of Emission Right Trading System in China

The pilot of China's emission right trading is in a relatively short time without wide range of implementation. The practice has encountered many theoretical and practical problems which need to be solved, but the Chinese government has determined to launch the national carbon emission right trading in 2017 which need us to determine the carbon emission right trading patterns suitable for the situation of the present China.

4.1 The Choice of the Emission Right Trading Mode for Our Country

Total amount-transaction mode is used in the United States most frequently, on the contrary, non continuous cutting pollutant emission mode is used seldom. The reason for this phenomenon is that Total amount-transaction mode has higher market liquidity and participation than the other two modes, and also it has low transaction costs. In accordance with China's current situation, emission right trading is a brand new system without too much practical experience and needs all transactions subjects to increase market activity, and needs to control the transaction costs in a moderate level, then we are supposed to think of a way to reduce the management costs of relevant departments. Obviously, Total amount-transaction mode fully meets all the needs of China's emission right trading market, so the suitable mode for China's emission right trading market is the Total amount-transaction mode.

Moreover, there are wide varieties of transactions subjects in the American emission right trading market which can be divided into three categories: standards, investors and environmentalists. It's the same to Germany's participation subjects in emission right trading market. The diversification of the main body of the transaction can help to satisfy different purpose of transactions. At the same time, it can vigorously promote emissions trading. China should draw lessons from the experience of foreign emission right trading system, increase the diversification of the attending subjects of the emission right trading in order to attract investors, speculators and environmentalists to enter the trading so as to increase transaction subject categories and improve level of trading activity.

Furthermore, there are large number of brokerage firms, consulting institutions and auction companies and other intermediaries as a bridge and link trading in the American emission right trading. Brokerage company plays a role of agent which is responsible for the buy and sell work of emission rights attached to provide price information for the parties of the transaction. The role of a consulting institution is to provide price and relevant information for the traders for reference under its own understanding on the trading market. The work of auction company is to sell emission rights obtained from enterprises or government departments for auction. Obviously, these intermediaries improve the emission right trading market and increase the level of activity in the market. Traders can get information through intermediaries and save many expenses, including searching for information cost and cost of buying procedures. All in all, the role of intermediaries is very important which means China's emission right trading market should also attach importance to the important role of intermediaries and encourage the establishment of relevant emission right trading intermediaries so as to lay the foundation for the development of emission right trading .

4.2 The Evaluation of Operation Effect of the Emission Right Transaction --Based on the Case of Electric Power Industry

Based on rich coal resource reserves in China, the electricity enterprise in our country mainly rely on coal-fired power to provide the required energy, while the proportion of renewable energy is not large. The amount of sulfur dioxide generated by coal combustion accounts for more than 80% of China's total emissions of sulfur dioxide, amount of sulfur dioxide from power plants burning coal accounts for more than 40% of China's total emissions of sulfur dioxide. That is to say, the power industry is one of the main sources of emissions of sulfur dioxide, but obviously the number of power generation enterprises in China will not reduce, nothing could prevent the expansion of power generation enterprises, so the control of emissions of sulfur dioxide of power industry is crucial.

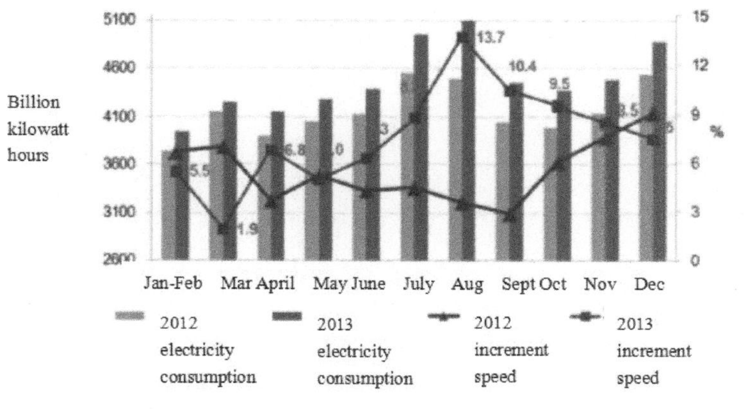

Figure 4. 2012 to 2013 the electricity consumption of the whole society and the growth rate of statistics

We Can see in Figure 4, the electricity consumption of the whole society has increased and with the continued development of the economy, it will have been showing a rising trend, apparently in China power industry in recent years and even decades will has been in growth ,reducing the number of power generation enterprises is clearly not realistic, then the control of emissions of sulfur dioxide of power industry becomes the most important to control the air pollution.

Table 1. The proportion of thermal power in gross generating capacity from 2002 to 2015 in China

Year	Proportion
2015	73.1
2014	74.9
2013	80.4
2012	78.6
2011	82.8
2010	80.3
2009	81.7
2008	81.8
2007	84.2
2006	82.4
2005	81.6
2004	82.6
2003	82.3
2002	81.7
2001	81.2

From the table above, we can see thermal power occupies an important position in gross generating capacity in our country. Next I will compare the difference between implementing or not implementing the emission right trading through intuitive calculation result according to the data of sulfur dioxide emissions in China, and focus on the analysis of the difference between the cost of implementing or not implementing the emission right trading, and also put forward some opinions and suggestions for the development of emission right trading.

If Electric power enterprises do not implement the emissions trading system, they must use the coal desulfurization process. The cost of desulfurization treatment includes the purchase of equipment and the equipment running cost. The table below counts the amount and cost of emissions of sulfur dioxide of China's electric power industry, the data of Year 2015 in the table is estimated according to < China electric power market analysis and research >:

Table 2. Statistics of sulfur dioxide emissions and cost in China's electric power industry

Year	Sulfur dioxide emissions (Million ton)	Target of Sulfur dioxide emission control (Million ton)	Desulfurization investment cost (Million yuan)	Desulfurization process operating cost (Million yuan)	Payment for Sulfur dioxide emissions(Million yuan)
2011	1706	851	1013245	855000	538683
2012	1757	808	1014367	949000	511464
2013	1810	767	1117680	1043000	485511
2014	1864	729	1176807	1135000	461457
2015	1920	693	1178098	1227000	438669
2016	1968	658	1104675	1310000	416514
2017	2017	625	1257654	1392000	395625
2018	2067	594	1379009	1473000	376002
2019	2119	570	1490987	1549000	360810
2020	2160	550	1528752	1610000	348150
2021	2205	523	1539630	1652000	324768
2022	2273	517	1570215	1694000	309421
2023	2324	506	1621734	1720000	288360
2024	2395	484	1679032	1751000	263945
2025	2430	462	1745953	1784000	241753
合计	31015	9337	20417838	21144000	5761132

According to the table above, total Desulfurization cost = investment cost + operation cost =41561838 million yuan approximately equal to 4156 billion yuan. By comparison, excessive emissions of sulfur dioxide should be payed 5761132 million yuan, approximately equal to 576 billion yuan.

At this time, enterprises can choose to buy emission rights for excessive emission of sulfur dioxide, emission rights pricing has become the key of the problem. In order that the market can produce enough demand and supply, the minimum of emission rights pricing must be less than the worst level of social handling pollution cost which is the biggest cost of pollution control for those enterprises with lag technology so as to satisfy the emission right requirements, also the maximum of emission rights pricing must be higher than the optimal social cost of pollution control which is the least cost of pollution treatment for those enterprise with advanced technology so as to ensure the supply of emission rights.

The Shanghai municipal government has put forward a pricing formula based on water pollution:

$$P=(2A+5B)*\lambda*C*D \tag{1}$$

In the above formula, P is the price of emission rights, A is the investment for reducing a unit of certain types of pollutants, B is operation cost needed for the reduction of a unit of certain pollutants, C is the weight for pollution factor, D is the weight for the functional area, λ is transaction cost coefficient.

Obviously we can see from the above equation, the main factors affecting the price of emission rights are the capital and the running costs of pollution control.

The pricing formula based on sulfur dioxide emission rights can be modeled on the above equation, main influencing factors which are the invested capital and running costs have existed, the ratio of investment capital and running costs is 2:5 or is 1:2.5, so the weight coefficient of investment costs based on sulfur dioxide is 1 / (1+2.5) about to 0.285, then the weight coefficient of running cost is 1-0.285=0.715. The equation follows the mathematical formula of price = cost / number, also we can say it calculates the price of emission right according to a unit of sulfur dioxide. And also we should plus the condition of transaction costs which is never be zero, so that it conforms to the actual situation, the transaction costs can be the cost for sulfur dioxide emissions, the specific formula is as follows:

$$P=(0.285A+0.715B)/Q+E/Q \tag{2}$$

In the formula, A is the investment funds to reduce emissions of sulfur dioxide, B is the operating costs to reduce the sulfur dioxide emissions, Q is the amount of sulfur dioxide emissions, E is the cost for per unit of sulfur dioxide emissions. Substitute the types in the equation with numbers:

$$P=(0.285*20417838+0.715*21144000)/31015+5761132/31015=860.81 \tag{3}$$

Results shows that, the price based on sulfur dioxide emission rights is \$860.81/ton, then the total costs to reduce emissions of sulfur dioxide is (31015-9337) *861.81=1868.23 billion yuan. Obviously, the price is lower than the needed operation cost to run the desulfurization equipment or the charges required to pay for sulfur dioxide emissions over emissions standards, and if the enterprises have high level of capacity for pollution control, they can sell the residual sulfur dioxide emissions for profit. In this way, the implementation of emission right trading system can not only save the cost for the enterprises, but also provide the enterprises with power of improving the level of pollution control.

5. Suggestions for the Implementation of Emission Right Trading in China

In order to control greenhouse gas emissions and promote low-carbon development, the central government and the local government and even enterprises are collaboratively promoting the construction of the national carbon emission right trading market. As the executive organ of the state power, the government has a wide range of functions and powers, which has the power to make the rules of the emission right trading system, so the government and relevant department will be playing an important role of guidance and guarantee in the construction of emission right trading system.

Firstly, it is necessary to strengthen the propaganda of environmental protection and emission rights related knowledge. At this stage, our people's awareness of environmental protection is still to be strengthened. At this time, the government should take on the responsibility of the popularization of environmental protection knowledge and the relevant knowledge of emission rights. There are a lot of methods to strengthen propaganda, but the government needs to take corresponding measures. For example, for the ordinary people with relatively low cultural level, the government can take measures like community lecture, community questionnaire like quiz to intensify propaganda, and to improve the mass awareness of environmental protection, and to guide people how to really achieve environmental protection in daily life. For the masses with medium culture level, the government can choose to conduct propaganda in units of the enterprises, and at the same time, emphasize knowledge about emission right. This will make enterprise workers become the supervisors of emission right trading system.

The government needs to attach enough importance to the education about environmental protection and related knowledge about emission right in institutions of higher learning. After all, the possibility for personnel of institutions of higher learning to engage in cutting-edge technology in the future is larger. Strengthening the education about environmental protection for college students can influence students, and also urge students to make environmental protection as the topic of the thesis. It can not only educate students themselves, but also expand the influence of environmental protection through research.

Then selecting the suitable method of initial allocation ways of emission rights considering about China's national conditions is very important. In the 1990s, the United States put forward three kinds of initial distribution ways of emission right trading system which are auction, fixed price sale and free distribution in the <Clean Air Act> amendment, and its initial distribution way is free distribution. Obviously, our country can not just copy the American experience. What we need is to choose a suitable initial distribution with a clear analysis of our country's condition. There is no monitoring and forecasting system about the capacity for the environment to bear the environment pollutants in our country. Then the prediction of the capacity for the environment to bear the environment pollutants must be lacking. In addition, emission right must be in short supply in the state with too many enterprises' demand for the emission right, which makes it becomes a scarce commodity with value, then the most suitable way of the initial allocation considering China's national condition is distribution with payment.

Next putting building the data system on the basis of total amount control on the agenda cannot be ignored. The premise of emission right trading system is total control, it provides the limit amount of pollutants within a certain area, so the core issue of emission right trading system is how to accurately measure the maximum value of pollutants that a region can accommodate. But now in China the data system based on the total amount control is still blank. Without the premise of implementation of emission right trading system, it will be impossible to carry out the system. Total amount control needs a large amount of statistics based on the capacity for the environment to bear the environment pollutants in need of a lot of supporting data which requires a great deal of time, manpower and material resources. At present, our country is not only lack of the related research institutions, but also lack of relevant databases, so to put building the data system on the basis of total amount control on the agenda is the top priority of our government.

Indeed, enterprises as the major participants of the emission right trading system are playing main responsibility in the various links and various aspects in the whole operating process of emission right trading. Only when enterprises really take the environmental protection as one of the goals of their own development, can they form the long-term and effective support force for environmental protection. Thus, improving the cognitive level of emission right trading system and environmental protection further is especially important. Even though, many enterprises have realized that extensive economic growth mode has been against with China's sustainable economic development policy, and they are aware of the importance of environmental protection. But for enterprises to actively participate in the emission right trading system with a fair attitude is not in place. The successful implement of the emission right trading system cannot be separated from the support and maintenance from enterprises as main participants as well as the active participating attitude of enterprises. When enterprises don't have enough emission right, they should choose to buy consciously the emission rights in the trading market; when they possess remaining emission rights, they ought to sell the emission rights in the market with the attitude of fairness as well as consciousness. It is prohibited to make a deal of emission rights in the black market and in disguise to improve emission rights prices on purpose or for "hoarding" mind to refuse to sell emission rights.

6. Concluding Remarks

According to China's current environmental situation and economic development situation, the implementation of emission right trading system is imperative, but absolutely can not directly copy the experience of developed countries, we must draw lessons from the successful experience and choose the most suitable implementation mechanism according to China's actual situation. The emission right trading system is still blank in China which is a good thing because it can completely start from zero without any other factors of interference, but also is not a good thing because it shows that our country has been lagging behind the western developed countries for decades in the implementation of emission right trading system. And now the government and enterprises must get together to strive to implement emission right trading system so as to catch up these developed countries.

Acknowledgement

This paper is supported in part by my advisor Duan Jindong. He has spared no effort to point out some parts of my paper in need of modification. Also he has spent a lot of time answering any question from me. I have to thank for his patience, hard work as well as his sense of responsibility.

Fund Project: Research on the pricing mechanism of emission rights under the specific regional environment

(No. kfjj20160105). This work is supported by' Foundation of Graduate Innovation Center in NUAA ' and 'the Fundamental Research Funds for the Central Universities'.

References

Qiaoling, T. (2011). A brief discussion on the <American clean energy and Security Act> and its impact on emissions trading system. *Financial Services Law Review, 1,* 219-241.

Qunfei, D. (2015). The problems and Countermeasures of the current emission trading market mechanism. *Ecological Economy, 1*, 103-108.

Ren, R., & Shuxun, Z. (2016). Research on the reform ideas of emission trading mechanism based on the total amount control. *Environmental Science and Management, 3*, 19-24.

Xiuyuan, X. (2014). The problems and solutions of emission trading in China. *Pricing Theory and Practice, 8*, 58-60.

Zhengge, T., & Renjun, C. (2015). Emissions trading mechanism in Chinese can realize the Potter effect? *Economic Research, 7*, 160-173.

Zhongquan, C., Yusen, X., & Xinliang, Z. (2015). The role of emission trading mechanism for pollution control in industrial. *Technology and Economy, 1*, 82-88.

20

Investigating the Effects of Migrant Remittances on the Economic Growth of Cameroon

Moses A. Ofeh[1] & Ali T. Muandzevara[2]

[1] Department of Economics, Higher Teacher Training College Bambili, University of Bamenda, Cameroon

[2] Government High School, Wabanne-Fontem, Cameroon

Correspondence: Moses A. Ofeh, Department of Economics, Higher Teacher Training College Bambili, University of Bamenda, Cameroon. E-mail: ofeh2002@yahoo.fr

Abstract

Low and unsteady economic growth rates and strategies for fostering growth are major issues of concern for Cameroon. The paper attempted to investigate the effects of remittances on the economic growth of Cameroon. To achieve the objective for a clearer understanding of the dynamics of migrant remittances in relation to economic growth in Cameroon, the least squares method of multiples regression was exploited to analysze data collected from 1980 to 2013. The results revealed that migrant remittances to the tune of 1.5% positively but insignificantly explained economic growth in Cameroon.Further, consumption expenditure; government expenditure and exports were found to positively but significantly explain growth while investment expenditure was found to positively but insignificantly determine growth. Only imports alone stood to negatively and significantly influence economic growth in Cameroon.The value of R-squared Adjusted showed that 85% of variation in GDP was explained by variations in the independent variables specified in the model. Therefore, any policy measure aimed at improving upon the level of economic growth in Cameroon must give consideration to migrant remittances.

Keywords: Cameroon, economic growth, migrants, remittances

1. Introduction

Migrants, remittances and economic growth are burning issues confronting sending and hosting countries of migrants today due to the influence of migrant's activities in the sending and receiving countries. While some authors view migrants' remittances and related activities as having positive impacts on economic growth, others argue that migrants' remittances do not contribute to economic growth in the recipient countries. In fact, remittance is a new phenomenon in the global financial system because of its size and impact on the world economic systems. Data from World Bank (2011) indicates that global remittance stood at 440.1 billion dollars in 2011 and remittance was 0.31% of the global GDP in 2009. The microeconomics of remittances has been focused since the early 1980s on the role of information and social interaction in explaining transfer behaviors. This has led to a change in the way economic researchers look at the determinants of remittances in terms of motives. From a more macroeconomic perspective, new growth theories have also greatly altered the directions for research on the impact of migration and remittances. Previous findings in the 1970s and 1980s were centered on the short run effects of international transfer mainly within the framework of static trade models. Gradually, focus has shifted to long run considerations notably the role of migrant remittances in the dynamics of inequality and growth.

In 2010, officially recorded migrant remittances to developing countries reached $ 334 billion (World Bank, 2010). According to the United Nations, there were about 214 million international migrants in 2010. In relative terms, this corresponds to over 3% of the world population. This percentage does not seem exceptionally high, especially when compared to the proportion of other cross boarder transactions such as trade and investment. However, the social and political relevance of migration goes beyond numbers. Migration involves people, not just as production factors but equally the related plans, dreams, frustrations, hopes and interest of the people.

For many developing countries, remittances constitute a large source of foreign income relative to other financial flows. Remittances have shifted seriously to reducing poverty and promoting human development. Evidently, this is well documented and often well reported to anchor and influence the overall development process (Ratha, 2007; Das & Serieux, 2010).

In fact, one of the most conspicuous signs of the process of globalization is the increase in migratory flows among countries. In an increasingly integrated world, people within significant controls move across national borders seeking for greener opportunities on foreign soils.

In general, studies from Asia offer more positive assessments of migrant remittances in promoting development than studies from other regions. This is probably due to three factors.Firstly, studies in Asia have endeavored more to measure and assess the indirect effects of remittances rather than focusing solely on direct effects that are the remittances themselves. Secondly, many Asian countries notably Korea, Thailand, and Indonesia have implemented macroeconomic policies favorable to market development. Finally, several Asian governments have implemented specific policies and strategies to encourage the repatriation of foreign earnings and capture remittances for the purpose of development. (Athukorala, 1993).

There is a growing debate on how migrants' remittances are used and to what extent they contribute to the migrant's country of origin (Ratha, 2003). Developed countries serve as the origin of total remittances, with the United States of America playing the leading role. It is believed that remittances from south-south are important and even from north-south flows but one thing is certain about this which is the pacity of data.

Geographic barriers are pushed aside, distances are shortened by modern means of communication, and alternative ways of life are shared and presented as desired. All of these have facilited migration. In recent times the direction of movement is gradually reversing from the developed to the developing in search for virgin nature and its pleasantries.

The concrete reason for most households in Cameroon to have someone abroad so that they can lean on for remittance help is finance (Baye, 2005). Locally and prestigiously, those abroad in Cameroon are called 'Bush-fallers'. Remittances as part of GDP of 2008 in Cameroon were 0.8% and since 2001 migrant remittances have experienced considerable increase. The estimates of the World Bank in 2009 indicated that migrants remittances to Cameroon as from 2000 were 11million US dollars, 103 million US dollars in 2004 and 167million US dollars in 2008. The World Bank ranked Cameroon among the top 10 recipients of remittances within the group with estimated remittance of 0.1billion US dollars (World Bank, 2011). It is difficult to evaluate the real value of migrant remittances on Cameroon economic growth since most remittances are sent informally. At the same time, migration entails brain-drain that hinders economic growth (Berry & Soligo, 1969, and Rivera, 1982). Also the real impact of migrant remittances on Cameroon's economy could be minimized by volatile exchange rates and domestic inflation. Considering the many growth challenges face by Camerooons, the main objective of the paper is to access the effects of migrants' remittances on the economic growth of Cameroon.

2. Literature Review

Concepts on remittances are varied. The World Bank's definition considers remittances to include workers' remittances, compensations of employee, migrant transfers, all of which are obtained from the balance of payment accounts of receivers and remitters. The international monetary fund considers remittances by excluding the "transfers of migrants" as it claims are in most cases unrelated to remittances and hence misleading. Simply, transfers of migrants refer to capital transfers of financial assets made by migrants as they move from one country to another and stay for more than one year. Remittances are money sent by migrant workers in foreign countries to countries of origin. This means, remittances include monetary and non-monetary items sent back home to their families by migrants (Berhane, 2005).

The motives for sending money home by immigrants can broadly be classified into two: altruism and self-interest motives. These two classifications can be further broken down into: altruism, exchange, insurance, investment, inheritance and strategic motives of which can be added education level of migrant, time passed abroad and gender.

The fundamental reason why money is sent home is altruism. According to Lopez Cordova and Olmedo (2006) and Sandhya Mahapatro et al. (2015), it is a situation in which the transfer does not entail any present or future compensation nor does it represent payment for any past debt. According to Lucas and Stark (1985), the remitter derives utility from the well-being of recipients at home and that the amount of remittance and the income are negatively violated. Those that support this theory include Chipeta and Kachaka (2004) who suggested that altruistic motives were behind remittance in Malawi. The reasons for altruistic behavior of remitter may be to mitigate poverty, low income shocks, drought, which affects wellbeing of the family. Most papers have found evidence consistent with altruism behavior, but Lucas and Stark (1985) and Agarwal and Horowitz (2002) have considered altruism against alternate family arrangements. Lucas and Stark found evidence in favor of self-interested behavior in Botswana while Agarwal and Horowitz found evidence in favor of altruism in Guyana.

Another reason for remittance is the exchange motive and it involves sending money for services rendered which may involve taking care of the children of migrated persons, housing properties, and repayment of loans borrowed by emigrants to cover emigration cost or education (Prabel & Dilip, 2012; Kwabena et al., 2014). This is in agreement with the study of Cox et al. (1998) that surveyed households in Peru, and found evidence consistent with the exchange motive for migrant remittances. The exchange motive was theorized as displaying a three waves shape. In the first stage, remittances are assumed to be repayments for informal and implicit loans contracted by migrants for investment in education and migration cost. In the second stage, they are loans made by migrants to young relatives to finance their education until they are themselves ready to migrate (Sara, 2015; Hasan, 2015). In this light, the amount remitted is expected to diminish in aggregated numbers because not all migrants are expected to give a loan to family members. Thirdly, before returning to country of origin, migrants invest accumulated capital at home, therefore the amount of remittances increase (Mausumi, 2015). Latter the next generations of emigrants repay the loan to the former emigrant lender who may have retired in the home country. Given the nature of the loan, remittances cannot consequently be reduced over time.

Investment is held as another reason for migrant remittances. The migrant may send money for the purchase of land, house or financial assets or start a small business in his/her country because he/she knows the local market more than the current host country. According to Ruiz-Arranz (2006); Emmanuel (2013) remitted funds are particularly used for investment where the financial sector does not meet the credit needs of local entrepreneurs. There are many evidences from various studies on the use of remittances for investment purpose. The investment motive directly translate growth (Gyan, Mukti, & Kamal, 2011); Asu Siddigue et al. (2012) The study of Woodruff and Zenteno (2001) in Mexico revealed that about one fifth of the capitals invested in 6000 micro enterprises in urban Mexico were financed by remittances. Yang (2008) suggested that households in Philippines that received remittances and benefited from exchange shocks spent more hours in self-employment and were more likely to start capital intensive entrepreneurial enterprises. The survey of 112 Nigerian migrant households in Chicago and a matched sample of 61 families in Nigeria by Osili (2004) found that a third of remittances were spent on housing investment in the preceding years.

Remittances are also emitted for insurance motives. Here, migrants and the remitter household members can enter into some contract wherein migrants would insure shortfalls in their incomes. Such arrangements are encouraging because government sponsored social insurances are generally poor or non-existent according to Yan and Choi (2005); Richard (2011). Also, the rural areas are exposed to risk of crop failure, price fluctuations, insecurity of land tenancies, livestock diseases and inadequate agricultural wages as Stark and levhari, (1982) put it. And so there is need for such contracts wherein migrants intend to insure the farmers left behind in order to neutralize the effects of bad yield or harvest. This was in line with funds sent by migrants in assisting to keep children in school in Ecuador during periods of distress caused by adverse shocks as in the opinion of Calero et al. (2009). Remittances quickened disaster recovery and reconstruction after a devastating earthquake in Pakistan in 2005.

Migrant remittances may also be motivated by inheritance. Schrieder and knerr (2000) carried out a study in Cameroon and asserted that the reasons for remittances were to keep a reasonable inheritance. In the Republic of Dominican, Dela Briere et al. (2002) suggested that remittances were conditioned by future inheritance.

The migrant's saving motive is also a fertile reason for remittances. Here, the assumption is that the migrant has the intention to return home with a certain amount of savings –the saving target. Thus, remittance flows during the migrant's stay abroad result from a bargaining process between the migrant and his or her family. The claim of migrant family left at home on the migrant income is considered as the demand side and the ability of migrant to remit as the supply side. Therefore the expectation of future incomes are continuously being revised and a nexus of interrelated factors are adjusted including the length of stay, the intensity of work, and the flow of remittances for the family's consumption. On the other hand, the family is regarded as having as its goal an income (including remittances) larger than that of the neighbors, in order to justify the decision to send some family members abroad. Therefore in Cameroon and elsewhere many unorthodox means such as artificial marriages, diplomatic imunities, under the canopy of an influential person, leapping without looking and others have been used to get family members abroad ('Paris at all cost', for leaving Cameroon for France). Empirical evidence for the support of saving target hypothesis was found for Greek-German migration in the period 1960-1982 and for migration from seven Mediterranean countries (Algeria, Egypt, Jordan, Morocco, Syria, Tunisia and Turkey), the remittances being positively correlated to the per capita income in the host as well as in the home country (Glytsos et al., 1998, 2002).

Lucas (2004) and Ozge Bilgili et al. (2015) summarized the answers to the question whether migration for permanent settlement resulted in lower remittances than temporary migration. Temporary migrants might have higher incentives to remit to those left behind than permanent migrants according to Galor and Stark (1990). It is discovered that, the longer migrants stay abroad, the lesser are the bonds to the sending economy and the lower are the remittances. Also, if migrants are better paid, they will leave longer in the destination countries. Thus, they could (if they wish) remit more, Lucas therefore, concluded that remittances may initially rise, and eventually decline with duration of stay which may suggest an optimal length of stay to maximize migrants' remittance flows in order to balance greater earning powers against diminishing attachments.

2.1 Transmission Modes of migrants' Remittances in Cameroon

Most remittances are made in the form of money. To a much lesser extent, they take the form of goods (such as staple foods or electronic items) or services (religious ceremonies or airline tickets). The focus of our study is on the financial infrastructure for money transfers. Other modes of remittances are touched on to remind readers of the demand for non-financial remittance services. Remittance channels are classified into two categories being the formal and informal.

Formal channels include money transfer services by banks and non-bank financial institutions such as foreign exchange bureaus and dedicated money transfer operators (MTOs), the best known of which are Western Union and Money Gram. The vast majority of MTOs transactions in Camroon are receipts of funds. Information concerning cross-borders money flows is only available on funds sent through formal channels. According to the IMF balance of payments statistics year book (2008), the total value of remittances transmitted through formal arrangements globally was estimated at US $433 billions. Russell (1996) and Taylor (1999) observed that less than 50% of remittances passed through formal channels. Micro-level field studies indicated that clandestine or in-kind transfers were substantial (Lozano, 1993; Massey & Parrado, 1994).

Informal channels of remittance transfers in Cameroon are similar to those found in other countries. The similarities are probably due in part to the long standing trade and migration links between these countries and Africa (El-Qorchi et al., 2002). It is still very common to send money with friends, relatives, drivers of taxis or buses or to carry it oneself. Other informal systems are modeled on hawala or hundi services or are single destination services provided by individual business people. Indian Diaspora and Somalia refugee's communities in East Africa for example have long had such systems. In Eastleigh a neighborhood of Nairobi known as "Mogadishu", informal agents with radios or satellite phones in Somalia operate money transfer businesses at home (Omer, 2002, Kabucho et al., 2003). Informal channels are common in Cameroon due to weak formal financial infrastructures and lack of access to financial services especially in rural and low income populated areas in Cameroon.

3. Methodology

3.1 Model Specification

Based on the main objective of the paper, a multiple regression model, linear in parameters (β_i) was used to express the relation among the concerned variables as in equation 1 below.

$$LogGDP_t = \beta_o + \beta_1 logC_t + \beta_2 logI_t + \beta_3 logG_t + \beta_4 logX_t + \beta_5 LogM_t + \beta_6 logRem_t + U_t$$

Where t = time, Log GDP= natural log of Gross Domestic Product used as a proxy for economic growth, LogC = natural log of consumption expenditure, LogI = natural log of investment, LogG = natural log of government expenditure, LogX = natural log of export, LogM=natural log of import, LogRem = natural log of migrants' remittances, and Ut = Stochastic error term .The aprior expectations of the model are such that: $\beta_o>0$ and $\beta_i>0$.

3.2 Estimation Technique

Graphs are used to express the trends of the variables and descriptive tables are used to figure out central tendencies information as well as deviations in the data collected. Pairwise correlation matrix is used to inform on the relationship among the variables specified in the model.The OLS technique; because of its BLUE property is therefore exploited to estimate the parameters of the model.

The parameters of the model are acknowledged and validated on the basis of economic, statistic and econometric conventional criteria that go respectively with value and sign of estimated parameters, the t-statistics and p-values to justify whether the coefficients of the parameters are significant; and the stationarity of the series to detect the presence of multicollinearity, autocorrelation and heteroscedasticity.

4. Presentation and Discussion of Results

4.1 Trend Analysis Results

The graphical analysis of the data collected allows for an understanding of the nature of the trend of the major variables (GDP and remittances) over the time period. This is to find out whether the variable has a stochastic, deterministic or linear trend as well as whether the variable trends with or without drift.

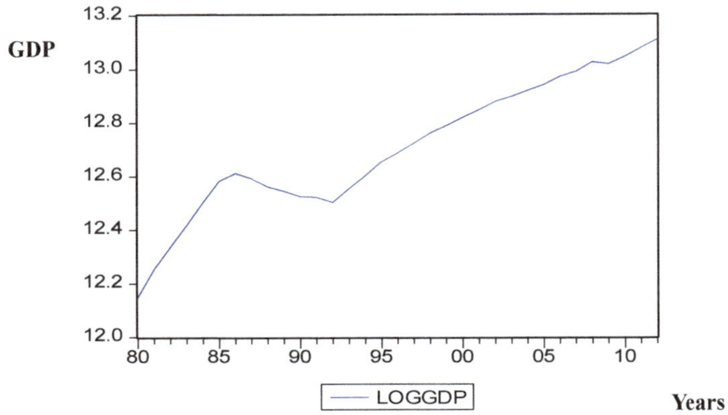

Figure 1. Trends of GDP in Cameroon from (1980-2012)

Source: Computed by Authors using E-views 5.0.

The GDP in Cameroon over the 33 years period shows that the trend is positive and more deterministic since the trend is almost linear, though there was a sharp increase and a subsequent decline in the 80s. The trend has a positive drift as the value for GDP in 1980 which is the start year is positive. Relating the trend with economic happenings in Cameroon, we discovered that from 1980, there was a steady rise in GDP in Cameroon; which clearly reflected the period of good economic performance attributed to the oil boom of the late 70s and subsequent inheritance in the early 80s. The downward sloping nature of the curve of GDP in the late 80s reflected the economic crisis of the late 80s experienced in Cameroon. The low economic performance continued and became worst in the early 90s when the structural adjustment program (SAP) of the World Bank was adopted as a panasea to reverse the dwelling economy. The economy of Cameroon took back a positive growth trend around 1994 which reflected the period when Cameroon joined the Heavily Indebted Poor Countries (HIPC) initiatives of the World Bank. Since the mid 90s, Cameroon has witnessed a low but positive growth trend.

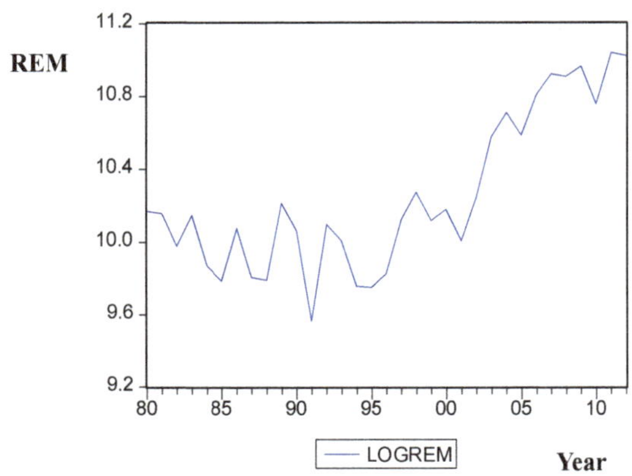

Figure 2. Trends of workers remittances in Cameroon trom (1980-2012)

Source: Computed by Authors using E-views 5.0.

Going by the trend of remittances in Cameroon, we discovered that the trend was positive with a positive drift. However, the trend revealed a series of shocks or fluctuations making predictions about the future level of remittances pretty difficult. The stochastic nature showed that the lowest annual receipts of remittances were recorded in 1991 and the highest in 2011. The trends of the other variables considered in the paper generally have had upward tendencies but exhibiting various degrees of variations depending on the econonomic events in Cameroon for the time frame (see Appendix 1).

4.1.1 Descriptive Analysis

Table 1. Descriptive analysis

	LOGGDP	LOGC	LOGINV	LOGG	LOGEXP	LOGIMP	LOGREM
Mean	12.71	12.55	11.97	11.75	9 .46	9.52	10.25
Median	12.69	12.54	11.96	11.68	9 .40	9.46	10.15
Maximum	13.11	12.96	12.40	12.25	9.87	9.93	11.04
Minimum	12.15	11.99	11.47	11.14	9.26	9.27	9.56
Std. Dev.	0.25	0.26	0.23	0.29	0.18	0.18	0.43
Skewness	-0.22	-0.21	-0.02	-0.04	0.85	0.78	0.53
Kurtosis	2.28	2.13	2.12	2.46	2 .42	2.47	2.07
Jarque-Bera	0.97	1.28	1.06	0.40	4.41	3.73	2.72
Probability	0.62	0.53	0.59	0.82	0.11	0.15	0.26
Observation	33	33	33	33	33	33	33

Source: Computed by Authors using E-views 5.0.

The descriptive analysis table 1 shows the main variables of the study (GDP and remittances) and the others. From the analysis, the mean value of the log of GDP over the period under study is 12.71 with a median of 12.69. The maximum amount of the log of GDP over the period is 13.11 with a minimum of 12.15 and a standard deviation of 0.25. The Log of GDP is leftly skewed over the period. On the other hand, the maximum amount of the log of remittances over the period is 11.04 with a minimum of 9.565 and a standard deviation of 0.43. The Log of remittances is rightly skewed over the period. The statistics about the other variables are glearing from the table.

Most economic time series data are non-stationary and to avoid the situation with such data that can lead to spurious analysis and wrong predictions (Ahmed, 2010), we engaged all the necessary tests to take care of correlation, stationarity and heteroscedasticity (see Appendices 2 for correlation, 3 for stationarity and 4 for multicolinearity).From the correlation matrix table in Appendix 2, it was realised that all the diagonals are 1. This means that there exists a perfect positive correlation between each variable and itself. All the other values of correlation in the table showed very strong positive relationships between the variables .For stationarity of the variables, the Augmented Dickey-Fuller test was carried out and the results are presented in Appendix 3. The results of the ADF test showed that all the variables are non stationary at level which is very common with macroeconomic time series and hence the existence of a unit roots. However, they all achieved stationarity after first difference as all the ADF test statistics were more negative than their critical counterparts at 10% level of significance. This allowed us to run the regression normally.

4.2 Regression Analysis

Table 2. Regression analysis results

Dependent Variable: D (LOGGDP)
Method: least Squares
Sample (adjusted): 1981 2012
Included observations: 32 after adjusting endpoints

Variable	Coefficient	Std. Error	t-Statistic	Prob.
D(LOGC)	0.68	0.09	7.81	0.00
D(LOGINV)	0.08	0.05	1.46	0.15
D(LOGG)	0.19	0.07	2.66	0.014
D(LOGEXP)	0.17	0.06	2.75	0.01
D(LOGIMP)	-0.17	0.06	-2.90	0.01
4hj'D(LOGREM)	0.01	0.01	1.39	0.18
C	0.00	0.003	0.24	0.81
R-squared	0.88	Mean dependent var		0.03
Adjusted R-squared	0.85	S.D. dependent var		0.03
S.E. of regression	0.01	Akaike info criterion		-5.70
Sum squared resid	0.00	Schwarz criterion		-5.38
Log likelihood	98.27	F-statistic		31.27
Durbin-Watson stat	2.12	Prob (F-statistic)		0.00

Source: Computed by Authors using E-views 5.0.

From the regression results in Table 2, the coefficient of consumption is 0.69, being positive meaning that there exists a positive relationship between consumption and economic growth. This conforms to our apriori theoretical expectation of the coefficient. In this connection, a 100 percentage increase in consumption expenditure will lead to a 68.31 percent increase in GDP in Cameroon with a standard deviation of 0.09. The p-value of consumption expenditure shows that the test is significant even at 1% level of significance. Therefore, we reject the null hypothesis and consider consumption expenditure to significantly affect economic growth in Cameroon.

With investment expenditure, results show that there exists a positive relationship between investment expenditure and GDP in Cameroon. This is confirming to the apriori theoretical expectations. Specifically, the coefficient shows that a 100% increases in investment expenditure will lead to 7.9% increase in GDP with a standard deviation of 0.05. The p-value of investment expenditure shows that the test is insignificant even at 10% level of significance. Thus we fail to reject the null hypothesis meaning investment expenditure in Cameroon does not significantly affect economic growth in Cameroon. The insignificant results may be as a result of the fact that most investments in Cameroon are public which are characterised with inefficiency and mismanagement, thus not yielding the desired effects on economic growth. More so, the coefficient of government expenditure is 0.19 and it is positive showing a positive relationship between government expenditures and economic growth in Cameroon as expected. The coefficient shows that a 100% increase in government expenditure will lead to 18.6% increase in GDP. The p-value of government expenditure is significant at 5% level of significance which allows for the rejection of the null hypothesis meaning government expenditure in Cameroon significantly affects economic growth.

The positive coefficient of exports, 0.17 from the results shows that, there exist a positive relationship between exports and GDP in Cameroon. This is in conformity with our expectations about exports. Precisely, the magnitude of the coefficient shows that a 100% increase in exports will lead to a 16.61% increase in GDP. The p-value of exports is significant at 5%, giving us the platform to reject the null hypothesis and hence the conclusion that exports significantly affects economic growth in Cameroon.The results equally show a negative relationship between imports and economic growth in Cameroon (-0.17). This contracts the expectations. Precisely, a 10 % in crease in import is capable of reducing economic growth in Cameroon to the tune of 1.6%. The p-value of the coefficient of imports is significant even at 1% level of significance and this permits a rejection of the null hypothesis and hence imports negatively and significantly affect economic growth in Cameroon. This is evidently true as more imports, above all consumables allows for outflow of currency, dampening exports and domestic production.

Finally the coefficient of migrant workers remittances is 0.01 which is positive portraying a positive relationship between remittances and economic growth. This is in conformity with the stated expectations about remittances. The coefficient shows that a 100% increase in remittances is capable of inducing GDP in Cameroon to the value of 1.45%. However, the p-value of remittances is insignificant even at 10% level of significance. Thus we fail to reject the null hypothesis showing that remittances do not significantly affect economic growth in Cameroon.

The coefficient of the R-squared Adjusted is 0.85 showing that more than 85% of variations in GDP were caused or explained by variations in the independent variables specified in the model. This means that there was a goodness of fits in our analysis. Also, the p-value of the F-statistic revealed that the model was overall significant at even 1% level of significance, which buttressed that the results were 99% reliable.

The DW statistics was 2.12 which when taken to the DW table, it felt in the region of no autocorrelation hence absence of autocorrelation in the analysis.To further validate the analysis, the Breusch-Pagan, Cook-Weisberg test for heteroskedasticity showed an insignificant Chi^2 probability even at 10% (see Appendix 4).This implies that we fail to reject the null hypothesis thus concluding that there is constant variance in our analysis. This means there was the absence of heteroskedasticity (or the presence of homoskedasticity) in the analysis which further validated our predictions.

5. Summary of Findings, Recommendations and Conclusion

5.1 Summary of Findings

In the paper, we set out to investigate the effect of migrant remittances on the economic growth of Cameroon. In order to achieve the objective, other macro economic variables that prior studies have considered to influence economic growth were included in the model. In order to confirm the relationship and the effects of migrant remittances on the economic growth of Cameroon, correlation analysis, regression analysis and other econometric tests were conducted on the macroeconomic variables data collected. Consumption expenditure, government expenditure, and exports and were found to positively and significantly influence economic growth in Cameroon while investment expenditure and migrants' remittances on the other hand were found to positively but insignificantly influence economic growth in Cameroon. Only imports negatively and significantly influence economic growth.

However, any policy measure aimed at improving upon the level of economic growth in Cameroon must take into consideration the effect of migrants' remittances and investment expenditure since they have the correct apriori expectation signs.

5.2 Recommendations

The government should increase her expenditure on major infrastructures like roads, schools, hospitals, sea ports, payment of salaries, social securities like pension and family allowances; all considered government expenditure capable of positively influencing economic growth. Cameroonian entrepreneurs should be encouraged to exploit the world market by penetrating with domestic goods to keep exportation above importation. Cameroonians in the Diaspora should be encouraged not only to remit more funds but to transfer the acquired knowledge and technologies back home. They should also be advised to set up cottage industries in Cameroon for the teeming unemployed youths. Also, there is need for prudence in the management of funds sent home by migrants. Such monies are expected to be channeled into productive ventures and not for profligacy. In addition to the above, Cameroon can have the full benefit of improved migrants' remittances under a globalized world economy by creating an investment climate that is favourable to foreign investors and Cameroonians in the Diaspora.

5.3 Conclusion

In this study, we have developed a model for examining the effects of migrants' remittances on the economic growth of Cameroon. Four out of the six explanatory variables via Consumption expenditure, Government expenditure and Exports have been found to exert a significant positive effect on economic growth in Cameroon. Migrants' remittances and Investment expenditure turned out to contribute positively but insignificantly to economic growth in Cameroon while only imports have shown a significant negative effect, contrarily to expextations.

References

Agarwal, R., & Horowitz, A. (2002). Are International Remittances Altruism or Insurance? Evidences from Guyana using multiple-migrant households. *World Development, 30*(11), 2033-2044.

Ahmed, B. (2010). Testing Non-Stationarity in Selected Macroeconomic Series from Sudan. *African Journal of Economic Policy, 17*(2).

Asu Siddigue et al. (2012). Remittances and Economic growth: Empirical Evidence from Bangladash India and Sri Lanka. *Journal of Development Studies.*

Authokorala, P. (1993). Improving the contribution of migrants' remittances to development, the experience of Asian labor-exporting countries. *International Migration, 31*, 103-124.

Baye, M. F. (2005). Structure of Sectoral Decomposition of aggregate poverty changes in Cameroon. Paper presented at *the international conference on shared Growth in Africa-Accra* (pp. 21-22). Organized Cornell University/ISSR/The World Bank.

Behane, T. (2005). Remittances as a tool for Development and Reconstruction in Eritria: An Economic Analysis. *Journal of Middle Eastern Geopolitics, 1*(2), 21-32.

Berry R. A., & Soligo, R. (1969). Some welfare aspects of international migration. *Journal of Political Economy, 77*, 778-794.

Calero et al. (2009). Remittances, Liquidity constraints and Human Capital Investment in Ecuador. *World Development*, 3716, 1143-1154.

Clipeta, C., & Kachaka, W. (2004). *The Role of migrants Remittances in an Unstable Lower Income Economy, A Case Study of Malaxui*. Report Submitted to the Global Development Network, Washington DC USA.

Cox D. et al. (1998). Motives for Private Transfer over the Life- cycle, An Analytical Framework and evidence from Peru. *Journal of Development Economics, 55*, 57-80.

Das, A., & Serieux, J. (2010). *Remittance and Reverse Flows in Developing Countries*. IDEAS Working paper series No 02/2010.

El-Qorchi, M., Samuel, M., & John, F. W. (2002). Hawala; How does this formal funds transfer system work, and should it be regulated? *Finance and Development, 39*(4). International monetary Fund, Washington DC.

Emmanuel, K. K. C. (2013). Remittances, Investment and Growth in Sub-Saharan Africa. *Journal of International Trade and Economic Development, 22*(7).

Galor, O., & Stark, O. (1990). Migrants' Savings, the Probability of return migration and migrants' performance. *International Economic Review, 31*, 463-467

Glytsos et al. (1998, 2002). Migrants' Remittances in the MENA Region, Issues and Policies for Consideration Forum. *Newsletter of the Economic Research Forum for the Arab Countries, Iran and Turkey, 5*(1), May.

Gyan, P., Mukti, U., & Kamal, U. (2011). Remittances and Economic Growth in Developing Countries. *The European Journal of Development Research, 20*(3).

Hasan, M. (2015). Impact of the Destination State on Migrants' Remmitances: A study of remitting among Bengladeshi Migrants in the USA, the UAE and Japan. *Migration and Development, 5*(1). http://dx.doi.org/10.1080/21632324.2015.1022007

Kabbbucho, K., & Sander, L. et al. (2003). *Pasing the Buch, Money Transfer Systems: The Practice and Potential for Products in Kenya, Nairobi, Micro Save-Africa*. Retrieved from http://www.livelihoods.org/hot_topics/docs/RemitKenya pdf

Kwabena, G. B. et al. (2012). Remittances and Investment in Education: Evidence from Ghana. *Journal of International Trade and Economic Development.*

Lopez, C. E., & Olmedo, A. (2006). *International remittances and development, existing evidence, policies and recommendations preliminary version.* WTALLIITD Occasional Paper Series, No. 41.

Lozano, A. F. (1993). *Bringing it Back Home: Remittances to the United States*. Monograph 37, Center for U.S. –Mexican studies, University of California at San Diego.

Lucas, R. E. B., & Stark, O. (1985). Motivation to Remit: Evidence from Botswana. *Journal of Political Economy, 93*(5), 901-18.

Lucas. (2004). *International Migration to High Income Countries, some consequences for Economic Development in the sending Countries.* Mimeo, Boston University.

Massey, D. S., & Parrado, E. (1994). Migradollars: The Remittances and Savings of Mexican Migrants to the United States. *Population Research and Policy Review, 13*, 3-30.

Mausumi, M. (2015). Migration, Development and Welfare: Findings from a Household survey in two selected Villages in Bagladash. *Migration and Development, 5*(3). http://dx.doi.org/10.1080/21632324.2015.1053304

Omer, A. S. (2002). *Supporting systems and procedures for the effective regulation and monitoring of Somali remittance Companies (Hawala)*. United Nations Development Programme, Somalia.

Osili, U. O. (2004). Migrant and House Investment, Theory and Evidence from Nigeria. *Economic Development and Cultural Change, 52*(4), 821-50.

Ozge, B. et al. (2015). To return permanently or to return temporarily? Explaining migrants' intentions. *Migration and Development, 6,* 20.

Prabal, K. D., & Dilip, R. (2012). Impact of remittances on household income asset and humancapital: Evidence from SriLanka. *Migration and Development*. http://dx.doi.org/10.1080/21632324.2012.719348

Ratha, D. (2003). Workers remittances, an important and stable source of external development finance in World Bank, Global development finance. *Striving for Stability in Development Finance, 1*, 157-75.

Ratha. (2007). *Leveraging remittances for Development, Migration Policy Institute.* World Bank, Washington DC.

Richard, H., & Adams, J. R. (2011). Evaluating the Economic Impact of International Remittances on Developing Countries Using Household Survey: A literature review. *Journal of Development Studies.*

Rivera-Batiz, F. L. (1982). International Migration, non- traded goods and economic welfare in source country. *Journal of Development Economics, 11*, 81-90.

Ruiz Arranz, M. (2006). *Boosting Economic Growth.* Institute of Development Studies.

Russel, & Taylor. (1999). The New Economic of Labour Migration and the role of remittances in the migration process. *International Migration, 37*(1), 63-88.

Sandhya, M. et al. (2015). Remittances and Money expenditure Patterns in India and Selected State. *Migration and Development*. http://dx.doi.org/10.1080/216322324.2015.1044316

Sara, R. T. (2015). The Role of Migrants' networks in Global migration Governance and Development. *Migration and Development, 5*(3). http://dx.doi.org/10.1080/21632324.2015.1068504

Schriender, G., & Knerr, B. (2000). Labour Migration as a Social Security Mechanism for Small Households in sub-Saharan Africa: The case of Cameroon. *Oxford Development Studies, 28*(2), 223-236. http://dox.doi.org/10.1080/713688309

Stark, O., & Levhari, D. (1982). On migration and Risk in LDCs. *Economic development and Cultural Change, 31*, 191-6.

Taylor, J. (1999). The New Economic of labour Migration and the role of remittances in the migration process. *International Migration, 37*(1), 63-88.

Woodruff, C., & Zenteno, R. (2001). *Remittances and Micro-Enterprises in Mexico Mimeo.* University of California at San Diego.

World Bank. (2011). *Migration and Remittance Fact Book*. Washington DC.

Yang, D. (2008). International Migration Remittances and Households Investment: Evidence from Philippines, Migrants Exchange Rate Shocks. *Economic Journal*, 591-630.

Yang, D., & Choi, H. (2005). Are *Remittances Insurance? Evidence from Rainfall Shocks in the Philippines.* University of Michigan School of Public Policy, Department of Economics Discussion Paper 53.

Appendix

Appendix 1

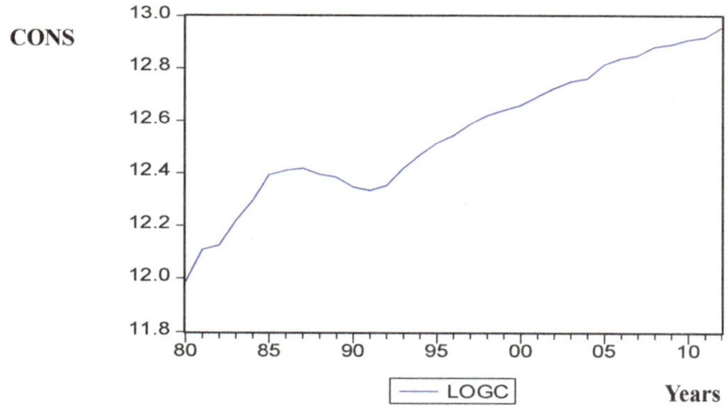

Figure 1a. Trends of consumption in Cameroon from (1980-2012)

Source: Computed by Authors using E-views 5.0.

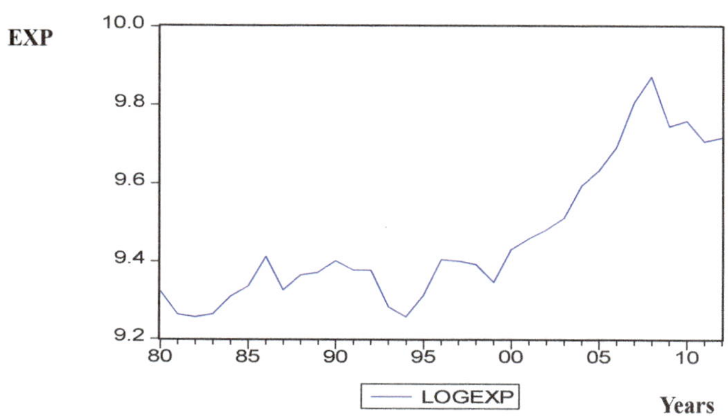

Figure 1b. Trends of exports in Cameroon from (1980-2012)

Source: Computed by Author using E-views 5.0.

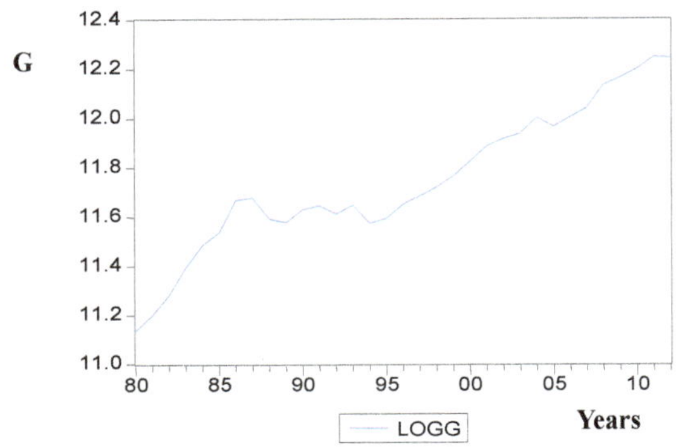

Figure 1c. Trends of government expenditure in Cameroon from (1980-2012)

Source: Computed by Author using E-views 5.0).

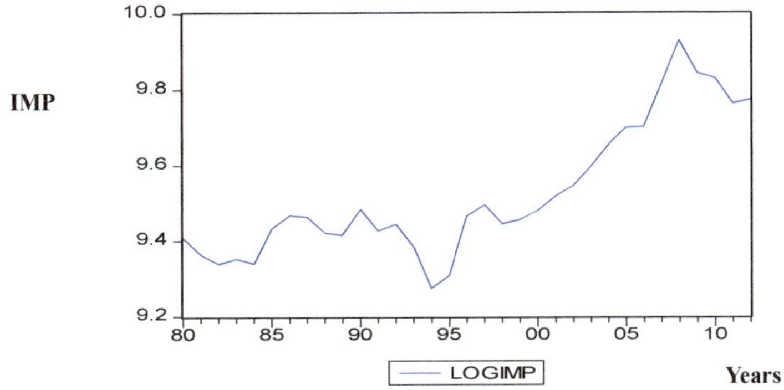

Figure 1d. Trends of imports in Cameroon from (1980-2012)

Source: Computed by Authorr using E-views 5.0.

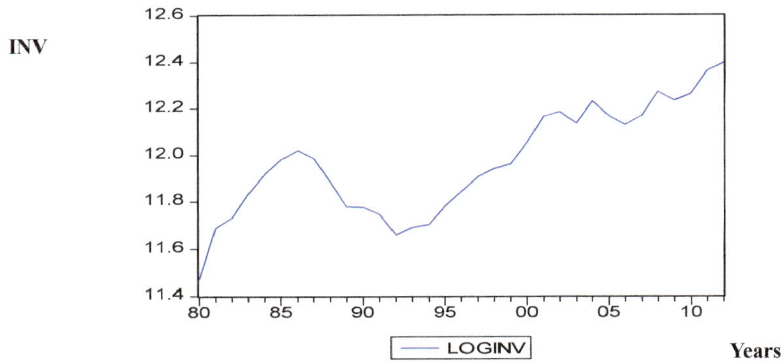

Figure 1e. Trends of investment in Cameroon from (1980-2012)

Source: Computed by Author using E-views 5.0.

Appendix 2.

Pairwise Correlation Matrix

	LOGGDP	LOGC	LOGINV	LOGG	LOGEXP	LOGIMP	LOGREM
LOGGDP	1.000000						
LOGC	0.996941	1.000000					
LOGINV	0.921359	0.897392	1.000000				
LOGG	0.979030	0.973264	0.909962	1.000000			
LOGEXP	0.858213	0.855042	0.827148	0.886023	1.000000		
LOGIMP	0.838677	0.835467	0.831373	0.876268	0.985212	1.000000	
LOGREM	0.744277	0.746125	0.746502	0.765066	0.888662	0.894371	1.000000

Source: Computed by Author using E-views 5.0.

Appendix 3.

Augmented Dickey-Fuller (ADF) Unit Root Test

Variable	Test Statistics at Level	Test Statistics after First Difference	Critical Value at 10%	Degree Of Integration
LOGGDP	-0.45	-3.23	-2.62	I(1)
LOGC	-0.61	-3.31	-2.62	I(1)
LOGINV	-0.44	-2.94	-2.62	I(1)
LOGG	-1.16	-3.28	-2.62	I(1)
LOGEXP	-0.70	-3.61	-2.62	I(1)
LOGIMP	-0.89	-4.61	-2.62	I(1)
LOGREM	-0.42	-6.97	-2.62	I(1)

Source: Computed by Authors using results from E-views 5.0.

Appendix 4.

Variance Inflation Factor (VIF) Test for Multicollinearity

Variable	VIF	1/VIF
Logimp	41.52	0.02
logexp	40.61	0.02
Logg	28.02	0.04
Logc	21.66	0.05
Loginv	6.40	0.16
Logrem	5.29	0.19
Mean VIF	23.92	

Source: computed by Author using STATA 11.

21

An Appraisal of the Activities of Central Depository Bangladesh Limited (CDBL)

Tanbir Ahmed Chowdhury[1] & Farzana Huda[2]

[1] Faculty of Business and Economics, East West University, Dhaka, Bangladesh

[2] Department of Business Administration, East West University, Dhaka, Bangladesh

Correspondence: Tanbir Ahmed Chowdhury, Professor Dr., Dean, Faculty of Business and Economics, East West University, A/2 Jahirul Islam City, Aftabnagar, Dhaka 1212, Bangladesh. E-mail: tanbir@mail.ewubd.edu

Abstract

In Bangladesh the establishment of Central Depository Bangladesh Limited (CDBL) added value to the stock market and plays a vital role in the progress of economic development. CDBL is engaged in the operations of the Central Depository System (CDS), a major financial market infrastructure in Bangladesh established as a part of the overall financial sector development. This study tried to analyze the growth and development of CDBL. Seven trend equations have been tested for different activities of CDBL.It is observed that CDBL was able to achieve a stable growth of listed securities in CDS, depository participants, settlement of securities transactions, documentation of CDBL, total assets and net income during the period of 2007-2015. Square of correlation coefficient (r^2) has also been tested for all trend equations. It indicates the prospect of CDBL in Bangladesh is relatively bright.

Keywords: central depository system, dematerialization, rematerilisation, earnings per share, net income

1. Introduction

In the developing economy firms and enterprises raised their capital by selling their common stock to expand business through capital market. The pattern of corporate finance in Bangladesh has undergone transformation at different times. Before liberation in 1971 the managing agency system provided the nucleus of finance for the corporate sector due to shyness of investor, imperfect capital market and lack of strong networks of financial system. After independence, Bangladesh witnessed drastic changes in the financial structure, particularly in view of the shift in Government policy toward socialistic approach of development. In consistent with the broader national objectives the abolition of managing agency system, suspension of stock exchange activities, nationalization of all banks, insurance companies and major industries, reorientation of credit and industrial policy took place. In 1975, a policy shift was adopted with the change of Government emphasizing private sectors. This shift in reliance from public to private sectors resulted reactivating Dhaka Stock Exchange in 1976. The only bourse of the country at that time and setting up of Investment Corporation of Bangladesh (ICB) intended to facilitate development of stock market. The second stock exchange of the country, Chittagong Stock exchange, was established on December, 1995 in Chittagong.

Early 1990s stock market in Bangladesh pretense a turmoil which creates the inevitability of Central Depository System (CDS), an electronic book entry system for custody and transfer of securities. CDS was introduced to replace the manual system of physical handling and settlement of shares at the stock exchange. This study will provide a pragmatic scenario of CDS from its inception to till date by breakdown of its escalation in terms of purpose, cost to revenue outline, contribution to the capital market, favorable to the participants and as a whole the economic development of Bangladesh.

2. Literature Review

Ali et al. (2011) examined the stock markets role in the capital formation in Pakistan from the period 1st January 2001 to 31st December 2008. The stock market size of capital, number of listed companies and liquidity positions has been examined in the study. The study revealed that Karachi Stock exchange is the oldest and biggest Stock exchange of Pakistan and it is the first mover to adapt institutional developments, new policies and procedures in the business of securities exchange and shares a big role in the capital formation in Pakistan. In recent years all stock exchanges have implemented the advanced technology and fully automated trading systems. This has changed the stock markets role in the capital formation as great boom has been observed during the study period.

Schmiedel (2006) investigated the existence and extent of economies of scale in depository and settlement system from 16 settlement institutions across different regions for the years 1993-2000 indicates the existence of significant economies of scale. The degree of such economies differs by size of settlement institution and region. While smaller settlement service providers reveal a high potential of economies for scale, larger institutions show an increasing trend toward cost effectiveness. Clearing and settlement systems in countries in Europe and Asia report substantially larger economies of scale than those of the US system. European cross-border settlement seems to be more cost intensive than that on a domestic level, reflecting chiefly complexities of EU international securities settlement systems and differences in the scope of international settlement service providers. The evidence also revealed that investments in implementing new systems and upgrades of settlement technology continuously improved cost effectiveness over the sample period.

According to Kamal (2006) investors should determine the cutoff point in between risk and return. The study tried to find out the impact of Central Depository System (CDS) listing, which is a new concept for shares instead of money. It holds securities of investors in electronic form. The very operation of CDS begins from the opening of a BO account can be opened with any participant of CDBL. The study also analyzed the operation of CDBL and its affects toward investors, issuers and brokers.

Corrado et al. (2000) examined that Central Depository System affects investors, insurers and brokers to a large extent. Investors are able to hold their securities in dematerialized form in a CDBL account; this removes the problems associated with physical certificates. Investors must have dematerialized Securities in their account before they instruct a stock broker to sell off. Securities resulting from a stock exchange bought trade will automatically be added to the investors account. Investors may rematerialize their securities or they may instruct with another participant or to a direct depository account. Securities in the account may be pledged to a bank or other financial institution without the need to withdraw them from the depository system. Investors, who have accounts in their own name, may request CDBL to issue them with a statement (to confirm the information given to them by their participant).

Hurkat and Ved (1999) discussed the role of depository system in many advanced countries in the stock and capital markets the world over. They also analyzed the services offered by depository system, dematerialization, re-materialization, trading and fee or charges, comparison of a bank and a depository for the benefits of the depository.

Shah (1996) highlighted that resolution of the single vs. multiple depositories, immobilization vs. dematerialization and role of capital adequacy norms for the custodians which really helpful in quick implementation of depository system in India.

Aggarwal and Dixit (1996) indicated the legal framework for depository system in India like benefits of the paperless trading, responsibilities of depository or participants and eligibility criteria, etc.

Sarkar (1996) analyzed the implications of the scrip less trading and share transfer based on book entry merely due to the existence of the depository ordinance 1995.

Gurusamy (1996) explained that the introduction of depository system would help in transfer of securities in the capital market by a mere book entry. He also pointed out the advantages of depository system such as delay in transfer, registration, fake certificates, soaring cost of transactions, more paper work, non availability of depositories in when the transfer of securities take place by physical delivery.

3. Objectives of the Study

The overall objectives of the study are:

- To present an overview of Central Depository system around the world.
- To appraise the activities of CDBL.
- To appraise the performance of CDBL.
- To identify the problems of CDBL.
- To suggest remedial measures for the development of CDBL.

4. Scope and Methodology of the Study

Both quantitative and qualitative analysis has been done in this study. All the information has been collected from secondary sources like published information, annual report, brochures, magazines and various articles. The study tried to analyze the performance and activities of CDBL from year 2007 to 2015 through the various statistical measures like growth percentage, trend equation, square of correlation coefficient etc.

5. Central Depository System- Around the world

Stock market is one of the most important financial institutions of any economy. Hafer and Hein (2007) notified that growth of new businesses or economy would not be possible without availability of stocks and development of financial markets and institutions like central depository system can ensure in the development of investors' confidence in the markets. There are now 62 approved central securities depositories all over the world.

5.1 Japan Securities Depository Center, Inc. (JASDEC)

JASDEC is a central securities depository in Japan designated under the Act on Transfer of Bonds, Shares, etc. JASDEC was established as a not-for-profit foundation in 1984 and incorporated as a stock company in 2002. In 2009, JASDEC accomplished dematerialization of stock certificates issued by all listed companies. With this step, new Book-entry Transfer System for stocks, corporate bonds and other securities has been fully established. JASDEC also provides pre-settlement matching system. JASDEC DVP Clearing Corporation, wholly owned by JASDEC, operates DVP settlement system for non-exchange transaction deliveries. As of the end of FY 2011 (March 2012), JASDEC's account balance of all the securities valued at JPY 696 trillion (US$8.7 trillion). In FY 2011, JASDEC settled 83 millions of cases in securities transactions.

5.2 Hong Kong Securities Clearing Company Limited (HKSCC)

Hong Kong Securities Clearing Company Limited was incorporated in 1989 and launched the central clearing and settlement system (CCASS) in 1992 based on the immobilisation of share certificates in a central depository operated by HKSCC. Physical certificates deposited into CCASS become immobilized and are transformed into electronic records to effect settlement. All stock held in the CCASS Depository are fungible and not earmarked for a particular or transaction. CCASS depository offers physical shares deposit for settlement or for custodial safekeeping purpose as well as physical share withdrawal services to Direct Clearing Participants, General Clearing Participant, Custodian Participants as well as Investor Participants and Stock Pledge Participants. CCASS participants are responsible to HKSCC for the good title of the securities deposited into CCASS.

5.3 Bursa Malaysia Depository Sdn. Bhd.

Bursa Malaysia Depository Sdn. Bhd. is a wholly-owned subsidiary of Bursa Malaysia Berhad was established in April 1990 with a paid up capital of RM25 million and commenced operations in November 1992. It is the sole central depository for the Malaysian securities market, providing depository services for Exchange Traded Funds (ETF), equities and fixed income securities listed on the stock exchange. Bursa Malaysia has focused on various initiatives aimed at improving its product and service offerings, increasing the liquidity and velocity of its markets, improving the efficiency of its businesses and achieving economies of scale in its operations. On 18 March 2005, Bursa Malaysia was listed on the Main Board of Bursa Malaysia Securities Berhad with a 17% or RM0.50 premium over its retail price of RM3.00.

5.4 Thailand Securities Depository Co., Ltd. (TSD)

Thailand Securities Depository Co., Ltd. (TSD) is a subsidiary of the Stock Exchange of Thailand was established on November 16, 1994 with a registered capital of THB 200 million, and commenced operations on January 1, 1995. TSD is the sole Central Securities Depository (CSD) in Thailand using scrip less system. The services provided by TSD are securities deposit, withdrawal, transfer, pledge and revocation. Investors can conduct the transactions through depository participants. TSD is also responsible for managing the foreign holding proportion of the securities traded on the main board and foreign board of the Stock Exchange of Thailand to comply with related rules and regulations.

5.5 National Securities Depository Limited (NSDL)

India had a vibrant capital market which is more than a century old, the paper-based settlement of trades caused substantial problems like bad delivery and delayed transfer of title till recently. The enactment of Depositories Act in August 1996 paved the way for establishment of NSDL, the first depository in India. NSDL, the first and largest depository in India, established in August 1996 and promoted by institutions of national stature responsible for economic development of the country has since established a national infrastructure of international standards that handles most of the securities held and settled in dematerialised form in the Indian capital market.

Using innovative and flexible technology systems, NSDL works to support the investors and brokers in the capital market of the country. NSDL aims at ensuring the safety and soundness of Indian marketplaces by developing settlement solutions that increase efficiency, minimise risk and reduce costs. NSDL play a central role in developing products and services that will continue to nurture the growing needs of the financial services industry.

5.6 PT Kustodian Sentral Efek Indonesia (KSEI)

PT Kustodian Sentral Efek Indonesia (KSEI - Indonesian Central Securities Depository), is the Securities Depository and Settlement Institution in the Indonesian capital market. KSEI was established on December 23, 1997 in Jakarta and obtained its operational license on November 11, 1998. Within the structure of the Indonesian capital market, KSEI is one of the few Self Regulatory Organizations (SROs), which includes PT Bursa Efek Indonesia (BEI) and PT Kliring Penjaminan Efek Indonesia (KPEI). In regards to the capital market, under the provisions of Law number 8 Year 1995, KSEI takes its role as LPP in the Indonesian capital market by providing orderly, fair, and efficient central Securities depository and transaction settlement services.

KSEI started its operational activities which handles Securities settlements in script form. On January 9, 1998 KSEI took over a similar function from PT Kliring Deposit Efek Indonesia (KDEI), which were once the Clearing Depository and Settlement Institution (LKPP). Afterwards, on July 17, 2000, KSEI together with BEI and KPEI made a breakthrough by implementing scrip less trading and central depository activities in the Indonesian capital market. KSEI shares are owned by its service users, namely: the SROs (IDX and KPEI), Custodian Banks, Securities Companies, and Registrars.

5.7 Singapore Exchange Limited (SGX)

SGX was formed on 1 December 1999 as a holding company and as of 31 January 2010, SGX had 774 listed companies with a combined market capitalisation of S$650 billion. The revenues of SGX are mainly from the securities market (75%) and derivatives market (25%). SGX reported a net profit of $165.8 million for the first half of its financial year 2010.

5.8 China Securities Depository and Clearing Corporation Limited (SD&C)

China Securities Depository and Clearing Corporation Limited (SD&C) was established in accordance with the Securities Law of the People's Republic of China and the Company Law of the People's Republic of China. The total registered capital is RMB1.2billion which is being the largest operations of this type in the world. Shanghai Stock Exchange and Shenzhen Stock Exchange are shareholders of SD&C, each holding 50% equities. SD&C was founded on 30 March, 2001 in line with related requirements by the Securities Law on establishing centralized securities registration and settlement operation.

In September 2001, SD&C Shanghai branch and Shenzhen Branch were established. As of 1 October 2001, the SD&C undertook all the securities registration and settlement business that used to be handled by Shanghai and Shenzhen Stock Exchanges, which marked the establishment of a centralized national securities registration and settlement framework. The mission of the SD&C is to build an open, flexible and unified securities registration, clearing and settlement system in line with international standards and practices, better serving market players and supporting the development of China's securities market by improving market efficiency and effectively managing risks.

6. Central Depository System in Bangladesh

Early 1990s all securities are held in physical form which is called script based system i.e physical movement of securities certificates along with transfer deeds and registration with the company. Script based system of securities transactions involves enormous paper work involving certificates and deeds. It is also time consuming, bad deliveries due to signature difference, mistakes in completion of transfer of deeds, tearing and mutilation of certificates, fake certificates, and cost of transfer: stamp duty, postal delays and charges etc.

To lessen the obscurity of script base system and to make the capital market vibrant, depository system has been initiated which assist listed companies in the handling of script less transfer of ownership of shares, debentures, mutual funds and also government bonds and treasury bills in the electronic form .

The Depositories Act, 1999 provides a legal basis for the regulation of depositories in Bangladesh. It gives regulatory responsibility to the Securities and Exchange Commission (SEC) and enables the commission to make regulations concerning the operation of the depository. The Commission has published the Depository Regulations, 2000 which set out the criteria for companies that wish to establish depository systems. The Commission has also published the Depository (User) Regulations, 2003 which are concerned with the organizations that may become participants of the depository. CDBL has been granted a Certificate of Business

Commencement from the Securities and Exchange Commission to begin operations. The CDBL By-laws define the acts and responsibilities of the CDBL, Depository Participants and Issuers.

CDBL was incorporated on 20th August 2000 in Bangladesh as a public limited company for running a central depository operation in Bangladesh. The Company is sponsored by the country's Nationalized Commercial Banks (NCBs), Investment Corporation of Bangladesh (ICB), Private Commercial Banks (PCBs), Foreign Banks, Merchant Banks, Publicly listed Companies, Insurance Companies and Dhaka & Chittagong Stock Exchanges with the collaboration of the Asian Development Bank (ADB). The Company received registration from the Securities & Exchange Commission (SEC) on 11th September 2001 under Depositories Regulations 2000 and subsequently obtained business commencement certificate on 23rd December 2003 from the SEC.

7. Legal & Regulatory Structure

The Depositories Act, 1999 provides a legal basis for the regulation of depositories in Bangladesh. It gives regulatory responsibility to the Securities and Exchange Commission and enables the commission to make regulations concerning the operation of the depository. The Commission has published the Depository Regulations, 2000 which set out the criteria for companies that wish to establish depository systems. The Commission has also published the Depository (User) Regulations, 2003 which are concerned with the organizations that may become participants of the depository. CDBL has been granted a Certificate of Business Commencement from the Securities and Exchange Commission to begin operations. The CDBL Bye Laws, defines the acts and responsibilities of the CDBL, Depository Participants, and Issuers. CDBL is regulated by the Securities and Exchange Commission (SEC).

8. Products & Services of CDBL

8.1 Dematerialization

Dematerialization is a process by which physical certificates are converted into electronic form for credit to the investors account in the depository. Once a security is eligible for holding in CDBL then all stock exchange trades must be settled through the depository. This means that sellers must have securities in the depository (i.e. the securities must have been dematerialized) before the broker can execute the sale order. To dematerialize securities investors should take their share certificates to a participant. The participant will request the investor to complete a dematerialization request form. The participant will take the documents to the issuer who (if the certificate is valid) will update the register by moving the securities from the certificated portion of the register to the depository portion. The issuer will then confirm the dematerialization to the depository and the depository will credit the securities to the investor's account. The participant will be able to see the balances in all the accounts that he controls through a computer link with CDBL. Investors do not need to wait until they wish to sell to dematerialize their holdings. Once a security is eligible, investors may open accounts and lodge securities at any time.

8.2 Direct Accounts

CDBL is offering a service to investors who wish to hold their securities in dematerialized form but do not wish to use a stockbroker or a bank to do so. Investors will be asked, by CDBL, to complete an account opening form. They will then be able to dematerialize existing holdings by giving the certificates to CDBL or to their stockbrokers and completing the dematerialization request form. When they wish to sell their securities they should instruct CDBL in writing to transfer the required number of securities to the stockbroker. When they buy they should instruct their stockbroker to transfer the securities to the Director Account on the settlement day. It is not necessary, in this case, to instruct CDBL. CDBL will not handle funds and investors must make arrangements to settle payments directly with their stockbrokers. CDBL will issue statements directly to the account holder on a monthly basis, if there are any movements and on a quarterly basis, if there are no movements.

8.3 Rematerialisation

To rematerialise securities that are in a CDBL account the account holder must instruct the participant through which he holds his account by completing a rematerialisation request form. The participant will instruct CDBL and the securities will then be debited from the account upon confirmation by the issuer. The issuer will transfer the holding from the depository portion of its register to the certificated portion of its register. The issuer will provide the investor with a share certificate within 30 days of a rematerialisation request.

8.4 Buying and Selling

The introduction of CDBL does not make any difference to the process of buying and selling although it does make a difference to the settlement of such trades. Where investors have a CDBL account through their broker then the act of giving a sell order to the broker also authorizes him to move Sucrets from the account to settle the sale. The broker will move the securities when he enters the order into the market. If the order is executed then the securities are used to settle the sale. If the order is not executed then the broker will move the securities back to the investor's account. Where investors have a CDBL account through a custodian (who is not a broker) then they must advise their custodian that they have sold as they do for physical securities. However, the securities must be in a CDBL account before they are sold and the broker may wish to check this fact with the custodian before executing the order. On the settlement date of a bough trade the broker will move securities to the account of the buying investors (provided the investor has paid). Investors may leave the securities in their account (ready for sale when they wish to sell or to avoid the need to hold certificates) or they may request the participant to rematerialize the securities.

8.5 Fees & Deposits

CDBL will charge fees to participants, issuers and Direct Account Holders, who are also required to lodge security deposits with CDBL, which are refundable upon termination. CDBL does not charge fees directly to account holders. Participants are charged fees which they may recover from investors holding accounts with them. Prospective Direct Account Holders should contact CDBL for an up to date fees & deposits schedule.

9. An Appraisal of the Activities of CDBL

This section evaluates the activities, development and prospect of CDBL from year 2007 to 2015. In esteem to this analysis various variables i.e. number of shares, listed securities, depository participants (DPS), number of shares settled in CDS, documentation, dematerialization of securities, settlement of securities transaction, net income, total assets, retained earnings, EPS and their growth percentage has been considered to evaluate the escalation of CDBL. This study also measured the trend equations and r^2 for the different mentioned variables.

9.1 Growth of Number of Shares in the CDS

Number of shares held in the CDS (Table 1) increased by 383,505,144 taking the total from 714.417 million as at 30th June '07 to 1,097.922 million as at 30th June '08. Market value of the shares held in CDS as at 30th June '07 amounted to around Tk. 166.08 billion which increased to Tk. 406.35 billion as at 30th June '08 registering a gain of around 145%. From year 2008 to 2009 number of shares held in the CDS increased by 68.87% which market value of around Tk. 406.35 billion as at 30th June '08 increased to Tk. 592.17 billion as at 30th June '09 scheduling a gain of around 46%. With the increase in securities held in the depository, share transfers in the depository relating to settlement of stock exchange trades during the year were significantly higher compared to the previous year, furthermore, transactions value up over 65 percent resulting in an upsurge in the income stream. For the duration of year 2010 this number increased by 3,558,695,047 (around 192%) taking the total from 1,854,028,146 as at 30th June '09 to 5,412,723,193 as at 30th June '10 wherever market value of these shares increased to Tk. 1,395.95 billion as at 30th June '10 recording a gain of around 136%. Besides that because of number of shares splits to Tk. 10 per share from Tk. 100 per share number of shares held in the CDS increased to 16,995,251,631 (around 214%) and 31,828,867,329 (87.28%) as at 30th June 2011 to 2012 indexing an increase of around 16% of market value of shares (Tk. 1,624,89 billion) and decreased to Tk.1,354.68 billion as at 30th June 2012 rolling a decline of around 17% (Tk.1,354.68 billion).

On the other hand Market value of the shares held in CDS as at 30th June 2012 amounted to around Tk. 1,354.68 billion which increased to Tk.1,399.16 billion as at 30th June 2013 registering a gain of over 3%. Number of shares held in the CDS increased during the year by 7,531,192,268 (around 20%) taking the total from 36,877.129 million as at 30th June 2013 to 44,408.321 million as at 30th June 2014. Market value of the shares held in CDS as at 30th June 2013 amounted to around Tk. 1,399.16 billion which increased to Tk.1, 577.07 billion as at 30th June 2014 registering a gain around 13%.

Conversely number of shares held in the CDS increased around 15% during the year by 6,465,981,153 taking the total from 44,408,321,318 as at 30th June 2014 to 50,874,302,471 as at 30th June 2015. Market value of the shares held in CDS as at 30th June 2014 amounted to around Tk. 1,577.07 billion which increased to Tk. 1,776.16 billion as at 30th June 2015 registering a gain around 13%.

Table 1. Growth of number of shares in the CDS

Year	Number of Shares in the CDS (Millions)	Growth (%)
2007	714.41	--
2008	1097.92	53.68
2009	1854.02	68.87
2010	5412.72	191.94
2011	16995.25	213.99
2012	31828.86	87.28
2013	36877	15.86
2014	44408	20.42
2015	50874	14.56

Source: Author's calculation using the different issues of Annual Report of CDBL
Note. US $1 = BDT 78.

9.2 Growth of Listed Securities in CDS

Table 2 demonstrated Listed Securities in CDS which increases from year 2007 to year 2015. By griping to this development 32 publicly listed companies came into the CDS during the year taking the total from 118 as at 30th June '07 to150 as on 30th June '08. On the other hand 31 publicly listed companies came into the CDS while 2 companies i.e. Beximco Fisheries Ltd. and Shinepukur Holdings Ltd. went out of the CDS count having merged with BEXIMCO Ltd. during the year taking the total from 150 as at 30th June '08 to 179 as at 30th June '09. From year 2009 to year 2010 listed securities showed 25.70% growth while the trend gradually decreased to 22.22% to 6.18% during year 2011 to year 2012.Conversely from year 2013 to 2014 listed securities decreased to 5.48% to 4.55% because of listed securities at DSE stood at 315 at the end of the year made up of 263 companies, 41 mutual funds, 8 debentures and 3 corporate bonds excluding 221 Bangladesh Government Treasury Bonds at 30th June 2014.In year 2015 listed securities increased by 7.45% from the preceding year.

Table 2. Growth of listed securities in CDS

Year	Listed Securities in CDS	Growth (%)
2007	118	--
2008	150	27.12
2009	179	19.33
2010	225	25.70
2011	275	22.22
2012	292	6.18
2013	308	5.48
2014	322	4.55
2015	346	7.45

Source: Author's calculation using the different issues of Annual Report of CDBL
Note. US $1 = BDT 78.

9.3 Growth of Depository Participants of CDBL

The participants of CDBL are called Depository Participant (DP). Table-3 showed that Depository Participants (DP) increased by 28, 22, 28, 28, 17, 18, 13 and 10 during the year ended 30th June '08 to 30th June 2015. The growth of Depository Participants (DP) increased from year 2007 to 2015 but it is fluctuating every year and at the end 30th June 2015 growth was 2.66% which was much below of the preceding years.

Table 3. Growth of depository participants of CDBL

Year	Depository Participants to CDBL	Growth (%)
2007	222	--
2008	250	12.61
2009	272	8.80
2010	300	10.29
2011	328	9.33
2012	345	5.18
2013	363	5.22
2014	376	3.58
2015	386	2.66

Source: Author's calculation using the different issues of Annual Report of CDBL
Note. US $1 = BDT 78.

9.4 Growth of Documentation of CDBL

Table 4 showed growth of documentation of CDBL. The table imitated that growth of documentation of CDBL fluctuate every year from year 2008 to year 2015. But in year 2008 growth was highest which 61% is and in year 2012 growth was lowest which 59%.

Table 4. Growth of documentation of CDBL

Year	Documentation	Growth (%)
2007	101939	--
2008	164320	61
2009	140000	-15
2010	205000	46
2011	235000	15
2012	97500	-59
2013	110000	13
2014	72,500	-34
2015	56,374	-22

Source: Author's calculation using the different issues of Annual Report of CDBL

Note. US $1 = BDT 78.

9.5 Growth of Dematerialization of Securities of CDBL

Table 5 showed growth pattern of dematerialization of securities of CDBL. The table reflected number of dematerialization of securities increasing but at a decreasing trend from year 2008 to 2011. But from year 2012, 2013 and 2015 it is decreased by 70%, 50% and 73%.

Table 5. Growth of dematerialization of securities of CDBL

Year	Dematerialization of Securities (Million BDT)	Growth (%)
2007	3.75	--
2008	7.90	111
2009	9.29	18
2010	17.41	87
2011	23.22	33
2012	6.97	-70
2013	3.48	-50
2014	4.21	21
2015	1.14	-73

Source: Author's calculation using the different issues of Annual Report of CDBL

Note. US $1 = BDT 78.

9.6 Growth of Settlement of Securities Transactions of CDBL

Table 6 illustrated growth of Settlement of Securities Transactions of CDBL. The table reflected that Settlement of Securities Transactions of CDBL increasing at a decreasing trend from year 2008 to 2011. But from year 2012, 2013 and 2015 it is decreased by 54%, 35% and 17%.

Table 6. Growth of settlement of securities transactions of CDBL

Year	Settlement of Securities Transactions (Million BDT)	Growth (%)
2007	88.54	--
2008	302.92	242
2009	508.07	68
2010	867.11	71
2011	1241.11	43
2012	569.85	-54
2013	369.35	-35
2014	469.75	27
2015	389.82	-17

Source: Author's calculation using the different issues of Annual Report of CDBL

Note. US $1 = BDT 78.

9.7 Growth of Net Profit of CDBL

From Table 7 it is reflected that outstanding financial results have been achieved in the year 2008 where net profit is increased by 254.40% compared to the previous year as a result of growth in income from depository operations of around 203%. From year 2009 to 2011 net profit increased by around 55%, 59% and 72% as a consequence of the favorable market conditions and the tight lid maintained expenditure. However, after 2011 net Profit of CDBL decreased by 20% in 2012 and it continue falling in year 2013and year 2015 as the incapability of the company to handle the expenditure. So it is reflected from the table that net profit of CDBL has shown up and down trends during the period of 2007-2015.

Table 7. Net profit of CDBL

Year	Net Profit (Million BDT)	Growth (%)
2007	99.55	
2008	352.82	254.40
2009	545.70	54.67
2010	867.15	58.91
2011	1492.69	72.14
2012	1194.08	-20.00
2013	878.47	-26.43
2014	978.59	11.40
2015	884.74	-9.59

Source: Author's calculation using the different issues of Annual Report of CDBL.
Note. US $1 = BDT 78.

9.8 Growth of Total Assets of CDBL

Conversely Table 8 exposed total assets of the company which showed an increasing trend from year 2007 to 2010 reflecting well supervision of both current and fixed asset. The growth trend of the assets during 2008, 2009 and 2010 was around 68%, 58% and 67%. The trend was drastically decreased by 72% during 2011 due to a financial or operational problem of the company. After 2011 total assets increased year after year and the growth rate peak in year 2013 which is 781.46%.

Table 8. Total assets of CDBL

Year	Total Assetsm (Million BDT)	Growth (%)
2007	485.29	--
2008	812.29	67.38
2009	1278.41	57.38
2010	2128.96	66.53
2011	595.90	-72.01
2012	629.98	5.72
2013	5553.10	781.46
2014	6182.47	11.33
2015	6411.76	3.71

Source: Author's calculation using the different issues of Annual Report of CDBL.
Note. US $1 = BDT 78.

9.9 Growth of Earnings Per Share (EPS)

The growth pattern of EPS has been revealed from Table 9. It is depicted from the table that the growth of EPS showed negative in 2009, 2011, 2012, 2013 and 2014 which was -22.65%, -25.54%, -36.01% and -10.22%. The EPS of the company uphold ups and down trend through year 2007 to 2012. During year 2008 EPS was dramatically increased by around 256%. Furthermore it declined to Tk. 5.97 from Tk. 9.33 reflecting the effect of the bearish market during the year on the income of the company. The lowest growth observed in 2012. The growth percentage of EPS showed very dissatisfactory depiction year after year.

Table 9. Earnings per share of CDBL

Year	Earnings per share(BDT)	Growth (%)
2007	2.87	--
2008	10.2	255.40
2009	7.89	-22.65
2010	12.53	58.81
2011	9.33	-25.54
2012	5.97	-36.01
2013	4.89	-18.09
2014	4.39	-10.22
2015	4.42	0.68

Source: Author's calculation using the different issues of Annual Report of CDBL.
Note. US $1 = BDT 78.

9.10 Growth of Paid-Up-Capital and Retained Earnings

Table 10 explicated paid –up-capital and retained Earnings of CDBL. Retained earnings used to maintain current operations, or to invest in new ventures. Retained Earnings Growth is the percent increase/decrease of a company's retained net income over time. CDBL retained earnings illustrated an upward sloping trend from year 2007 to 2011 indicated that the growth is accompanied by subsequent increases in sales and profitability. Due to financial recession the trend decreased by around 9% in year 2012, 90.40% in year 2013and 2.60% in year 2015 but consequently increased by 15.46% in year 2014.

CDBL paid –up- capital remained constant from year 2007 to 2009 maintained a zero growth rate. Although in year 2010 it was Tk. 690 million which was reached the threshold of Tk. 500 million set by SEC for mandatory share issuance to the public. After that it raised by around 132% and 25% during year 2011 and 2012. The company issued 40,000,000 bonus shares in year 2012 which has increased the paid up capital of the company to Tk. 2 billion. After year 2012 paid-up-capital remained constant up to year 2015.

Table 10. Paid-up-capital & retained earnings of CDBL

Year	Paid-Up-Capital (Million BDT)	Growth (%)	Retained Earnings (Million BDT)	Growth (%)
2007	346	--	104	--
2008	346	0.00	422	307.18
2009	346	0.00	878	108.11
2010	690	99.42	1364	55.43
2011	1600	131.88	5807	325.59
2012	2000	25.00	5294	-8.84
2013	2000	0.00	508	-90.40
2014	2000	0.00	587	15.46
2015	2000	0.00%	572	-2.60%

Source: Author's calculation using the different issues of Annual Report of CDBL.
Note. US $1 = BDT 78.

9.11 Trend Equation of CDBL

Table 11 showed the summary of trend equation and r^2 of number of shares in the CDS, listed securities in CDS, depository participants to CDBL, dematerialization of securities, settlement of securities transactions of CDBL, net profit, total assets and EPS.

It is observed from the table that number of shares in the CDS trend equation is positive and goodness of fit is higher than 0.50 i.e. 0.60. On the other hand trend equation of listed securities in CDS is positive and goodness of fit is more than 0.50. It is exposed from the table that a trend equation of depository participant to CDBL is positive and goodness of fit is more than 0.50. Dematerialization of securities of CDBL trend equation is not positive and goodness of fit is very low i.e. 0.19. Trend equation of settlement of securities transactions of CDBL is negative and goodness of fit is very low i.e. 0.02. The table also showed that trend equation of net profit of CDBL is positive but goodness of fit of the equation is low i.e. 0.22.Trend equation and r^2 of total assets of CDBL is positive but Goodness of fit is not in a satisfactory level which is 0.17 and trend equation of EPS is negative where Goodness of fit is 0.42.

Table 11. Trend equation and r^2

Particulars	Yc= a+bx	r2
Number of Shares in the CDS	Yc=20.45+246.11x	0.62
Listed Securities in CDS	Yc=20.45+246.11x	0.48
Depository Participants to CDBL	Yc=14.48+315.78x	0.46
Dematerialization of Securities	Yc=-1.15+8.6x	0.19
Settlement of Securities Transactions	Yc=20.45+246.11x	0.02
Net Profit	Yc= 72.4 -810.43x	0.22
Total Assets	Yc=391.58+2675.35x	0.17
EPS	Yc=20.45+246.11x	0.41

10. Findings and Conclusion

The establishment of CDBL added value to the stock market of Bangladesh and attracted more investors' especially foreign investors. Before the establishment of CDBL process of transferring and delivering ownership was too lengthy and risky. After implementing automated trading system in DSE & CSE and introducing central depository system, the stock market of Bangladesh became more effective and credible to the investors (Bepari & Mollik).

The proceedings of CDBL in the coming year appear to be excellent though the stock market may be vulnerable to overheating which invariably leads to a bubble burst at some stage. The increasing number of users of the Company's CDS is most stirring and intensely appreciated. The Company has nonetheless made investments to be technologically well placed with new up-graded scalable systems to handle any extraordinary upsurge in trade volumes at the stock exchanges efficiently and deliver significant improvements in its service to depository participants and issuers.

It has been observed that net income, depository participants, dematerialization of securities, settlement of securities, number of shares, listed securities of CDBL has increased from the previous year during 2007-2015 which indicated that CDBL is able to perform activities efficiently. Every year the company's total assets increased.

Seven trend equations have been tested for different activities of CDBL. Among them the trend value of all activities except EPS, settlement of securities and dematerialization of securities is positive. Square of correlation coefficient (r^2) has also been tested for all trend equations. The r^2 of depository participants and listed securities in CDS is more than 0.5 which indicates the prospect of CDBL is bright.

The growth percentage of EPS of CDBL was very low and fluctuating. In order to increase activities and income CDBL need to increase income. It has been identified that the growth rate of net income and EPS is not satisfactory. CDBL should try to increase the growth rate.

We are quite optimistic that if the given suggestions of this paper are implemented then CDBL will be able to overcome its present problems and may contribute in the rapid development of the economy of Bangladesh.

References

Azim, M., Ahmed, E., & D'Netto, B. (2011). Corporate Social Disclosure in Bangladesh: A Study of the Financial Sector. *International Review of Business Research Papers, 7*, 37-55.

Chaity, N. S., & Sharmin, S. (2012). Efficiency Measures of Capital Market: A Case of Dhaka Stock Exchange. *International Journal of Business and Management, 7*(1).

Islam. K. A. R. (2007). The prospects, possibilities and challenges of Bangladesh capital market. *The Financial Express.*

Kanan, S. (2008). Market Comparable Approach. *Journal of Financial Services Research, 24*, 121-148.

Mujeri, M. K., & Rahman, M. H. (2009). *Financing Long Term Investments in Bangladesh: Capital Market Development Issues.* Paper provided by esocialsciences.com in its series Working Papers with number id: 2060.

Saha, A. K. (2012). Capital Market in Bangladesh: An Overview. *International Journal of Science and Research (IJSR), 1*(3).

Sing, S., & Goyal, S. (2011). Analysis Factor Affecting the decision making of the investors in Depository system. *Journal of Banking, Financial Services and Insurance Research, 1*, 13-38.

Solaiman, S. M. (2006). Recent Reforms and the Development of the Securities Market in Bangladesh. *Journal of Asian and African Studies, 41*(3). https://doi.org/10.1177/0021909606063878

Permissions

All chapters in this book were first published in IJEF, by Canadian Center of Science and Education; hereby published with permission under the Creative Commons Attribution License or equivalent. Every chapter published in this book has been scrutinized by our experts. Their significance has been extensively debated. The topics covered herein carry significant findings which will fuel the growth of the discipline. They may even be implemented as practical applications or may be referred to as a beginning point for another development.

The contributors of this book come from diverse backgrounds, making this book a truly international effort. This book will bring forth new frontiers with its revolutionizing research information and detailed analysis of the nascent developments around the world.

We would like to thank all the contributing authors for lending their expertise to make the book truly unique. They have played a crucial role in the development of this book. Without their invaluable contributions this book wouldn't have been possible. They have made vital efforts to compile up to date information on the varied aspects of this subject to make this book a valuable addition to the collection of many professionals and students.

This book was conceptualized with the vision of imparting up-to-date information and advanced data in this field. To ensure the same, a matchless editorial board was set up. Every individual on the board went through rigorous rounds of assessment to prove their worth. After which they invested a large part of their time researching and compiling the most relevant data for our readers.

The editorial board has been involved in producing this book since its inception. They have spent rigorous hours researching and exploring the diverse topics which have resulted in the successful publishing of this book. They have passed on their knowledge of decades through this book. To expedite this challenging task, the publisher supported the team at every step. A small team of assistant editors was also appointed to further simplify the editing procedure and attain best results for the readers.

Apart from the editorial board, the designing team has also invested a significant amount of their time in understanding the subject and creating the most relevant covers. They scrutinized every image to scout for the most suitable representation of the subject and create an appropriate cover for the book.

The publishing team has been an ardent support to the editorial, designing and production team. Their endless efforts to recruit the best for this project, has resulted in the accomplishment of this book. They are a veteran in the field of academics and their pool of knowledge is as vast as their experience in printing. Their expertise and guidance has proved useful at every step. Their uncompromising quality standards have made this book an exceptional effort. Their encouragement from time to time has been an inspiration for everyone.

The publisher and the editorial board hope that this book will prove to be a valuable piece of knowledge for researchers, students, practitioners and scholars across the globe.

List of Contributors

Amaechi N. Nwaokoro
College of Business, Albany State University, Albany, Georgia, USA

Trilochan Tripathy and Bijon Pani
XLRI-Xavier School of Management, Jamshedpur, India

Vasiliki A. Basdekidou
SRFA Aristotle University of Thessaloniki, Greece

Mohammad Zahed Hossain
Senior Lecturer, Department of Business Administration, Leading University, Sylhet

Muhamad Muda and Siti Nurazira Daud
Faculty of Economic and Muamalat, Universiti Sains Islam Malaysia, Nilai, Malaysia

Ibrahim Mohamed Ibrahim Eldeeb
Master candidate in Faculty of Economic and Muamalat, Universiti sainsIslamMalaysia, Nilai, Malaysia

Pam Zahonogo
Université OuagaII, Burkina Faso

Nikolaos Dritsakis
Professor, Department of Applied Informatics, School of Information Sciences, University of Macedonia, Thessaloniki, Greece

Georgios Savvas
Post-Graduate Student, Master of Science in Applied Informatics, Department of Applied Informatics, School of Information Sciences, University of Macedonia, Greece

Ali Dadpay
Professor of Economics, The Bill Munday School of Business, St. Edward's University, United States

Najah Hassan Salamah
Department of Marketing, Faculty of Economic and Administration, King Abdul-Aziz University, Saudi Arabia

Muneer Shaik
Research Scholar, Institute for Financial Management and Research, India

S. Maheswaran
Senior Professor, Institute for Financial Management and Research, India

Nayef Al-Shammari and Huda Al-Rashid
Department of Economics, College of Business Administration, Kuwait University, Kuwait

Zi-Yu Li, Jia-Yu Zhong and Xiao-Xu Yan
Innovation Practice Base of Mathematical Modeling, Electrical and Information College of Jinan University, Zhuhai, China

Yuan-Biao Zhang
Innovation Practice Base of Mathematical Modeling, Electrical and Information College of Jinan University, Zhuhai, China
Key Laboratory of Product Packaging and Logistics of Guangdong Higher Education Institutes, Jinan University, Zhuhai, China

Xin-Guang Lv
Key Laboratory of Product Packaging and Logistics of Guangdong Higher Education Institutes, Jinan University, Zhuhai, China

Xiao-Xu Yan, Xin-Kun Lv and Zi-Yu Li
Innovation Practice Base of Mathematical Modeling, Electrical and Information College of Jinan University, Zhuhai, China

Yuan-Biao Zhang
Innovation Practice Base of Mathematical Modeling, Electrical and Information College of Jinan University, Zhuhai, China
Key Laboratory of Product Packaging and Logistics of Guangdong Higher Education Institutes, Jinan University, Zhuhai, China

Ming Qi
School of Business Administration, China University of Petroleum (Beijing), China

Bader Mustafa Al-Sharif, Amjad Qwader and Zaher Abdel Fattah Al-Slehat
Faculty of Business, Tafila Technical University, At-Tafila, Jordan

Nguyen Minh Ha and Nguyen Hung Lam
Graduate School, Ho Chi Minh City Open University, Vietnam

Rashmi Soni
K J Somaiya Institute of Management Studies and Research, Mumbai, India

Vasiliki A. Basdekidou
SRFA Aristotle University of Thessaloniki, Greece

Ding Shanshan
Graduate of Economics and Management College, Nanjing University of Aeronautics and Astronautics, Nanjing, China

Duan Jindong
Professor of Economics and Management College, Nanjing University of Aeronautics and Astronautics, Nanjing, China

Moses A. Ofeh
Department of Economics, Higher Teacher Training College Bambili, University of Bamenda, Cameroon

Ali T. Muandzevara
Government High School, Wabanne-Fontem, Cameroon

Tanbir Ahmed Chowdhury
Faculty of Business and Economics, East West University, Dhaka, Bangladesh

Farzana Huda
Department of Business Administration, East West University, Dhaka, Bangladesh

Index

S

T

U

V

W